C-5009   CAREER EXAMINATION SERIES

This is your
PASSBOOK for...

NYC Public Safety Exam

Test Preparation Study Guide
Questions & Answers

NLC®

NATIONAL LEARNING CORPORATION®

COPYRIGHT NOTICE

This book is SOLELY intended for, is sold ONLY to, and its use is RESTRICTED to individual, bona fide applicants or candidates who qualify by virtue of having seriously filed applications for appropriate license, certificate, professional and/or promotional advancement, higher school matriculation, scholarship, or other legitimate requirements of education and/or governmental authorities.

This book is NOT intended for use, class instruction, tutoring, training, duplication, copying, reprinting, excerption, or adaptation, etc., by:

1) Other publishers
2) Proprietors and/or Instructors of "Coaching" and/or Preparatory Courses
3) Personnel and/or Training Divisions of commercial, industrial, and governmental organizations
4) Schools, colleges, or universities and/or their departments and staffs, including teachers and other personnel
5) Testing Agencies or Bureaus
6) Study groups which seek by the purchase of a single volume to copy and/or duplicate and/or adapt this material for use by the group as a whole without having purchased individual volumes for each of the members of the group
7) Et al.

Such persons would be in violation of appropriate Federal and State statutes.

PROVISION OF LICENSING AGREEMENTS – Recognized educational, commercial, industrial, and governmental institutions and organizations, and others legitimately engaged in educational pursuits, including training, testing, and measurement activities, may address request for a licensing agreement to the copyright owners, who will determine whether, and under what conditions, including fees and charges, the materials in this book may be used them. In other words, a licensing facility exists for the legitimate use of the material in this book on other than an individual basis. However, it is asseverated and affirmed here that the material in this book CANNOT be used without the receipt of the express permission of such a licensing agreement from the Publishers. Inquiries re licensing should be addressed to the company, attention rights and permissions department.

All rights reserved, including the right of reproduction in whole or in part, in any form or by any means, electronic or mechanical, including photocopying, recording, or by any information storage and retrieval system, without permission in writing from the Publisher.

Copyright © 2024 by
National Learning Corporation

212 Michael Drive, Syosset, NY 11791
(516) 921-8888 • www.passbooks.com
E-mail: info@passbooks.com

PASSBOOK® SERIES

THE *PASSBOOK® SERIES* has been created to prepare applicants and candidates for the ultimate academic battlefield – the examination room.

At some time in our lives, each and every one of us may be required to take an examination – for validation, matriculation, admission, qualification, registration, certification, or licensure.

Based on the assumption that every applicant or candidate has met the basic formal educational standards, has taken the required number of courses, and read the necessary texts, the *PASSBOOK® SERIES* furnishes the one special preparation which may assure passing with confidence, instead of failing with insecurity. Examination questions – together with answers – are furnished as the basic vehicle for study so that the mysteries of the examination and its compounding difficulties may be eliminated or diminished by a sure method.

This book is meant to help you pass your examination provided that you qualify and are serious in your objective.

The entire field is reviewed through the huge store of content information which is succinctly presented through a provocative and challenging approach – the question-and-answer method.

A climate of success is established by furnishing the correct answers at the end of each test.

You soon learn to recognize types of questions, forms of questions, and patterns of questioning. You may even begin to anticipate expected outcomes.

You perceive that many questions are repeated or adapted so that you can gain acute insights, which may enable you to score many sure points.

You learn how to confront new questions, or types of questions, and to attack them confidently and work out the correct answers.

You note objectives and emphases, and recognize pitfalls and dangers, so that you may make positive educational adjustments.

Moreover, you are kept fully informed in relation to new concepts, methods, practices, and directions in the field.

You discover that you are actually taking the examination all the time: you are preparing for the examination by "taking" an examination, not by reading extraneous and/or supererogatory textbooks.

In short, this PASSBOOK®, used directedly, should be an important factor in helping you to pass your test.

NYC PUBLIC SAFETY EXAM

The Public Safety Exam is designed to offer you the opportunity to take one multiple-choice test for multiple titles and have your name available for hiring to any of the included titles if you meet the minimum qualification requirements.

SANITATION ENFORCEMENT AGENT

Sanitation Enforcement Agents, under supervision, are responsible for enforcement of certain laws, rules and regulations of the New York City Health and Administrative Codes, New York State Public Health Law (Canine Waste), New York City Traffic Regulations; and prepare and issue summonses for certain violations thereof. Under supervision, they may inspect commercial and residential establishments, streets and sidewalks; direct and control traffic around Department of Sanitation operations. During snow events, they may assist with the coordination of the activities of snow shovelers. They operate and monitor hand-held communication devices; assist in the preparation of cases relating to summonses issued, for trial in court or before an Administrative Tribunal; operate a motor vehicle; and perform related work.

SCHOOL SAFETY AGENT

School Safety Agents patrol designated areas of school buildings and surrounding areas; identify and prevent infiltration of unlawful or prohibited items through scanning; give routine information to visitors and direct them to the proper personnel and offices; request identification of, and remove from the premises, any unauthorized persons; aid sick and injured persons and call for medical, police or fire assistance, when needed; notify supervisors of all emergency incidents and complete any related documentation; respond to altercations between students and other persons, and attempt to separate the involved persons and resolve conflicts; maintain records of persons entering and leaving buildings; monitor security camera systems to ensure facility entrances are secure; identify persons violating Department of Education Rules and Regulations; apprehend persons violating the Penal Law and notify the proper administrative personnel; prepare reports and testify in regard to these violations at Superintendent's or Principal's hearings and/or in court; monitor and use radios to request assistance from co-workers; and may operate motor vehicles. All School Safety Agents perform related work.

SPECIAL OFFICER

Special Officers under supervision, perform Special Officer work of ordinary difficulty and responsibility relating to physical security, safety, loss prevention and maintenance of order. They patrol designated areas of public buildings, other facilities, and surrounding areas to maintain order, preserve the peace, and safeguard life and property against fire, vandalism, theft, etc.; give routine information to visitors and service recipients and direct them to the proper individuals and offices; discourage and eject loiterers and disorderly persons and when appropriate, arrest and issue summonses to law violators on premises; transport, escort and/or arrange for transport of persons in custody to police precincts and have arrests recorded on police blotter; prepare and transmit all necessary documents relating to arrests; testify in court on arrests; report security instances and unusual occurrences by telephone or radio and make subsequent written reports; as required, provide assistance to the sick, injured, mentally and physically disabled, and call for ambulances and/or medical attention when necessary and complete and forward forms; record daily actions in memo book; maintain records of persons entering or leaving building; keep bulletin board in their area current by adding and removing materials; may make clock rounds as required; may control vehicular traffic on grounds and/or premises; may operate a motor vehicle; monitor and report unusual events from security systems as required; distribute and maintain accountability for designated equipment or property; monitor and control access by the means of electronic security measures, such as closed circuit television; access control readers; may operate hydraulic access devices; attend, complete, and maintain training requirements as per State and Agency mandates; make written entries into location log book; and perform related work.

TRAFFIC ENFORCEMENT AGENT

At Assignment Level I, under supervision, Traffic Enforcement Agents patrol an assigned area in order to enforce laws, rules and regulations relating to movement, parking, stopping and standing of vehicles. They prepare and issue paper and electronic summonses for violations; prepare and issue summonses to vehicles and motorists; testify at administrative hearing offices and court; report inoperative or missing parking meters and traffic conditions requiring attention; prepare required reports; operate a motor vehicle; operate portable and vehicle radios and other electronic equipment; and perform related work.

SCOPE OF THE EXAMINATION
The written test will cover knowledge, skills and abilities in such areas as:

1. **Information Ordering**: following correctly a rule or set of rules or actions in a certain order. The rule or set of rules used must be given. The things or actions to be put in order can include numbers, letters, words, pictures, procedures, sentences, and mathematical or logical operations.
2. **Memorization**: remembering information, such as words, numbers, pictures and procedures. Pieces of information can be remembered by themselves or with other pieces of information.
3. **Number Facility**: the degree to which adding, subtracting, multiplying and dividing can be done quickly and correctly. These can be steps in other operations like finding percentages.
4. **Problem Sensitivity**: being able to tell when something is wrong or is likely to go wrong. Problem sensitivity includes being able to identify the whole problem as well as the elements of the problem.
5. **Spatial Orientation**: determining where you are in relation to the location of some object or where the object is in relation to you.
6. **Time Management**: Skill in managing one's own time and the time of others to promote effective use of work hours.
7. **Written Expression**: using English words or sentences in writing so that others will understand.

HOW TO TAKE A TEST

I. YOU MUST PASS AN EXAMINATION

A. *WHAT EVERY CANDIDATE SHOULD KNOW*

Examination applicants often ask us for help in preparing for the written test. What can I study in advance? What kinds of questions will be asked? How will the test be given? How will the papers be graded?

As an applicant for a civil service examination, you may be wondering about some of these things. Our purpose here is to suggest effective methods of advance study and to describe civil service examinations.

Your chances for success on this examination can be increased if you know how to prepare. Those "pre-examination jitters" can be reduced if you know what to expect. You can even experience an adventure in good citizenship if you know why civil service exams are given.

B. *WHY ARE CIVIL SERVICE EXAMINATIONS GIVEN?*

Civil service examinations are important to you in two ways. As a citizen, you want public jobs filled by employees who know how to do their work. As a job seeker, you want a fair chance to compete for that job on an equal footing with other candidates. The best-known means of accomplishing this two-fold goal is the competitive examination.

Exams are widely publicized throughout the nation. They may be administered for jobs in federal, state, city, municipal, town or village governments or agencies.

Any citizen may apply, with some limitations, such as the age or residence of applicants. Your experience and education may be reviewed to see whether you meet the requirements for the particular examination. When these requirements exist, they are reasonable and applied consistently to all applicants. Thus, a competitive examination may cause you some uneasiness now, but it is your privilege and safeguard.

C. *HOW ARE CIVIL SERVICE EXAMS DEVELOPED?*

Examinations are carefully written by trained technicians who are specialists in the field known as "psychological measurement," in consultation with recognized authorities in the field of work that the test will cover. These experts recommend the subject matter areas or skills to be tested; only those knowledges or skills important to your success on the job are included. The most reliable books and source materials available are used as references. Together, the experts and technicians judge the difficulty level of the questions.

Test technicians know how to phrase questions so that the problem is clearly stated. Their ethics do not permit "trick" or "catch" questions. Questions may have been tried out on sample groups, or subjected to statistical analysis, to determine their usefulness.

Written tests are often used in combination with performance tests, ratings of training and experience, and oral interviews. All of these measures combine to form the best-known means of finding the right person for the right job.

II. HOW TO PASS THE WRITTEN TEST

A. NATURE OF THE EXAMINATION

To prepare intelligently for civil service examinations, you should know how they differ from school examinations you have taken. In school you were assigned certain definite pages to read or subjects to cover. The examination questions were quite detailed and usually emphasized memory. Civil service exams, on the other hand, try to discover your present ability to perform the duties of a position, plus your potentiality to learn these duties. In other words, a civil service exam attempts to predict how successful you will be. Questions cover such a broad area that they cannot be as minute and detailed as school exam questions.

In the public service similar kinds of work, or positions, are grouped together in one "class." This process is known as *position-classification*. All the positions in a class are paid according to the salary range for that class. One class title covers all of these positions, and they are all tested by the same examination.

B. FOUR BASIC STEPS

1) Study the announcement

How, then, can you know what subjects to study? Our best answer is: "Learn as much as possible about the class of positions for which you've applied." The exam will test the knowledge, skills and abilities needed to do the work.

Your most valuable source of information about the position you want is the official exam announcement. This announcement lists the training and experience qualifications. Check these standards and apply only if you come reasonably close to meeting them.

The brief description of the position in the examination announcement offers some clues to the subjects which will be tested. Think about the job itself. Review the duties in your mind. Can you perform them, or are there some in which you are rusty? Fill in the blank spots in your preparation.

Many jurisdictions preview the written test in the exam announcement by including a section called "Knowledge and Abilities Required," "Scope of the Examination," or some similar heading. Here you will find out specifically what fields will be tested.

2) Review your own background

Once you learn in general what the position is all about, and what you need to know to do the work, ask yourself which subjects you already know fairly well and which need improvement. You may wonder whether to concentrate on improving your strong areas or on building some background in your fields of weakness. When the announcement has specified "some knowledge" or "considerable knowledge," or has used adjectives like "beginning principles of..." or "advanced ... methods," you can get a clue as to the number and difficulty of questions to be asked in any given field. More questions, and hence broader coverage, would be included for those subjects which are more important in the work. Now weigh your strengths and weaknesses against the job requirements and prepare accordingly.

3) Determine the level of the position

Another way to tell how intensively you should prepare is to understand the level of the job for which you are applying. Is it the entering level? In other words, is this the position in which beginners in a field of work are hired? Or is it an intermediate or advanced level? Sometimes this is indicated by such words as "Junior" or "Senior" in the class title. Other jurisdictions use Roman numerals to designate the level – Clerk I, Clerk II, for example. The word "Supervisor" sometimes appears in the title. If the level is not indicated by the title, check the description of duties. Will you be working under very close supervision, or will you have responsibility for independent decisions in this work?

4) Choose appropriate study materials

Now that you know the subjects to be examined and the relative amount of each subject to be covered, you can choose suitable study materials. For beginning level jobs, or even advanced ones, if you have a pronounced weakness in some aspect of your training, read a modern, standard textbook in that field. Be sure it is up to date and has general coverage. Such books are normally available at your library, and the librarian will be glad to help you locate one. For entry-level positions, questions of appropriate difficulty are chosen -- neither highly advanced questions, nor those too simple. Such questions require careful thought but not advanced training.

If the position for which you are applying is technical or advanced, you will read more advanced, specialized material. If you are already familiar with the basic principles of your field, elementary textbooks would waste your time. Concentrate on advanced textbooks and technical periodicals. Think through the concepts and review difficult problems in your field.

These are all general sources. You can get more ideas on your own initiative, following these leads. For example, training manuals and publications of the government agency which employs workers in your field can be useful, particularly for technical and professional positions. A letter or visit to the government department involved may result in more specific study suggestions, and certainly will provide you with a more definite idea of the exact nature of the position you are seeking.

III. KINDS OF TESTS

Tests are used for purposes other than measuring knowledge and ability to perform specified duties. For some positions, it is equally important to test ability to make adjustments to new situations or to profit from training. In others, basic mental abilities not dependent on information are essential. Questions which test these things may not appear as pertinent to the duties of the position as those which test for knowledge and information. Yet they are often highly important parts of a fair examination. For very general questions, it is almost impossible to help you direct your study efforts. What we can do is to point out some of the more common of these general abilities needed in public service positions and describe some typical questions.

1) General information

Broad, general information has been found useful for predicting job success in some kinds of work. This is tested in a variety of ways, from vocabulary lists to questions about current events. Basic background in some field of work, such as sociology or economics, may be sampled in a group of questions. Often these are principles which have become familiar to most persons through exposure rather than through formal training. It is difficult to advise you how to study for these questions; being alert to the world around you is our best suggestion.

2) Verbal ability

An example of an ability needed in many positions is verbal or language ability. Verbal ability is, in brief, the ability to use and understand words. Vocabulary and grammar tests are typical measures of this ability. Reading comprehension or paragraph interpretation questions are common in many kinds of civil service tests. You are given a paragraph of written material and asked to find its central meaning.

3) Numerical ability

Number skills can be tested by the familiar arithmetic problem, by checking paired lists of numbers to see which are alike and which are different, or by interpreting charts and graphs. In the latter test, a graph may be printed in the test booklet which you are asked to use as the basis for answering questions.

4) Observation

A popular test for law-enforcement positions is the observation test. A picture is shown to you for several minutes, then taken away. Questions about the picture test your ability to observe both details and larger elements.

5) Following directions

In many positions in the public service, the employee must be able to carry out written instructions dependably and accurately. You may be given a chart with several columns, each column listing a variety of information. The questions require you to carry out directions involving the information given in the chart.

6) Skills and aptitudes

Performance tests effectively measure some manual skills and aptitudes. When the skill is one in which you are trained, such as typing or shorthand, you can practice. These tests are often very much like those given in business school or high school courses. For many of the other skills and aptitudes, however, no short-time preparation can be made. Skills and abilities natural to you or that you have developed throughout your lifetime are being tested.

Many of the general questions just described provide all the data needed to answer the questions and ask you to use your reasoning ability to find the answers. Your best preparation for these tests, as well as for tests of facts and ideas, is to be at your physical and mental best. You, no doubt, have your own methods of getting into an exam-taking mood and keeping "in shape." The next section lists some ideas on this subject.

IV. KINDS OF QUESTIONS

Only rarely is the "essay" question, which you answer in narrative form, used in civil service tests. Civil service tests are usually of the short-answer type. Full instructions for answering these questions will be given to you at the examination. But in case this is your first experience with short-answer questions and separate answer sheets, here is what you need to know:

1) Multiple-choice Questions

Most popular of the short-answer questions is the "multiple choice" or "best answer" question. It can be used, for example, to test for factual knowledge, ability to solve problems or judgment in meeting situations found at work.

A multiple-choice question is normally one of three types—
- It can begin with an incomplete statement followed by several possible endings. You are to find the one ending which *best* completes the statement, although some of the others may not be entirely wrong.
- It can also be a complete statement in the form of a question which is answered by choosing one of the statements listed.

- It can be in the form of a problem – again you select the best answer.

Here is an example of a multiple-choice question with a discussion which should give you some clues as to the method for choosing the right answer:

When an employee has a complaint about his assignment, the action which will *best* help him overcome his difficulty is to
  A. discuss his difficulty with his coworkers
  B. take the problem to the head of the organization
  C. take the problem to the person who gave him the assignment
  D. say nothing to anyone about his complaint

In answering this question, you should study each of the choices to find which is best. Consider choice "A" – Certainly an employee may discuss his complaint with fellow employees, but no change or improvement can result, and the complaint remains unresolved. Choice "B" is a poor choice since the head of the organization probably does not know what assignment you have been given, and taking your problem to him is known as "going over the head" of the supervisor. The supervisor, or person who made the assignment, is the person who can clarify it or correct any injustice. Choice "C" is, therefore, correct. To say nothing, as in choice "D," is unwise. Supervisors have and interest in knowing the problems employees are facing, and the employee is seeking a solution to his problem.

2) True/False Questions

The "true/false" or "right/wrong" form of question is sometimes used. Here a complete statement is given. Your job is to decide whether the statement is right or wrong.

SAMPLE: A roaming cell-phone call to a nearby city costs less than a non-roaming call to a distant city.

This statement is wrong, or false, since roaming calls are more expensive.

This is not a complete list of all possible question forms, although most of the others are variations of these common types. You will always get complete directions for answering questions. Be sure you understand *how* to mark your answers – ask questions until you do.

V. RECORDING YOUR ANSWERS

Computer terminals are used more and more today for many different kinds of exams.
For an examination with very few applicants, you may be told to record your answers in the test booklet itself. Separate answer sheets are much more common. If this separate answer sheet is to be scored by machine – and this is often the case – it is highly important that you mark your answers correctly in order to get credit.

An electronic scoring machine is often used in civil service offices because of the speed with which papers can be scored. Machine-scored answer sheets must be marked with a pencil, which will be given to you. This pencil has a high graphite content which responds to the electronic scoring machine. As a matter of fact, stray dots may register as answers, so do not let your pencil rest on the answer sheet while you are pondering the correct answer. Also, if your pencil lead breaks or is otherwise defective, ask for another.

Since the answer sheet will be dropped in a slot in the scoring machine, be careful not to bend the corners or get the paper crumpled.

The answer sheet normally has five vertical columns of numbers, with 30 numbers to a column. These numbers correspond to the question numbers in your test booklet. After each number, going across the page are four or five pairs of dotted lines. These short dotted lines have small letters or numbers above them. The first two pairs may also have a "T" or "F" above the letters. This indicates that the first two pairs only are to be used if the questions are of the true-false type. If the questions are multiple choice, disregard the "T" and "F" and pay attention only to the small letters or numbers.

Answer your questions in the manner of the sample that follows:

32. The largest city in the United States is
    A. Washington, D.C.
    B. New York City
    C. Chicago
    D. Detroit
    E. San Francisco

1) Choose the answer you think is best. (New York City is the largest, so "B" is correct.)
2) Find the row of dotted lines numbered the same as the question you are answering. (Find row number 32)
3) Find the pair of dotted lines corresponding to the answer. (Find the pair of lines under the mark "B.")
4) Make a solid black mark between the dotted lines.

VI. BEFORE THE TEST

Common sense will help you find procedures to follow to get ready for an examination. Too many of us, however, overlook these sensible measures. Indeed, nervousness and fatigue have been found to be the most serious reasons why applicants fail to do their best on civil service tests. Here is a list of reminders:

- Begin your preparation early – Don't wait until the last minute to go scurrying around for books and materials or to find out what the position is all about.
- Prepare continuously – An hour a night for a week is better than an all-night cram session. This has been definitely established. What is more, a night a week for a month will return better dividends than crowding your study into a shorter period of time.
- Locate the place of the exam – You have been sent a notice telling you when and where to report for the examination. If the location is in a different town or otherwise unfamiliar to you, it would be well to inquire the best route and learn something about the building.
- Relax the night before the test – Allow your mind to rest. Do not study at all that night. Plan some mild recreation or diversion; then go to bed early and get a good night's sleep.
- Get up early enough to make a leisurely trip to the place for the test – This way unforeseen events, traffic snarls, unfamiliar buildings, etc. will not upset you.
- Dress comfortably – A written test is not a fashion show. You will be known by number and not by name, so wear something comfortable.

- Leave excess paraphernalia at home – Shopping bags and odd bundles will get in your way. You need bring only the items mentioned in the official notice you received; usually everything you need is provided. Do not bring reference books to the exam. They will only confuse those last minutes and be taken away from you when in the test room.
- Arrive somewhat ahead of time – If because of transportation schedules you must get there very early, bring a newspaper or magazine to take your mind off yourself while waiting.
- Locate the examination room – When you have found the proper room, you will be directed to the seat or part of the room where you will sit. Sometimes you are given a sheet of instructions to read while you are waiting. Do not fill out any forms until you are told to do so; just read them and be prepared.
- Relax and prepare to listen to the instructions
- If you have any physical problem that may keep you from doing your best, be sure to tell the test administrator. If you are sick or in poor health, you really cannot do your best on the exam. You can come back and take the test some other time.

VII. AT THE TEST

The day of the test is here and you have the test booklet in your hand. The temptation to get going is very strong. Caution! There is more to success than knowing the right answers. You must know how to identify your papers and understand variations in the type of short-answer question used in this particular examination. Follow these suggestions for maximum results from your efforts:

1) Cooperate with the monitor

The test administrator has a duty to create a situation in which you can be as much at ease as possible. He will give instructions, tell you when to begin, check to see that you are marking your answer sheet correctly, and so on. He is not there to guard you, although he will see that your competitors do not take unfair advantage. He wants to help you do your best.

2) Listen to all instructions

Don't jump the gun! Wait until you understand all directions. In most civil service tests you get more time than you need to answer the questions. So don't be in a hurry. Read each word of instructions until you clearly understand the meaning. Study the examples, listen to all announcements and follow directions. Ask questions if you do not understand what to do.

3) Identify your papers

Civil service exams are usually identified by number only. You will be assigned a number; you must not put your name on your test papers. Be sure to copy your number correctly. Since more than one exam may be given, copy your exact examination title.

4) Plan your time

Unless you are told that a test is a "speed" or "rate of work" test, speed itself is usually not important. Time enough to answer all the questions will be provided, but this does not mean that you have all day. An overall time limit has been set. Divide the total time (in minutes) by the number of questions to determine the approximate time you have for each question.

5) Do not linger over difficult questions

If you come across a difficult question, mark it with a paper clip (useful to have along) and come back to it when you have been through the booklet. One caution if you do this – be sure to skip a number on your answer sheet as well. Check often to be sure that you have not lost your place and that you are marking in the row numbered the same as the question you are answering.

6) Read the questions

Be sure you know what the question asks! Many capable people are unsuccessful because they failed to *read* the questions correctly.

7) Answer all questions

Unless you have been instructed that a penalty will be deducted for incorrect answers, it is better to guess than to omit a question.

8) Speed tests

It is often better NOT to guess on speed tests. It has been found that on timed tests people are tempted to spend the last few seconds before time is called in marking answers at random – without even reading them – in the hope of picking up a few extra points. To discourage this practice, the instructions may warn you that your score will be "corrected" for guessing. That is, a penalty will be applied. The incorrect answers will be deducted from the correct ones, or some other penalty formula will be used.

9) Review your answers

If you finish before time is called, go back to the questions you guessed or omitted to give them further thought. Review other answers if you have time.

10) Return your test materials

If you are ready to leave before others have finished or time is called, take ALL your materials to the monitor and leave quietly. Never take any test material with you. The monitor can discover whose papers are not complete, and taking a test booklet may be grounds for disqualification.

VIII. EXAMINATION TECHNIQUES

1) Read the general instructions carefully. These are usually printed on the first page of the exam booklet. As a rule, these instructions refer to the timing of the examination; the fact that you should not start work until the signal and must stop work at a signal, etc. If there are any *special* instructions, such as a choice of questions to be answered, make sure that you note this instruction carefully.

2) When you are ready to start work on the examination, that is as soon as the signal has been given, read the instructions to each question booklet, underline any key words or phrases, such as *least, best, outline, describe* and the like. In this way you will tend to answer as requested rather than discover on reviewing your paper that you *listed without describing*, that you selected the *worst* choice rather than the *best* choice, etc.

3) If the examination is of the objective or multiple-choice type – that is, each question will also give a series of possible answers: A, B, C or D, and you are called upon to select the best answer and write the letter next to that answer on your answer paper – it is advisable to start answering each question in turn. There may be anywhere from 50 to 100 such questions in the three or four hours allotted and you can see how much time would be taken if you read through all the questions before beginning to answer any. Furthermore, if you come across a question or group of questions which you know would be difficult to answer, it would undoubtedly affect your handling of all the other questions.

4) If the examination is of the essay type and contains but a few questions, it is a moot point as to whether you should read all the questions before starting to answer any one. Of course, if you are given a choice – say five out of seven and the like – then it is essential to read all the questions so you can eliminate the two that are most difficult. If, however, you are asked to answer all the questions, there may be danger in trying to answer the easiest one first because you may find that you will spend too much time on it. The best technique is to answer the first question, then proceed to the second, etc.

5) Time your answers. Before the exam begins, write down the time it started, then add the time allowed for the examination and write down the time it must be completed, then divide the time available somewhat as follows:
    - If 3-1/2 hours are allowed, that would be 210 minutes. If you have 80 objective-type questions, that would be an average of 2-1/2 minutes per question. Allow yourself no more than 2 minutes per question, or a total of 160 minutes, which will permit about 50 minutes to review.
    - If for the time allotment of 210 minutes there are 7 essay questions to answer, that would average about 30 minutes a question. Give yourself only 25 minutes per question so that you have about 35 minutes to review.

6) The most important instruction is to *read each question* and make sure you know what is wanted. The second most important instruction is to *time yourself properly* so that you answer every question. The third most important instruction is to *answer every question*. Guess if you have to but include something for each question. Remember that you will receive no credit for a blank and will probably receive some credit if you write something in answer to an essay question. If you guess a letter – say "B" for a multiple-choice question – you may have guessed right. If you leave a blank as an answer to a multiple-choice question, the examiners may respect your feelings but it will not add a point to your score. Some exams may penalize you for wrong answers, so in such cases *only*, you may not want to guess unless you have some basis for your answer.

7) Suggestions
    a. Objective-type questions
        1. Examine the question booklet for proper sequence of pages and questions
        2. Read all instructions carefully
        3. Skip any question which seems too difficult; return to it after all other questions have been answered
        4. Apportion your time properly; do not spend too much time on any single question or group of questions

5. Note and underline key words – *all, most, fewest, least, best, worst, same, opposite,* etc.
6. Pay particular attention to negatives
7. Note unusual option, e.g., unduly long, short, complex, different or similar in content to the body of the question
8. Observe the use of "hedging" words – *probably, may, most likely,* etc.
9. Make sure that your answer is put next to the same number as the question
10. Do not second-guess unless you have good reason to believe the second answer is definitely more correct
11. Cross out original answer if you decide another answer is more accurate; do not erase until you are ready to hand your paper in
12. Answer all questions; guess unless instructed otherwise
13. Leave time for review

b. Essay questions
1. Read each question carefully
2. Determine exactly what is wanted. Underline key words or phrases.
3. Decide on outline or paragraph answer
4. Include many different points and elements unless asked to develop any one or two points or elements
5. Show impartiality by giving pros and cons unless directed to select one side only
6. Make and write down any assumptions you find necessary to answer the questions
7. Watch your English, grammar, punctuation and choice of words
8. Time your answers; don't crowd material

8) Answering the essay question

Most essay questions can be answered by framing the specific response around several key words or ideas. Here are a few such key words or ideas:

M's: manpower, materials, methods, money, management
P's: purpose, program, policy, plan, procedure, practice, problems, pitfalls, personnel, public relations

a. Six basic steps in handling problems:
1. Preliminary plan and background development
2. Collect information, data and facts
3. Analyze and interpret information, data and facts
4. Analyze and develop solutions as well as make recommendations
5. Prepare report and sell recommendations
6. Install recommendations and follow up effectiveness

b. Pitfalls to avoid
1. *Taking things for granted* – A statement of the situation does not necessarily imply that each of the elements is necessarily true; for example, a complaint may be invalid and biased so that all that can be taken for granted is that a complaint has been registered

2. *Considering only one side of a situation* – Wherever possible, indicate several alternatives and then point out the reasons you selected the best one
3. *Failing to indicate follow up* – Whenever your answer indicates action on your part, make certain that you will take proper follow-up action to see how successful your recommendations, procedures or actions turn out to be
4. *Taking too long in answering any single question* – Remember to time your answers properly

IX. AFTER THE TEST

Scoring procedures differ in detail among civil service jurisdictions although the general principles are the same. Whether the papers are hand-scored or graded by machine we have described, they are nearly always graded by number. That is, the person who marks the paper knows only the number – never the name – of the applicant. Not until all the papers have been graded will they be matched with names. If other tests, such as training and experience or oral interview ratings have been given, scores will be combined. Different parts of the examination usually have different weights. For example, the written test might count 60 percent of the final grade, and a rating of training and experience 40 percent. In many jurisdictions, veterans will have a certain number of points added to their grades.

After the final grade has been determined, the names are placed in grade order and an eligible list is established. There are various methods for resolving ties between those who get the same final grade – probably the most common is to place first the name of the person whose application was received first. Job offers are made from the eligible list in the order the names appear on it. You will be notified of your grade and your rank as soon as all these computations have been made. This will be done as rapidly as possible.

People who are found to meet the requirements in the announcement are called "eligibles." Their names are put on a list of eligible candidates. An eligible's chances of getting a job depend on how high he stands on this list and how fast agencies are filling jobs from the list.

When a job is to be filled from a list of eligibles, the agency asks for the names of people on the list of eligibles for that job. When the civil service commission receives this request, it sends to the agency the names of the three people highest on this list. Or, if the job to be filled has specialized requirements, the office sends the agency the names of the top three persons who meet these requirements from the general list.

The appointing officer makes a choice from among the three people whose names were sent to him. If the selected person accepts the appointment, the names of the others are put back on the list to be considered for future openings.

That is the rule in hiring from all kinds of eligible lists, whether they are for typist, carpenter, chemist, or something else. For every vacancy, the appointing officer has his choice of any one of the top three eligibles on the list. This explains why the person whose name is on top of the list sometimes does not get an appointment when some of the persons lower on the list do. If the appointing officer chooses the second or third eligible, the No. 1 eligible does not get a job at once, but stays on the list until he is appointed or the list is terminated.

X. HOW TO PASS THE INTERVIEW TEST

The examination for which you applied requires an oral interview test. You have already taken the written test and you are now being called for the interview test – the final part of the formal examination.

You may think that it is not possible to prepare for an interview test and that there are no procedures to follow during an interview. Our purpose is to point out some things you can do in advance that will help you and some good rules to follow and pitfalls to avoid while you are being interviewed.

What is an interview supposed to test?

The written examination is designed to test the technical knowledge and competence of the candidate; the oral is designed to evaluate intangible qualities, not readily measured otherwise, and to establish a list showing the relative fitness of each candidate – as measured against his competitors – for the position sought. Scoring is not on the basis of "right" and "wrong," but on a sliding scale of values ranging from "not passable" to "outstanding." As a matter of fact, it is possible to achieve a relatively low score without a single "incorrect" answer because of evident weakness in the qualities being measured.

Occasionally, an examination may consist entirely of an oral test – either an individual or a group oral. In such cases, information is sought concerning the technical knowledges and abilities of the candidate, since there has been no written examination for this purpose. More commonly, however, an oral test is used to supplement a written examination.

Who conducts interviews?

The composition of oral boards varies among different jurisdictions. In nearly all, a representative of the personnel department serves as chairman. One of the members of the board may be a representative of the department in which the candidate would work. In some cases, "outside experts" are used, and, frequently, a businessman or some other representative of the general public is asked to serve. Labor and management or other special groups may be represented. The aim is to secure the services of experts in the appropriate field.

However the board is composed, it is a good idea (and not at all improper or unethical) to ascertain in advance of the interview who the members are and what groups they represent. When you are introduced to them, you will have some idea of their backgrounds and interests, and at least you will not stutter and stammer over their names.

What should be done before the interview?

While knowledge about the board members is useful and takes some of the surprise element out of the interview, there is other preparation which is more substantive. It *is* possible to prepare for an oral interview – in several ways:

1) Keep a copy of your application and review it carefully before the interview

This may be the only document before the oral board, and the starting point of the interview. Know what education and experience you have listed there, and the sequence and dates of all of it. Sometimes the board will ask you to review the highlights of your experience for them; you should not have to hem and haw doing it.

2) Study the class specification and the examination announcement

Usually, the oral board has one or both of these to guide them. The qualities, characteristics or knowledges required by the position sought are stated in these documents. They offer valuable clues as to the nature of the oral interview. For example, if the job involves supervisory responsibilities, the announcement will usually indicate that knowledge of modern supervisory methods and the qualifications of the candidate as a supervisor will be tested. If so, you can expect such questions, frequently in the form of a hypothetical situation which you are expected to solve. NEVER go into an oral without knowledge of the duties and responsibilities of the job you seek.

3) Think through each qualification required
Try to visualize the kind of questions you would ask if you were a board member. How well could you answer them? Try especially to appraise your own knowledge and background in each area, *measured against the job sought*, and identify any areas in which you are weak. Be critical and realistic – do not flatter yourself.

4) Do some general reading in areas in which you feel you may be weak
For example, if the job involves supervision and your past experience has NOT, some general reading in supervisory methods and practices, particularly in the field of human relations, might be useful. Do NOT study agency procedures or detailed manuals. The oral board will be testing your understanding and capacity, not your memory.

5) Get a good night's sleep and watch your general health and mental attitude
You will want a clear head at the interview. Take care of a cold or any other minor ailment, and of course, no hangovers.

What should be done on the day of the interview?
Now comes the day of the interview itself. Give yourself plenty of time to get there. Plan to arrive somewhat ahead of the scheduled time, particularly if your appointment is in the fore part of the day. If a previous candidate fails to appear, the board might be ready for you a bit early. By early afternoon an oral board is almost invariably behind schedule if there are many candidates, and you may have to wait. Take along a book or magazine to read, or your application to review, but leave any extraneous material in the waiting room when you go in for your interview. In any event, relax and compose yourself.

The matter of dress is important. The board is forming impressions about you – from your experience, your manners, your attitude, and your appearance. Give your personal appearance careful attention. Dress your best, but not your flashiest. Choose conservative, appropriate clothing, and be sure it is immaculate. This is a business interview, and your appearance should indicate that you regard it as such. Besides, being well groomed and properly dressed will help boost your confidence.

Sooner or later, someone will call your name and escort you into the interview room. *This is it.* From here on you are on your own. It is too late for any more preparation. But remember, you asked for this opportunity to prove your fitness, and you are here because your request was granted.

What happens when you go in?
The usual sequence of events will be as follows: The clerk (who is often the board stenographer) will introduce you to the chairman of the oral board, who will introduce you to the other members of the board. Acknowledge the introductions before you sit down. Do not be surprised if you find a microphone facing you or a stenotypist sitting by. Oral interviews are usually recorded in the event of an appeal or other review.

Usually the chairman of the board will open the interview by reviewing the highlights of your education and work experience from your application – primarily for the benefit of the other members of the board, as well as to get the material into the record. Do not interrupt or comment unless there is an error or significant misinterpretation; if that is the case, do not hesitate. But do not quibble about insignificant matters. Also, he will usually ask you some question about your education, experience or your present job – partly to get you to start talking and to establish the interviewing "rapport." He may start the actual questioning, or turn it over to one of the other members. Frequently, each member undertakes the questioning on a particular area, one in which he is perhaps most competent, so you can expect each member to participate in the examination. Because time is limited, you may also expect some rather abrupt switches in the direction the questioning takes, so do not be upset by it. Normally, a board member will not pursue a single line of questioning unless he discovers a particular strength or weakness.

After each member has participated, the chairman will usually ask whether any member has any further questions, then will ask you if you have anything you wish to add. Unless you are expecting this question, it may floor you. Worse, it may start you off on an extended, extemporaneous speech. The board is not usually seeking more information. The question is principally to offer you a last opportunity to present further qualifications or to indicate that you have nothing to add. So, if you feel that a significant qualification or characteristic has been overlooked, it is proper to point it out in a sentence or so. Do not compliment the board on the thoroughness of their examination – they have been sketchy, and you know it. If you wish, merely say, "No thank you, I have nothing further to add." This is a point where you can "talk yourself out" of a good impression or fail to present an important bit of information. Remember, *you close the interview yourself.*

The chairman will then say, "That is all, Mr. _____, thank you." Do not be startled; the interview is over, and quicker than you think. Thank him, gather your belongings and take your leave. Save your sigh of relief for the other side of the door.

How to put your best foot forward
Throughout this entire process, you may feel that the board individually and collectively is trying to pierce your defenses, seek out your hidden weaknesses and embarrass and confuse you. Actually, this is not true. They are obliged to make an appraisal of your qualifications for the job you are seeking, and they want to see you in your best light. Remember, they must interview all candidates and a non-cooperative candidate may become a failure in spite of their best efforts to bring out his qualifications. Here are 15 suggestions that will help you:

1) Be natural – Keep your attitude confident, not cocky
If you are not confident that you can do the job, do not expect the board to be. Do not apologize for your weaknesses, try to bring out your strong points. The board is interested in a positive, not negative, presentation. Cockiness will antagonize any board member and make him wonder if you are covering up a weakness by a false show of strength.

2) Get comfortable, but don't lounge or sprawl
Sit erectly but not stiffly. A careless posture may lead the board to conclude that you are careless in other things, or at least that you are not impressed by the importance of the occasion. Either conclusion is natural, even if incorrect. Do not fuss with your clothing, a pencil or an ashtray. Your hands may occasionally be useful to emphasize a point; do not let them become a point of distraction.

3) Do not wisecrack or make small talk
This is a serious situation, and your attitude should show that you consider it as such. Further, the time of the board is limited – they do not want to waste it, and neither should you.

4) Do not exaggerate your experience or abilities

In the first place, from information in the application or other interviews and sources, the board may know more about you than you think. Secondly, you probably will not get away with it. An experienced board is rather adept at spotting such a situation, so do not take the chance.

5) If you know a board member, do not make a point of it, yet do not hide it

Certainly you are not fooling him, and probably not the other members of the board. Do not try to take advantage of your acquaintanceship – it will probably do you little good.

6) Do not dominate the interview

Let the board do that. They will give you the clues – do not assume that you have to do all the talking. Realize that the board has a number of questions to ask you, and do not try to take up all the interview time by showing off your extensive knowledge of the answer to the first one.

7) Be attentive

You only have 20 minutes or so, and you should keep your attention at its sharpest throughout. When a member is addressing a problem or question to you, give him your undivided attention. Address your reply principally to him, but do not exclude the other board members.

8) Do not interrupt

A board member may be stating a problem for you to analyze. He will ask you a question when the time comes. Let him state the problem, and wait for the question.

9) Make sure you understand the question

Do not try to answer until you are sure what the question is. If it is not clear, restate it in your own words or ask the board member to clarify it for you. However, do not haggle about minor elements.

10) Reply promptly but not hastily

A common entry on oral board rating sheets is "candidate responded readily," or "candidate hesitated in replies." Respond as promptly and quickly as you can, but do not jump to a hasty, ill-considered answer.

11) Do not be peremptory in your answers

A brief answer is proper – but do not fire your answer back. That is a losing game from your point of view. The board member can probably ask questions much faster than you can answer them.

12) Do not try to create the answer you think the board member wants

He is interested in what kind of mind you have and how it works – not in playing games. Furthermore, he can usually spot this practice and will actually grade you down on it.

13) Do not switch sides in your reply merely to agree with a board member

Frequently, a member will take a contrary position merely to draw you out and to see if you are willing and able to defend your point of view. Do not start a debate, yet do not surrender a good position. If a position is worth taking, it is worth defending.

14) Do not be afraid to admit an error in judgment if you are shown to be wrong

The board knows that you are forced to reply without any opportunity for careful consideration. Your answer may be demonstrably wrong. If so, admit it and get on with the interview.

15) Do not dwell at length on your present job

The opening question may relate to your present assignment. Answer the question but do not go into an extended discussion. You are being examined for a *new* job, not your present one. As a matter of fact, try to phrase ALL your answers in terms of the job for which you are being examined.

Basis of Rating

Probably you will forget most of these "do's" and "don'ts" when you walk into the oral interview room. Even remembering them all will not ensure you a passing grade. Perhaps you did not have the qualifications in the first place. But remembering them will help you to put your best foot forward, without treading on the toes of the board members.

Rumor and popular opinion to the contrary notwithstanding, an oral board wants you to make the best appearance possible. They know you are under pressure – but they also want to see how you respond to it as a guide to what your reaction would be under the pressures of the job you seek. They will be influenced by the degree of poise you display, the personal traits you show and the manner in which you respond.

ABOUT THIS BOOK

This book contains tests divided into Examination Sections. Go through each test, answering every question in the margin. We have also attached a sample answer sheet at the back of the book that can be removed and used. At the end of each test look at the answer key and check your answers. On the ones you got wrong, look at the right answer choice and learn. Do not fill in the answers first. Do not memorize the questions and answers, but understand the answer and principles involved. On your test, the questions will likely be different from the samples. Questions are changed and new ones added. If you understand these past questions you should have success with any changes that arise. Tests may consist of several types of questions. We have additional books on each subject should more study be advisable or necessary for you. Finally, the more you study, the better prepared you will be. This book is intended to be the last thing you study before you walk into the examination room. Prior study of relevant texts is also recommended. NLC publishes some of these in our Fundamental Series. Knowledge and good sense are important factors in passing your exam. Good luck also helps. So now study this Passbook, absorb the material contained within and take that knowledge into the examination. Then do your best to pass that exam.

EXAMINATION SECTION

EXAMINATION SECTION
TEST 1

DIRECTIONS: Each question or incomplete statement is followed by several suggested answers or completions. Select the one that BEST answers the question or completes the statement. *PRINT THE LETTER OF THE CORRECT ANSWER IN THE SPACE AT THE RIGHT.*

Questions 1-4.

DIRECTIONS: Questions 1 through 4 are to be answered on the basis of the information provided in the paragraph below.

Rodent control must be planned carefully in order to insure its success. This means that more knowledge is needed about the habits and favorite breeding places of Domestic Rats, than any other kind. A favorite breeding place for Domestic Rats is known to be in old or badly constructed buildings. Rats find these buildings very comfortable for making nests. However, the only way to gain this kind of detailed knowledge about rats is through careful study.

1. According to the above paragraph, rats find comfortable nesting places   1._____

    A. in old buildings
    B. in pipes
    C. on roofs
    D. in sewers

2. The paragraph states that the BEST way to learn all about the favorite nesting places of rats is by   2._____

    A. asking people
    B. careful study
    C. using traps
    D. watching ratholes

3. According to the paragraph, in order to insure the success of rodent control, it is necessary to   3._____

    A. design better bait
    B. give out more information
    C. plan carefully
    D. use pesticides

4. The paragraph states that the MOST important rats to study are _____ rats.   4._____

    A. African   B. Asian   C. Domestic   D. European

Questions 5-8.

DIRECTIONS: Questions 5 through 8 are to be answered on the basis of the following paragraph.

A few people who live in old tenements have the bad habit of throwing garbage out of their windows, especially if there is an empty lot near their building. Sometimes the garbage is food, sometimes the garbage is half-empty soda cans. Sometimes the garbage is a little bit of both mixed together. These people just don't care about keeping the lot clean.

1

5. The paragraph states that throwing garbage out of windows is a   5._____
   A. bad habit   B. dangerous thing to do
   C. good thing to do   D. good way to feed rats

6. According to the paragraph, an empty lot next to an old tenement is sometimes used as   6._____
   a place to
   A. hold local gang meetings   B. play ball
   C. throw garbage   D. walk dogs

7. According to the paragraph, which of the following throw garbage out of their windows?   7._____
   A. Nobody   B. Everybody
   C. Most people   D. Some people

8. According to the paragraph, the kinds of garbage thrown out of windows are   8._____
   A. candy and cigarette butts
   B. food and half-empty soda cans
   C. fruit and vegetables
   D. rice and bread

Questions 9-12.

DIRECTIONS: Questions 9 through 12 are to be answered on the basis of the following paragraph.

The game that is recognised all over the world as an all-American game is the game of baseball. As a matter of fact, baseball heroes like Joe DiMaggio, Willie Mays, and Babe Ruth, were as famous in their day as movie stars Robert Redford, Paul Newman, and Clint Eastwood are now. All these men have had the experience of being mobbed by fans whenever they put in an appearance anywhere in the world. Such unusual popularity makes it possible for stars like these to earn at least as much money off the job as on the job. It didn't take manufacturers and advertising men long to discover that their sales of shaving lotion, for instance, increased when they got famous stars to advertise their product for them on radio and television.

9. According to the paragraph, baseball is known everywhere as a(n) _____ game.   9._____
   A. all-American   B. fast
   C. unusual   D. tough

10. According to the paragraph, being so well known means that it is possible for people like   10._____
    Willie Mays and Babe Ruth to
    A. ask for anything and get it
    B. make as much money off the job as on it
    C. travel anywhere free of charge
    D. watch any game free of charge

11. According to the paragraph, which of the following are known all over the world?   11._____
    A. Baseball heroes   B. Advertising men
    C. Manufacturers   D. Basketball heroes

12. According to the paragraph, it is possible to sell much more shaving lotion on television   12.____
    and radio if

    A. the commercials are in color instead of black and white
    B. you can get a prize with each bottle of shaving lotion
    C. the shaving lotion makes you smell nicer than usual
    D. the shaving lotion is advertised by famous stars

Questions 13-16.

DIRECTIONS: Questions 13 through 16 are to be answered on the basis of the following paragraph.

People are very suspicious of all strangers who knock at their door. For this reason, every pest control aide, whether man or woman, must carry an identification card at all times on the job. These cards are issued by the agency the aide works for. The aide's picture is on the card. The aide's name is typed in, and the aide's signature is written on the line below. The name, address, and telephone number of the agency issuing the card is also printed on it. Once the aide shows this ID card to prove his or her identity, the tenant's time should not be taken up with small talk. The tenant should be told briefly what pest control means. The aide should be polite and ready to answer any questions the tenant may have on the subject. Then, the aide should thank the tenant for listening and say goodbye.

13. According to the above paragraph, when she visits tenants, the one item a pest control   13.____
    aide must ALWAYS carry with her is a(n)

    A. badge   B. driver's license
    C. identification card   D. watch

14. According to the paragraph, a pest control aide is supposed to talk to each tenant he vis-   14.____
    its

    A. at length about the agency
    B. briefly about pest control
    C. at length about family matters
    D. briefly about social security

15. According to the paragraph, the item that does NOT appear on an ID card is the   15.____

    A. address of the agency
    B. name of the agency
    C. signature of the aide
    D. social security number of the aide

16. According to the paragraph, a pest control aide carries an identification card because he   16.____
    must

    A. prove to tenants who he is
    B. provide the tenants with the agency's address
    C. provide the tenant with the agency's telephone number
    D. save the tenant's time

Questions 17-20.

DIRECTIONS: Questions 17 through 20 are to be answered on the basis of the following paragraph.

Very early on a summer's morning, the nicest thing to look at is a beach, before the swimmers arrive. Usually all the litter has been picked up from the sand by the Park Department clean-up crew. Everything is quiet. All you can hear are the waves breaking, and the sea gulls calling to each other. The beach opens to the public at 10 A.M. Long before that time, however, long lines of eager men, women, and children have driven up to the entrance. They form long lines that wind around the beach waiting for the signal to move.

17. According to the paragraph, before 10 A.M., long lines are formed that are made up of 17.____

    A. cars
    B. clean-up crews
    C. men, women, and children
    D. Park Department trucks

18. The season referred to in the above paragraph is 18.____

    A. fall   B. summer   C. winter   D. spring

19. The place the paragraph is describing is a 19.____

    A. beach
    B. park
    C. golf course
    D. tennis court

20. According to the paragraph, one of the things you notice early in the morning is that 20.____

    A. radios are playing
    B. swimmers are there
    C. the sand is dirty
    D. the litter is gone

Questions 21-30.

DIRECTIONS: In Questions 21 through 30, select the answer which means MOST NEARLY the SAME as the capitalized word in the sentence.

21. He received a large REWARD. 21.____
    In this sentence, the word REWARD means

    A. capture
    B. recompense
    C. key
    D. praise

22. The aide was asked to TRANSMIT a message. In this sentence, the word TRANSMIT means 22.____

    A. change   B. send   C. take   D. type

23. The pest control aide REQUESTED the tenant to call the Health Department. 23.____
    In this sentence, the word REQUESTED means the pest control aide

    A. asked   B. helped   C. informed   D. warned

24. The driver had to RETURN the Health Department's truck. In this sentence, the word RETURN means 24.____

    A. borrow   B. fix   C. give back   D. load up

25. The aide discussed the PURPOSE of the visit. In this sentence, the word PURPOSE means

    A. date   B. hour   C. need   D. reason,

26. The tenant SUSPECTED the aide who knocked at her door. In this sentence, the word SUSPECTED means

    A. answered
    C. distrusted
    B. called
    D. welcomed

27. The aide was POSITIVE that the child hit her. In this sentence, the word POSITIVE means

    A. annoyed   B. certain   C. sorry   D. surprised

28. The tenant DECLINED to call the Health Department. In this sentence, the word DECLINED means

    A. agreed   B. decided   C. refused   D. wanted

29. The aide ARRIVED on time.
    In this sentence, the word ARRIVED means

    A. awoke   B. came   C. left   D. delayed

30. The salesman had to DELIVER books to each person he visited.
    In this sentence, the word DELIVER means

    A. give   B. lend   C. mail   D. sell

KEY (CORRECT ANSWERS)

1.	A	11.	A	21.	B
2.	B	12.	D	22.	B
3.	C	13.	C	23.	A
4.	C	14.	B	24.	C
5.	A	15.	D	25.	D
6.	C	16.	A	26.	C
7.	D	17.	C	27.	B
8.	B	18.	B	28.	C
9.	A	19.	A	29.	B
10.	B	20.	D	30.	A

TEST 2

DIRECTIONS: Each question or incomplete statement is followed by several suggested answers or completions. Select the one that BEST answers the question or completes the statement. *PRINT THE LETTER OF THE CORRECT ANSWER IN THE SPACE AT THE RIGHT.*

Questions 1-10.

DIRECTIONS: In Questions 1 through 10, pick the word that means MOST NEARLY the OPPOSITE of the capitalize word in the sentence.

1. It is possible to CONSTRUCT a rat-proof home. The opposite of CONSTRUCT is   1.____
   A. build   B. erect   C. plant   D. wreck

2. The pest control aide had to REPAIR the flat tire. The opposite of the word REPAIR is   2.____
   A. destroy   B. fix   C. mend   D. patch

3. The pest control aide tried to SHOUT the answer. The opposite of the word SHOUT is   3.____
   A. scream   B. shriek   C. whisper   D. yell

4. Daily VISITS are the best.   4.____
   The opposite of the word VISITS is
   A. absences   B. exercises   C. lessons   D. trials

5. It is important to ARRIVE early in the morning. The opposite of the word ARRIVE is   5.____
   A. climb   B. descend   C. enter   D. leave

6. Jorge is a group LEADER.   6.____
   The opposite of the word LEADER is
   A. boss   B. chief   C. follower   D. overseer

7. The EXTERIOR of the house needs painting.   7.____
   The opposite of the word EXTERIOR is
   A. inside   B. outdoors   C. outside   D. surface

8. He CONCEDED the victory.   8.____
   The opposite of the word CONCEDED is
   A. admitted   B. denied   C. granted   D. reported

9. He watched the team BEGIN.   9.____
   The opposite of the word BEGIN is
   A. end   B. fail   C. gather   D. win

10. Your handwriting is ILLEGIBLE.   10.____
    The opposite of the word ILLEGIBLE is
    A. clear   B. confused   C. jumbled   D. unclear

Questions 11-15.

DIRECTIONS: Questions 11 through 15 are to be answered by following the instructions given in each question. Note that 5 possible answers have been given for these questions ONLY. Therefore, for these questions, your choice may be A, B, C, D, or E.

11. Add:
    $12\frac{1}{2}$
    $2\frac{1}{4}$
    $3\frac{1}{4}$

    The CORRECT answer is

    A. 17 B. 174 C. 174 D. 17 3/4 E. 18

12. Subtract:
    150
    -80

    The CORRECT answer is

    A. 70 B. 80 C. 130 D. 150 E. 230

13. After cleaning up some lots in the East Bronx, five cleanup crews loaded the following amounts of garbage on trucks:
    Crew No. 1 loaded 2 1/4 tons
    Crew No. 2 loaded 3 tons
    Crew No. 3 loaded 1 1/4 tons
    Crew No. 4 loaded 2 1/4 tons
    Crew No. 5 loaded 1/2 ton
    The TOTAL number of tons of garbage loaded was

    A. 8 B. 8 1/4 C. 8 3/4 D. 9 E. 9 1/4

14. Subtract:
    17 3/4
    - 7 1/4

    The CORRECT answer is

    A. 7 1/2 B. 10 1/2 C. 14 1/4 D. 17 3/4 E. 25

15. Yesterday, Tom and Bill each received 10 leaflets about rat control. Each supermarket in the neighborhood was supposed to receive one of these leaflets. When the day was over, Tom had 8 leaflets left. Bill had no leaflets left. How many supermarkets got leaflets yesterday?

    A. 8 B. 10 C. 12 D. 18 E. 20

Questions 16-20.

DIRECTIONS: Questions 16 through 20 are to be answered ONLY on the basis of the information in the following statement and chart, DAILY WORK REPORT FORM (Chart A).

Assume that you are a member of the Pest Control Truck Crew Number 1. Julio Rivera is your Crew Chief. The crew is supposed to report to work at nine o'clock in the morning, Since you are the first to show up, at ten minutes before nine, on 5/24 Rivera asks you to help him out by filling in the Daily Work Report Form for him. Driver Hal Williams shows up at nine, and Driver Rick Smith shows up ten minutes after Williams.

DAILY WORK REPORT FORM (Chart A)

Block #1 Crew No.	Block #2 Date	
Block #3 TRUCKS IN USE Truck # # # # # # # # # #	Block #4 DRIVER'S NAME	Block #5 TIME OF ARRIVAL A.M. P.M.
Block #6 TRUCKS OUT OF ORDER # # # # #	Block #7 ADDRESS OF CLEAN-UP SITE No._____ Street_____	Block #8 Borough Block #9 Signature of Crew Chief

16. According to the above statement, the entry that belongs in Block #9 is

    A. Julio Rivera   B. June Stevens
    C. Jim Watson   D. Hal Williams

17. According to the above statement, the entry that should be made in Block #2 is

    A. 9:00 A.M.   B. 9:10 P.M.   C. 5/24   D. 7/24

18. The names of Hal Williams and Rick Smith should appear in Block #

    A. 4   B. 6   C. 7   D. 9

4 (#2)

19. Rick Smith's time of arrival should be entered in Block #5 as _____ A.M. 19.___
    A. 8:50   B. 8:55   C. 9:00   D. 9:10

20. According to the statement, the entry that should be made in Block #1 is 20.___
    A. zero   B. one   C. 5/24   D. 6/24

Questions 21-23.

DIRECTIONS: Questions 21 through 23 are to be answered on the basis of the statement shown below. Use DAILY WORK REPORT FORM (Chart A) on Page 3 as a guide.

Pete Marberg showed up at a quarter after nine, in the morning, but his truck, No. 22632441, was in the garage for repairs. Steve Marino showed up a half hour after Pete. He was assigned truck No. 6342003, which was in working order.

21. According to the above statement, truck No. 22632441 should be entered in Block # 21.___
    A. 3   B. 4   C. 6   D. 8

22. According to the above statement, Steve Marino showed up at 22.___
    A. 9:00 A.M.   B. 9:15 A.M.   C. 9:30 P.M.   D. 9:45 A.M.

23. According to the above statement, Steve Marino's truck number belongs in Block #3. The number entered there should be 23.___
    A. 22632441   B. 6342003   C. 6432003   D. 26232441

Questions 24-30.

DIRECTIONS: Questions 24 through 30 are to be answered ONLY on basis of the information in the statements above ea question and the following chart, DAILY GARBAGE COLLECTION REPORT (Chart B).

DAILY GARBAGE COLLECTION REPORT C Chart B)				
Block #1	Block #2	Block #3	Block #4	Block #5
No. of Trucks Used For Collection	Address of Garbage Pick-Up	Amount of Garbage Collected	Amount of Garbage Unloaded	Hours During Which Garbage Was Unloaded
#456	45 Southwest	1/2 ton	1/2 ton	From 7 AM — To 8 AM
TOTALS _____		Block #6 otal Amount of Garbage Collected By All Trucks	Block #7 Total Amount of Garbage Unloaded By All Trucks	Block #8 Total Amount of Time Spent Unloading Of All Trucks

24. Truck # 2437752 started unloading garbage at ten o'clock Monday morning and finished unloading its garbage that afternoon. The clock looked like this when the job was done.
    The time entries that should be recorded in Block #5 are
    A. 10 A.M. and 12:15 P.M.
    B. 10 P.M. and 12:30 A.M.
    C. 10 P.M. and 12:00 A.M.
    D. 10 A.M. and 3:00 P.M.

24._____

25. Truck # 8967432 had to pick up a load of garbage from 911 South Avenue. It took the crew until 11:00 A.M. to load the garbage.
    According to this statement, the item 911 South Avenue should be entered in Block #

    A. 1   B. 2   C. 3   D. 4

25._____

26. On Tuesday, truck # 124356 unloaded 4 ton of garbage, truck # 2437752 unloaded J ton of garbage, and truck # 435126 unloaded 1/2 ton of garbage.
    The TOTAL amount of garbage unloaded by the three trucks on Tuesday should be entered in Block #

    A. 3   B. 4   C. 5   D. 8

26._____

27. On Wednesday, it took truck # 4050607 from 2 P.M. to 6 P.M. to unload 1 ton of garbage. It took truck # 7040650 from 1 P.M. to 2 P.M. to unload 1/4 ton of garbage. These were the only trucks working that day.
    The TOTAL amount of time it took for both trucks to unload garbage was _____ hours.

    A. 5   B. 6   C. 7   D. 8

27._____

28. The amount of garbage collected by one truck should be entered in the DAILY GARBAGE COLLECTION REPORT FORM in Block #

    A. 3   B. 6   C. 7   D. 8

28._____

29. Truck # 557799010 reported to 1020 Hudson River Alley to pick up garbage from an empty lot.
    This information should be entered in the DAILY GARBAGE COLLECTION REPORT FORM in Block # _____ and Block # _____ .

    A. 1; 4   B. 2; 5   C. 1; 2   D. 2; 3

29._____

30. It took the Pest Control Truck crew from 8 in the morning to 12 noon to unload the garbage it collected the night before.
    This information should be entered in the DAILY GARBAGE COLLECTION REPORT FORM under Block #   30._____

    A. 4　　　　　　　B. 5　　　　　　　C. 6　　　　　　　D. 7

KEY (CORRECT ANSWERS)

1.	D	11.	E	21.	C
2.	A	12.	A	22.	D
3.	C	13.	E	23.	B
4.	A	14.	B	24.	D
5.	D	15.	C	25.	B
6.	C	16.	A	26.	B
7.	A	17.	C	27.	A
8.	B	18.	A	28.	A
9.	A	19.	D	29.	C
10.	A	20.	B	30.	B

EXAMINATION SECTION
TEST 1

DIRECTIONS: Each question or incomplete statement is followed by several suggested answers or completions. Select the one that BEST answers the question or completes the statement. *PRINT THE LETTER OF THE CORRECT ANSWER IN THE SPACE AT THE RIGHT.*

1. If you can't come to work in the morning because you do not feel well, you should

    A. call your supervisor and let him know that you are sick
    B. try to get someone else to take your place
    C. have your doctor call your office as proof that you are sick
    D. come to work anyway so that you won't lose your job

2. Many machines have certain safety devices for the operators.
   The MOST important reason for having these safety devices is to

    A. increase the amount of work that the machines can do
    B. permit repairs to be made on the machines without shutting them down
    C. help prevent accidents to people who use the machines
    D. reduce the cost of electric power needed to run the machines

3. While working on the job, you accidentally break a window pane. No one is around, and you are able to clean up the broken pieces of glass.
   It would then be BEST for you to

    A. leave a note near the window that a new glass has to be put in because it was accidentally broken
    B. forget about the whole thing because the window was not broken on purpose
    C. write a report to your supervisor telling him that you saw a broken window pane that has to be fixed
    D. tell your supervisor that you accidentally broke the window pane while working

4. There is a two-light fixture in the room where you are working. One of the light bulbs goes out, and you need more light to work by.
   You should

    A. change the fuse in the fuse box
    B. have a new bulb put in
    C. call for an electrician and stop work until he comes
    D. find out what is causing the short circuit

5. The BEST way to remove some small pieces of broken glass from a floor is to

    A. use a brush and dust pan
    B. pick up the pieces carefully with your hands
    C. use a wet mop and a wringer
    D. sweep the pieces into the corner of the room

6. When you are not sure about some instructions that your supervisor has given you on how to do a certain job, it would be BEST for you to

    A. start doing the work and stop when you come to the part that you do not understand
    B. ask the supervisor to go over the instructions which are not clear to you
    C. do the job immediately from beginning to the end, leaving out the part that you are not sure of
    D. wait until the supervisor leaves and then ask a more experienced worker to explain the job to you

7. When an employee first comes on the job, he is given a period of training by his supervisor.
   The MAIN reason for this training period is to

    A. make sure that the employee will learn to do his work correctly and safely
    B. give the employee a chance to show the supervisor that he can learn quickly
    C. allow the supervisor and the employee a chance to become friendly with each other
    D. find out which employees will make good supervisors later on

8. After you open a sealed box of supplies, you find that the box is not full and that some of the supplies are missing.
   You should

    A. use fewer supplies than you intended to
    B. seal the box and take it back to the storeroom
    C. get signed statements from other employees that when you opened the box, it was not full
    D. tell your supervisor about it

9. Suppose that after you have been on the job a few months, your supervisor shows you some small mistakes you are making in your work.
   You should

    A. tell your supervisor that these mistakes don't keep you from finishing your work
    B. ask your supervisor how you can avoid these mistakes
    C. try to show your supervisor that your way of doing the work is just as good as his way of doing it
    D. check with the other workers to find out if your supervisor is also finding fault with them

10. If your supervisor gives you an order to do a special job which you do not like to do, you should

    A. take a long time to do the job so that you won't get this job again
    B. do the job the best way you know how even though you don't like it
    C. make believe that you didn't hear your supervisor and do your regular work
    D. say nothing but tell another employee that the supervisor wants him to do this special job

11. If two employees who are working together on a job do not agree on how to do the job, it would be BEST

    A. for each worker to do the job in his own way until it is finished
    B. to put off doing the job until both workers agree to do it the same way
    C. to ask the supervisor to decide on the way the job is to be done
    D. for each worker to ask for a transfer to another assignment because they can't get along with each other

11._____

12. Suppose that in order to finish your work, you have to lift a heavy box off the floor onto an empty desk.
    You should

    A. leave the box where it is and tell your supervisor that you have finished your work
    B. lift the box by yourself very quickly so that your supervisor will see that you are a strong, willing worker
    C. ask another employee to give you a hand to lift the box off the floor
    D. complain to your supervisor that he should check a job before giving you such a tough assignment

12._____

13. Bulletin boards for the posting of official notices are usually put up near the place where employees check in and out each day.
    For an employee to spend a few minutes each day to read the new notices is

    A. *good;* these notices give him information about the Department and his own work
    B. *bad;* all important information is given to employees by their supervisors
    C. *good;* this is a way to "take a break" during the day
    D. *bad;* the notices can't help him in his work

13._____

14. Suppose that your supervisor gives you a job to do and tells you that he wants you to finish it in three hours.
    If you finish the work at the end of 2 hours, you should

    A. wait until the three hours are up and then tell your supervisor that you are finished
    B. go to your supervisor and tell him that you finished a half-hour ahead of time
    C. spend the next half-hour getting ready for the next job you think your supervisor may give you
    D. take a half-hour rest period because good work deserves a reward

14._____

15. Which one of the following is it LEAST important to include in an accident report?

    A. Name and address of the injured person
    B. Date, time, and place where the accident happened
    C. Name and address of the injured person's family doctor
    D. An explanation of how the accident happened

15._____

16. If, near the end of the day, you realize that you made a mistake in your work and you can't do the work over, you should

    A. forget about it because there is only a small chance that the mistake can be traced back to you
    B. wait a few days and take the blame for the mistake if it is caught
    C. ask the other employees to keep the mistake a secret so that no one can be blamed
    D. tell your supervisor about the mistake right away

16._____

17. Employees should wipe up water spilled on floors immediately.
The BEST reason for this is that water on a floor

   A. is a sign that employees are sloppy
   B. makes for a slippery condition that could cause an accident
   C. will eat into the wax protecting the floor
   D. is against health regulations

18. Another worker, who is a good friend of yours, leaves work an hour before quitting time to take care of a personal matter. When you leave later, you find that your friend did not sign out on the timesheet.
For you to sign out for your friend would be

   A. *good,* because he will do the same for you some day when you want to leave early
   B. *bad,* because other employees will also want you to do the same favor for them on other days
   C. *good,* because the timesheet should not have any empty spaces on it
   D. *bad,* because timesheets are official records which employees should keep honestly and accurately

19. While you are working, a person asks you how to get to an office which you know is one floor above you in the building where you work.
It would be BEST for you to tell this person that

   A. you can't answer any questions because you have to finish your work
   B. he should go back to the lobby and check the list of offices
   C. the office he is looking for is on the next floor
   D. he should call the office he is looking for to get exact instructions on how to get there

20. While you are at work, you find a sealed brown envelope under a desk. The envelope is marked *Personal - Hand Delivery* and is addressed to an official who has an office in the building where you are working.
You should

   A. drop the envelope into the nearest mailbox so that it can be delivered the next day
   B. look up the telephone number of the official and call him up to tell him what you have found
   C. put the envelope in your pocket and come in early the next day to deliver it personally to the official
   D. give the envelope to your supervisor right away and tell him where you found it

21. A messenger delivered 32 letters on Monday, 47 on Tuesday, 29 on Wednesday, 36 on Thursday, and 41 on Friday.
How many letters did he deliver altogether?

   A. 157   B. 185   C. 218   D. 229

22. Mr. White paid 4% sales tax on a $95 television set.
The amount of sales tax that he paid was

   A. $9.50   B. $4.00   C. $3.80   D. $.95

23. How many square feet are there in a room which is 25 feet long and 35 feet wide? 23.____
    _____ square feet.
    A. 600   B. 750   C. 875   D. 925

24. How much would it cost to send a 34 pound package by parcel post if the postage is 24.____
    $1.60 for the first 20 pounds and 7 for each additional pound?
    A. $2.34   B. $2.58   C. $2.66   D. $2.80

25. Adding together 1/2, 3/4, and 1/8, the total is 25.____
    A. 1 1/4   B. 1 1/2   C. 1 3/8   D. 1 3/4

26. If a piece of wood 40 inches long is cut into two pieces so that the larger piece is three 26.____
    times as long as the, smaller piece, the smaller piece is _____ inches.
    A. 4   B. 5   C. 8   D. 10

27. Two friends, Smith and Jones, together spend $1,800 to buy a car. 27.____
    If Smith put up twice as much money as Jones, then Jones' share of the cost of the car
    was
    A. $300   B. $600   C. $900   D. $1,200

28. In a certain agency, two-thirds of the employees are clerks and the remainder are typists. 28.____
    If there are 180 clerks, then the number of typists in this agency is
    A. 270   B. 90   C. 240   D. 60

Questions 29-35.

DIRECTIONS: Answer Questions 29 through 35 ONLY according to the information given in
the chart below.

EMPLOYEE RECORD

Name of Employee	Where Assigned	Number of Days Absent Vacation	Sick Leave	Yearly Salary
Carey	Laundry	18	4	$18,650
Hayes	Mortuary	24	8	$17,930
Irwin	Buildings	20	17	$18,290
King	Supply	12	10	$17,930
Lane	Mortuary	17	8	$17,750
Martin	Buildings	13	12	$17,750
Prince	Buildings	5	7	$17,750
Quinn	Supply	19	0	$17,250
Sands	Buildings	23	10	$18,470
Victor	Laundry	21	2	$18,150

29. The *only* employee who was NOT absent because of sickness is   29.___
    A. Hayes   B. Lane   C. Victor   D. Quinn

30. The employee with the HIGHEST salary is   30.___
    A. Carey   B. Irwin   C. Sands   D. Victor

31. The employee with the LOWEST salary is assigned to the _____ Bureau.   31.___
    A. Laundry   B. Mortuary   C. Building   D. Supply

32. Which one of these was absent or on vacation more than 20 days?   32.___
    A. Irwin   B. Lane   C. Quinn   D. Victor

33. The number of employees whose salary is LESS than $18,100 a year is   33.___
    A. 4   B. 5   C. 6   D. 7

34. MOST employees are assigned to   34.___
    A. Laundry   B. Mortuary   C. Buildings   D. Supply

35. From the chart, you can figure out for each employee   35.___
    A. how long he has worked in his present assignment
    B. how many days vacation he has left
    C. how many times he has been late
    D. how much he earns a month

KEY (CORRECT ANSWERS)

1.	A	16.	D
2.	C	17.	B
3.	D	18.	D
4.	B	19.	C
5.	A	20.	D
6.	B	21.	B
7.	A	22.	C
8.	D	23.	C
9.	B	24.	B
10.	B	25.	C
11.	C	26.	D
12.	C	27.	B
13.	A	28.	B
14.	B	29.	D
15.	C	30.	A

31.	D
32.	D
33.	C
34.	C
35.	D

TEST 2

DIRECTIONS: Each question or incomplete statement is followed by several suggested answers or completions. Select the one that BEST answers the question or completes the statement. *PRINT THE LETTER OF THE CORRECT ANSWER IN THE SPACE AT THE RIGHT.*

Questions 1-5.

DIRECTIONS: Answer Questions 1 to 5 ONLY according to the information given in the following passage.

EMPLOYEE LEAVE REGULATIONS

Peter Smith, as a full-time permanent City employee under the Career and Salary Plan, earns an "annual leave allowance" This consists of a certain number of days off a year with pay and may be used for vacation, personal business, and for observing religious holidays. As a newly appointed employee, during his first eight years of City service, he will earn an "annual leave allowance" of twenty days off a year (an average of 1 2/3 days off a month). After he has finished eight full years of working for the City, he will begin earning an additional five days off a year. His "annual leave allowance," therefore, will then be twenty-five days a year and will remain at this amount for seven full years. He will begin earning an additional two days off a year after he has completed a total of fifteen years of City employment. Therefore, in his sixteenth year of working for the City, Mr. Smith will be earning twenty-seven days off a year as his "annual leave allowance" (an average of 2 1/4 days off a month).

A "sick leave allowance" of one day a month is also given to Mr. Smith, but it can be used only in case of actual illness. When Mr. Smith returns to work after using "sick leave allowance," he must have a doctor's note if the absence is for a total of more than three days, but he may also be required to show a doctor's note for absences of one, two, or three days.

1. According to the above passage, Mr. Smith's *annual leave allowance* consists of a certain number of days off a year which he   1._____

    A. does not get paid for
    B. gets paid for at time and a half
    C. may use for personal business
    D. may not use for observing religious holidays

2. According to the above passage, after Mr. Smith has been working for the City for nine years, his *annual leave allowance* will be _____ days a year.   2._____

    A. 20   B. 25   C. 27   D. 37

3. According to the above passage, Mr. Smith will begin earning an average of 2 1/4 days off a month as his *annual leave allowance* after he has worked for the City for _____ full years.   3._____

    A. 7   B. 8   C. 15   D. 17

4. According to the above passage, Mr. Smith is given a *sick leave allowance* of   4._____

    A. 1 day every 2 months   B. 1 day per month
    C. 1 2/3 days per month   D. 2 1/4 days a month

19

5. According to the above passage, when he uses *sick leave allowance*, Mr. Smith may be required to show a doctor's note

   A. even if his absence is for only 1 day
   B. only if his absence is for more than 2 days
   C. only if his absence is for more than 3 days
   D. only if his absence is for 3 days or more

Questions 6-9.

DIRECTIONS: Answer Questions 6 to 9 ONLY according to the information given in the following passag

MOPPING FLOORS

When mopping hardened cement floors, either painted or unpainted, a soap and water mixture should be used. This should be made by dissolving 1/2 a cup of soft soap in a pail of hot water. It is not desirable, however, under any circumstances, to use a soap and water mixture on cement floors that are not hardened. For mopping this type of floor, it is recommended that the cleaning agent be made up of two ounces of laundry soda mixed in a pail of water.

Soaps are not generally used on hard tile floors because slippery films may build up on the floor. It is generally recommended that these floors be mopped using a pail of hot water in which has been mixed two ounces of washing powder for each gallon of water. The floors should then be rinsed thoroughly.

After the mopping is finished, proper care should be taken of the mop. This is done by first cleaning the mop in clear, warm water. Then, it should be wrung out, after which the strands of the mop should be untangled. Finally, the mop should be hung by its handle to dry.

6. According to the above passage, you should NEVER use a soap and water mixture when mopping _____ floors.

   A. hardened cement   B. painted
   C. unhardened cement   D. unpainted

7. According to the above passage, using laundry soda mixed in a pail of water as a cleaning agent is recommended for

   A. all floors
   B. all floors except hard tile floors
   C. some cement floors
   D. lineoleum floor coverings only

8. According to the above passage, the generally recommended mixture for mopping hard tile floors is

   A. 1/2 a cup of soft soap for each gallon of hot water
   B. 1/2 a cup of soft soap in a pail of hot water
   C. 2 ounces of washing powder in a pail of hot water
   D. 2 ounces of washing powder for each gallon of hot water

9. According to the above passage, the proper care of a mop after it is used includes   9._____

   A. cleaning it in clear cold water and hanging it by its handle to dry
   B. wringing it out, untangling and drying it
   C. untangling its strands before wringing it out
   D. untangling its strands while cleaning it in clear water

Questions 10-13.

DIRECTIONS: Answer Questions 10 to 13 ONLY according to the information given in the following passage.

HANDLING HOSPITAL LAUNDRY

In a hospital, care must be taken when handling laundry in order to reduce the chance of germs spreading. There is always the possibility that dirty laundry will be carrying dangerous germs. To avoid catching germs when they are working with dirty laundry, laundry workers should be sure that any cuts or wounds they have are bandaged before they touch the dirty laundry. They should also be careful when handling this laundry not to rub their eyes, nose, or mout. Just like all other hospital workers, laundry workers should also protect themselves against germs by washing and rinsing their hands thoroughly before eating meals and before leaving work at the end of the day.

To be sure that germs from dirty laundry do not pass onto clean laundry and thereby increase the danger to patients, clean and dirty laundry should not be handled near each other or by the same person. Special care also has to be taken with laundry that comes from a patient who has a dangerous, highly contagious disease so that as few people as possible come in direct contact with this laundry. Laundry from this patient, therefore, should be kept separate from other dirty laundry at all times.

10. According to the above passage, when working with dirty laundry, laundry workers   10._____
    should

    A. destroy laundry carrying dangerous germs
    B. have any cuts bandaged before touching the dirty laundry
    C. never touch the dirty laundry directly
    D. rub their eyes, nose, and mouth to protect them from germs

11. According to the above passage, all hospital workers should wash their hands thoroughly   11._____

    A. after eating meals to remove any trace of food from their hands
    B. at every opportunity to show good example to the patients
    C. before eating meals to protect themselves against germs
    D. before starting work in the morning to feel fresh and ready to do a good day's work

12. According to the above passage, the danger to patients will increase   12._____

    A. unless a worker handles dirty and clean laundry at the same time
    B. unless clean and dirty laundry are handled near each other
    C. when clean laundry is ironed frequently
    D. when germs pass from dirty laundry to clean laundry

13. According to the above passage, laundry from a patient with a dangerous, highly contagious disease should be

   A. given special care so that as few people as possible come in direct contact with it
   B. handled in the same way as any other dirty laundry
   C. washed by hand
   D. separated from the other dirty laundry just before it is washed

Questions 14-17.

DIRECTIONS: Answer Questions 14 to 17 ONLY according to the information given in the following passage.

EMPLOYEE SUGGESTIONS

To increase the effectiveness of the New York City governments the City asks its employees to offer suggestions when they feel an improvement could be made in some government operation. The Employees' Suggestions Program was started to encourage City employees to do this. Through this Program, which is only for City employees, cash awards may be given to those whose suggestions are submitted and approve Suggestions are looked for not only from supervisors but from all City employees as any City employee may get an idea which might be approved and contribute greatly to the solution of some problem of City government.

Therefore, all suggestions for improvement are welcome, whether they be suggestions on how to improve working conditions, or on how to increase the speed with which work is done, or on how to reduce or eliminate such things as waste, time losses, accidents, or fire hazards. There are, however, a few types of suggestions for which cash awards can not be given. An example of this type would be a suggestion to increase salaries or a suggestion to change the regulations about annual leave or about sick leave. The number of suggestions sent in has increased sharply during the past few years. It is hoped that it will keep increasing in the future in order to meet the City's needs for more ideas for improved ways of doing things.

14. According to the above passage, the main reason why the City asks its employees for suggestions about government operations is to

   A. increase the effectiveness of the City government
   B. show that the Employees' Suggestion Program is working well
   C. show that everybody helps run the City government
   D. have the employee win a prize

15. According to the above passage, the Employees' Suggestion Program can approve awards only for those suggestions that come from

   A. City employees
   B. City employees who are supervisors
   C. City employees who are not supervisors
   D. experienced employees of the City

16. According to the above passage, a cash award can not be given through the Employees' Suggestion Program for a suggestion about   16._____

    A. getting work done faster
    B. helping prevent accidents on the job
    C. increasing the amount of annual leave for City employees
    D. reducing the chance of fire where City employees work

17. According to the above passage, the suggestions sent in during the past few years have   17._____

    A. all been approved
    B. generally been well written
    C. been mostly about reducing or eliminating waste
    D. been greater in number than before

Questions 18-21.

DIRECTIONS: Answer Questions 18 to 21 ONLY according to the information given in the following passage.

ACCIDENT PREVENTION

Many accidents and injuries can be prevented if employees learn to be more careful. The wearing of shoes with thin or badly worn soles or open toes can easily lead to foot injuries from tacks, nails, and chair and desk legs. Loose or torn clothing should not be worn near moving machinery. This is especially true of neckties which can very easily become caught in the machine. You should not place objects so that they block or partly block hallways, corridors, or other passageways. Even when they are stored in the proper place, tools, supplies, and equipment should be carefully placed or piled so as not to fall, nor have anything stick out from a pile. Before cabinets, lockers, or ladders are moved, the tops should be cleared of anything which might injure someone or fall of If necessary, use a dolly to move these or other bulky objects.

Despite all efforts to avoid accidents and injuries, however, some will happen. If an employee is injured, no matter how small the injury, he should report it to his supervisor and have the injury treated. A small cut that is not attended to can easily become infected and can cause more trouble than some injuries which at first seem more serious. It never pays to take chances.

18. According to the above passage, the one statement that is NOT true is that   18._____

    A. by being more careful, employees can reduce the number of accidents that happen
    B. women should wear shoes with open toes for comfort when working
    C. supplies should be piled so that nothing is sticking out from the pile
    D. if an employee sprains his wrist at work, he should tell his supervisor about it

19. According to the above passage, you should NOT wear loose clothing when you are   19._____

    A. in a corridor   B. storing tools
    C. opening cabinets   D. near moving machinery

20. According to the above passage, before moving a ladder, you should　　　　20.___

    A. test all the rungs
    B. get a dolly to carry the ladder at all times
    C. remove everything from the top of the ladder which might fall off
    D. remove your necktie

21. According to the above passage, an employee who gets a slight cut should　　　　21.___

    A. have it treated to help prevent infection
    B. know that a slight cut becomes more easily infected than a big cut
    C. pay no attention to it as it can't become serious
    D. realize that it is more serious than any other type of injury

Questions 22-24.

DIRECTIONS: Answer Questions 22 to 24 ONLY according to the information given in the following passage.

GOOD EMPLOYEE PRACTICES

As a City employee, you will be expected to take an interest in your work and perform the duties of your job to the best of your ability and in a spirit of cooperation. Nothing shows an interest in your work more than coming to work on time, not only at the start of the day but also when returning from lunch. If it is necessary for you to keep a personal appointment at lunch hour which might cause a delay in getting back to work on time, you should explain the situation to your supervisor and get his approval to come back a little late before you leave for lunch.

You should do everything that is asked of you willingly and consider important even the small jobs that your supervisor gives you. Although these jobs may seem unimportant, if you forget to do them or if you don't do them right, trouble may develop later.

Getting along well with your fellow workers will add much to the enjoyment of your work. You should respect your fellow workers and try to see their side when a disagreement arises. The better you get along with your fellow workers and your supervisor, the better you will like your job and the better you will be able to do it.

22. According to the above passage, in your job as a City employee, you are expected to　　　　22.___

    A. show a willingness to cooperate on the job
    B. get your supervisor's approval before keeping any personal appointments at lunch hour
    C. avoid doing small jobs that seem unimportant
    D. do the easier jobs at the start of the day and the more difficult ones later on

23. According to the above passage, getting to work on time shows that you　　　　23.___

    A. need the job
    B. have an interest in your work
    C. get along well with your fellow workers
    D. like your supervisor

24. According to the above passage, the one of the following statements that is NOT true is   24._____
    A. if you do a small job wrong, trouble may develop
    B. you should respect your fellow workers
    C. if you disagree with a fellow worker, you should try to see his side of the story
    D. the less you get along with your supervisor, the better you will be able to do your job

Questions 25-35.   VOCABULARY

25. The porter cleaned the VACANT room.   25._____
    In this sentence, the word VACANT means nearly the same as

    A. empty   B. large   C. main   D. crowded

26. The supervisor gave a BRIEF report to his men.   26._____
    In this sentence, the word BRIEF means nearly the same as

    A. long   B. safety   C. complete   D. short

27. The supervisor told him to CONNECT the two pieces.   27._____
    In this sentence, the word CONNECT means nearly the same as

    A. join   B. paint   C. return   D. weigh

28. Standing on the top of a ladder is RISKY.   28._____
    In this sentence, the word RISKY means nearly the same as

    A. dangerous   B. sensible   C. safe   D. foolish

29. He RAISED the cover of the machine.   29._____
    In this sentence, the word RAISED means nearly the same as

    A. broke   B. lifted   C. lost   D. found

30. The form used for reporting the finished work was REVISED.   30._____
    In this sentence, the word REVISED means nearly the same as

    A. printed   B. ordered   C. dropped   D. changed

31. He did his work RAPIDLY.   31._____
    In this sentence, the word RAPIDLY means nearly the same as

    A. carefully   B. quickly   C. slowly   D. quietly

32. The worker was OCCASIONALLY late   32._____
    In this sentence, the word OCCASIONALLY means nearly the same as

    A. sometimes   B. often   C. never   D. always

33. He SELECTED the best tool for the job.   33._____
    In this sentence, the word SELECTED means nearly the same as

    A. bought   B. picked   C. lost   D. broke

34. He needed ASSISTANCE to lift the package.
    In this sentence, the word ASSISTANCE means nearly the same as

    A. strength   B. time   C. help   D. instructions

    34.___

35. The tools were ISSUED by the supervisor.
    In this sentence, the word ISSUED means nearly the same as

    A. collected   B. cleaned up
    C. given out   D. examined

    35.___

KEY (CORRECT ANSWERS)

1.	C		16.	C
2.	B		17.	D
3.	C		18.	B
4.	B		19.	D
5.	A		20.	C
6.	C		21.	A
7.	C		22.	A
8.	D		23.	B
9.	B		24.	D
10.	B		25.	A
11.	C		26.	D
12.	D		27.	A
13.	A		28.	A
14.	A		29.	B
15.	A		30.	D

31. B
32. A
33. B
34. C
35. C

EXAMINATION SECTION
TEST 1

DIRECTIONS: Each question or incomplete statement is followed by several suggested answers or completions. Select the one that BEST answers the question or completes the statement. *PRINT THE LETTER OF THE CORRECT ANSWER IN THE SPACE AT THE RIGHT.*

1. An employee who is not sure how to do a job that the supervisor has just assigned should

    A. ask another employee how to do the job
    B. ask the supervisor how to do the job
    C. do some other work until the supervisor gives further instructions
    D. do the best he can

2. An employee who is asked by the supervisor to work one hour overtime cannot stay because of previous arrangements made with the family. The employee should

    A. ask another employee who does not have a family to take over
    B. explain the situation to the supervisor and ask to be excused
    C. go home, but leave a note for the supervisor explaining the reason for not being able to stay
    D. refuse, giving the excuse that time-and-a-half is not being paid for overtime

3. A department's MAIN purpose in setting up employee rules and regulations is to

    A. explain the department's work to the public
    B. give an official history of the department
    C. help in the efficient running of the department
    D. limit the number of employees who break the rules

4. The MAIN reason an employee should be polite is that

    A. he may get into trouble if he is not polite
    B. he never knows when he may be talking to an official
    C. politeness is a duty which any employee owes the public
    D. politeness will make him appear to be alert and efficient

5. Public employees would *most probably* be expected by their supervisor to do

    A. a fair day's work according to their ability
    B. more work than the employees of other supervisors
    C. more work than the supervisor really knows they can do
    D. the same amount of work that a little better than average employee can do

6. Your supervisor gives you a special job to do without saying when it must be finished and then leaves for another job location. A little before quitting time you realize that you will not be able to finish the job that day. You should

    A. ask a few of the other employees to help you finish the job
    B. go home at quitting time and finish the job the next day
    C. stay on the job till you get in touch with your supervisor by phone and get further instructions
    D. work overtime till you finish the job

7. "While on duty an employee is not permitted to smoke in public." Of the following, the most likely reason for such a rule is that

   A. government employees must be willing to surrender some of their personal liberties
   B. lighted cigarettes create a fire hazard
   C. nicotine in tobacco will lessen a city employee's ability to perform assigned duties properly
   D. smoking on duty may make an unfavorable impression on the public

8. While you are on duty someone asks you how to get somewhere. Supposing that you know how to get there, you should

   A. give him the necessary directions
   B. make believe you did not hear him
   C. tell him it is not your duty to give information
   D. tell him you are too busy to give the information

9. The BEST way to make sure that a piece of important mail will be received is to send it by

   A. first class mail B. fourth class mail
   C. registered mail D. special delivery

10. Letters, if they don't weigh more than an ounce, need a

    A. 37¢ stamp B. 38¢ stamp
    C. 39¢ stamp D. 40¢ stamp

QUESTIONS 11-15.

Answer questions 11 to 15 ONLY on the basis of the information given in the following paragraph.

If an employee thinks he can save money, time, or material for the city or has an idea about how to do something better than it is being done, he should not keep it to himself. He should send his ideas to the Employee's Suggestion Program, using the special form which is kept on hand in all departments. An employee may send in as many ideas as he wishes. To make sure that each idea is judged fairly, the name of the suggestor is not made known until an award is made. The awards are certificates of merit or cash prizes ranging from $10 to $500.

11. According to the above paragraph, an employee who knows how to do a job in a better way should

    A. be sure it saves enough time to be worthwhile
    B. get paid the money he saves for the city
    C. keep it to himself to avoid being accused of causing a speed-up
    D. send his ideas to the Employee's Suggestion Program

12. In order to send his idea to the Employee's Suggestion Program, an employee should

    A. ask the Department of Personnel for a special form
    B. get the special form in his own department

C. mail the idea, using Special Delivery
D. send it on plain, white, letter-sized paper

13. An employee may send to the Employee's Suggestion Program 13.____

    A. as many ideas as he can think of
    B. no more than one idea each week
    C. no more than ten ideas in a month
    D. only one idea on each part of the job

14. The reason the name of an employee who makes a suggestion is not made known at first is to 14.____

    A. give the employee a larger award
    B. help the judges give more awards
    C. insure fairness in judging
    D. make sure no employee gets two awards

15. An employee whose suggestion receives an award may be given a 15.____

    A. bonus once a year
    B. cash price of up to $500
    C. certificate for $10
    D. salary increase of $500

QUESTIONS 16-18.

Answer questions 16 to 18 ONLY on the basis of the information given in the following paragraph.

According to the rules of the Department of Personnel, the work of every permanent City employee is reviewed and rated by his supervisor at least once a year. The civil service rating system gives the employee and his supervisor a chance to talk about the progress made during the past year as well as about those parts of the job in which the employee needs to do better. In order to receive a pay increase each year, the employee must have a satisfactory service rating. Service ratings also count toward an employee's final mark on a promotion examination.

16. According to the above paragraph, a permanent City employee is rated *at least* once 16.____

    A. before his work is reviewed
    B. every six months
    C. yearly by his supervisor
    D. yearly by the Department of Personnel

17. According to the above paragraph, under the rating system the supervisor and the employee can discuss how 17.____

    A. much more work needs to be done next year
    B. the employee did his work last year
    C. the work can be made easier next year
    D. the work of the Department can be increased

18. According to the above paragraph, a permanent City employee will NOT receive a yearly pay increase   18.____

    A. if he received a pay increase for the year before
    B. if he used his service rating for his mark on a promotion examination
    C. if his service rating is unsatisfactory
    D. unless he got some kind of a service rating

19. "Employees on duty represent their Department to the citizens and are expected to be neat and orderly in their dress at all times." According to this statement, neat and orderly dress of employees while on duty is important because   19.____

    A. citizens don't care about the appearance of city employees who are off duty
    B. employees who are neat and orderly in their dress make better citizens
    C. if an employee dresses neatly while at work, he will dress neatly when away from work
    D. people might judge a department by the appearance of its employees

20. "In the city there are 266 shoe factories which employ 10,000 workers while in all the other cities of the state there are 62 shoe factories which employ 27,000 workers." According to this statement, the shoe factories in the city   20.____

    A. are larger than the shoe factories in any other city in the state
    B. employ more workers than all the other shoe factories in the state
    C. make cheaper shoes than the shoe factories in other cities of the state
    D. are greater in number than the shoe factories in all the other cities of the state

21. "All mail matter up to and including eight ounces in weight which is not classified as first or second class mail is third class mail. If a package weighs more than eight ounces, it is put into the fourth class and sent as parcel-post mail." According to this statement, mail weighing eight ounces or less may be   21.____

    A. classified as parcel-post mail
    B. first, second, or third class mail
    C. second class mail but not third class
    D. third or fourth class mail

QUESTIONS 22-24.

Answer questions 22 to 24 ONLY on the basis of the information given in the following paragraph.

Keeping the City of New York operating day and night requires the services of more than 200,000 civil service workers-roughly the number of people who live in Syracuse. This huge army of specialists work at more than 2,000 different jobs. The City's civil service workers are able to do everything that needs doing to keep the City running. Their only purpose is the well-being, comfort and safety of the citizens of New York.

22. Of the following titles, the one that *most nearly* gives the meaning of the above paragraph is: 22.____

    A. "Civil Service in Syracuse"
    B. "Everyone Works"

C. "Job Variety"
D. "Serving New York City"

23. According to the above paragraph, in order to keep New York City operating 24 hours a day

    A. half of the civil service workers work days and half work nights
    B. more than 200,000 civil service workers are needed on the day shift
    C. the City needs about as many civil service workers as there are people in Syracuse
    D. the services of some people who live in Syracuse is required

24. According to the above paragraph, it is MOST reasonable to assume that in New York City's civil service

    A. a worker can do any job that needs doing
    B. each worker works at a different job
    C. some workers work at more than one job
    D. some workers work at the same jobs

QUESTIONS 25-28.

Answer questions 25 to 28 ONLY on the basis of the information given in the following paragraph.

The National and City flags are displayed daily from those public buildings which are equipped with vertical or horizontal flag staffs. Where a building has only one flag staff, only the National flag is displayed. When the National flag is to be raised at the same time as other flags, the National flag shall be raised about 6 feet in advance of the other flags; if the flags are raised separately, the National flag shall always be raised first. When more than one flag is flown on horizontal staffs, the National flag shall be flown so that it is to the extreme left as the observer faces the flag.
When more than one flag is displayed, they should all by the same size. Under no circumstances should the National flag be smaller in size than any other flag in a combination display. The standard size for flags flown from City buildings is 5' x 8'.

25. From the above paragraph, a REASONABLE conclusion about flag staffs on public buildings is that a public building

    A. might have no flag staff at all
    B. needs two flag staffs
    C. should have at least one flag staff
    D. usually has a horizontal and a vertical flag staff

26. According to the above paragraph, a public building that has only one flag staff should raise the National flag

    A. and no other flag
    B. at sunrise
    C. first and then the City flag
    D. six feet in advance of any other flag

27. According to the above paragraph, the order, from left to right, in which the National flag 27._____
flying from one of four horizontal staffs appear to a person who is facing the flag staffs is:

    A. Flag 1, flag 2, flag 3, National flag
    B. National flag, flag 1, flag 2, flag 3
    C. Flag 1, flag 2, National flag, flag 3
    D. Flag 1, National flag, flag 2, flag 3

28. According to the above paragraph, a combination display of flags on a City building 28._____
would *usually* have

    A. a 6' x 10' National flag
    B. all flags 5' x 8' size
    C. all other flags smaller than the National flag
    D. 5' x 8' National and City flags and smaller sized other flags

QUESTIONS 29-30.

Answer questions 29 to 30 ONLY on the basis of the information given in the following paragraph.

Supplies are to be ordered from the stock room once a week. The standard requisition form, Form SP 21, is to be used for ordering all supplies. The form is prepared in triplicate, one white original and two green copies. The white and one green copy are sent to the stock room, and the remaining green copy is to be kept by the orderer until the supplies are received.

29. According to the above paragraph, there is a limit on the 29._____

    A. amount of supplies that may be ordered
    B. day on which supplies may be ordered
    C. different kinds of supplies that may be ordered
    D. number of times supplies may be ordered in one year

30. According to the above paragraph, when the standard requisition form for supplies is, 30._____
prepared

    A. a total of four requisition blanks is used
    B. a white form is the original
    C. each copy is printed in two colors
    D. one copy is kept by the stock clerk

QUESTIONS 31-55.

Each of questions 31 to 55 consists of a word in capital letters followed by four suggested meanings of the word. For each question, choose the word or phrase which means *most nearly* the SAME as the word in capital letters.

31. ABOLISH 31._____

    A. count up   B. do away with
    C. give more   D. pay double for

32. ABUSE

    A. accept   B. mistreat
    C. respect   D. touch

33. ACCURATE

    A. correct   B. lost
    C. neat   D. secret

34. ASSISTANCE

    A. attendance   B. belief
    C. help   D. reward

35. CAUTIOUS

    A. brave   B. careful
    C. greedy   D. hopeful

36. COURTEOUS

    A. better   B. easy
    C. polite   D. religious

37. CRITICIZE

    A. admit   B. blame
    C. check on   D. make dirty

38. DIFFICULT

    A. capable   B. dangerous
    C. dull   D. hard

39. ENCOURAGE

    A. aim at   B. beg for
    C. cheer on   D. free from

40. EXTENT

    A. age   B. size
    C. truth   D. wildness

41. EXTRAVAGANT

    A. empty   B. helpful
    C. over   D. wasteful

42. FALSE

    A. absent   B. colored
    C. not enough   D. wrong

43. INDICATE

    A. point out   B. show up
    C. shrink from   D. take to

44. NEGLECT 44.____

    A. disregard   B. flatten
    C. likeness   D. thoughtfulness

45. PENALIZE 45.____

    A. make   B. notice
    C. pay   D. punish

46. POSTPONED 46.____

    A. put off   B. repeated
    C. taught   D. went to

47. PUNCTUAL 47.____

    A. bursting   B. catching
    C. make a hole in   D. on time

48. RARE 48.____

    A. large   B. ride up
    C. unusual   D. young

49. RELY 49.____

    A. depend   B. do again
    C. use   D. wait for

50. REVEAL 50.____

    A. leave   B. renew
    C. soften   D. tell

51. SERIOUS 51.____

    A. important   B. order
    C. sharp   D. tight

52. TRIVIAL 52.____

    A. alive   B. empty
    C. petty   D. troublesome

53. VENTILATE 53.____

    A. air out   B. darken
    C. last   D. take a chance

54. VOLUNTARY 54.____

    A. common   B. paid
    C. sharing   D. willing

55. WHOLESOME 55.____

    A. cheap   B. healthful
    C. hot   D. together

56. An employee earns $96 a day and works 5 days a week. He will earn $4,320 in _____ weeks.

    A. 5 B. 7 C. 8 D. 9

57. In a certain bureau the entire staff consists of 1 senior supervisor, 2 supervisors, 6 assistant supervisors and 54 associate workers. The percent of the staff who are NOT associate workers is *most nearly*

    A. 14 B. 21 C. 27 D. 32

58. In a certain bureau, five employees each earn $2,000 a month, another three employees each earn $2,400 a month and another two employees each earn $8,200 a month. The monthly payroll for those employees is

    A. 27,200 B. 27,600 C. 33,600 D. 36,000

59. An employee contributes 5% of his salary to the pension fund. If his salary is $2,400 a month, the amount of his contribution to the pension fund in a year is

    A. 960 B. 1,440 C. 1,920 D. 2,400

60. The amount of square feet in an area that is 50 feet long and 30 feet wide is

    A. 80 B. 150 C. 800 D. 1,500

61. An injured person who is unconscious should NOT be given a liquid to drink *mainly* because

    A. cold liquid may be harmful
    B. he may choke on it
    C. he may not like the liquid
    D. his unconsciousness may be due to too much liquid

62. The MOST important reason for putting a bandage on a cut is to

    A. help prevent germs from getting into the cut
    B. hide the ugly scar
    C. keep the blood pressure down
    D. keep the skin warm

63. In first aid for an injured person, the MAIN purpose of a tourniquet is to

    A. prevent infection
    B. restore circulation
    C. support a broken bone
    D. stop severe bleeding

64. Artificial respiration is given in first aid *mainly* to

    A. force air into the lungs
    B. force blood circulation by even pressure
    C. keep the injured person awake
    D. prevent shock by keeping the victim's body in motion

65. The aromatic spirits of ammonia in a first aid kit should be used to 65.____

    A. clean a dirty wound
    B. deaden pain
    C. revive a person who has fainted
    D. warm a person who is chilled

QUESTIONS 66-70.

Read the chart below showing the absences in Unit A for the period November 1 through November 15; then answer questions 66 to 70 according to the information given.

ABSENCE RECORD-UNIT A
November 1-15

Date:	1	2	3	4	5	6	7	8	9	10	11	12	13	14	15
Employee															
Ames	X	S	H					X			H			X	X
Bloom	X		H				X	X	S	S	H	S	S		X
Deegan	X	J	H	J	J	J	X	X			H				X
Howard	X		H					X			H			X	X
Jergens	X	M	H	M	M	M		X			H			X	X
Lange	X		H			S	X	X							X
Morton	X						X	X	V	V	H				X
O'Shea	X		H			0		X			H	X		X	X

Code for Types of Absence
X-Saturday or Sunday
H-Legal Holiday
P-Leave without pay
M-Military leave
J-Jury duty
V-Vacation
S-Sick leave
O-Other leave or absence

Note: If there is no entry against an employee's name under a date, the employee worked on that date.

66. According to the above chart, NO employee in Unit A was absent on 66.____

    A. leave without pay
    B. military leave
    C. other leave of absence
    D. vacation

67. According to the above chart, all but one of the employees in Unit A were present on the 67.____

    A. 3rd   B. 5th   C. 9th   D. 13th

11 (#1)

68. According to the above chart, the *only* employees who worked on a legal holiday when the other employees were absent are   68.____

   A. Deegan and Morton
   B. Howard and O'Shea
   C. Lange and Morton
   D. Morton and O'Shea

69. According to the above chart, the employee who was absent *only* on a day that was either a Saturday, Sunday or legal holiday was   69.____

   A. Bloom   B. Howard   C. Morton   D. O'Shea

70. The employee who had more absences than anyone else are   70.____

   A. Bloom and Deegan
   B. Bloom, Deegan, and Jergens
   C. Deegan and Jergens
   D. Deegan, Jergens, and O'Shea

KEY (CORRECT ANSWERS)

1. B	16. C	31. B	46. A	61. B
2. B	17. B	32. B	47. D	62. A
3. C	18. C	33. A	48. C	63. D
4. C	19. D	34. C	49. A	64. A
5. A	20. D	35. B	50. D	65. C
6. B	21. B	36. C	51. A	66. A
7. D	22. D	37. B	52. C	67. D
8. A	23. C	38. D	53. A	68. C
9. C	24. D	39. C	54. D	69. B
10. C	25. A	40. B	55. B	70. B
11. D	26. A	41. D	56. D	
12. B	27. B	42. D	57. A	
13. A	28. B	43. A	58. C	
14. C	29. D	44. A	59. B	
15. B	30. B	45. D	60. D	

TEST 2

DIRECTIONS: Each question consists of a statement. You are to indicate whether the statement is TRUE (T) or FALSE (F). *PRINT THE LETTER OF THE CORRECT ANSWER IN THE SPACE AT THE RIGHT.*

QUESTIONS 1-4.

Read the paragraph below about "shock" and then answer questions 1 to 4 according to the information given in the paragraph.

SHOCK

While not found in all injuries, shock is present in all serious injuries caused by accidents. During shock, the normal activities of the body slow down. This partly explains why one of the signs of shock is a pale, cold skin, since insufficient blood goes to the body parts during shock.

1. If the injury caused by an accident is serious, shock is sure to be present.   1.____

2. In shock, the heart beats faster than normal.   2.____

3. The face of a person suffering from shock is usually red and flushed.   3.____

4. Not enough blood goes to different parts of the body during shock.   4.____

QUESTIONS 5-8.

Read the paragraph below about carbon monoxide gas and then answer questions 5 to 8 according to the information given in this paragraph.

CARBON MONOXIDE GAS

Carbon monoxide is a deadly gas from the effects of which no one is immune. Any person's strength will be cut down considerably by breathing this gas, even though he does not take in enough to overcome him. Wearing a handkerchief tied around the nose and mouth offers some protection against the irritating fumes of ordinary smoke, but many people have died convinced that a handkerchief will stop carbon monoxide. Any person entering a room filled with this deadly gas should wear a mask equipped with an air hose, or even better, an oxygen breathing apparatus.

5. Some people get no ill effects from carbon monoxide gas until they are overcome.   5.____

6. A person can die from breathing carbon monoxide gas.   6.____

7. A handkerchief around the mouth and nose gives some protection against the effects of ordinary smoke.   7.____

8. It is better for a person entering a room filled with carbon monixide to wear a mask equipped with an air hose than an oxygen breathing apparatus.   8.____

QUESTIONS 9-17.

Read the paragraph below about moving an office and then answer questions 9 to 17 according to the information given in the paragraph.

MOVING AN OFFICE

An office with all its equipment is sometimes moved during working hours. This is a difficult task, and must be done in an orderly manner to avoid confusion. The operation should be planned in such a way as not to interrupt the progress of work usually done in the office and to make possible the accurate placement of the furniture and records in the new location. If the office moves to a place inside the same building, the desks and files are moved with all their contents. If the movement is to another building, the contents of each desk and file are placed in boxes. Each box is marked with a letter showing the particular section in the new quarters to which it is to be moved. Also marked on each box is the number of the desk or file on which the box is to be placed. Each piece of equipment must have a numbered tag. The number of each piece of equipment is put in soft chalk on the floor in the new office to show the proper location, and several floor plans are made to show where each piece of equipment goes. When the moving is done someone is stationed at each of the several exits of the old office to see that each box or piece of equipment has its destination clearly marked on it. At the new office someone stands at each of the several entrances with a copy of the floor plan, and directs the placing of the furniture and equipment according to the floor plan. No one should interfere at this point with the arrangements shown on the plan. Improvements in arrangement can be considered and made at a later date.

9. It is a hard job to move an office from one place to another during working hours. 9.____

10. Confusion CANNOT be avoided if an office is moved during working hours. 10.____

11. The work usually done in an office must be stopped for the day when the office is moved during working hours. 11.____

12. If an office is moved from one floor to another in the same building, the contents of a desk are taken out and put into boxes for moving. 12.____

13. If boxes are used to hold material from desks when moving an office, the box is numbered the same as the desk on which it is to be put. 13.____

14. Letters are marked in soft chalk on the floor at new quarters to show where the desks should go when moved. 14.____

15. When the moving begins, a person is put at each exit of the old office to check that each box and piece of equipment has clearly marked on it where it is to go. 15.____

16. A person stationed at each entrance of the new quarters to direct the placing of the furniture and equipment has a copy of the floor plan of the new quarters. 16.____

17. If, while the furniture is being moved into the new office, a person helping at a doorway gets an idea of a better way to arrange the furniture, he should change the planned arrangement and make a record of the change. 17.____

3 (#2)

QUESTIONS 18-25.

Read the paragraph below about polishing brass fixtures and then answer questions 18 to 25 according to the information given in this paragraph.

POLISHING BRASS FIXTURES

Uncoated brass should be polished in the usual way using brass polish. Special attention need be given only to brass fixtures coated with lacquer. The surface of these fixtures will not endure abrasive cleaners or polishes and should be cleaned regularly with mild soap and water. Lacquer seldom fails to properly protect the surface of brass for the period guaranteed by the manufacturer. But, if the attendant finds darkening or corrosion, or any other symptom of failure of the lacquer, he should notify his foreman. If the guarantee period has not expired, the foreman will have the article returned to the manufacturer. If the guarantee period is over, it is necessary to first remove the old lacquer, refinish and then relacquer the fixture at the agency's shop. It is emphasized that all brass polish contains some abrasive. For this reason, no brass polish should be used on lacquered brass.

18. All brass fixtures should be cleaned in a special way. 18.____

19. A mild brass polish is good for cleaning brass fixtures coated with clear lacquer. 19.____

20. Lacquer coating on brass fixtures usually protects the surfaces for the period of the manufacturer's guarantee. 20.____

21. If an attendant finds corrosion in any lacquered brass article, he should relacquer the article. 21.____

22. The attendant should notify his foreman of failure of lacquer on a brass fixture only if the period of guarantee has expired. 22.____

23. The brass fixtures relacquered at the agency's shops are those on which the manufacturer's guarantee has expired. 23.____

24. Before a brass fixture Is relacquered, the old lacquer should be taken off. 24.____

25. Brass polish should NOT be used on lacquered surfaces because it contains acid. 25.____

QUESTIONS 26-50.

Questions 26 to 50 relate to word meaning.

26. "The foreman had received a few requests." In this sentence, the word 'requests' means *nearly* the SAME as 'complaints.' 26.____

27. "The procedure for doing the work was modified." In this sentence, the word 'modified' means *nearly* the SAME as 'discovered.' 27.____

28. "He stressed the importance of doing the job right ." In this sentence, the word 'stressed' means *nearly* the SAME as 'discovered.' 28.____

29. "He worked with rapid movements." In this sentence, the word 'rapid' means *nearly* the SAME as 'slow.' 29.____

30. "The man resumed his work when the foreman came in." In this sentence, the word 'resumed' means *nearly* the SAME as 'stopped.' 30.____

31. "The interior door would not open." In this sentence, the word 'interior' means *nearly* the SAME as 'inside.'   31.____

32. "He extended his arm." In this sentence, the word 'extended' means *nearly* the SAME as 'stretched out.'   32.____

33. "He answered promptly." In this sentence, the word 'promptly' means *nearly* the SAME as 'quickly.'   33.____

34. "He punctured a piece of rubber." In this sentence, the word 'punctured' means *nearly* the SAME as 'bought.'   34.____

35. "A few men were assisting the attendant." In this sentence, the word 'assisting' means *nearly* the SAME as 'helping.'   35.____

36. "He opposed the idea of using a vacuum cleaner for this job." In this sentence, the word 'opposed' means *nearly* the SAME as 'suggested.'   36.____

37. "Four employees were selected." In this sentence, the word 'selected' means *nearly* the SAME as 'chosen.'   37.____

38. "This man is constantly supervised." In this sentence, the word 'constantly' means *nearly* the SAME as 'rarely.'   38.____

39. "One part of soap to two parts of water is sufficient." In this sentence, the word 'sufficient' means *nearly* the SAME as 'enough.'   39.____

40. "The fire protection system was inadequate." In this sentence, the word 'inadequate' means *nearly* the SAME as 'enough.'   40.____

41. "The nozzle of the hose was clogged." In this sentence, the word 'clogged' means *nearly* the SAME as 'brass.'   41.____

42. "He resembles the man who worked here before." In this sentence, the word 'resembles,' means *nearly* the SAME as 'replaces.'   42.____

43. "They eliminated a number of items." In this sentence, the word 'eliminated' means *nearly* the SAME as 'bought.'   43.____

44. "He is a dependable worker." In this sentence, the word 'dependable' means *nearly* the SAME as 'poor.'   44.____

45. "Some wood finishes color the wood and conceal the natural grain." In this sentence, the word 'conceal' means *nearly* the SAME as 'hide.'   45.____

46. "Paint that is chalking sometimes retains its protective value." In this sentence, the word 'retains' means *nearly* the SAME as 'keeps.'   46.____

47. "Wood and trash had accumulated." In this sentence, the word 'accumulated' means *nearly* the SAME as 'piled up.'   47.____

48. An 'inflammable' liquid is one that is easily set on fire.   48.____

49. "The amounts were then compared." In this sentence, the word 'compared' means *nearly* the SAME as 'added.' 49.____

50. "The boy had fallen into a shallow pool." In this sentence, the work 'shallow' means *nearly* the SAME as 'deep.' 50.____

KEY (CORRECT ANSWERS)

1.	T	11.	F	21.	F	31.	T	41.	F
2.	F	12.	F	22.	F	32.	T	42.	F
3.	F	13.	T	23.	T	33.	T	43.	F
4.	T	14.	F	24.	T	34.	F	44.	F
5.	F	15.	T	25.	F	35.	T	45.	T
6.	T	16.	T	26.	F	36.	F	46.	T
7.	T	17.	F	27.	T	37.	T	47.	T
8.	F	18.	F	28.	F	38.	F	48.	T
9.	T	19.	F	29.	F	39.	T	49.	F
10.	F	20.	T	30.	F	40.	F	50.	F

EXAMINATION SECTION

TEST 1

DIRECTIONS: Each question consists of a statement. You are to indicate whether the statement is TRUE (T) or FALSE (F). *PRINT THE LETTER OF THE CORRECT ANSWER IN THE SPACE AT THE RIGHT.*

Questions 1-7.

DIRECTIONS: Questions 1 through 7 are to be answered SOLEY on the basis of the information contained in the following paragraph.

RESPONSIBILITY OF PARENTS

In a recent survey, ninety percent of the people interviewed felt that parents should be held responsible for the delinquency of their children. Forty-eight out of fifty states have laws holding parents criminally responsible for contributing to the delinquency of their children. It is generally acceptged that parents are a major influence in the early moral development of their children. Yet, in spite of all this evidence, practical experience seems to prove that "punish the parents" laws are wrong. Legally, there is some question about the constitutionality of such laws. How far can one person be held responsible for the actions of another? Further, although there are many such laws, the fact remains that they are rarely used, and where they are used they fail in most cases to accomplish the end for which they were intended.

1. Nine out of ten of those interviewed held that parents should be reponsible for the delinquency of their children. 1.____

2. Forty-eight percent of the states have laws holding parents responsible for contributing to the delinquency of their children. 2.____

3. Most people feel that parents have little influence on the early moral development of their children. 3.____

4. Experience seems to indicate that laws holding parents responsible for children's delinquency are wrong. 4.____

5. There is no doubt that laws holding parents responsible for delinquency of their children are within the Constitution. 5.____

6. Laws holding parents responsible for delinquent children are not often enforced. 6.____

7. "Punish the parent" laws *usually* achieve their purpose. 7.____

Questions 8-13.

DIRECTIONS: Questions 8 through 13 are to be answered SOLELY on the basis of the information contained in the following paragraphs.

CONTROL OF RABIES

The history of rabies in many countries proveds the need for strong preventive measures. England is a good example. Rabies ran rampant in the British Isles during the American Revolution. In the 19th Century, the country began to enforce stric measures: licensing of all dogs, muzzling all dogs and quanrantining all incoming animals for 6 months' observation. An additional measure was the capturing and killing of all unlicensed "strays."

As a result, rabies was completely eradicated, and similar measures have achieved the same results in Ireland, Denmark, Norway, Sweden, Australia, and Hawaii.

8. Rabies was prevalent in England around the year 1776. 8.____

9. By enforcement of strict measures in the 1800's, rabies was eliminated in England. 9.____

10. The only measures enforced in England for the control of rabies were the licensing and muzzling of all dogs. 10.____

11. Unlicensed dogs without owners were put to death when found. 11.____

12. A total of six countries, including England, obtained good results in combating rabies. 12.____

13. Rabies has been eliminated in three Scandinavian countries. 13.____

Questions 14-25.

DIRECTION: Questions 14 through 25 are to be answered SOLELY on the basis of the information contained in the following paragraphs.

RESCUE BREATHING

"Mouth-to-mouth," or "rescue breathing," is the easiest, most efficient, and quickest method of getting oxygen into a suffocating victim of drowning, heart attack, electricl shock, poisoning or other cause of interruption of breathing. It is superior to other types of artificial respiration because the victim does not have to be moved and the rescuer can continue for hours without exhaustion. No special equipment is needed.

Begin rescue breathing immediately. The victim's head should be lower than his body. Tilt his head back as far as possible so his jaw juts out. Keep the air passage to his lungs straight at all times. Open your mouth as wide as possible and seal your lips over the adult victim's mouth or his nose and the child victim's mouth and nose. Blow in air until his chest rises. Remove your mouth and listen to him breathe out. Then blow again and fill his lungs.

For the first minute, blow thirty times into a child, then twenty times a minute. With an adult, blow twenty times for the first minute, then ten to twelve times a minute. Do not stop breathing for the victim, however long it takes, until he begins breathing for himself – or is dead.

14. The FASTEST wasy to get oxygen into the lungs of a suffocating person is by mouth-to-mouth breathing.   14.____

15. The "rescue breathing" method of artificial respiration should be used ONLY in cases of drowning.   15.____

16. Rescue breathing is NOT the only kind of artificial respiration.   16.____

17. The person who applies mouth-to-mouth breathing will NOT tire easily.   17.____

18. Special equipment used in rescue breathing should be kept handy at all times.   18.____

19. Rescue breathing should be commenced at the earliest possible moment.   19.____

20. The suffocating victim should be placed so that his body is NOT higher than his head.   20.____

21. In "rescue breathing," the head of the victim should be bent forward so oxygen will be more easily forced in the lungs.   21.____

22. In mouth-to-mouth breathing, air may be blown into the victim's nose.   22.____

23. When "rescue breathing" is applied to children, air should be blown into the lungs thirty times djuring the first minute.   23.____

24. It is NEVER necessary to continue rescue breathing for longer than about five minutes.   24.____

25. Mouth-to-mouth breathing is ALWAYS successful in reviving the victim.   25.____

Questions 26-45.

DIRECTIONS: Questions 26 through 45 relate to word meaning.

26. "His ideas about the best method of doing the work were flexible." In this sentence, the word "flexible" means NEARLY THE SAME as "unchangeable".   26.____

27. "Many difficulties were encountered." In this sentence, the word "encountered" means NEARLY THE SAME as "met".   27.____

28. "The different parts of the refuse must be segregated." In this sentence, the word "segregated" means NEARLY THE SAME as "combined".   28.____

29. "The child was obviously hurt." In this sentence, the word "obviously" means NEARLY THE SAME as "accidentally".

30. "Some kind of criteria for judging service necessity must be established." In this sentence, the word "criteria" means NEARLY THE SAME as "standards".

31. "A small segment of the membership favored the amendment." In this sentence, the word "segment" means NEARLY THE SAME as "part".

32. "The effectiveness of an organization depends upon the quality and integrity of its rank and file." In this sentence, the word "integrity" means NEARLY THE SAME as "quantity".

33. "He adhered to his opinion." In this sentence, the word "adhered" means NEARLY THE SAME as "stuck to".

34. "The suspects were interrogated at the police station." In this sentence, the word "interrogated" means NEARLY THE SAME as "identified".

35. "Flanking the fireplace are shelves holding books." In this sentence, the word "flanking" means NEARLY THE SAME as "above".

36. "He refused to comment on the current Berlin crisis." In this sentence, the word "current" means NEARLY THE SAME as "shocking".

37. "Nothing has been done to remedy the situation." In this sentence, the word "remedy" means NEARLY THE SAME as "correct".

38. "The reports had been ignored." In this sentence, the word "ignored" means NEARLY THE SAME as "prepared".

39. "A firm was hired to construct the building." In this sentence, the word "construct" means NEARLY THE SAME as "build".

40. "The commissioner spoke about the operations of his department. In this sentence, the word "operations" means NEARLY THE SAME as "problems."

41. "The metal was corroded." In this sentence, the word "corroded" means NEARLY THE SAME as "polished".

42. "The price of this merchandise fluctuates from day to day." In this sentence, the word "fluctuates" means the OPPOSITE of "remains steady".

43. "The patient was in acute pain." In this sentence, the word "acute" means the OPPOSITE of "slight".

44. "The essential data appear in the report." In this sentence, the word "data" means the OPPOSITE of "facts".   44.____

45. "The open lounge is spacious." In this sentence, the word "spacious" means the OPPOSITE of "well-lighted".   45.____

46. A good first aid measure for a person who has fainted is to place his head lower than the rest of his body.   46.____

47. Many accidents are caused by carelessness of employees while at work.   47.____

48. If, at work, you are unable to lift a very heavy object, you should rest a couple of minutes and try again.   48.____

49. A victim of a bad fall who has suffered some broken bones should be moved to a comfortable spot *immediately*.   49.____

50. The safest and quickest way to remove a burned out light bulb from a ceiling fixture is to stand on a chair on top of a desk or table.   50.____

51. The legal age for voting in New York State was reduced to 18 years.   51.____

52. The purpose of a primary election is to select party candidates for the general election.   52.____

53. If three men working at the same rate of speed finish a job in 4½ hours, then two of them could do the job in 6¾ hours.   53.____

54. If a typist shares four boxes of envelopes with four other typists, each will have one box of envelopes.   54.____

55. An article bought for $100 must be sold for $125 in order to make a profit of 20% of the selling price.   55.____

56. ½ of ⅛ is ¼.   56.____

57. Ten square feet of carpet will cover the floor of a room 10 feet by 10 feet.   57.____

Questions 58-65.

DIRECTION: Questions 58 through 65 are to be answered SOLELY on the basis of the information contained in the following table.

SUMMONS RECORD

District	No. of Summonses Issued 2014	No. of Summonses Issued 2015	No. of Summonses Dismissed 2014	No. of Summonses Dismissed 2015
Oakdale	3,250	3,147	650	631
Marlboro	2,410	2,320	670	718
Eastchester	3,502	3,710	800	825
Kensington	10,423	10,218	2,317	2,343
Glendridge	5,100	5,250	1,200	1,213
Seaside	4,864	4,739	1,469	1,375
Darwin	3,479	3,661	815	826
Ulster	4,100	3,789	1,025	1,000
Totals	37,128	?	8,946	?

58. In most of the districts, the number of summonses dismissesd was GREATER in 2015 than in 2014. 58.____

59. In most of the districts, the number of summonses issued was SMALLER in 2014 than in 2015. 59.____

60. The district which had the SMALLEST number of summonses issued in 2014 also had the SMALLEST number of summonses dismissed in 2014. 60.____

61. The two districts which issued the LARGEST number of summonses in 2015 also dismissed the LARGEST number of summonses in 2015. 61.____

62. The district that was second in the number of summonses issued both years was also second in the number of summonses dismissed both years. 62.____

63. The total number of summonses dismissed in 2015 is 15 less than the total number dismissed in 2014. 63.____

64. In 2015 there was a greater difference between the two districts with the smallest and largest number of summonses dismissesd than in 2014. 64.____

65. The total number of summonses issued in 2014 is 294 GREATER than the total number of summonses issued in 2015. 65.____

KEY (CORRECT ANSWERS)

1.	T	16.	T	31.	T	46.	T	61.	F
2.	F	17.	T	32.	F	47.	T	62.	F
3.	F	18.	F	33.	T	48.	F	63.	T
4.	T	19.	T	34.	F	49.	F	64.	T
5.	F	20.	F	35.	F	50.	F	65.	T
6.	T	21.	F	36.	F	51.	F		
7.	F	22.	T	37.	T	52.	T		
8.	T	23.	T	38.	F	53.	T		
9.	T	24.	F	39.	T	54.	F		
10.	F	25.	F	40.	F	55.	T		
11.	T	26.	F	41.	F	56.	F		
12.	F	27.	T	42.	T	57.	F		
13.	T	28.	F	43.	T	58.	T		
14.	T	29.	F	44.	F	59.	F		
15.	F	30.	T	45.	F	60.	F		

TEST 2

DIRECTIONS: Each question or incomplete statement is followed by several suggested answers or completions. Select the one that BEST answers the question or completes the statement. *PRINT THE LETTER OF THE CORRECT ANSWER IN THE SPACE AT THE RIGHT.*

Questions 1-20.

DIRECTIONS: Each of Questions 1 through 20 consists of a word in capital letters followed by four suggested meanings of the word. Select the word or phrase which means MOST NEARLY the same as the word in capital letters.

1. ABRUPT
   A. smooth   B. safe   C. sudden   D. slow

2. ALLEVIATE
   A. relieve   B. join   C. agree with   D. raise

3. ALLOT
   A. permit   B. assign   C. exclude   D. accept

4. ALTER
   A. divide   B. argue   C. opposite   D. change

5. APPARENT
   A. unimportant   B. obvious   C. connected   D. loose

6. BRITTLE
   A. easily broken   B. narrow
   C. made of metal   D. shiny

7. CAPSIZE
   A. protest   B. press down   C. overturn   D. fill

8. CONSPICUOUS
   A. colorful   B. point out   C. cooperate   D. noticeable

9. CONSTRICT
   A. collect   B. compress   C. convince   D. circulate

10. DELETE
    A. follow   B. refuse   C. hesitate   D. erase

11. FLUCTUATE
    A. fill gradually   B. change continually
    C. take apart   D. shake loose

50

12. IMPLY
    A. excuse   B. fold over   C. examine   D. suggest

13. MAINTAIN
    A. slow down   B. draw back   C. keep up   D. damage

14. OBSCURE
    A. empty   B. at an angle   C. receive   D. not clean

15. SCRUTINIZE
    A. ask politely
    B. without mistakes
    C. look at carefully
    D. do on purpose

16. SEVER
    A. separate   B. shift   C. serious   D. strict

17. SPHERICAL
    A. doubtful   B. round   C. at the edge   D. balanced

18. TAUT
    A. tight   B. thick   C. tall   D. timely

19. TERMINATE
    A. stop   B. investigate   C. speed up   D. prefer

20. VARIABLE
    A. questionable   B. hard   C. changeable   D. responsible

Questions 21-25.

DIRECTIONS: Each of Questions 21 through 25 consists of four sentences. One of the sentences in each group contains an error in grammar, sentence structure or English usage. For each question, select the sentence which is INCORRECT.

21. A. The driver of the north-bound car, who was responsible for the accident, escaped without injury.
    B. The Duncan parking meter was the better of the two meters used in the test.
    C. After a long day of driving, he was real tired.
    D. The car appeared suddenly over the top of the hill.

22. A. The man stopped his work because the sun was very hot.
    B. The car sped down the road it suddenly swerved toward the ditch along the side of the road.
    C. On today's modern highways there are many cars; some are new and others are fit only for the junkyard.
    D. Traffic congestion is a current problem which is hard to solve.

23.
- A. Neither the driver nor the pedestrian are to blame for the accident.
- B. In his report he included all the pertinent data.
- C. A new set of rules and regulations has been adopted.
- D. He asserted that there was no basis for the motorist's complaint of unequal treatment.

24.
- A. Standing or stopping at an intersection is a violation of the law.
- B. Reckless driving, especially at sunset, is a major cause of accidents.
- C. Before starting a car, you should adjust the rear view mirror and fasten your seat belt.
- D. Pulling up at the gas station, the gas tank was filled up before they began their trip.

25.
- A. Because the accident report was incomplete, a question arose as to who was at fault.
- B. They told both he and I that the suggestion was accepted.
- C. He was allowed to choose whomever he wanted for the job.
- D. The final decision was reached after everyone told his side of the incident.

Questions 26-30.

DIRECTIONS: Each of Questions 26 through 30 consists of a group of four words. Examine each group carefully, then in the space at the right, print one of the following letters:
- A – if only ONE word in the group is spelled correctly.
- B – if TWO words in the group are spelled correctly.
- C – if THREE words in the group are spelled correctly.
- D – if ALL FOUR words in the group are spelled correctly.

26. Wendsday, particular, similar, hunderd

27. realize, judgment, opportunities, consistent

28. equel, principle, assistense, commitee

29. simultaneous, privilege, advise, ocassionaly

30. necissery, official, Febuary, distence

Questions 31-37.

DIRECTIONS: Questions 31 through 37 are to be answered on the basis of the information given in the following passage.

The parking meter was designed 30 years ago primarily as a mechanism to assist in reducing parking overtime at the curb, to increase parking turnover, and to facilitate enforcement of parking regulations. That the meter has accomplished these basic functions is attested to by its use in an increasing number of cities.

4 (#2)

A recent survey of cities in the United States indicates that overtime parking was reduced 75% or more in 47% of the cities surveyed, and to a lesser degree in 43% of the cities surveyed, making a total of 90% of the cities surveyed where the parking meter was found to be effective in reducing overtime parking at the curb.

A side effect of the reduction in overtime parking is the increase in parking turnover. Approximately 89% of the places surveyed found meters useful in this respect. Meters also encourage even spacing of cars at the curb. Unmetered curb parking is often so irregular that it wastes space or makes parking and departure difficult.

The effectiveness of parking meters, in the final analysis, rests upon the enforcement of the regulations by squads of enforcement agents who will diligently patrol the metered area. The task of checking parking time is made easier with meters, since violations can be checked from a moving vehicle or by visual sightings of an agent on foot patrol, and the laborious process of chalking tires is greatly reduced. It is reported that, after meters have been installed, it takes on the average only 25% of the time formerly required to patrol the same area.

The fact that a parker activates a mechanism that immediately begins to count time, that will indicate exactly when the parking time has expired, and that will advertise such a fact by showing a red flag, tends to make a parker more conscious of his parking responsibilities than the hit and miss system of possible detection by a patrolman.

31. According to the above passage, when the parking meter was introduced, one of its major purposes was NOT to
    A. cut down overtime curb parking
    B. make curb parking available to more parkers
    C. bring in revenue from parking fees
    D. make it easier to enforce parking regulations

32. In the cities surveyed, the installation of parking meters
    A. was *effective* to some degree in all the cities surveyed
    B. was *ineffective* in only 1 out of every 10 cities surveyed
    C. *reduced* overtime parking at least 75% in most cities surveyed
    D. *slightly reduced* overtime parking in 43% of the cities surveyed

33. When overtime parking is reduced by the installation of parking meters, an accompanying result is
    A. an increase in the amount of parking space
    B. the use of the available parking spaces by more cars
    C. the faster the movement of traffic
    D. a decrease in the number of squads required to enforce traffic regulations

34. According to the above passage, on streets which have parking meters, as compared with streets with are un-metered,
    A. there is less waste of parking space
    B. parking is more difficult
    C. parking time limits are irregular
    D. drivers waste more time looking for an empty parking space

35. According to the above passage, the use of parking meters will NOT be effective unless
    A. parking areas are patrolled in automobiles
    B. it is combined with chalking of tires
    C. the public cooperates
    D. there is strict enforcement of parking regulations

36. According to the above passage, ONE reason why there is greater compliance with parking regulations when parking time is regulated by meter rather than by a foot patrolman chalking tires is that
    A. overtime parking becomes glaringly evident to everyone
    B. the parker is himself responsible for operating the timing mechanism
    C. there is no personal relationship between parker and enforcing officer
    D. the timing of elapsed parking time is accurate

37. In the last paragraph of the above passage, the words "a parker activates a mechanism" refers to the fact that a motorist
    A. starts the timing device of the meter working
    B. parks his car
    C. checks whether the meter is working
    D. starts the engine of his car

Questions 38-40.

DIRECTIONS: Questions 38 through 40 are to be answered on the basis of the information given in the following passage.

When markings upon the curb or the pavement of a street designate parking space, no person shall stand or park a vehicle in such designated parking space so that any part of such vehicle occupies more than one such space or protrudes beyond the markings designating such a space, except that a vehicle which is of a size too large to be parked within a single designated parking space shall be parked with the front bumper at the front of the space with the rear of the vehicle extending as little as possible into the adjoining space to the rear, or vice-versa.

38. The regulations quoted above applies to parking at ANY
    A. curb or pavement
    B. metered spaces
    C. street where parking is permitted
    D. spaces with marked boundaries

39. The regulations quoted above PROHIBITS the occupying of more than one indicated parking space by
    A. any vehicle
    B. large vehicles
    C. small vehicles
    D. vehicles in spaces partially occupied

40. In the regulations quoted above, the term "vice-versa" refers to a vehicle of a size too large parked with

    A. front bumper flush with front of parking space it occupies
    B. front of vehicle extending into front of parking space
    C. rear bumper flush with rear of parking space it occupies
    D. rear of vehicle protruding into adjoining parking space

40.____

KEY (CORRECT ANSWERS)

1.	C	11.	B	21.	C	31.	C
2.	A	12.	D	22.	B	32.	B
3.	B	13.	C	23.	A	33.	B
4.	D	14.	D	24.	D	34.	A
5.	B	15.	C	25.	B	35.	D
6.	A	16.	A	26.	B	36.	A
7.	C	17.	B	27.	D	37.	A
8.	D	18.	A	28.	A	38.	D
9.	B	19.	A	29.	C	39.	C
10.	D	20.	C	30.	A	40.	C

SCANNING MAPS

One section of the exam tests your ability to orient yourself within a given region on a map. Using the map accompanying questions 1 through 3; choose the best way of getting from one point to another.

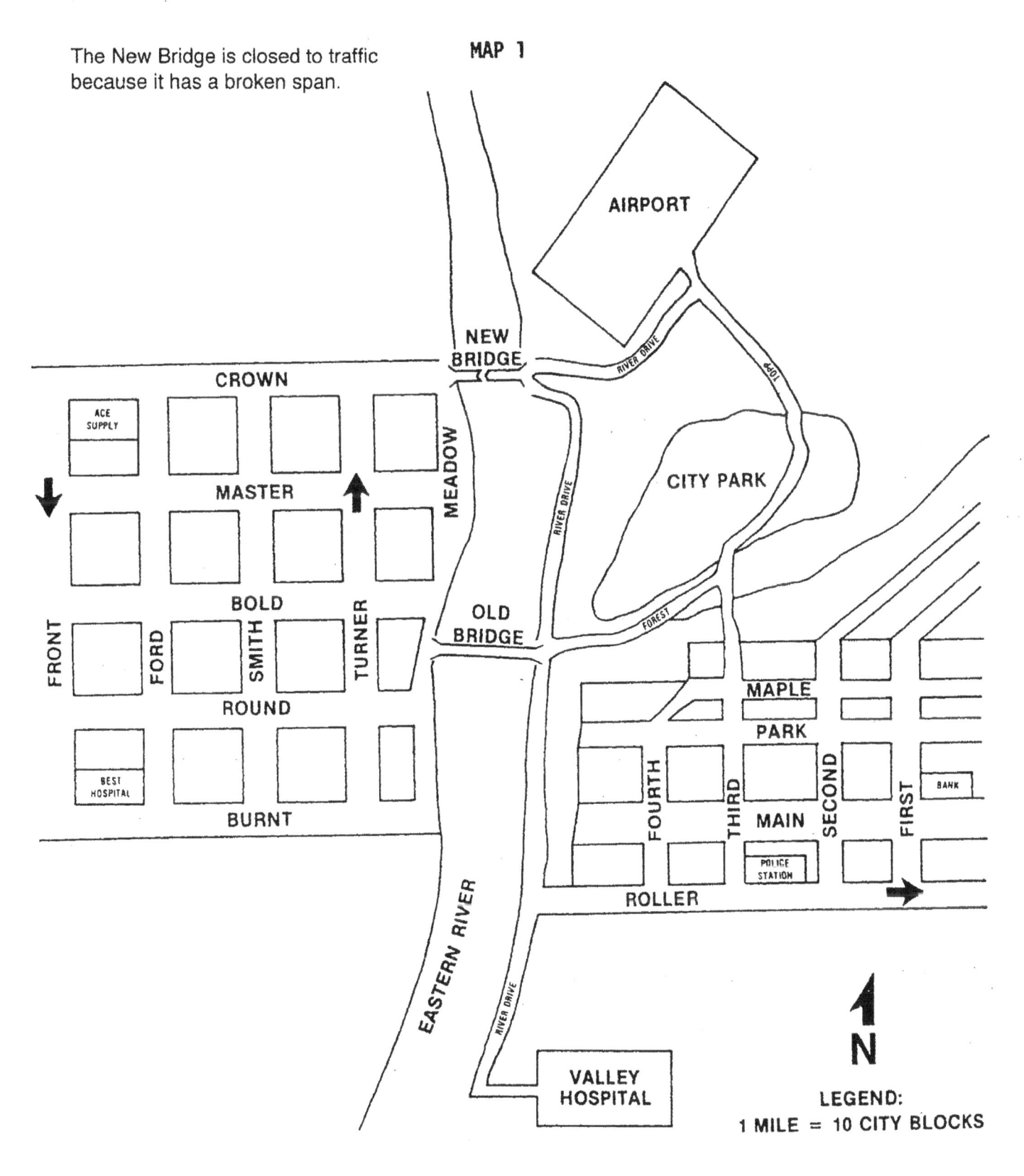

The New Bridge is closed to traffic because it has a broken span.

MAP 1

LEGEND:
1 MILE = 10 CITY BLOCKS

Arrows (───▶) indicate on-way traffic and direction of traffic. A street marked by an arrow is one way for the entire length of the street.

SAMPLE QUESTIONS

1. Officers in a patrol car which is at the Airport receive a call for assistance at Best Hospital. The shortest route without breaking the law is:
   A. Southwest on River Drive, right on Forest, cross Old Bridge, south on Meadow, and west on Burnt to hospital entrance.
   B. Southwest on River Drive, right on New Bridge, left on Meadow, west on Burnt to hospital entrance.
   C. Southwest on River Drive, right on Old Bridge, left on Turner, right on Burnt to hospital entrance.
   D. North on River Drive to Topp, through City Park to Forest, cross Old Bridge, left on Meadow, west on Burnt to hospital entrance.

2. After returning to the police station, the officers receive a call to pick up injured persons at an accident site (located on the east side of New Bridge) and return to Valley Hospital. The shortest route without breaking the law is:

   A. West on Roller, north on River Drive, left to accident scene at New Bridge, then north on River Drive to hospital entrance.
   B. North on Third, left on Forest, north on River Drive, left to accident scene at new Bridge, then south on River Drive to hospital entrance.
   C. East on Roller, left on First, west on Maple, north on Third, left on Forest, north on River Drive to accident scene at New Bridge, then south on River Drive to hospital entrance.
   D. North on Third, left on Forest, cross Old Bridge, north on Meadow to New Bridge, south on Meadow, east over Old Bridge, then south on River Drive to hospital entrance.

3. While at the Valley Hospital, the officers receive a call asking them to pick up materials at the Ace Supply and return them to the police station. The shortest route without breaking the law is:
   A. North on River Drive, cross New Bridge, west on Crown to Ace Supply, then south on Front, east on Burnt, north on Meadow, cross Old Bridge, east on Forest, south on Third to police station.
   B. North on River Drive, right on Roller to police station, then north on Third, left on Forest, cross Old Bridge, north on Meadow, west on Crown to Ace Supply.
   C. North on River Drive, cross Old Bridge, north on Meadow, west on Crown to Ace Supply, then east on Crown, south on Meadow, cross Old Bridge, east on Forest, south on Third to police station.
   D. North on River Drive, cross Old Bridge, south on Meadow, west on Burnt, north on Front to Ace Supply, then east on Crown, south on Meadow, cross Old Bridge, east on Forest, south on Third to police station.

KEY (CORRECT ANSWERS)

1. A
2. B
3. C

MAP READING

EXAMINATION SECTION
TEST 1

DIRECTIONS: Each question or incomplete statement is followed by several suggested answers or completions. Select the one that BEST answers the question or completes the statement. *PRINT THE LETTER OF THE CORRECT ANSWER IN THE SPACE AT THE RIGHT.*

Questions 1-3.

DIRECTIONS: Questions 1 through 3 are to be answered SOLELY on the basis of the map which appears on the next page. The flow of traffic is indicated by the arrow. If there is only one arrow shown, then traffic flows only in the direction indicated by the arrow. If there are two arrows shown, then traffic flows in both directions. You must follow the flow of traffic.

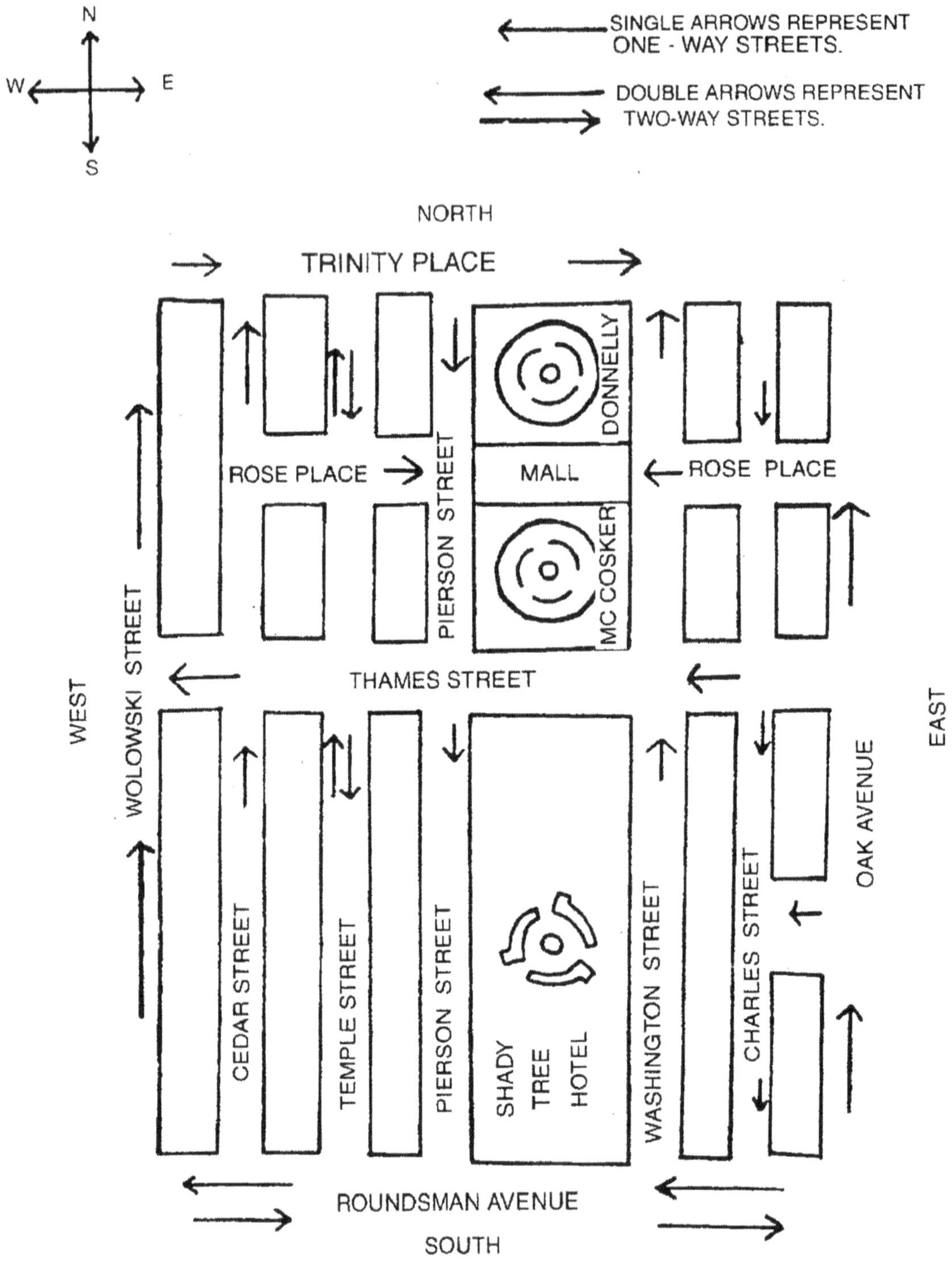
N
W
E
S
SINGLE ARROWS REPRESENT ONE - WAY STREETS.
DOUBLE ARROWS REPRESENT TWO-WAY STREETS.
NORTH
TRINITY PLACE
DONNELLY
ROSE PLACE
PIERSON STREET
MALL
ROSE PLACE
MC COSKER
WOLOWSKI STREET
THAMES STREET
WEST
EAST
OAK AVENUE
CEDAR STREET
TEMPLE STREET
PIERSON STREET
SHADY TREE HOTEL
WASHINGTON STREET
CHARLES STREET
ROUNDSMAN AVENUE
SOUTH

1. Police Officers Simms and O'Brien are located at Roundsman Avenue and Washington Street. The radio dispatcher has assigned them to investigate a motor vehicle accident at the corner of Pierson Street and Rose Place.
Which one of the following is the SHORTEST route for them to take in their patrol car, making sure to obey all traffic regulations?
Travel

   A. west on Roundsman Avenue, then north on Temple Street, then east on Thames Street, then north on Pierson Street to Rose Place
   B. east on Roundsman Avenue, then north on Oak Avenue, then west on Rose Place to Pierson Street
   C. west on Roundsman Avenue, then north on Temple Street, then east on Rose Place to Pierson Street
   D. east on Roundsman Avenue, then north on Oak Avenue, then west on Thames Street, then north on Temple Street, then east on Rose Place to Pierson Street

2. Police Officers Sears and Castro are located at Cedar Street and Roundsman Avenue. They are called to respond to the scene of a burglary at Rose Place and Charles Street. Which one of the following is the SHORTEST route for them to take in their patrol car, making sure to obey all traffic regulations?
Travel

   A. east on Roundsman Avenue, then north on Oak Avenue, then west on Rose Place to Charles Street
   B. east on Roundsman Avenue, then north on Washington Street, then east on Rose Place to Charles Street
   C. west on Roundsman Avenue, then north on Wolowski Street, then east on Trinity Place, then south on Charles Street to Rose Place
   D. east on Roundsman Avenue, then north on Charles Street to Rose Place

3. Police Officer Glasser is in an unmarked car at the intersection of Rose Place and Temple Street when he begins to follow two robbery suspects. The suspects go south for two blocks, then turn left for two blocks, then make another left turn for one more block. The suspects realize they are being followed and make a left turn and travel two more blocks and then make a right turn.
In what direction are the suspects now headed?

   A. North   B. South   C. East   D. West

Questions 4-6.

DIRECTIONS: Questions 4 through 6 are to be answered SOLELY on the basis of the following map. The flow of traffic is indicated by the arrows. If there is only one arrow shown, then traffic flows only in the direction indicated by the arrow. If there are two arrows shown, then traffic flows in both directions. You must follow the flow of traffic.

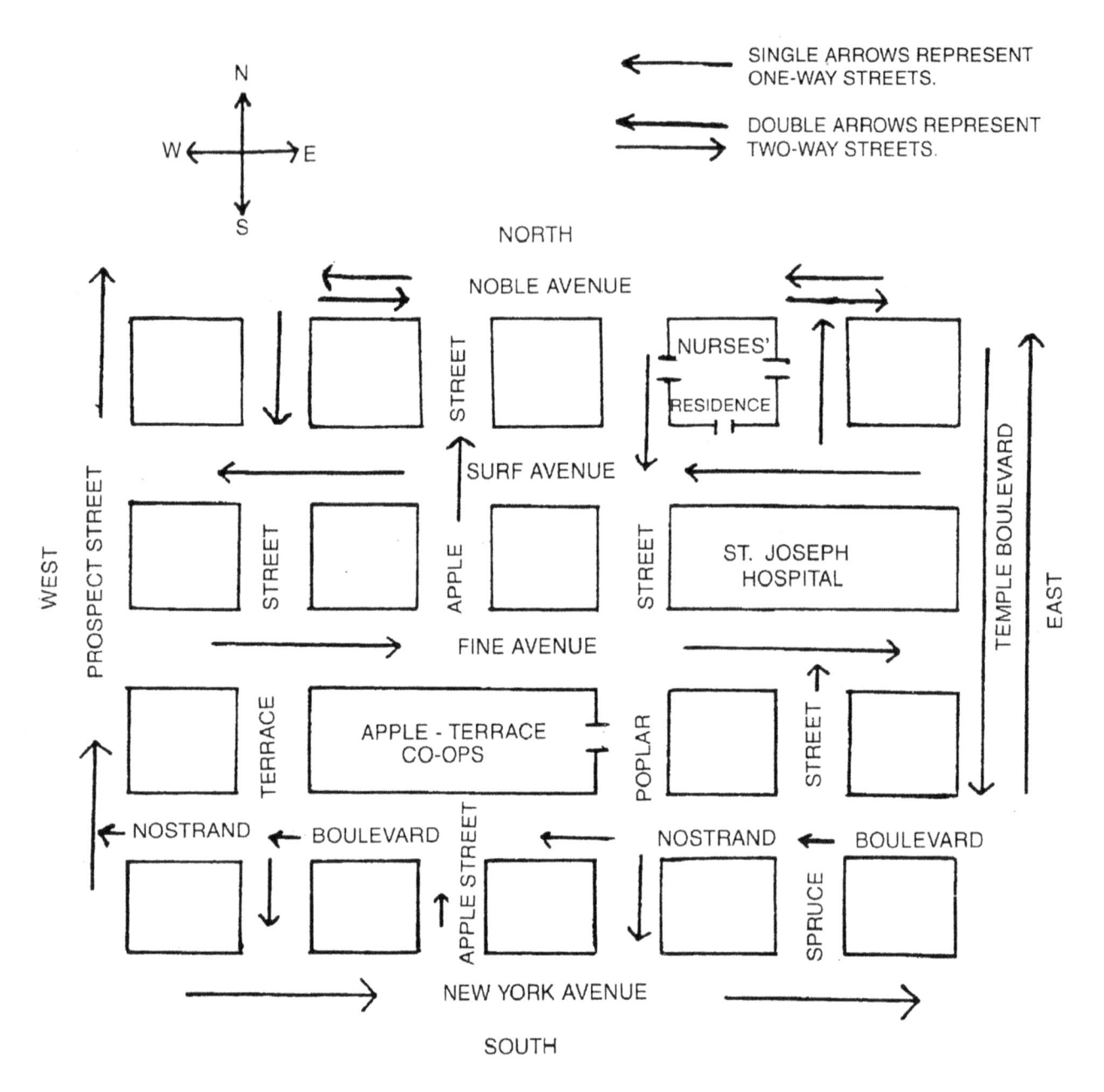

4. Police Officers Gannon and Vine are located at the intersection of Terrace Street and Surf Avenue when they receive a call from the radio dispatcher stating that they need to respond to an attempted murder at Spruce Street and Fine Avenue.
Which one of the following is the SHORTEST route for them to take in their patrol car, making sure to obey all traffic regulations?
Travel _____ to Spruce Street.

- A. west on Surf Avenue, then north on Prospect Street, then east on Noble Avenue, then south on Poplar Street, then east on Fine Avenue
- B. east on Surf Avenue, then south on Poplar Street, then east on Fine Avenue
- C. west on Surf Avenue, then south on Prospect Street, then east on Fine Avenue
- D. south on Terrace Street, then east on Fine Avenue

5. Police Officers Sears and Ronald are at Nostrand Boulevard and Prospect Street. They receive a call assigning them to investigate a disruptive group of youths at Temple Boulevard and Surf Avenue.
    Which one of the following is the SHORTEST route for them to take in their patrol car, making sure to obey all traffic regulations?
    Travel

    A. north on Prospect Street, then east on Surf Avenue to Temple Boulevard
    B. north on Prospect Street, then east on Noble Avenue, then south on Temple Boulevard to Surf Avenue
    C. north on Prospect Street, then east on Fine Avenue, then north on Temple Boulevard to Surf Avenue
    D. south on Prospect Street, then east on New York Avenue, then north on Temple Boulevard to Surf Avenue

5._____

6. While on patrol at Prospect Street and New York Avenue, Police Officers Ross and Rock are called to a burglary in progress near the entrance to the Apple-Terrace Co-ops on Poplar Street midway between Fine Avenue and Nostrand Boulevard.
    Which one of the following is the SHORTEST route for them to take in their patrol car, making sure to obey all traffic regulations?
    Travel _____ Poplar Street.

    A. east on New York Avenue, then north
    B. north on Prospect Avenue, then east on Fine Avenue, then south
    C. north on Prospect Street, then east on Surf Avenue, then south
    D. east on New York Avenue, then north on Temple Boulevard, then west on Surf Avenue, then south

6._____

Questions 7-8.

DIRECTIONS: Questions 7 and 8 are to be answered SOLELY on the basis of the map which appears below. The flow of traffic is indicated by the arrows. If there is only one arrow shown, then traffic flows only in the direction indicated by the arrow. If there are two arrows shown, then traffic flows in both directions. You must follow the flow of traffic.

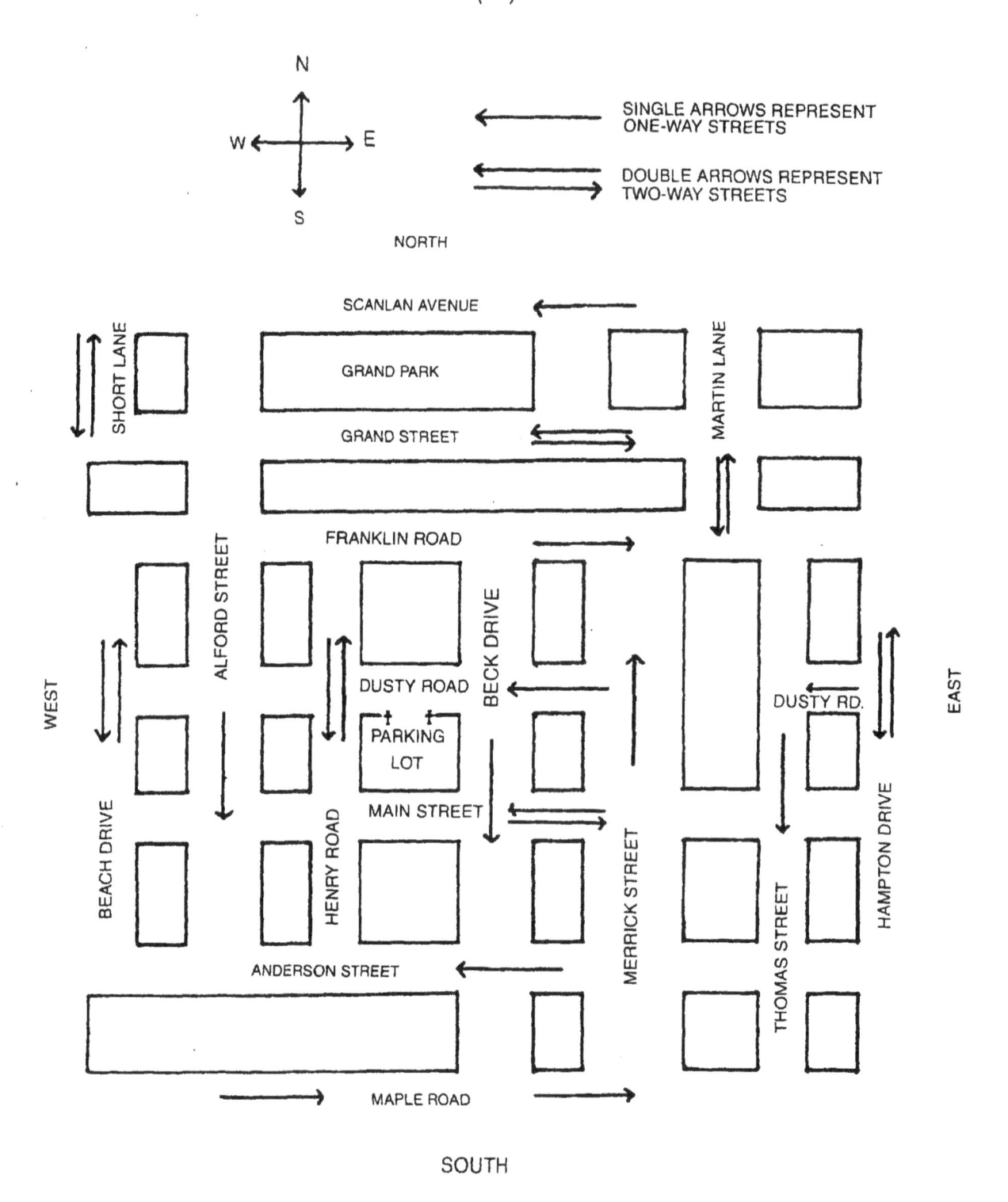

7. Police Officers Gold and Warren are at the intersection of Maple Road and Hampton Drive. The radio dispatcher has assigned them to investigate an attempted auto theft in the parking lot on Dusty Road.
Which one of the following is the SHORTEST route for the officers to take in their patrol car to get to the entrance of the parking lot on Dusty Road, making sure to obey all traffic regulations?
Travel _____ to the parking lot entrance.

A. north on Hampton Drive, then west on Dusty Road
B. west on Maple Road, then north on Beck Drive, then west on Dusty Road
C. north on Hampton Drive, then west on Anderson Street, then north on Merrick Street, then west on Dusty Road
D. west on Maple Road, then north on Merrick Street, then west on Dusty Road

8. Police Officer Gladden is in a patrol car at the intersection of Beach Drive and Anderson Street when he spots a suspicious car. Police Officer Gladden calls the radio dispatcher to determine if the vehicle was stolen. Police Officer Gladden then follows the vehicle north on Beach Drive for three blocks, then turns right and proceeds for one block and makes another right. He then follows the vehicle for two blocks, and then they both make a left turn and continue driving. Police Officer Gladden now receives a call from the dispatcher stating the car was reported stolen and signals for the vehicle to pull to the side of the road.
In what direction was Police Officer Gladden heading at the time he signaled for the other car to pull over?

A. North   B. East   C. South   D. West

Questions 9-10.

DIRECTIONS: Questions 9 and 10 are to be answered SOLELY on the basis of the map which appears on the following page. The flow of traffic is indicated by the arrows. If there is only one arrow shown, then traffic flows only in the direction indicated by the arrow. If there are two arrows shown, then traffic flows in both directions. You must follow the flow of traffic.

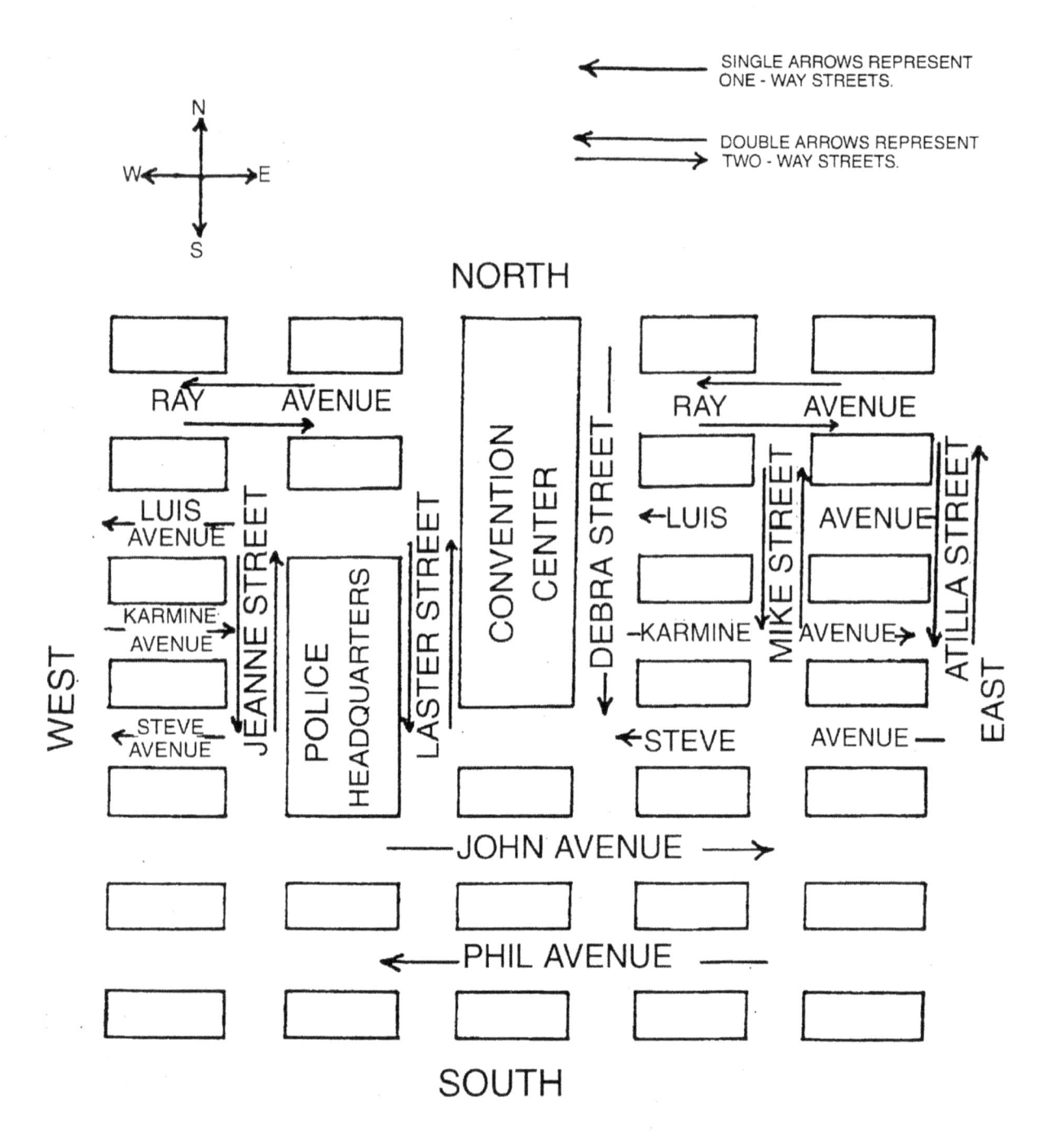

9. While in a patrol car located at Ray Avenue and Atilla Street, Police Officer Ashley receives a call from the dispatcher to respond to an assault at Jeanne Street and Karmine Avenue.
Which one of the following is the SHORTEST route for Officer Ashley to follow in his patrol car, making sure to obey all traffic regulations?
Travel

- A. south on Atilla Street, west on Luis Avenue, south on Debra Street, west on Steve Avenue, north on Lester Street, west on Luis Avenue, then one block south on Jeanne Street
- B. south on Atilla Street, then four blocks west on Phil Avenue, then north on Jeanne Street to Karmine Avenue

C. west on Ray Avenue to Debra Street, then five blocks south to Phil Avenue, then west to Jeanne Street, then three blocks north to Karmine Avenue
D. south on Atilla Street, then four blocks west on John Avenue, then north on Jeanne Street to Karmine Avenue

10. After taking a complaint report from the assault victim, Officer Ashley receives a call from the dispatcher to respond to an auto larceny in progress at the corner of Debra Street and Luis Avenue.
Which one of the following is the SHORTEST route for Officer Ashley to follow in his patrol car, making sure to obey all traffic regulations?
Travel

    A. south on Jeanne Street to John Avenue, then east three blocks on John Avenue, then north on Mike Street to Luis Avenue, then west to Debra Street
    B. south on Jeanne Street to John Avenue, then east two blocks on John Avenue, then north on Debra Street to Luis Avenue
    C. north on Jeanne Street two blocks, then east on Ray Avenue for one block, then south on Lester Street to Steve Avenue, then one block east on Steve Avenue, then north on Debra Street to Luis Avenue
    D. south on Jeanne Street to John Avenue, then east on John Avenue to Atilla Street, then north three blocks to Luis Avenue, then west to Debra Street

10._____

Questions 11-13.

DIRECTIONS: Questions 11 through 13 are to be answered SOLELY on the basis of the following map. The flow of traffic is indicated by the arrows. You must follow the flow of traffic.

10 (#1)

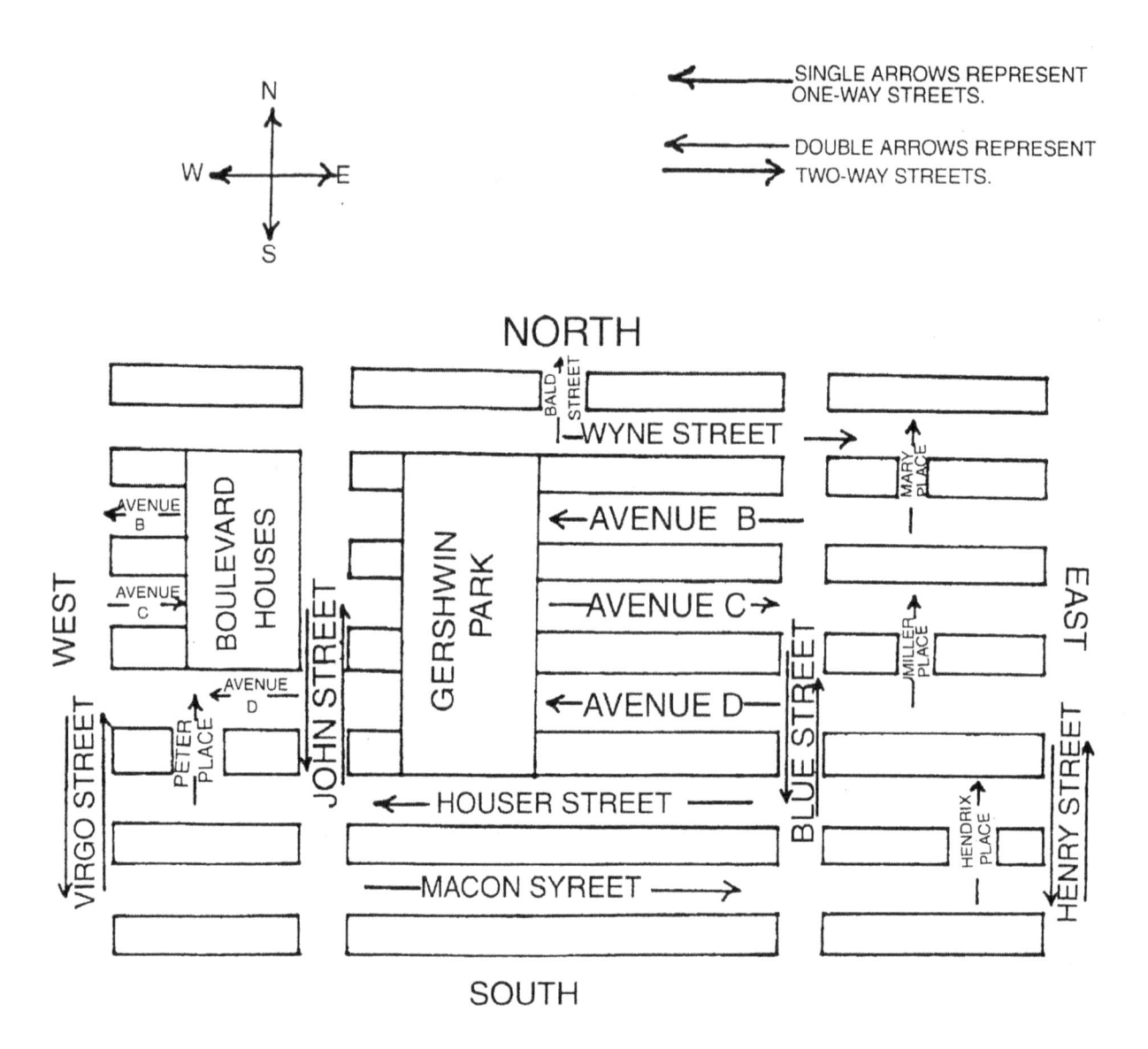

11. Police Officers Ranking and Fish are located at Wyne Street and John Street. The radio dispatcher has assigned them to investigate a motor vehicle accident at the corner of Henry Street and Houser Street.
Which one of the following is the SHORTEST route for them to take in their patrol car, making sure to obey all traffic regulations?
Travel

   A. four blocks south on John Street, then three blocks east on Houser Street to Henry Street
   B. two blocks east on Wyne Street, then two blocks south on Blue Street, then two blocks east on Avenue C, then two blocks south on Henry Street
   C. two blocks east on Wyne Street, then five blocks south on Blue Street, then two blocks east on Macon Street, then one block north on Henry Street
   D. five blocks south on John Street, then three blocks east on Macon Street, then one block north to Houser Street

12. Police Officers Rizzo and Latimer are located at Avenue B and Virgo Street. They respond to the scene of a robbery at Miller Place and Avenue D.
Which one of the following is the SHORTEST route for them to take in their patrol car, making sure to obey all traffic regulations?
Travel _____ to Miller Place.

   A. one block north on Virgo Street, then four blocks east on Wyne Street, then three blocks south on Henry Street, then one block west on Avenue D
   B. four blocks south on Virgo Street, then two blocks east on Macon Street, then two blocks north on Blue Street, then one block east on Avenue D
   C. three blocks south on Virgo Street, then east on Houser Street to Henry Street, then one block north on Henry Street, then one block west on Avenue D
   D. four blocks south on Virgo Street, then four blocks east to Henry Street, then north to Avenue D, then one block west

13. Police Officer Bendix is in an unmarked patrol car at the intersection of John Street and Macon Street when he begins to follow a robbery suspect. The suspect goes one block east, turns left, travels for three blocks, and then turns right. He drives for two blocks and then makes a right turn. In the middle of the block, the suspect realizes he is being followed and makes a u-turn. In what direction is the suspect now headed?

   A. North B. South C. East D. West

Questions 14-15.

DIRECTIONS: Questions 14 and 15 are to be answered SOLELY on the basis of the following map. The flow of traffic is indicated by the arrows. If there is only one arrow shown, then traffic flows only in the direction indicated by the arrow. If there are two arrows shown, then traffic flows in both directions. You must follow the flow of traffic.

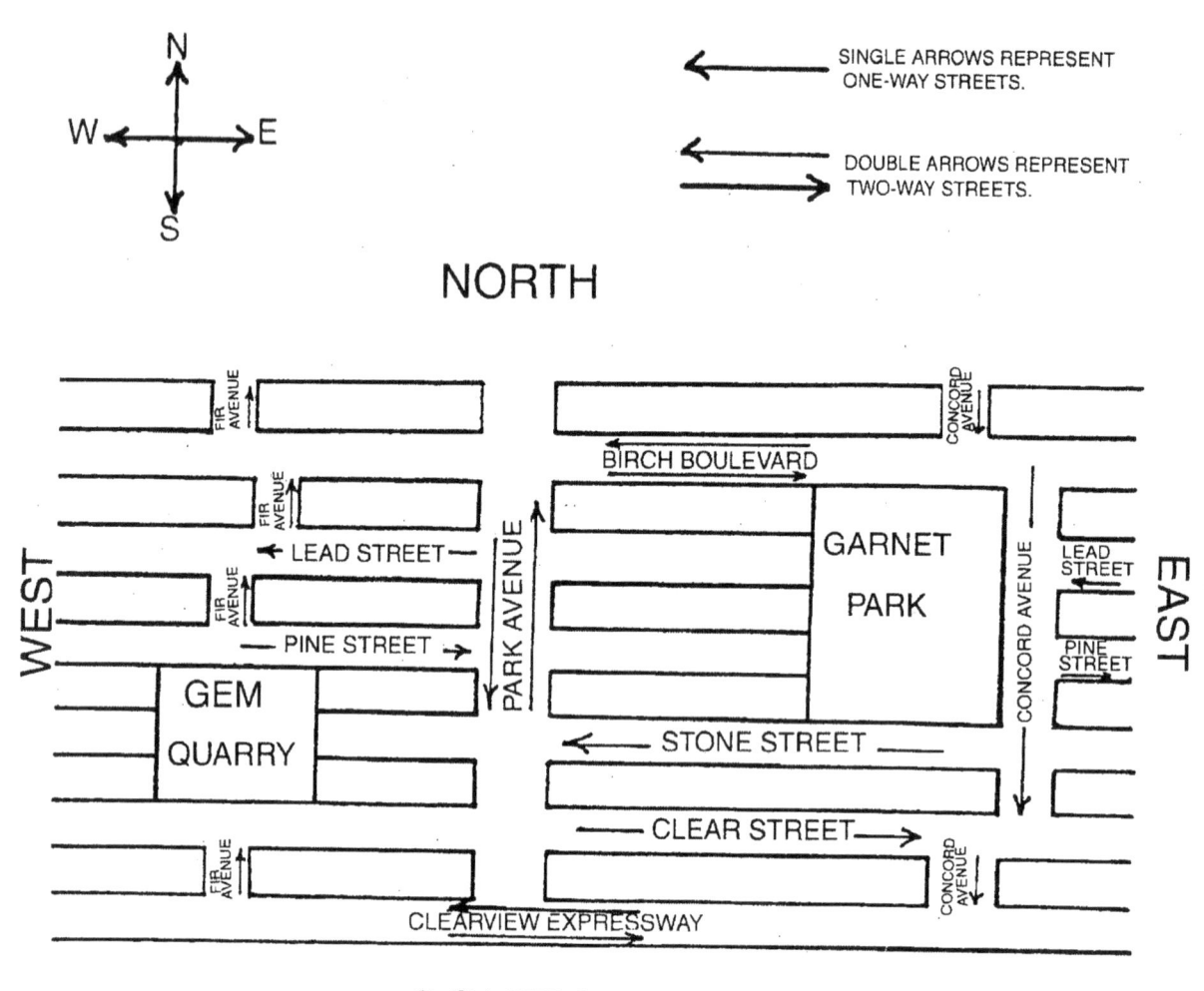

14. You are located at Fir Avenue and Birch Boulevard and receive a request to respond to a disturbance at Fir Avenue and Clear Street.
Which one of the following is the MOST direct route for you to take in your patrol car, making sure to obey all traffic regulations?
Travel

   A. one block east on Birch Boulevard, then four blocks south on Park Avenue, then one block east on Clear Street
   B. two blocks east on Birch Boulevard, then three blocks south on Concord Avenue, then two blocks west on Stone Street, then one block south on Park Avenue, then one block west on Clear Street
   C. one block east on Birch Boulevard, then five blocks south on Park Avenue, then one block west on the Clearview Expressway, then one block north on Fir Avenue
   D. two blocks south on Fir Avenue, then one block east on Pine Street, then three blocks south on Park Avenue, then one block east on the Clearview Expressway, then one block north on Fir Avenue

15. You are located at the Clearview Expressway and Concord Avenue and receive a call to respond to a crime in progress at Concord Avenue and Pine Street. Which one of the following is the MOST direct route for you to take in your patrol car, making sure to obey all traffic regulations?
    Travel

    A. two blocks west on the Clearview Expressway, then one block north on Fir Avenue, then one block east on Clear Street, then four blocks north on Park Avenue, then one block east on Birch Boulevard, then two blocks south on Concord Avenue
    B. one block north on Concord Avenue, then one block west on Clear Street, then one block north on Park Avenue, then one block east on Stone Street, then one block north on Concord Avenue
    C. one block west on the Clearview Expressway, then four blocks north on Park Avenue, then one block west on Lead Street, then one block south on Fir Avenue
    D. one block west on the Clearview Expressway, then five blocks north on Park Avenue, then one block east on Birch Boulevard, then two blocks south on Concord Avenue

15.____

Questions 16-20.

DIRECTIONS: Questions 16 through 20 are to be answered SOLELY on the basis of the following map. The flow of traffic is indicated by the arrows. You must follow the flow of traffic.

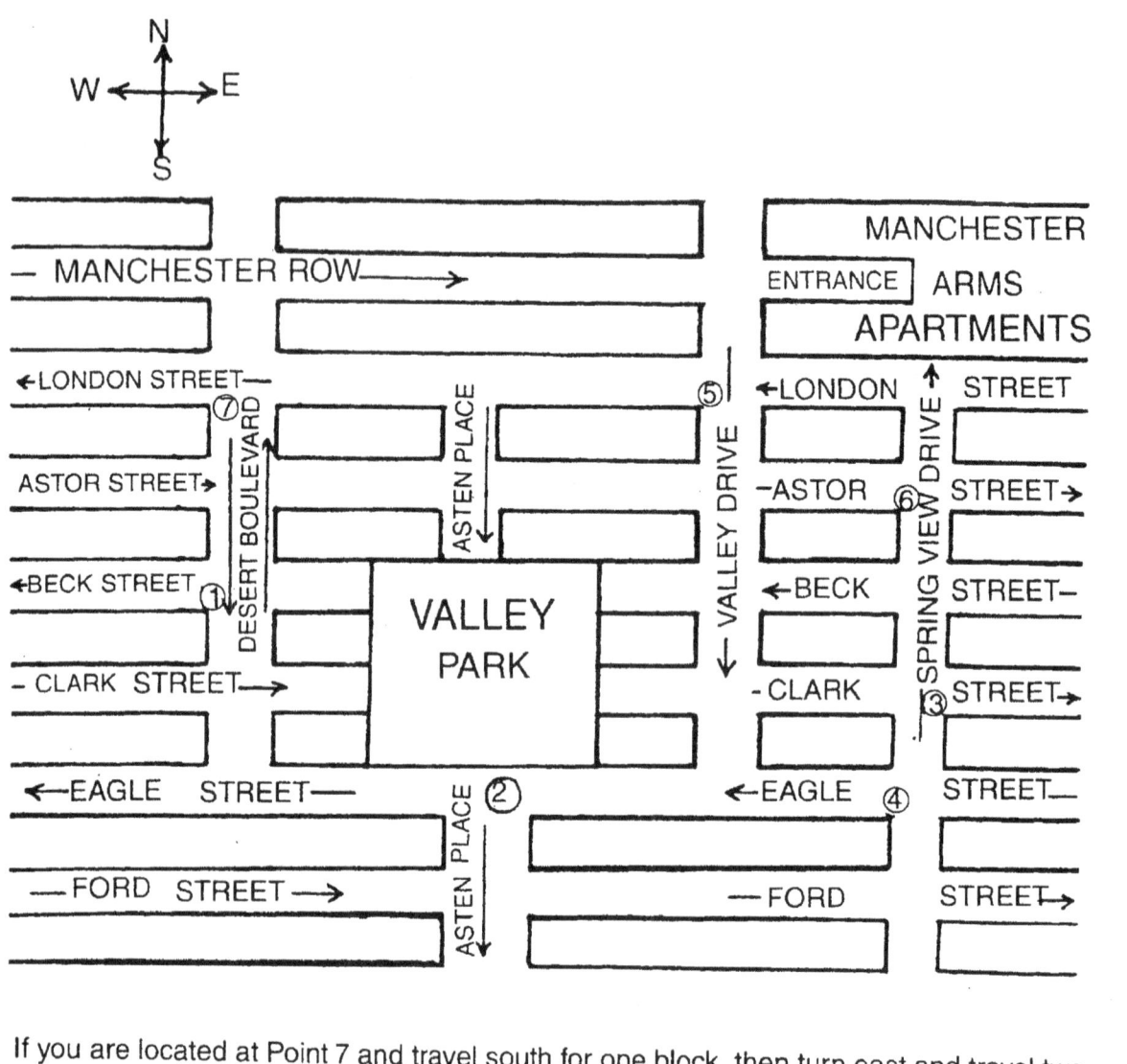

16. If you are located at Point 7 and travel south for one block, then turn east and travel two blocks, then turn south and travel two blocks, then turn east and travel one block, you will be CLOSEST to Point

    A. 2   B. 3   C. 4   D. 6

17. If you are located at Point 3 and travel north for one block, and then turn west and travel one block, and then turn south and travel two blocks, and then turn west and travel one block, you will be CLOSEST to Point

    A. 1   B. 2   C. 4   D. 6

18. You are located at Astor Street and Spring View Drive. You receive a call of a crime in progress at the intersection of Beck Street and Desert Boulevard.
    Which one of the following is the MOST direct route for you to take in your patrol car, making sure to obey all traffic regulations?
    Travel

    A. one block north on Spring View Drive, then three blocks west on London Street, then two blocks south on Desert Boulevard
    B. three blocks west on Astor Street, then one block south on Desert Boulevard

C. one block south on Spring View Drive, then three blocks west on Beck Street
   D. three blocks south on Spring View Drive, then three blocks west on Eagle Street, then two blocks north on Desert Boulevard

19. You are located on Clark Street and Desert Boulevard and must respond to a disturbance at Clark Street and Spring View Drive.
   Which one of the following is the MOST direct route for you to take in your patrol car, making sure to obey all traffic regulations?
   Travel

   A. two blocks north on Desert Boulevard, then three blocks east on Astor Street, then two blocks south on Spring View Drive
   B. one block south on Desert Boulevard, then three blocks east on Eagle Street, then one block north on Spring View Drive
   C. two blocks north on Desert Boulevard, then two blocks east on Astor Street, then three blocks south on Valley Drive, then one block east on Eagle Street, then one block north on Spring View Drive
   D. two blocks north on Desert Boulevard, then two blocks east on Astor Street, then two blocks south on Valley Drive, then one block east on Clark Street

19._____

20. You are located at Valley Drive and Beck Street and receive a call to respond to the corner of Asten Place and Astor Street.
   Which one of the following is the MOST direct route for you to take in your patrol car, making sure to obey all traffic regulations?
   Travel _____ on Astor Street.

   A. one block north on Valley Drive, then one block west
   B. two blocks south on Valley Drive, then one block east on Eagle Street, then three blocks north on Spring View Drive, then two blocks west
   C. two blocks south on Valley Drive, then two blocks west on Eagle Street, then three blocks north on Desert Boulevard, then one block east
   D. one block south on Valley Drive, then one block east on Clark Street, then two blocks north on Spring View Drive, then two blocks west

20._____

KEY (CORRECT ANSWERS)

1. C	11. B
2. A	12. A
3. A	13. A
4. D	14. C
5. C	15. D
6. B	16. B
7. C	17. B
8. B	18. A
9. A	19. D
10. A	20. C

MAP READING
EXAMINATION SECTION
TEST 1

DIRECTIONS: Each question or incomplete statement is followed by several suggested answers or completions. Select the one that BEST answers the question or completes the Statement. *PRINT THE LETTER OF THE CORRECT ANSWER IN THE SPACE AT THE RIGHT.*

Questions 1-5.

DIRECTIONS: Questions 1 through 5 are to be answered SOLELY on the basis of the following information and map.

An employee may be required to assist civilians who seek travel directions or referral to city agencies and facilities.

The following is a map of part of a city, where several public offices and other institutions are located. Each of the squares represents one city block. Street names are as shown. If there is an arrow next to the street name, it means the street is one-way only in the direction of the arrow. If there is no arrow next to the street name, two-way traffic is allowed.

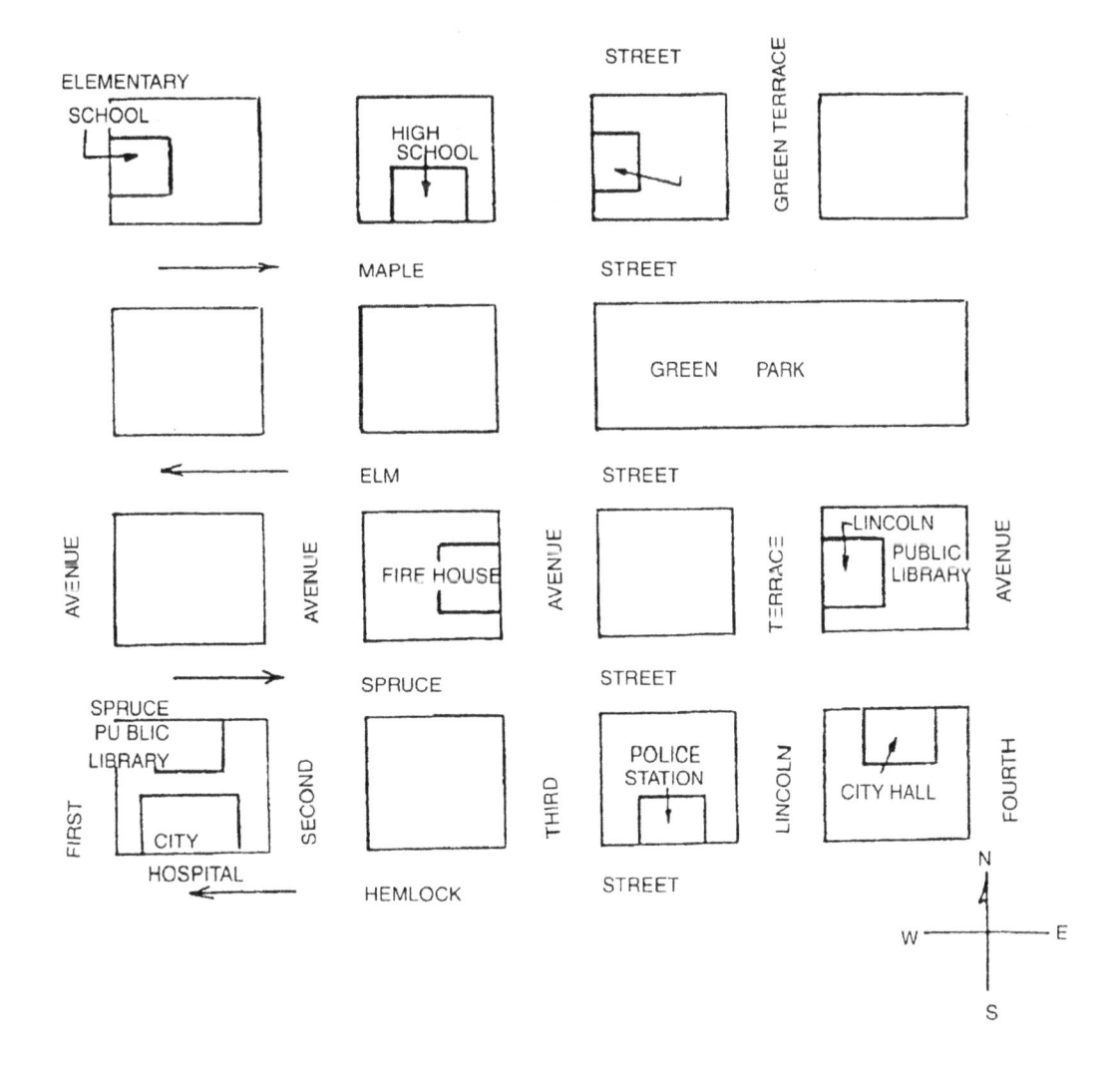

75

1. A woman whose handbag was stolen from her in Green Park asks a firefighter at the firehouse where to go to report the crime.
   The firefighter should tell the woman to go to the

   A. police station on Spruce Street
   B. police station on Hemlock Street
   C. city hall on Spruce Street
   D. city hall on Hemlock Street

2. A disabled senior citizen who lives on Green Terrace telephones the firehouse to ask which library is closest to her home.
   The firefighter should tell the senior citizen it is the

   A. Spruce Public Library on Lincoln Terrace
   B. Lincoln Public Library on Spruce Street
   C. Spruce Public Library on Spruce Street
   D. Lincoln Public Library on Lincoln Terrace

3. A woman calls the firehouse to ask for the exact location of City Hall.
   She should be told that it is on

   A. Hemlock Street, between Lincoln Terrace and Fourth Avenue
   B. Spruce Street, between Lincoln Terrace and Fourth Avenue
   C. Lincoln Terrace, between Spruce Street and Elm Street
   D. Green Terrace, between Maple Street and Pine Street

4. A delivery truck driver is having trouble finding the high school to make a delivery. The driver parks the truck across from the firehouse on Third Avenue facing north and goes into the firehouse to ask directions.
   In giving directions, the firefighter should tell the driver to go _____ to the school.

   A. north on Third Avenue to Pine Street and then make a right
   B. south on Third Avenue, make a left on Hemlock Street, and then make a right on Second Avenue
   C. north on Third Avenue, turn left on Elm Street, make a right on Second Avenue and go to Maple Street, then make another right
   D. north on Third Avenue to Maple Street, and then make a left

5. A man comes to the firehouse accompanied by his son and daughter. He wants to register his son in the high school and his daughter in the elementary school. He asks a firefighter which school is closest for him to walk to from the firehouse.
   The firefighter should tell the man that the

   A. high school is closer than the elementary school
   B. elementary school is closer than the high school
   C. elementary school and high school are the same distance away
   D. elementary school and high school are in opposite directions

Questions 6-8.

DIRECTIONS: Questions 6 through 8 are to be answered SOLELY on the basis of the following map and information. The flow of traffic is indicated by the arrows. If there is only one arrow shown, then traffic flows in the direction indicated by the arrow. If there are two arrows, then traffic flows in both directions. You must follow the flow of traffic

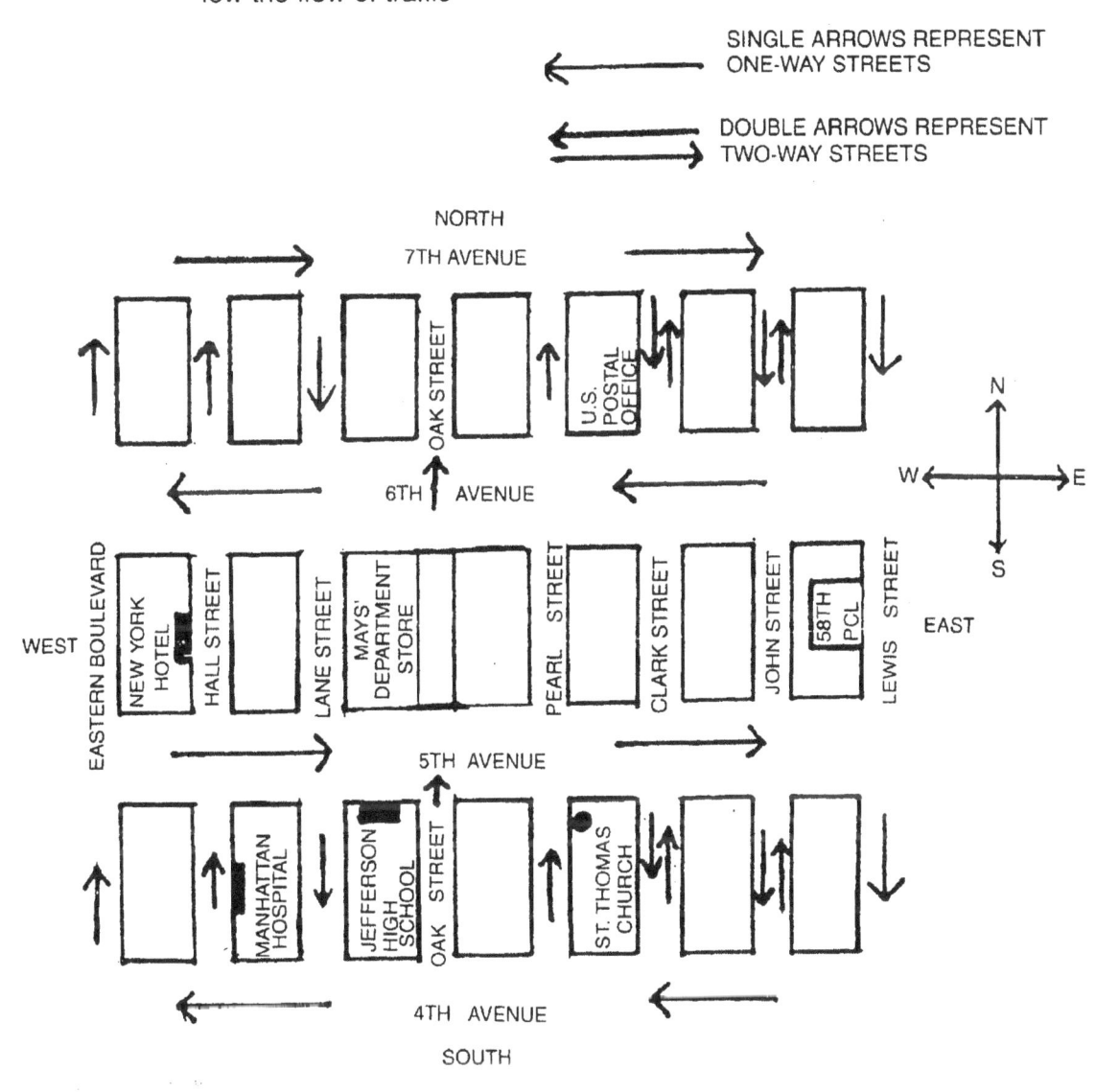

6. Traffic Enforcement Agent Fox was on foot patrol at John Street between 6th and 7th Avenues when a motorist driving southbound asked her for directions to the New York Hotel, which is located on Hall Street between 5th and 6th Avenues. Which one of the following is the SHORTEST route for Agent Fox to direct the motorist to take, making sure to obey all traffic regulations?
Travel _____ to the New York Hotel.

   A. north on John Street, then east on 7th Avenue, then north on Lewis Street, then west on 4th Avenue, then north on Eastern Boulevard, then east on 5th Avenue, then north on Hall Street
   B. south on John Street, then west on 6th Avenue, then south on Eastern Boulevard, then east on 5th Avenue, then north on Hall Street

C. south on John Street, then west on 6th Avenue, then south on Clark Street, then east on 4th Avenue, then north on Eastern Boulevard, then east on 5th Avenue, then north on Hall Street
D. south on John Street, then west on 4th Avenue, then north on Hall Street

7. Traffic Enforcement Agent Murphy is on motorized patrol on 7th Avenue between Oak Street and Pearl Street when Lt. Robertson radios him to go to Jefferson High School, located on 5th Avenue between Lane Street and Oak Street. Which one of the following is the SHORTEST route for Agent Murphy to take, making sure to obey all the traffic regulations?
Travel east on 7th Avenue, then south on _____, then east on 5th Avenue to Jefferson High School.

A. Clark Street, then west on 4th Avenue, then north on Hall Street
B. Pearl Street, then west on 4th Avenue, then north on Lane Street
C. Lewis Street, then west on 6th Avenue, then south on Hall Street
D. Lewis Street, then west on 4th Avenue, then north on Oak Street

7.____

8. Traffic Enforcement Agent Vasquez was on 4th Avenue and Eastern Boulevard when a motorist asked him for directions to the 58th Police Precinct, which is located on Lewis Street between 5th and 6th Avenues.
Which one of the following is the SHORTEST route for Agent Vasquez to direct the motorist to take, making sure to obey all traffic regulations.
Travel north on Eastern Boulevard, then east on _____ on Lewis Street to the 58th Police Precinct.

A. 5th Avenue, then north
B. 7th Avenue, then south
C. 6th Avenue, then north on Pearl Street, then east on 7th Avenue, then south
D. 5th Avenue, then north on Clark Street, then east on 6th Avenue, then south

8.____

Questions 9-13.

DIRECTIONS: Questions 9 through 13 are to be answered SOLELY on the basis of the following map and the following information.

Toll collectors answer motorists' questions concerning directions by reading a map of the metropolitan area. Although many alternate routes leading to destinations exist on the following map, you are to choose the MOST direct route of those given.

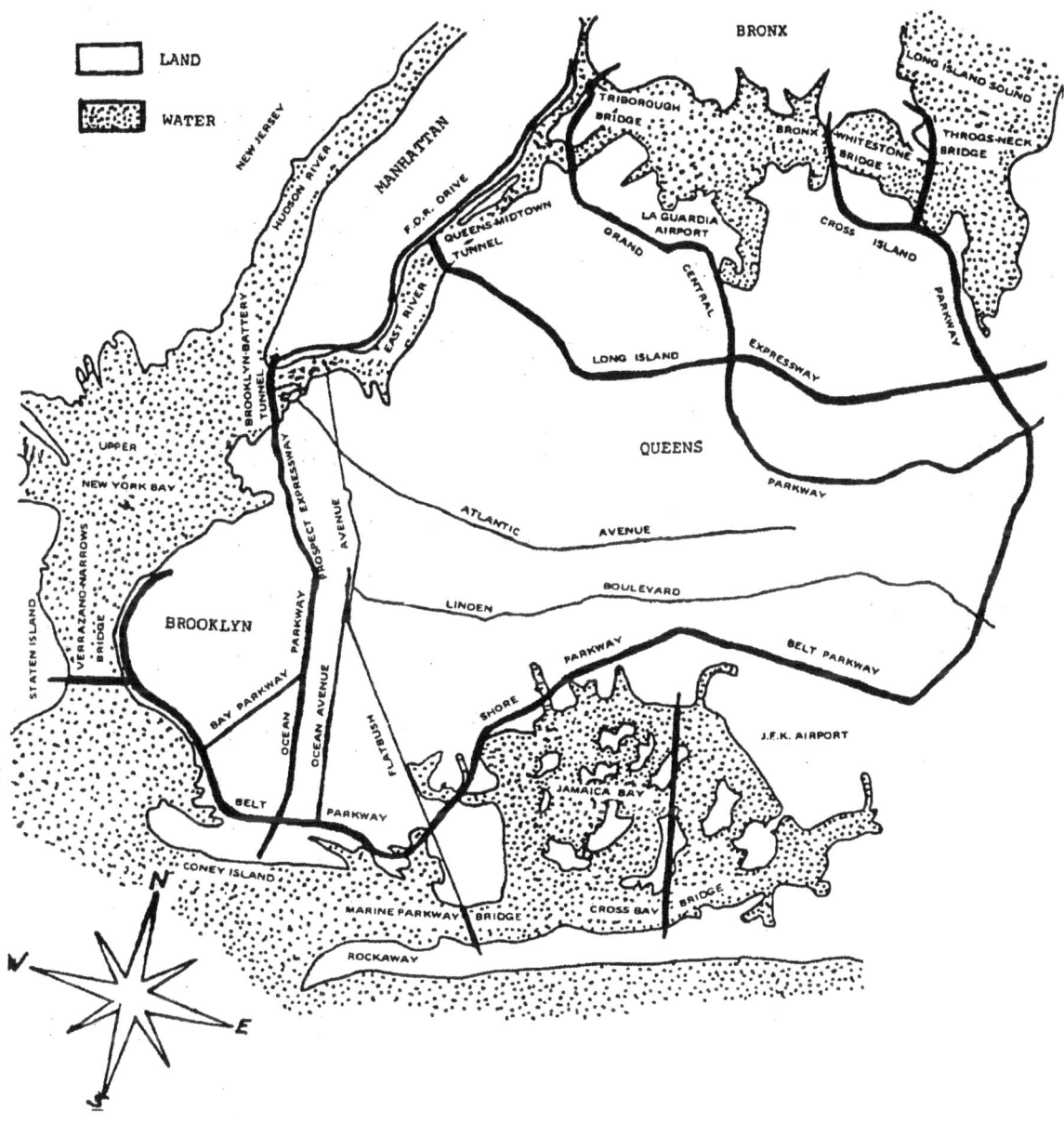

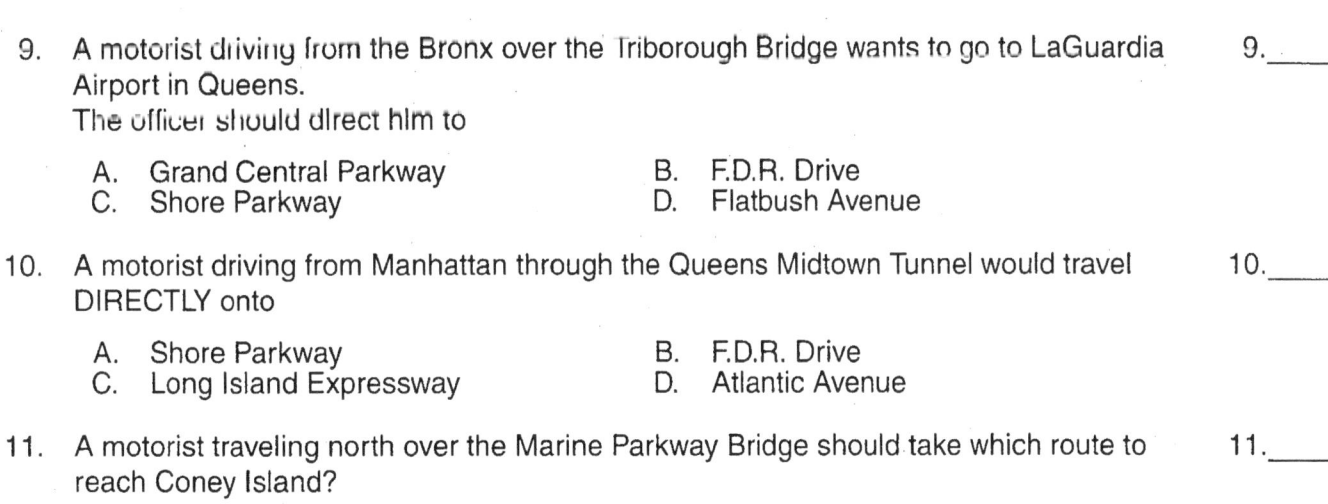

5 (#1)

9. A motorist driving from the Bronx over the Triborough Bridge wants to go to LaGuardia Airport in Queens.
The officer should direct him to

    A. Grand Central Parkway   B. F.D.R. Drive
    C. Shore Parkway   D. Flatbush Avenue

9.____

10. A motorist driving from Manhattan through the Queens Midtown Tunnel would travel DIRECTLY onto

    A. Shore Parkway   B. F.D.R. Drive
    C. Long Island Expressway   D. Atlantic Avenue

10.____

11. A motorist traveling north over the Marine Parkway Bridge should take which route to reach Coney Island?

    A. Shore Parkway East   B. Belt Parkway West
    C. Linden Boulevard   D. Ocean Parkway

11.____

12. Which facility does NOT connect the Bronx and Queens? 12._____

   A. Triborough Bridge
   B. Bronx-Whitestone Bridge
   C. Verrazano-Narrows Bridge
   D. Throgs-Neck Bridge

13. A motorist driving from Manhattan arrives at the toll booth of the Brooklyn-Battery Tunnel and asks directions to Ocean Parkway. 13._____
    To which one of the following routes should the motorist FIRST be directed?

   A. Atlantic Avenue
   B. Bay Parkway
   C. Prospect Expressway
   D. Ocean Avenue

Questions 14-16.

DIRECTIONS: Questions 14 through 16 are to be answered SOLELY on the basis of the following map. The flow of traffic is indicated by the arrows. If there is only one arrow shown, then traffic flows only in the direction indicated by the arrow. If there are two arrows, then traffic flows in both directions. You must follow the flow of traffic.

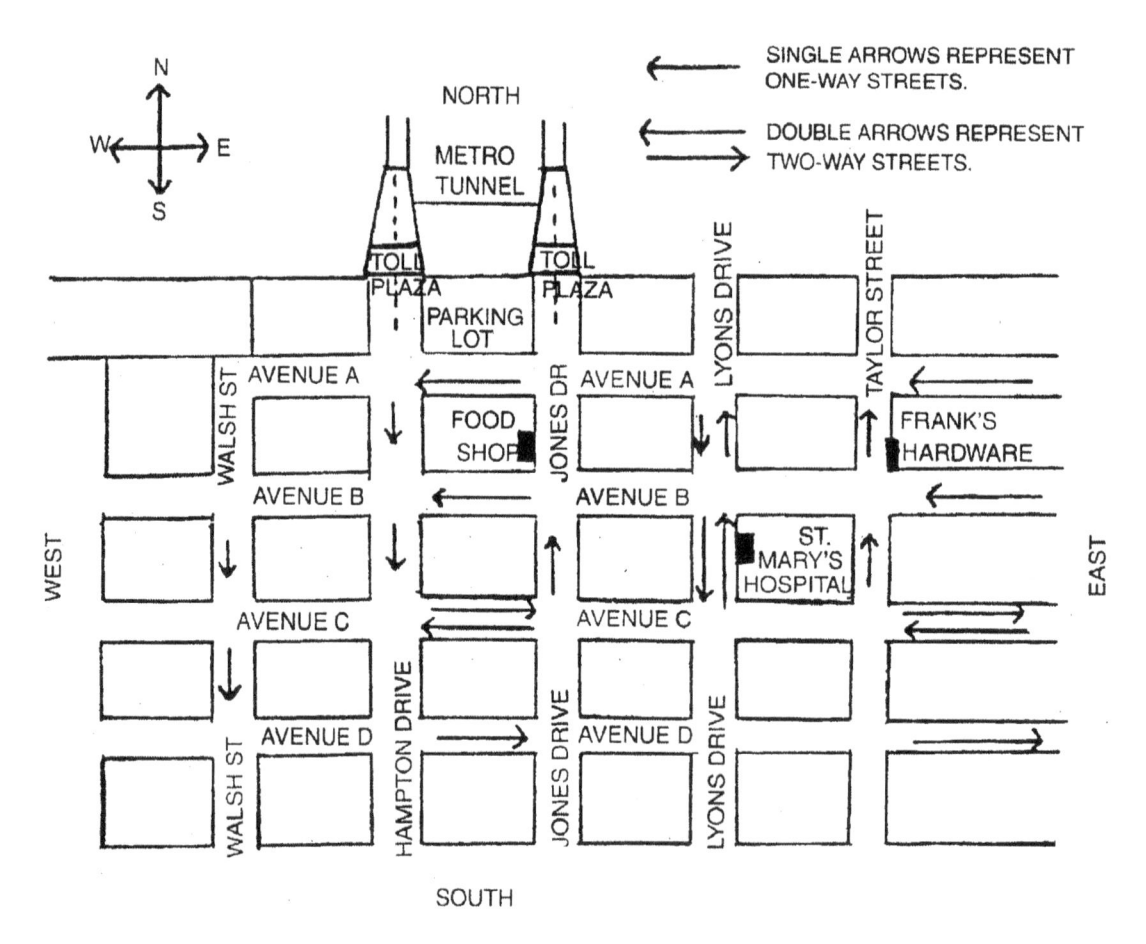

14. A motorist is exiting the Metro Tunnel and approaches the bridge and tunnel officer at the toll plaza. He asks the officer how to get to the food shop on Jones Drive. Which one of the following is the SHORTEST route for the motorist to take, making sure to obey all traffic regulations? 14._____
    Travel south on Hampton Drive, then left on _____ on Jones Drive to the food shop.

	A.	Avenue A, then right	B.	Avenue B, then right
	C.	Avenue D, then left	D.	Avenue C, then left

15. A motorist heading south pulls up to a toll booth at the exit of the Metro Tunnel and asks 15.____
Bridge and Tunnel Officer Evans how to get to Frank's Hardware Store on Taylor Street.
Which one of the following is the SHORTEST route for the motorist to take, making
sure to obey all traffic regulations?
Travel south on Hampton Drive, then east on

    A. Avenue B to Taylor Street
    B. Avenue D, then north on Taylor Street to Avenue B
    C. Avenue C, then north on Taylor Street to Avenue B
    D. Avenue C, then north on Lyons Drive, then east on Avenue B to Taylor Street

16. A motorist is exiting the Metro Tunnel and approaches the toll plaza. She asks Bridge 16.____
and Tunnel Officer Owens for directions to St. Mary's Hospital.
Which one of the following is the SHORTEST route for the motorist to take, making
sure to obey all traffic regulations?
Travel south on Hampton Drive, then _____ on Lyons Drive to St. Mary's Hospital.

    A. left on Avenue D, then left
    B. right on Avenue A, then left on Walsh Street, then left on Avenue D, then left
    C. left on Avenue C, then left
    D. left on Avenue B, then right

Questions 17-18.

DIRECTIONS: Questions 17 and 18 are to be answered SOLELY on the basis of the map which appears on the following page. The flow of traffic is indicated by the arrows. If there is only one arrow shown, then traffic flows only in the direction indicated by the arrow. If there are two arrows shown, then traffic flows in both directions. You must follow the flow of traffic.

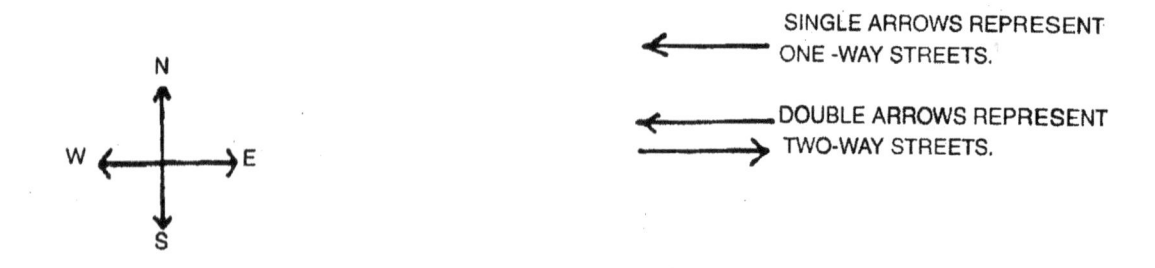

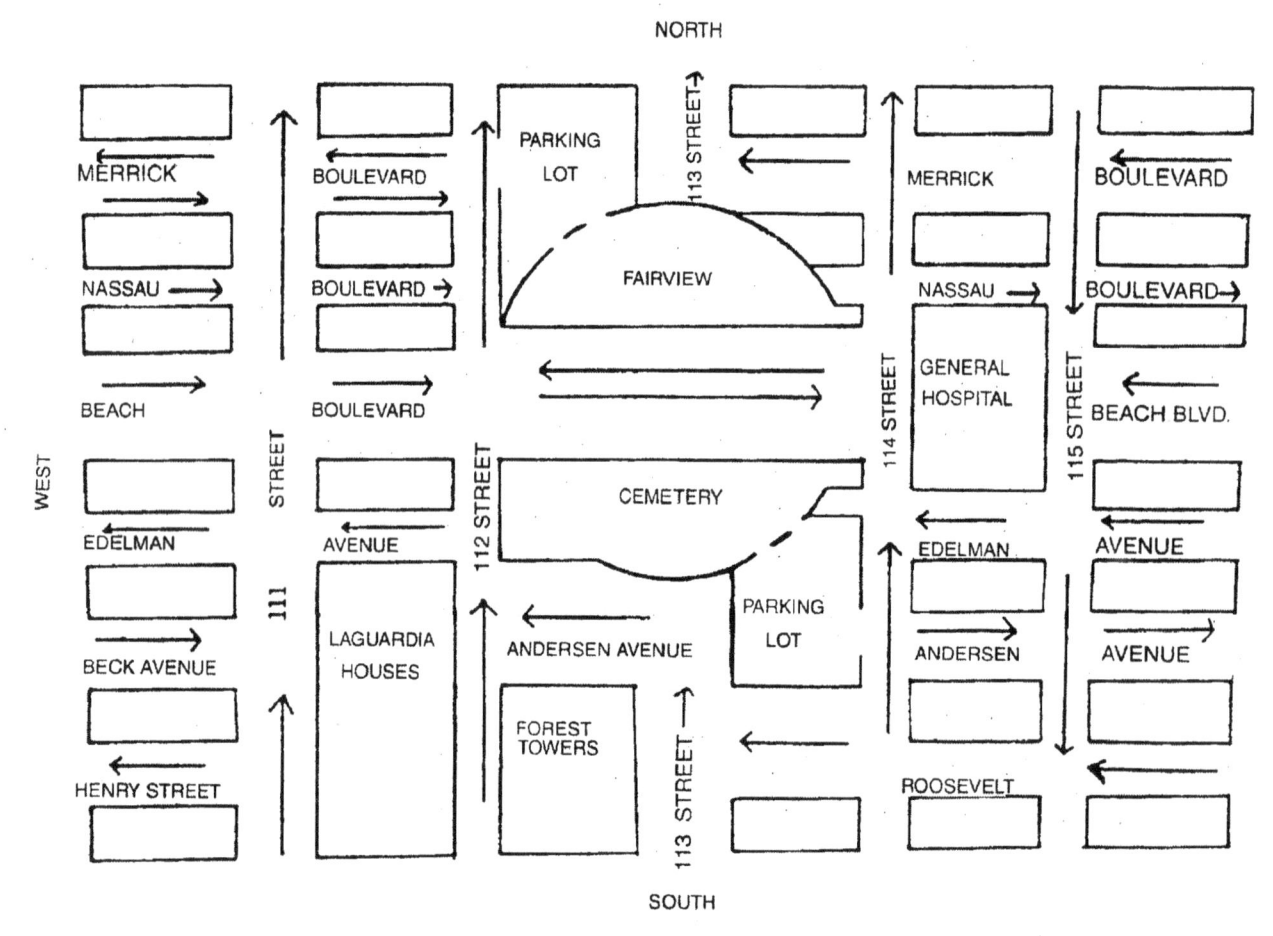

17. Police Officers Glenn and Albertson are on 111th Street at Henry Street when they are dispatched to a past robbery at Beach Boulevard and 115th Street.
Which one of the following is the SHORTEST route for the officers to follow in their patrol car, making sure to obey all traffic regulations?
Travel north on 111th Street, then east on _____ south on 115th Street.

   A. Edelman Avenue, then north on 112th Street, then east on Beach Boulevard, then north on 114th Street, then east on Nassau Boulevard, then one block
   B. Beach Boulevard, then north on 114th Street, then east on Nassau Boulevard, then one block
   C. Merrick Boulevard, then two blocks
   D. Nassau Boulevard, then south on 112th Street, then east on Beach Boulevard, then north on 114th Street, then east on Nassau Boulevard, then one block

18. Later in their tour, Officers Glenn and Albertson are driving on 114th Street. If they make a left turn to enter the parking lot at Andersen Avenue, and then make a u-turn, in what direction would they now be headed?

    A. North   B. South   C. East   D. West

18.____

Questions 19-20.

DIRECTIONS: Questions 19 and 20 are to be answered SOLELY on the basis of the following map. The flow of traffic is indicated by the arrows. If there is only one arrow shown, then traffic flows only in the direction indicated by the arrow. If there are two arrows shown, then traffic flows in both directions. You must follow the flow of traffic.

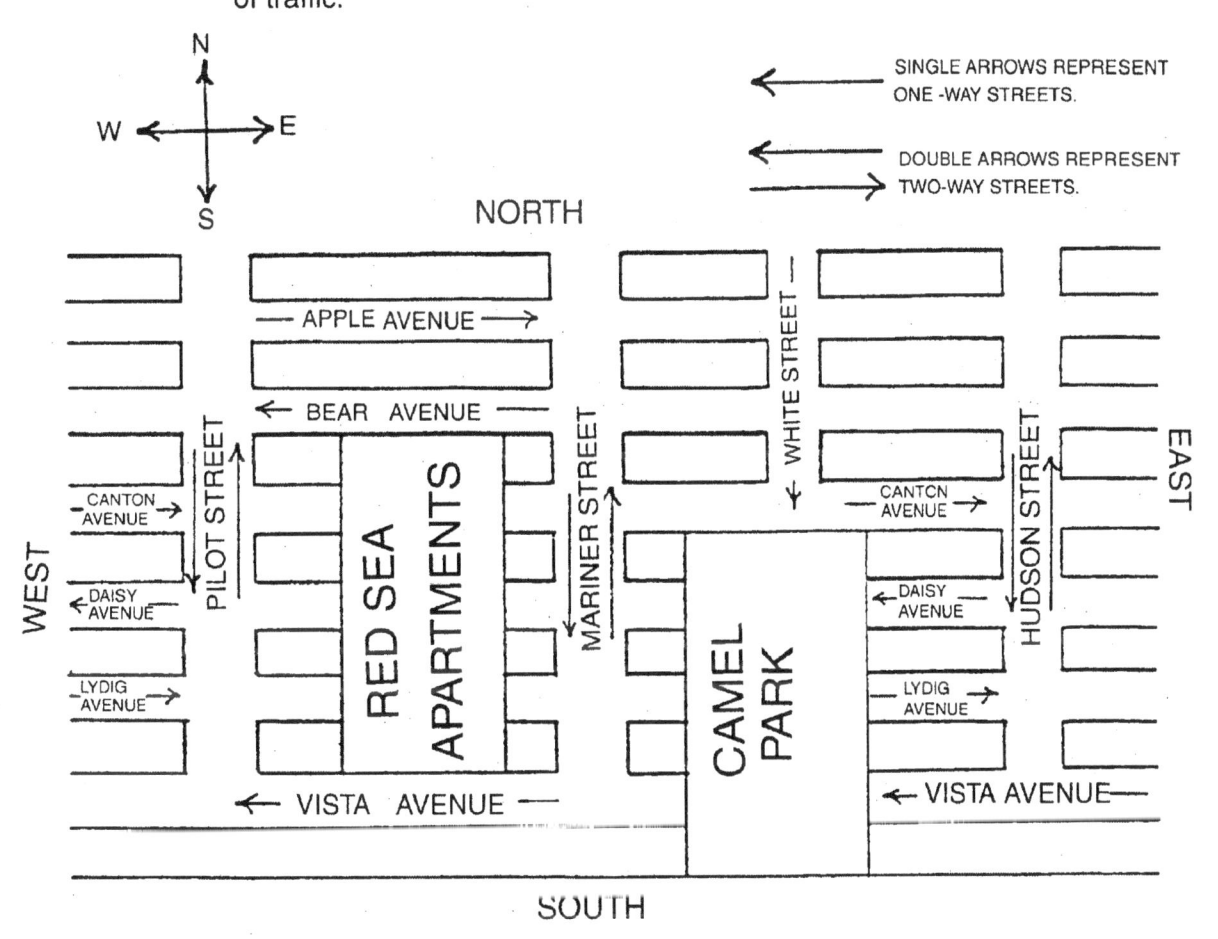

19. You are located at Apple Avenue and White Street. You receive a call to respond to the corner of Lydig Avenue and Pilot Street.
Which one of the following is the MOST direct route for you to take in your patrol car, making sure to obey all traffic regulations?
Travel _____ on Pilot Street.

    A. two blocks south on White Street, then one block east on Canton Avenue, then one block north on Hudson Street, then three blocks west on Bear Avenue, then three blocks south

    B. one block south on White Street, then two blocks west on Bear Avenue, then three blocks south

19.____

C. two blocks west on Apple Avenue, then four blocks south
D. two blocks south on White Street, then one block west on Canton Avenue, then three blocks south on Mariner Street, then one block west on Vista Avenue, then one block north

20. You are located at Canton Avenue and Pilot Street. You receive a call of a crime in progress at the intersection of Canton Avenue and Hudson Street.
Which one of the following is the MOST direct route for you to take in your patrol car, making sure to obey all traffic regulations?
Travel

    20.____

   A. two blocks north on Pilot Street, then two blocks east on Apple Avenue, then one block south on White Street, then one block east on Bear Avenue, then one block south on Hudson Street
   B. three blocks south on Pilot Street, then travel one block east on Vista Avenue, then travel three blocks north on Mariner Street, then travel two blocks east on Canton Avenue
   C. one block north on Pilot Street, then travel three blocks east on Bear Avenue, then travel one block south on Hudson Street
   D. two blocks north on Pilot Street, then travel three blocks east on Apple Avenue, then travel two blocks south on Hudson Street

---

KEY (CORRECT ANSWERS)

1.	B	11.	B/D
2.	D	12.	C
3.	B	13.	C
4.	C	14.	D
5.	A	15.	C
6.	D	16.	C
7.	A	17.	B
8.	B	18.	C
9.	A	19.	B
10.	C	20.	D

EXAMINATION SECTION

TEST 1

DIRECTIONS: Each question or incomplete statement is followed by several suggested answers or completions. Select the one that BEST answers the question or completes the statement. *PRINT THE LETTER OF THE CORRECT ANSWER IN THE SPACE AT THE RIGHT.*

Questions 1-4.

DIRECTIONS: Questions 1 through 4 measure your ability to recognize objects, people, events, parts of maps, or crime, accident, or other scenes to which you have been exposed.

Below and on the following pages are twenty illustrations. Study them carefully. In the test, you will be shown pairs of drawings. For each pair, you will be asked which is or are from the twenty illustrations in this part.

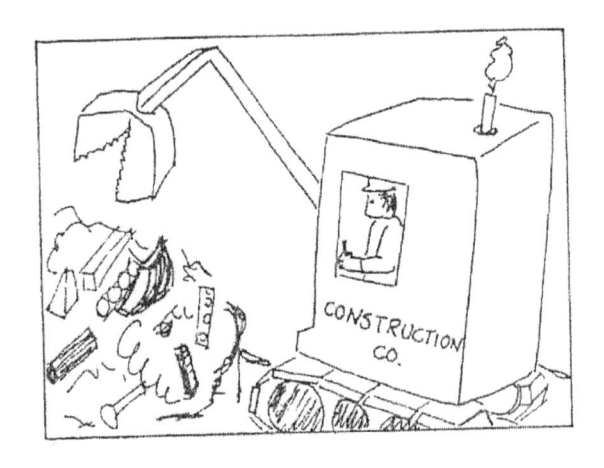

2 (#1)

3 (#1)

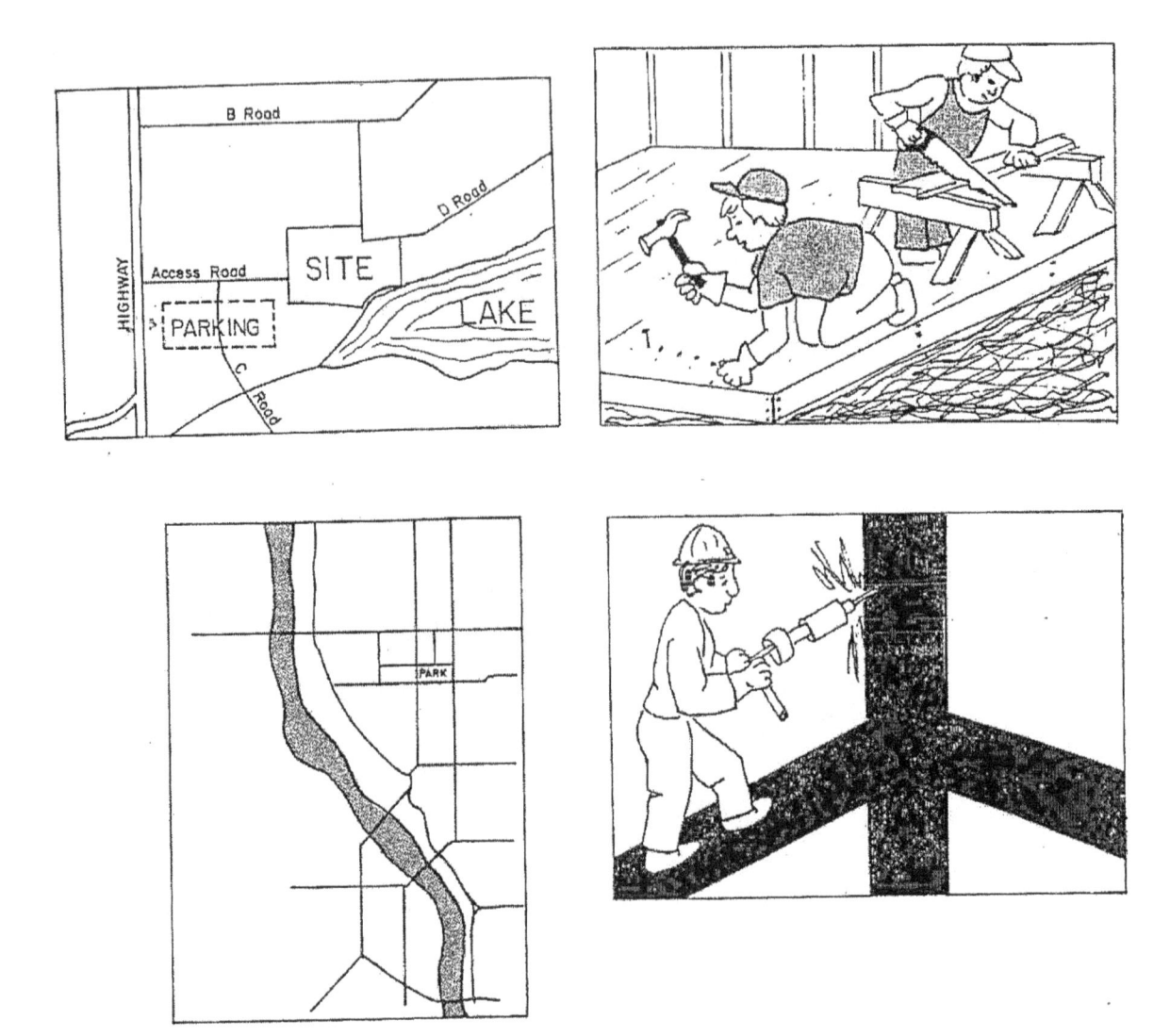

4 (#1)

5 (#1)

Questions 1-4.

DIRECTIONS: In Questions 1 through 4, select the choice that corresponds to the scene(s) that is(are) from the illustrations for this section. *PRINT THE LETTER OF THE CORRECT ANSWER IN THE SPACE AT THE RIGHT.*

1. I   II   2.____

   A. I only
   B. II only
   C. Both I and II
   D. Neither I nor II

2. I   II   2.

   A. I only
   B. II only
   C. Both I and II
   D. Neither I nor II

89

3.

A. I only
C. Both I and II
B. II only
D. Neither I nor II

3.____

4.

A. I only
C. Both I and II
B. II only
D. Neither I nor II

4.____

Questions 5-6.

DIRECTIONS: Questions 5 and 6 measure your ability to notice and interpret details accurately. You will be shown a picture, below, and then asked a set of questions about the picture. You do NOT need to memorize this picture. You may look at the picture when answering the questions.

5.

5.____

Details in the picture lend some support to or do NOT tend to contradict which of the following statements about the person who occupies the room?
I. The person is very careless.
II. The person smokes.
The CORRECT answer is:
 A. I only
 B. II only
 C. Both I and II
 D. Neither I nor II

6. The number on the piece of paper on the desk is MOST likely a 6.____
 A. ZIP code
 B. street number
 C. social security number
 D. telephone area code

Questions 7-10.

DIRECTIONS: Questions 7 through 10 measure your ability to recognize objects or people in differing views, contexts, or situations. Each question consists of three pictures; one labeled I and one labeled II. In each question, you are to determine whether A – I only, B – II only, C – Both I and II, and D – Neither I nor II COULD be the subject.

The Subject is *always* ONE person or ONE object. The Subject picture shows the object or person as it, he, or she appeared at the time of initial contact. Pictures I and II show objects from a different viewpoint than that of the Subject picture. For example, if the Subject picture presents a front view, I and II may present back views, side views, or a back and a side view. Also, art objects may be displayed differently, may have a different base or frame or method of hanging.

When the subject is a person, I or II will be a picture of a different person or will be a picture of the same person after some change has taken place. The person may have made a deliberate attempt to alter his or her appearance, such as wearing (or taking off a wig, growing (or shaving off) a beard or mustache, or dressing as a member of the opposite sex. The change may also be a natural one, such as changing a hair style, changing from work clothes to play clothes, or from play clothes to work clothes, or growing older, thinner, or taller. None has had cosmetic surgery.

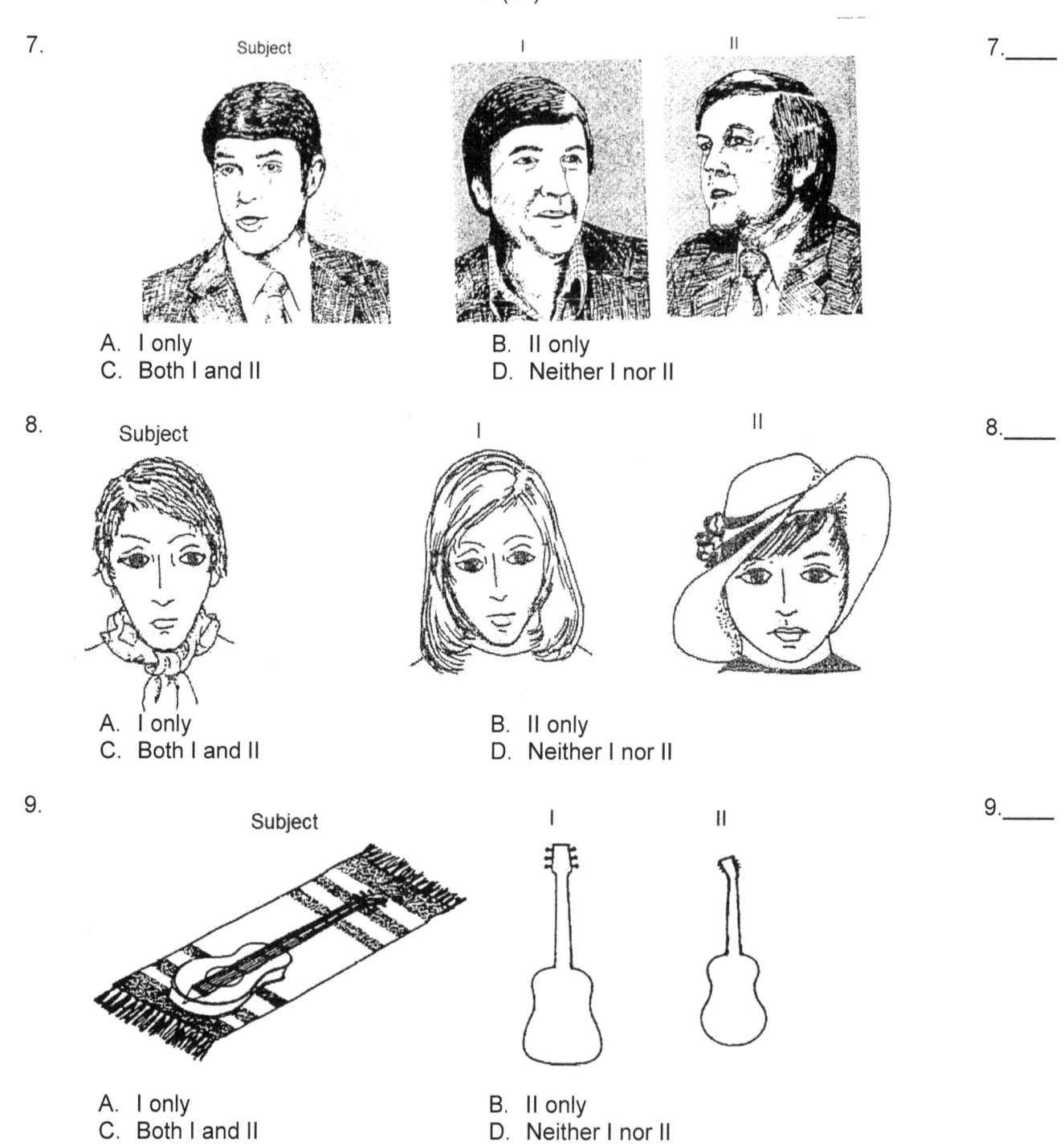

7.

Subject | I | II

A. I only
B. II only
C. Both I and II
D. Neither I nor II

7.____

8.

Subject | I | II

A. I only
B. II only
C. Both I and II
D. Neither I nor II

8.____

9.

Subject | I | II

A. I only
B. II only
C. Both I and II
D. Neither I nor II

9.____

10. Subject   I   II

10._____

A. I only
B. II only
C. Both I and II
D. Neither I nor II

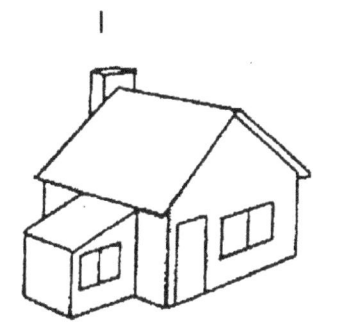

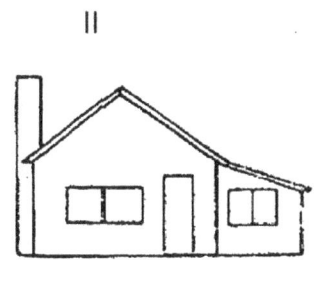

KEY (CORRECT ANSWERS)

1.	B	6.	B
2.	D	7.	D
3.	A	8.	A
4.	A	9.	D
5.	B	10.	D

VISUAL RECALL

EXAMINATION SECTION
TEST 1

DIRECTIONS: Each question or incomplete statement is followed by several suggested answers or completions. Select the one that BEST answers the question or completes the statement. *PRINT THE LETTER OF THE CORRECT ANSWER IN THE SPACE AT THE RIGHT.* This test consists of four(4) pictures with questions following each picture. Study each picture for three (3) minutes. Then answer the questions based upon what you remember without looking back at the pictures.

Questions 1-5

DIRECTIONS: Questions 1 through 5 are based on the drawing below showing a view of a waiting area in a public building.

1. A desk is shown in the drawing. Which of the following is on the desk? A(n)

   A. plant
   B. telephone
   C. in-out file
   D. *Information* sign

2. On which floor is the waiting area?

   A. Basement
   B. Main floor
   C. Second floor
   D. Third floor

3. The door <u>immediately to the right</u> of the desk is a(n)

   A. door to the Personnel Office
   B. elevator door
   C. door to another corridor
   D. door to the stairs

4. Among the magazines on the tables in the waiting area are

   A. TIME and NEWSWEEK
   B. READER'S DIGEST and T.V. GUIDE
   C. NEW YORK and READER'S DIGEST
   D. TIME and T.V. GUIDE

5. One door is partly open.
   This is the door to

   A. the Director's office
   B. the Personnel Manager's office
   C. the stairs
   D. an unmarked office

Questions 6-9.

DIRECTIONS: Questions 6 through 9 are based on the drawing below showing the contents of a male suspect's pockets.

6. The suspect had a slip in his pockets showing an appointment at an out-patient clinic on 6.____

   A. February 9, 2009
   B. September 2, 2008
   C. February 19, 2008
   D. September 12, 2009

7. The transistor radio that was found on the suspect was made by 7.____

   A. RCA   B. GE   C. Sony   D. Zenith

8. The coins found in the suspect's pockets have a TOTAL value of 8.____

   A. 56¢   B. 77¢   C. $1.05   D. $1.26

9. All except one of the following were found in the suspect's pockets. 9.____
   Which was NOT found?
   A

   A. ticket stub   B. comb
   C. subway token   D. pen

Questions 10-13.

DIRECTIONS: Questions 10 through 13 are based on the picture showing the contents of a woman's handbag. Assume that all of the contents are shown in the picture.

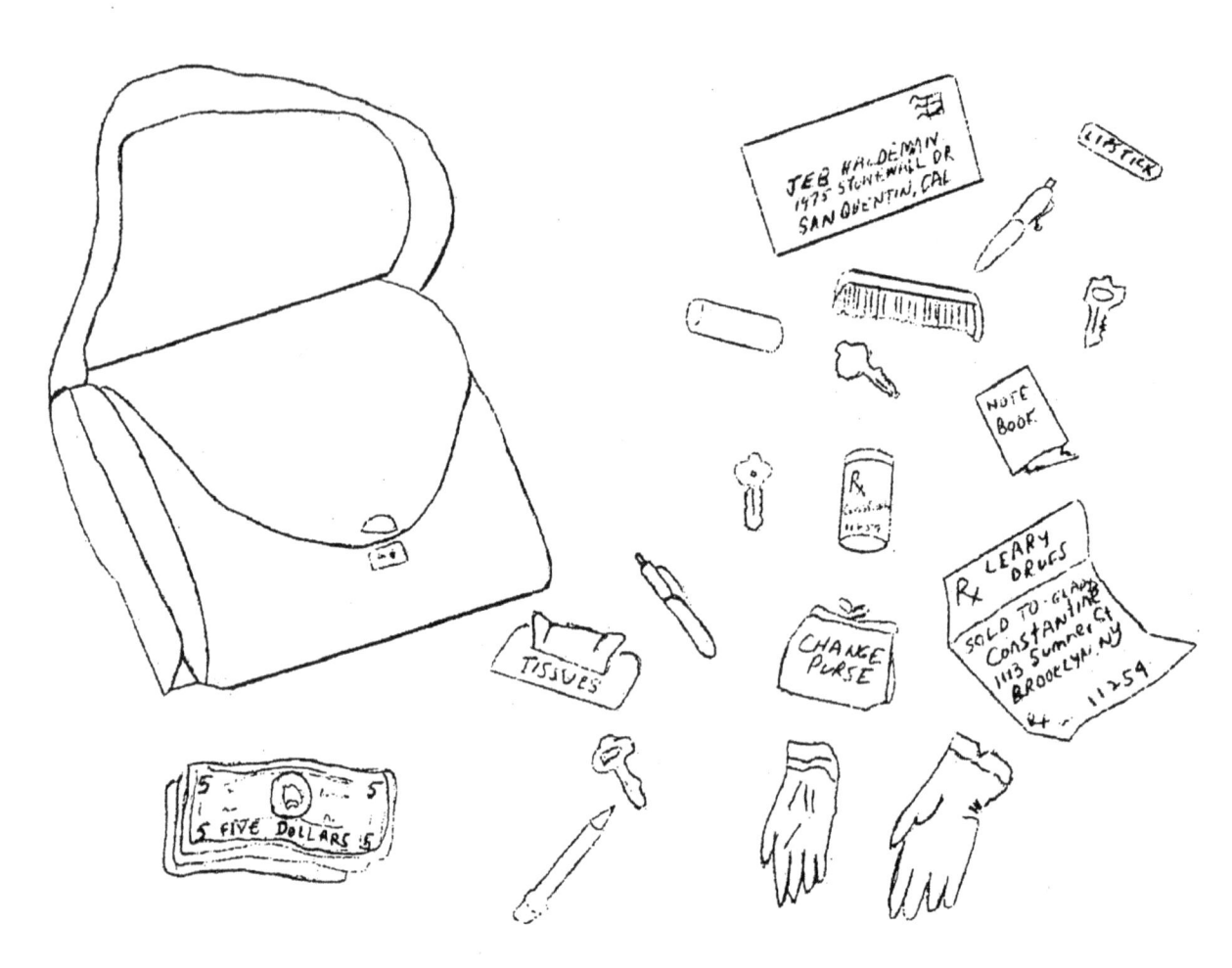

10. Where does Gladys Constantine live?
   _____ Street in _____.

   A. Chalmers; Manhattan B. Summer; Manhattan
   C. Summer; Brooklyn   D. Chalmers; Brooklyn

11. How many keys were in the handbag?

   A. 2   B. 3   C. 4   D. 5

12. How much money was in the handbag?
   _____ dollar(s).

   A. Exactly five   B. More than five
   C. Exactly ten   D. Less than one

13. The sales slip found in the handbag shows the purchase of which of the following?

   A. The handbag   B. Lipstick
   C. Tissues   D. Prescription medicine

Questions 14-18.

DIRECTIONS: Questions 14 through 18 are based on the street scene on the following page. A robbery may be in progress down the block from where you are standing. Study and memorize the details before answering these questions.

5 (#1)

14. The man carrying the two shopping bags is wearing 14._____

    A. khaki shorts and work boots
    B. a hat and black jacket
    C. a zip-up fleece and glasses
    D. a casual shirt and jeans

15. The building at the center of the photo is a(n) 15._____

    A. hotel   B. bank   C. restaurant   D. office building

16. The sidewalk is lined on the street side with 16._____

    A. parking meters   B. safety pillars
    C. street vendors   D. flower beds

17. Among the people standing in front of the center building is a 17._____

    A. man wearing khaki pants
    B. woman wearing knee-high boots
    C. young boy chasing another young boy
    D. man wearing a sports jersey

18. Reflections in the store windows indicate that 18._____

    A. there are food carts parked in the street
    B. a white truck is driving nearby
    C. it is a very sunny day
    D. a man is sitting on a curb nearby

KEY (CORRECT ANSWERS)

1.	D	11.	C
2.	C	12.	B
3.	B	13.	D
4.	D	14.	C
5.	B	15.	A
6.	A	16.	D
7.	C	17.	A
8.	D	18.	B
9.	D		
10.	C		

SPATIAL RELATIONS
EXAMINATION SECTION
TEST 1

DIRECTIONS: In each of Questions 1 to 11 the front and top views of an object are given. Of the views labeled 1, 2, 3, and 4, select the one that CORRECTLY represents the right side view of each object for third angle projection.

1.

   A. 1   B. 2   C. 3   D. 4

1.____

2.

   A. 1   B. 2   C. 3   D. 4

2.____

3.

   A. 1   B. 2   C. 3   D. 4

3.____

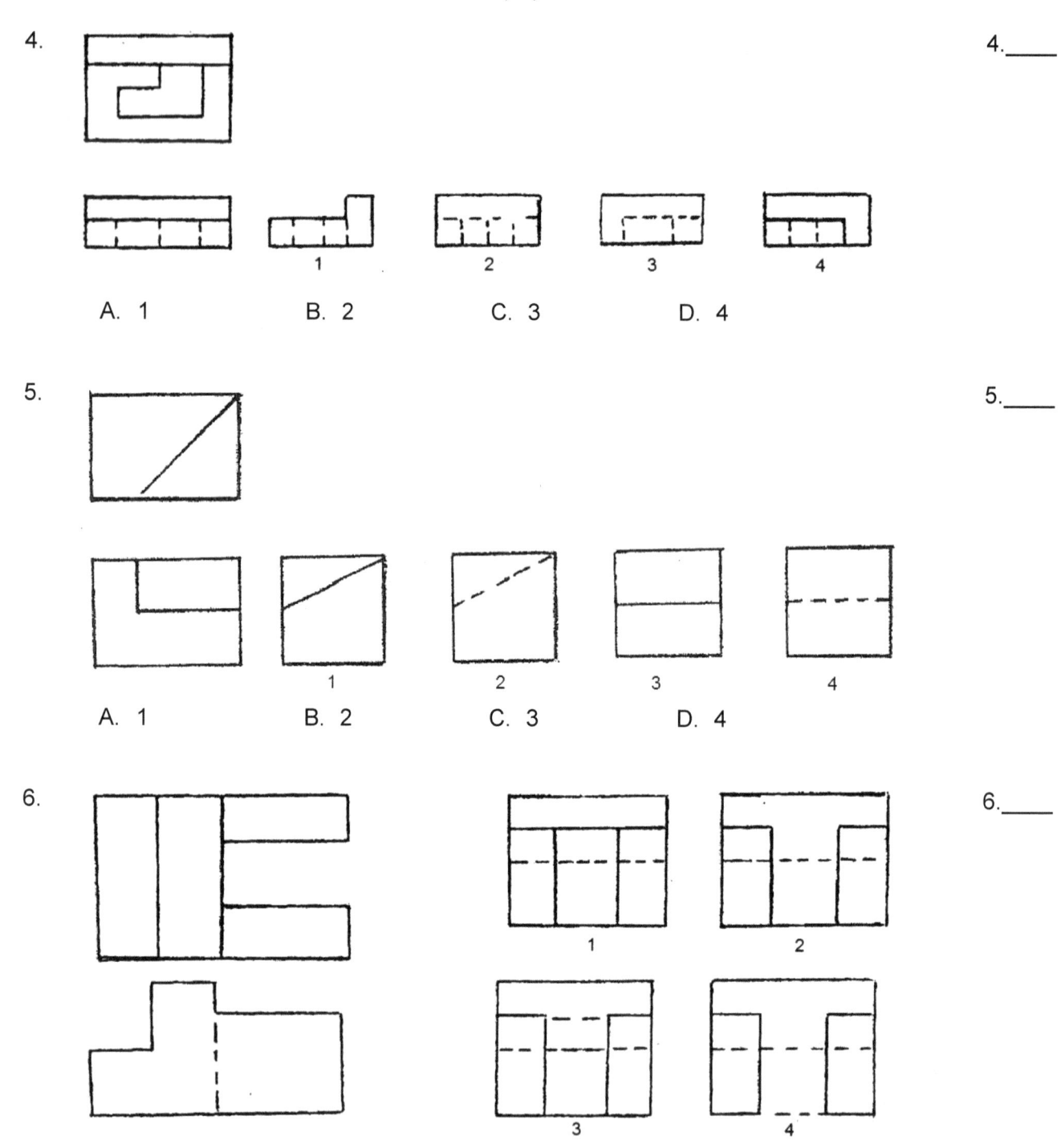

4.

A. 1   B. 2   C. 3   D. 4

4.___

5.

A. 1   B. 2   C. 3   D. 4

5.___

6.

A. 1   B. 2   C. 3.   D. 4

6.___

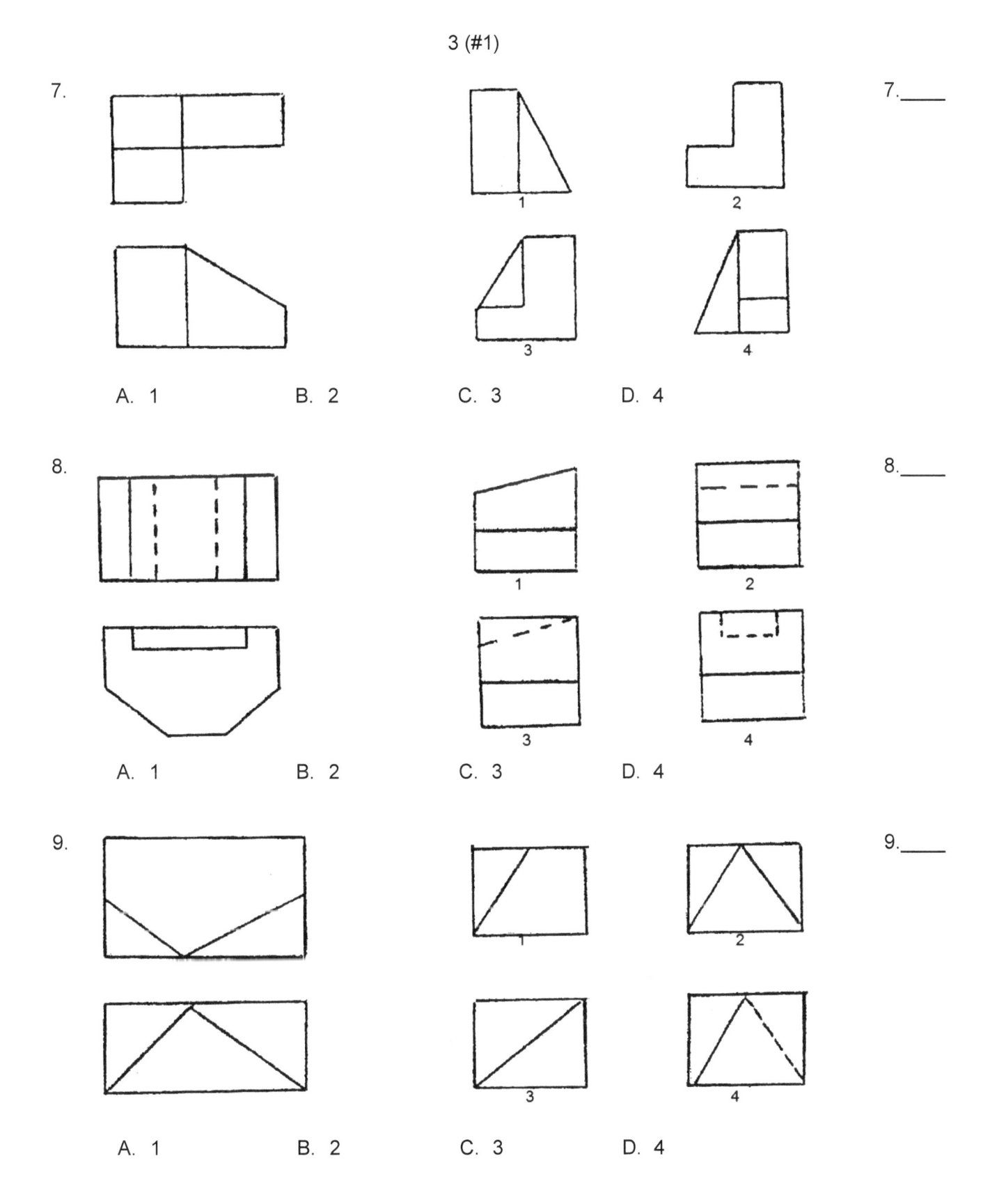

7.

A. 1   B. 2   C. 3   D. 4

7.____

8.

A. 1   B. 2   C. 3   D. 4

8.____

9.

A. 1   B. 2   C. 3   D. 4

9.____

10.

A. 1   B. 2   C. 3   D. 4

10.____

11.

TOP VIEW

FRONT VIEW

A. 1   B. 2   C. 3   D. 4

11.____

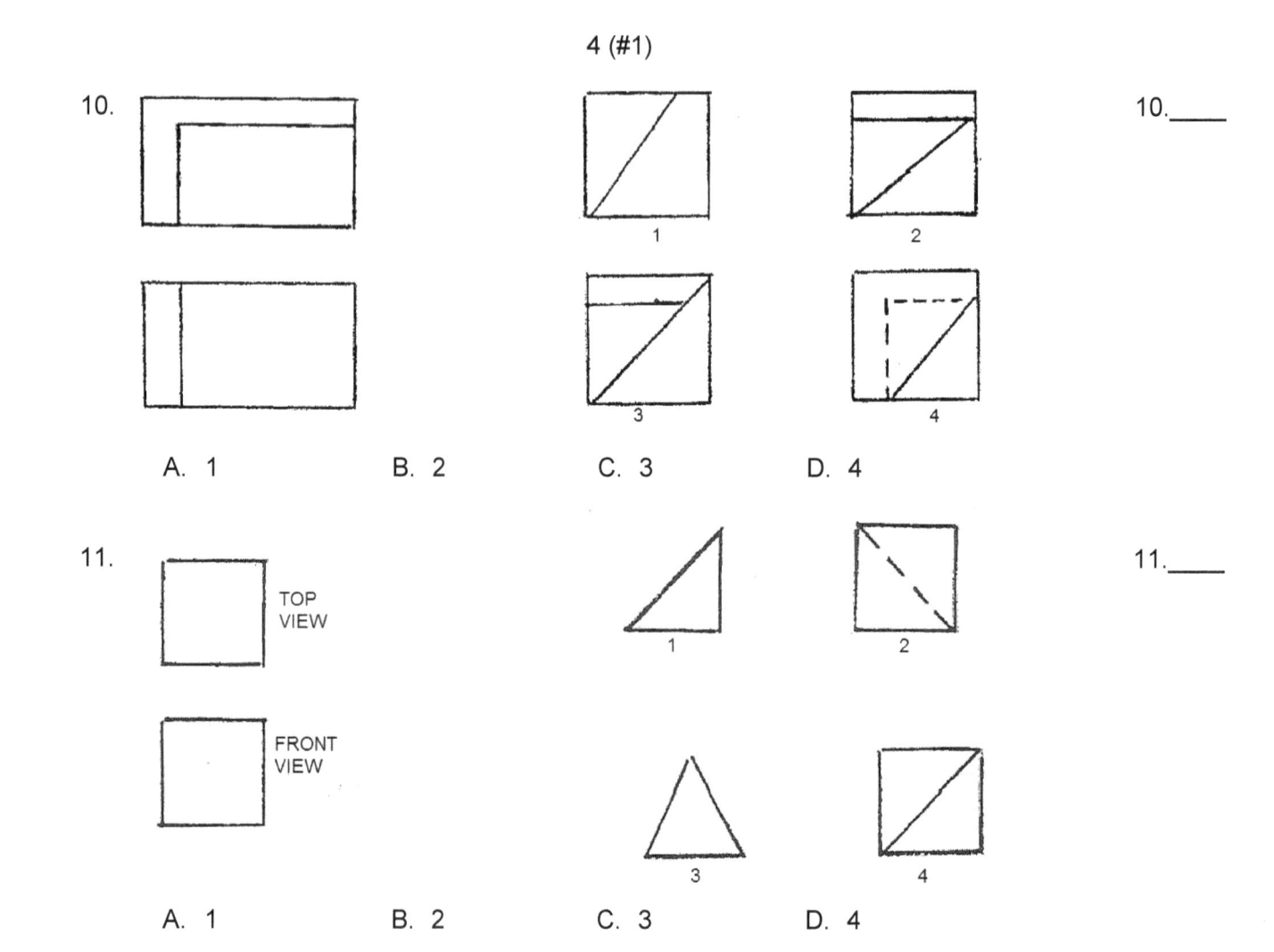

Questions 12-16.

DIRECTIONS: In each of Questions 12 to 25 inclusive, two views of an object are given. Of the views labeled 1, 2, 3, and 4, select the one that CORRECTLY represents the right side view of each object.

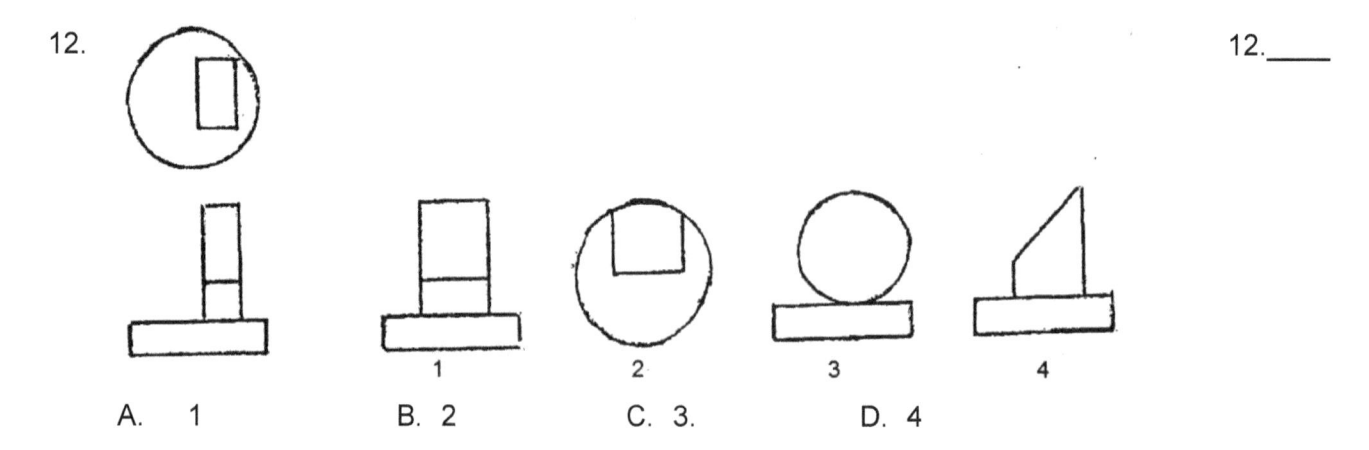

12.

A. 1   B. 2   C. 3.   D. 4

12.____

104

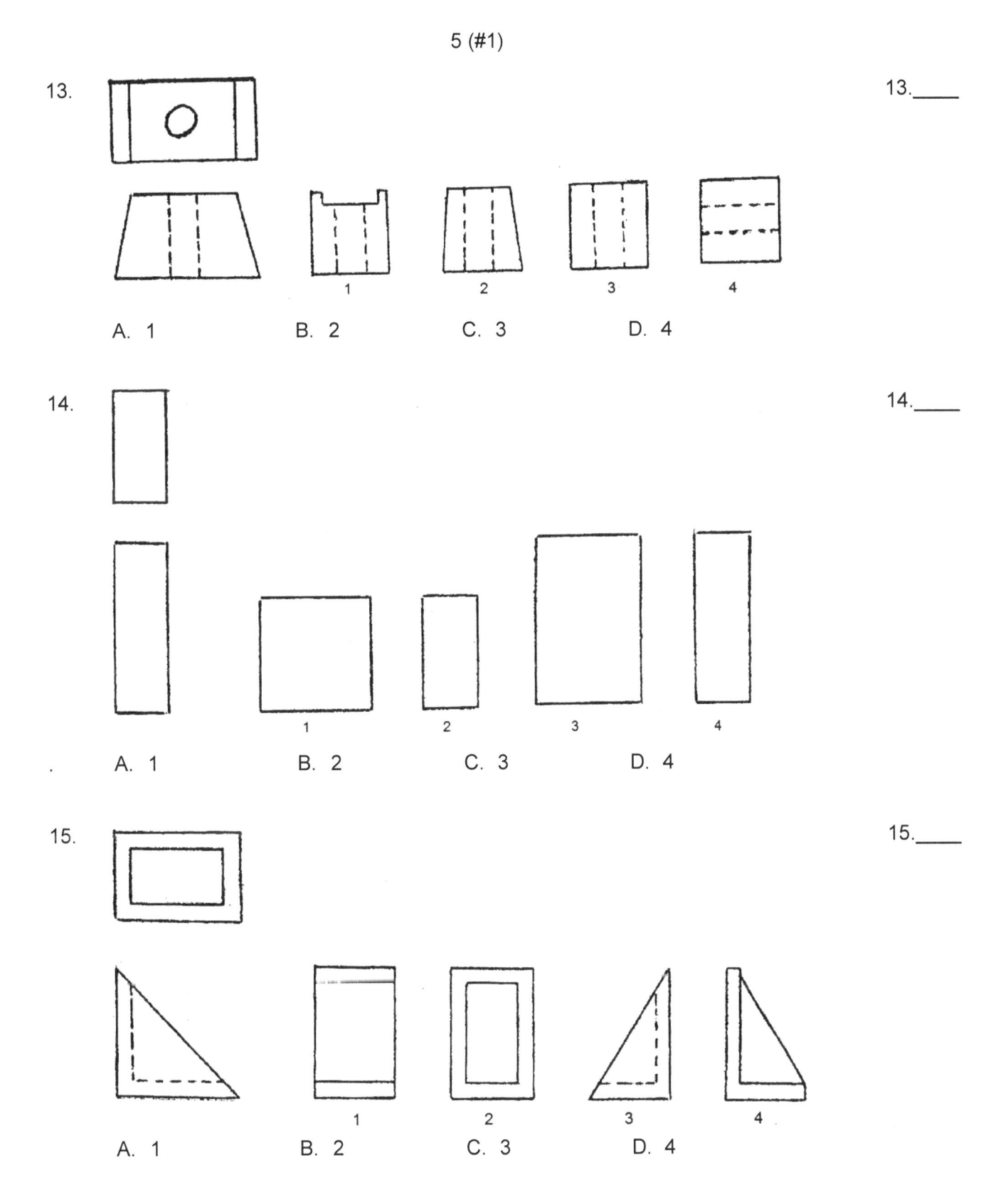

5 (#1)

13.

A. 1   B. 2   C. 3   D. 4

13.____

14.

A. 1   B. 2   C. 3   D. 4

14.____

15.

A. 1   B. 2   C. 3   D. 4

15.____

105

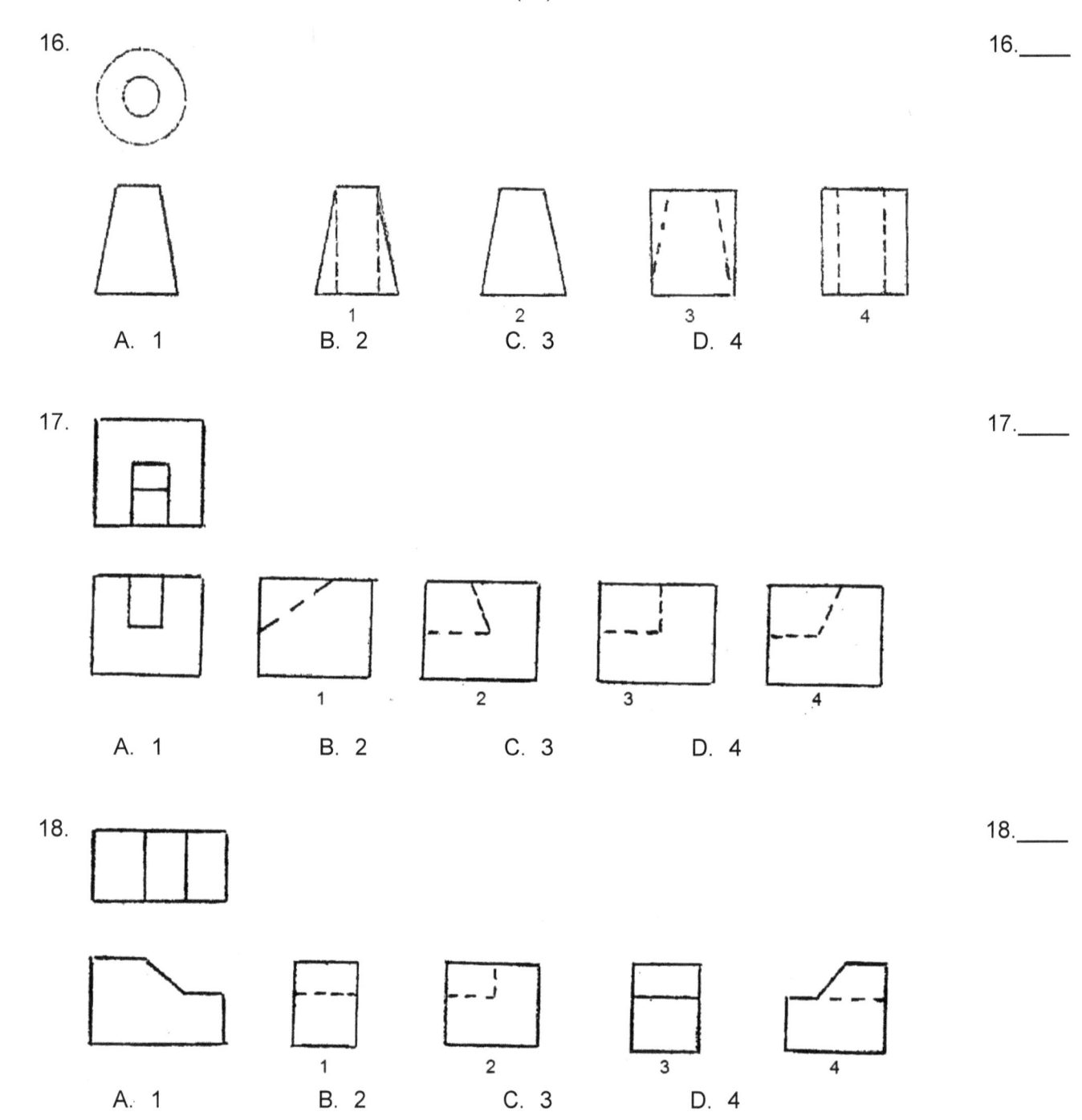

16.

A. 1   B. 2   C. 3   D. 4

16.____

17.

A. 1   B. 2   C. 3   D. 4

17.____

18.

A. 1   B. 2   C. 3   D. 4

18.____

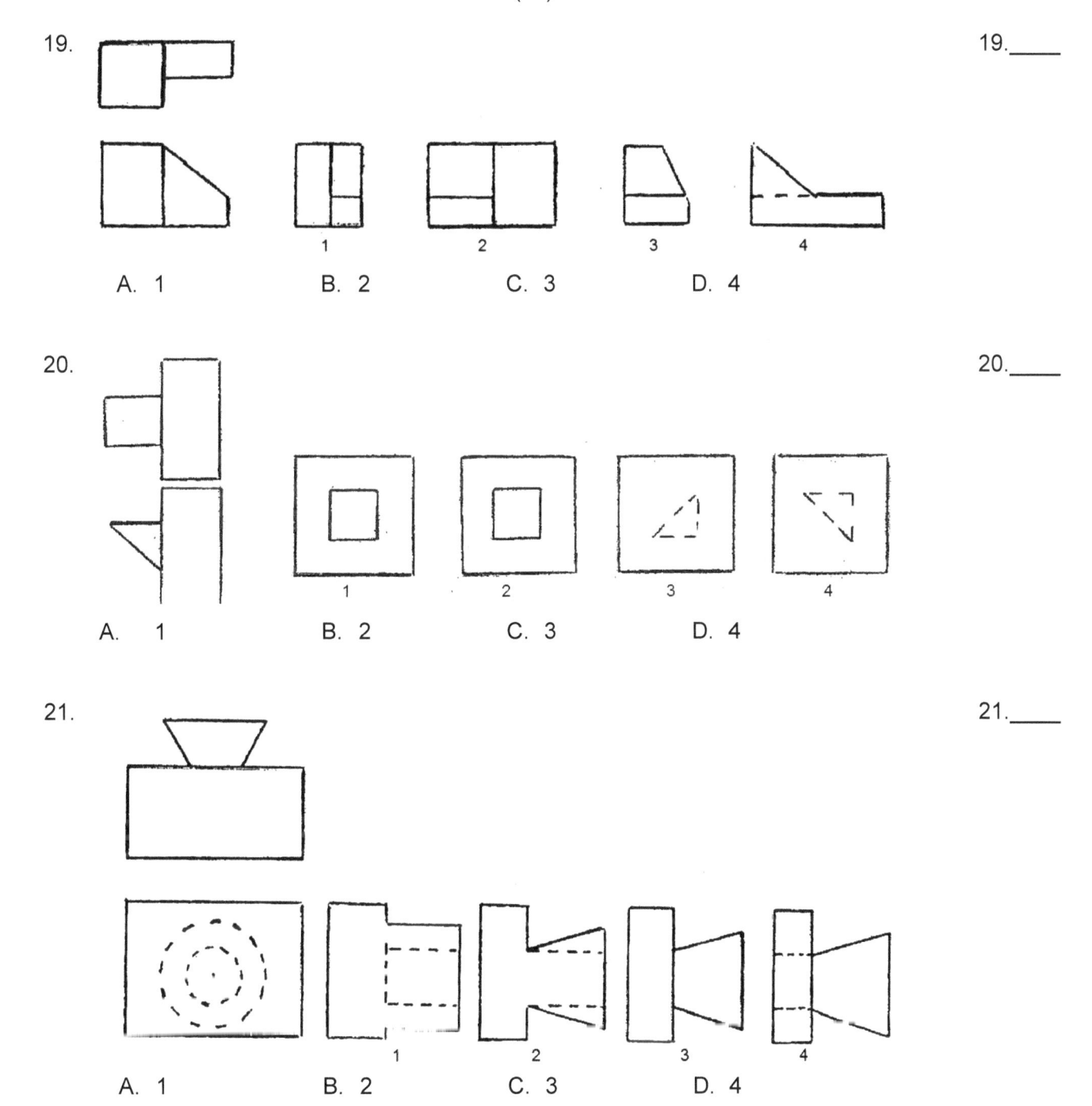

19. _____

20. _____

21. _____

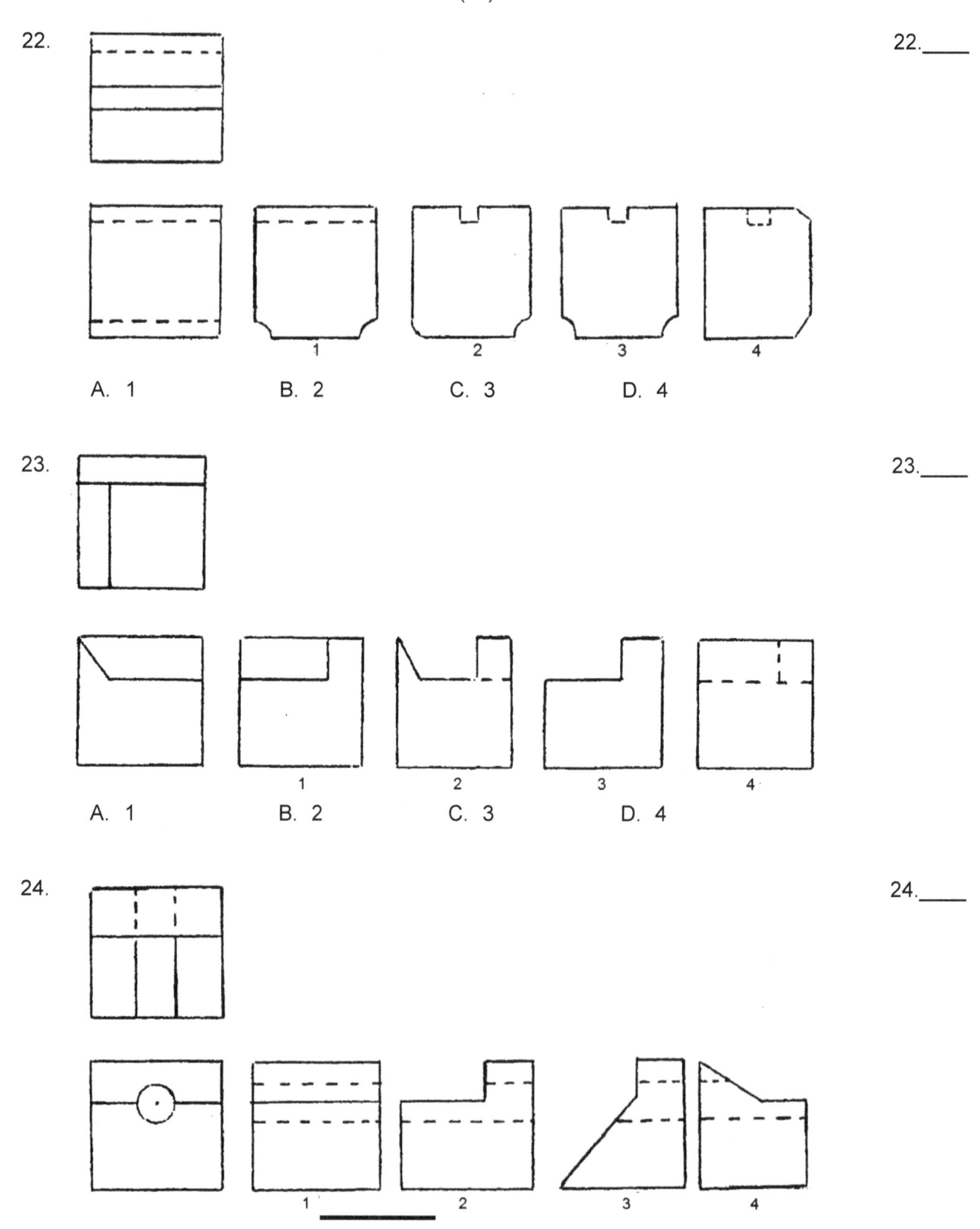

22.

A. 1   B. 2   C. 3   D. 4

22.____

23.

A. 1   B. 2   C. 3   D. 4

23.____

24.

24.____

25.

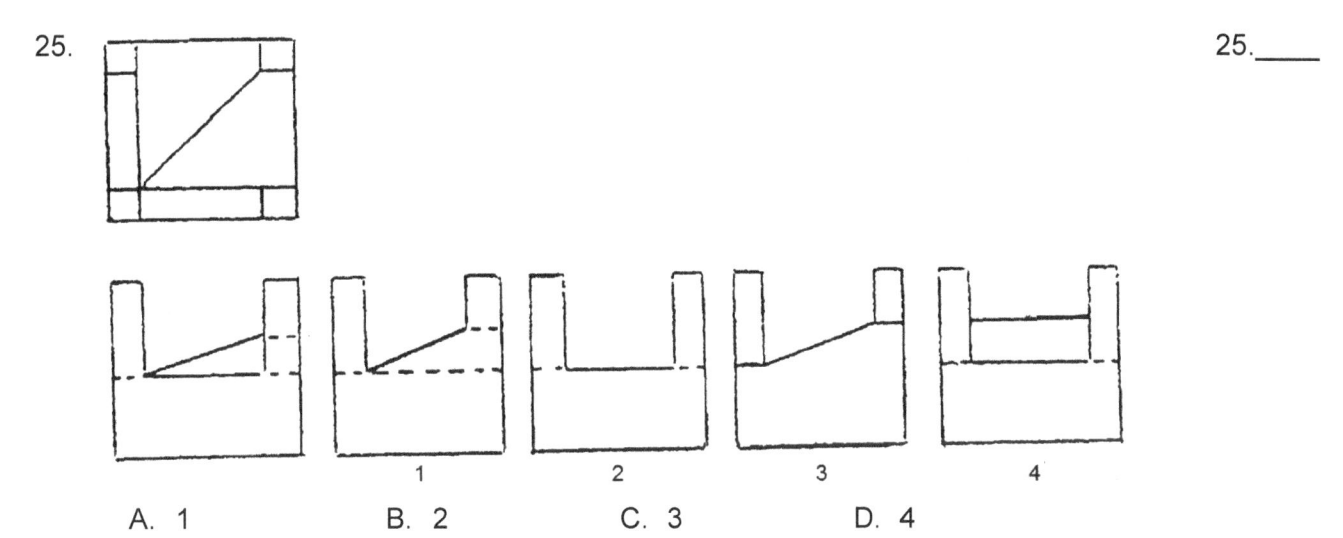

A. 1   B. 2   C. 3   D. 4

Questions 26-30.

DIRECTIONS: In Questions 26 through 30 which follow, the plan and front elevation of an object are shown on the left, and on the right are shown four figures, one of which and only one represents the right side elevation. Mark in the space at the right the letter which represents the right side elevation. In the sample below, which figure correctly represents the right side elevation?

SAMPLE QUESTION

Plan

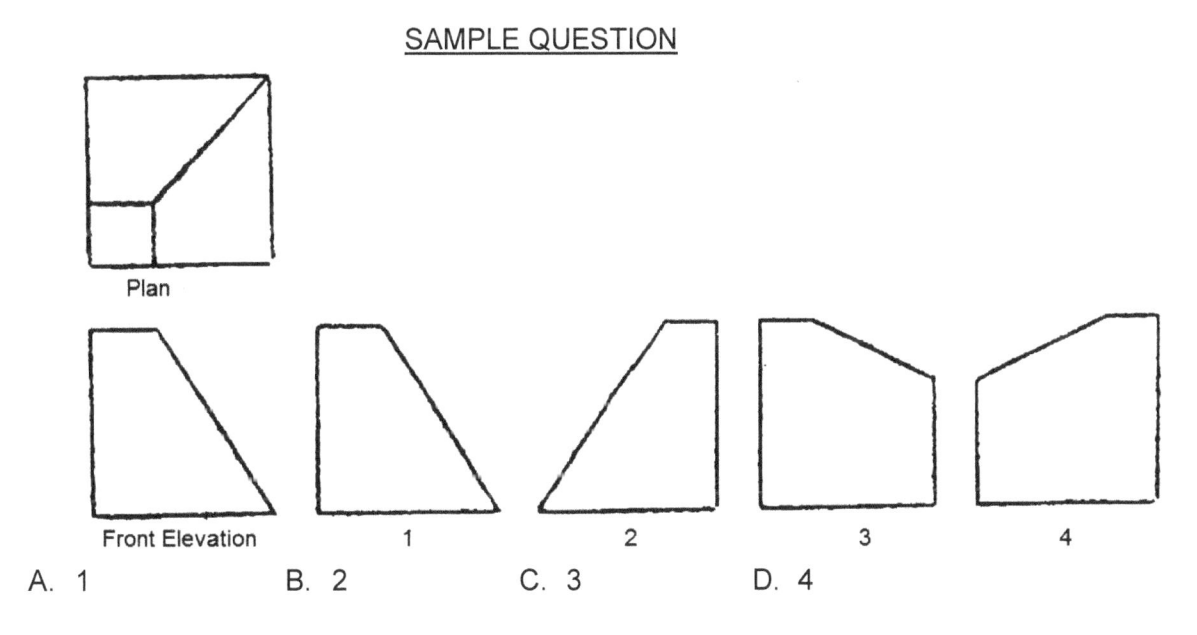

Front Elevation   1   2   3   4

A. 1   B. 2   C. 3   D. 4

The correct answer is A.

109

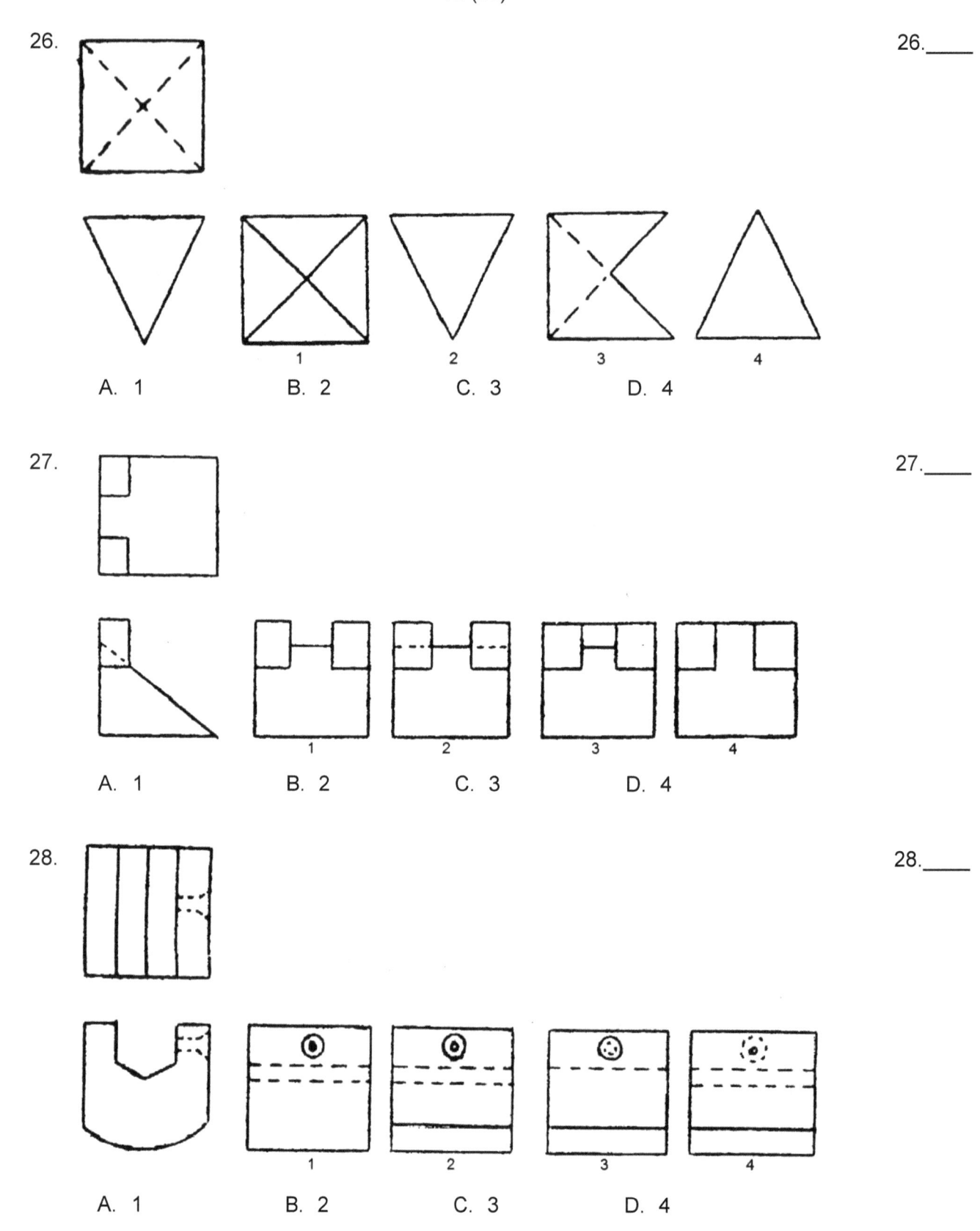

26.

A. 1   B. 2   C. 3   D. 4

27.

A. 1   B. 2   C. 3   D. 4

28.

A. 1   B. 2   C. 3   D. 4

26.____

27.____

28.____

29.

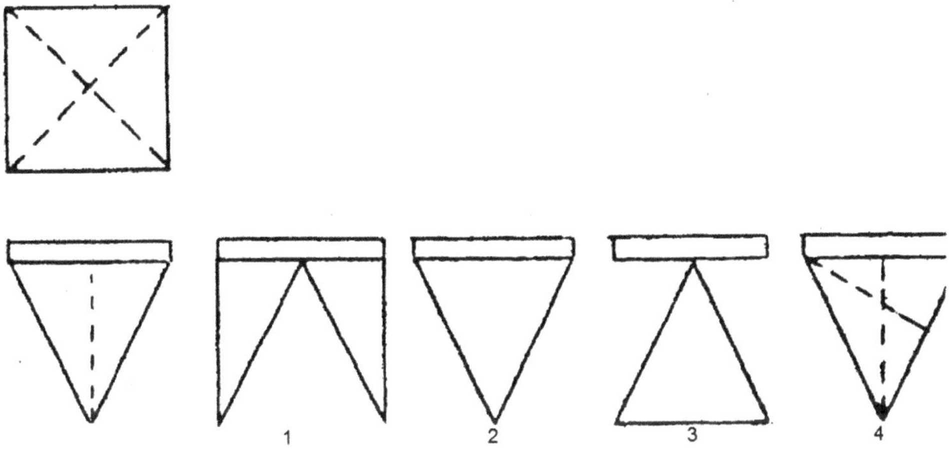

A. 1   B. 2   C. 3   D. 4

29.____

30.

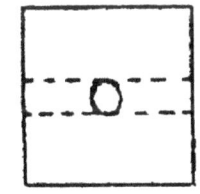

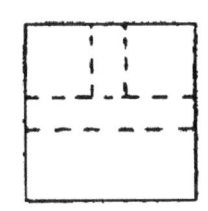

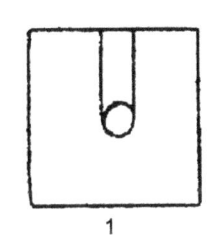

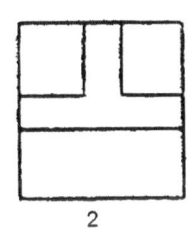

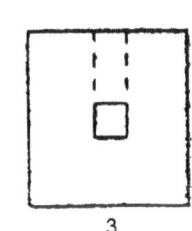

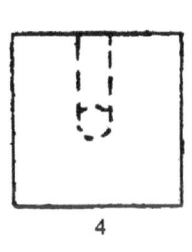

A. 1   B. 2   C. 3   D. 4

30.____

KEY (CORRECT ANSWERS)

1.	B	11.	A	21.	C
2.	D	12.	D	22.	B
3.	A	13.	C	23.	A
4.	A	14.	C	24.	B
5.	C	15.	B	25.	A
6.	B	16.	B	26.	B
7.	D	17.	D	27.	A
8.	C	18.	C	28.	B
9.	A	19.	A	29.	A
10.	A	20.	B	30.	C

TEST 2

Questions 1-10.

DIRECTIONS: Questions 1 through 10 deal with relationships between sets of figures. For each question, select that choice (A, or B, or C, or D) which has the SAME relationship to Figure 3 that Figure 2 has to Figure 1.

SAMPLE: Study Figures 1 and 2 in the Sample. Notice that Figure 1 has been turned clockwise 1/4 of a turn to get Figure 2. Taking Figure 3 and turning it clockwise 1/4 of a turn, we get choice A, the correct answer.

2 (#2)

Questions 11-16.

DIRECTIONS: Questions 11 through 16 show the top view of an object in the first column, the front view of the same object in the second column and four drawings in the third column, one of which correctly represents the RIGHT side of the object. Select the CORRECT right side view.

As a guide, the first one is an illustrative example, the correct answer of which is C.

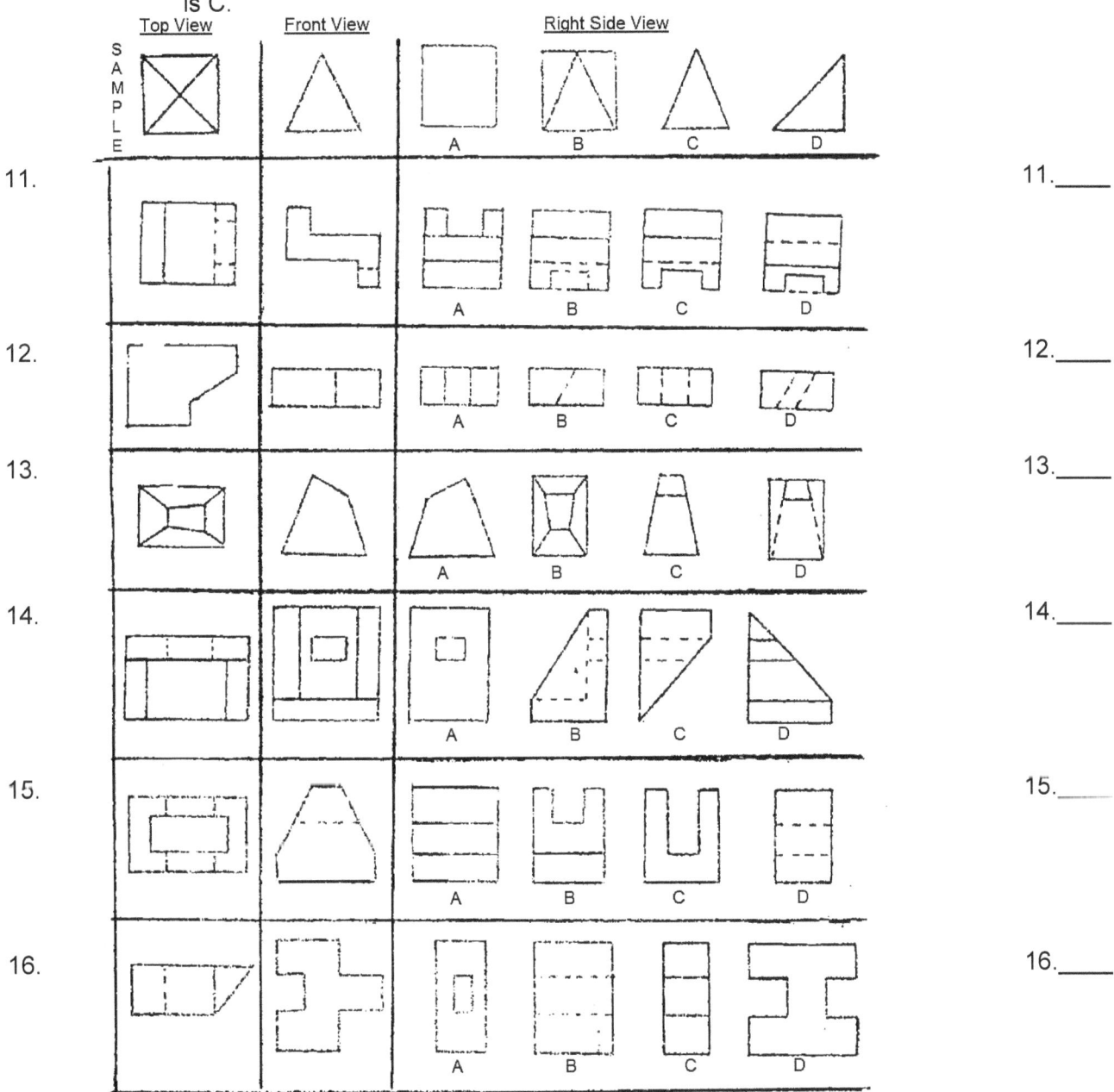

11. _____

12. _____

13. _____

14. _____

15. _____

16. _____

113

Questions 17-20.

DIRECTIONS: In each of the following groups of drawings, the top view and front elevation of an object are shown on the left. At the right are four drawings, one of which represents the end elevation of the object as seen from the right. Select the drawing which represents the correct end elevation and print the letter in the space at the right.

The first group is shown as an example only.
The correct answer in this group is C.

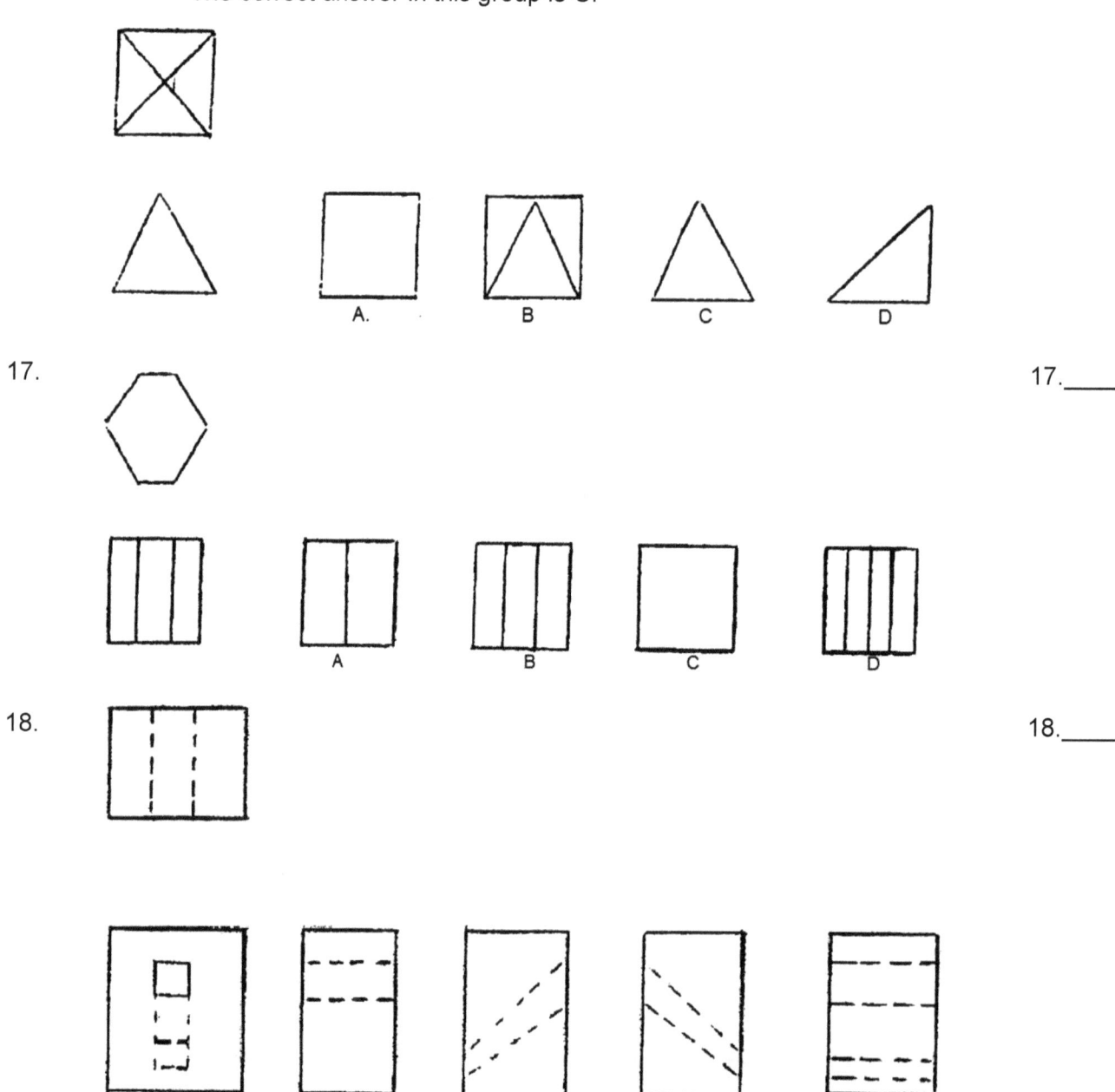

17.

17.____

18.

18.____

4 (#2)

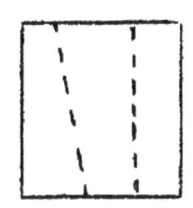

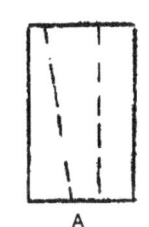

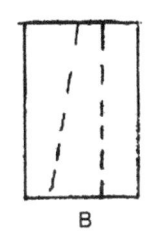

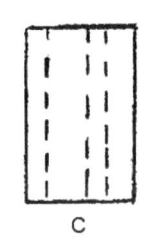

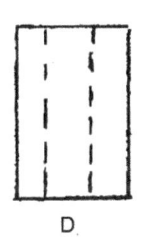

19.

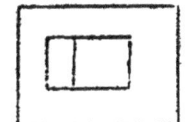

20.

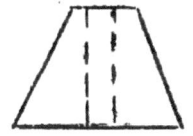

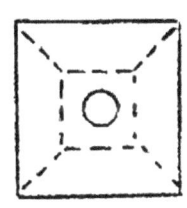

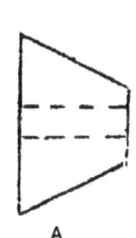

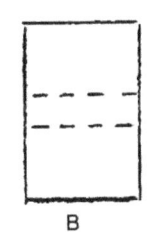

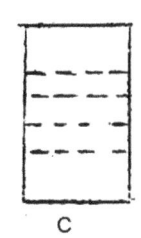

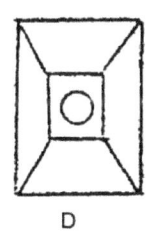

KEY (CORRECT ANSWERS)

1.	C	6.	C	11.	C	16.	C
2.	B	7.	A	12.	A	17.	A
3.	D	8.	B	13.	C	18.	C
4.	A	9.	B	14.	B	18.	D
5.	B	10.	D	15.	B	19.	A

EVALUATING INFORMATION AND EVIDENCE
EXAMINATION SECTION
TEST 1

DIRECTIONS: Each question or incomplete statement is followed by several suggested answers or completions. Select the one that BEST answers the question or completes the statement. *PRINT THE LETTER OF THE CORRECT ANSWER IN THE SPACE AT THE RIGHT.*

Questions 1-9

Questions 1 through 9 measure your ability to (1) determine whether statements from witnesses say essentially the same thing and (2) determine the evidence needed to make it reasonably certain that a particular conclusion is true.

1. Which of the following pairs of statements say essentially the same thing in two different ways?   1._____
    I. All Hoxie steelworkers are at least six feet tall. No steelworker is less than six feet tall.
    II. Some neutered pit bulls are not dangerous dogs. Some dangerous dogs are neutered pit bulls.

    A. I only
    B. I and II
    C. II only
    D. Neither I nor II

2. Which of the following pairs of statements say essentially the same thing in two different ways?   2._____
    I. If we are in training today, it is definitely Wednesday. Every Wednesday there is training.
    II. You may go out tonight only after you clean your room. If you clean your room, you may go out tonight.

    A. I only
    B. I and II
    C. II only
    D. Neither I nor II

3. Which of the following pairs of statements say essentially the same thing in two different ways?   3._____
    I. The case will be dismissed if either the defendant pleads guilty and agrees to perform community service, or the defendant pleads guilty and makes a full apology to the victim.
    The case will be dismissed if the defendant pleads guilty and either agrees to perform community service or makes a full apology to the victim.
    II. Long books are fun to read.
    Books that aren't fun to read aren't long.

    A. I only
    B. I and II
    C. II only
    D. Neither I nor II

117

4. Which of the following pairs of statements say essentially the same thing in two different ways?

      I. If you live in a mansion, you have a big heating bill. If you do not have a big heating bill, you do not live in a mansion.
      II. Some clerks can both type and read shorthand. Some clerks can neither type nor read shorthand.

  A. I only
  B. I and II
  C. II only
  D. Neither I nor II

4._____

5. Summary of Evidence Collected to Date:
      I. Three students - Bob, Mary and Stan - each received a grade of A, C and F on the civil service exam.
      II. Stan did not receive an F on the exam.

Prematurely Drawn Conclusion: Stan received an A.

Which of the following pieces of evidence, if any, would make it *reasonably certain* that the conclusion drawn is true?

  A. Bob received an F
  B. Mary received a C
  C. Bob did not receive an A
  D. None of these

5._____

6. Summary of Evidence Collected to Date:
      I. At Walco, all the employees who work the morning shift work the evening shift as well.
      II. Some Walco employees who work the evening shift also work the afternoon shift.

Prematurely Drawn Conclusion: If Ron, a Walco employee, works the morning shift, he does not work the afternoon shift.

Which of the following pieces of evidence, if any, would make it *reasonably certain* that the conclusion drawn is true?

  A. Ron works only two shifts
  B. Ron works the evening shift
  C. All Walco employees work at least one shift
  D. None of these

6._____

7. Summary of Evidence Collected to Date:

All the family counselors at the agency have an MTF certification and an advanced degree.

Prematurely Drawn Conclusion: Any employee of the agency who has an advanced degree is a family counselor.

Which of the following pieces of evidence, if any, would make it *reasonably certain* that the conclusion drawn is true?

7._____

A. Nobody at the agency who has an advanced degree is employed as anything other than a family counselor
B. Everyone who has an MTF certification is a family counselor
C. Each person at the agency who has an MTF certification also has an advanced degree
D. None of these

8. Summary of Evidence Collected to Date: 8.____
Margery, a worker at the elder agency, is working on recreational programs.
Prematurely Drawn Conclusion: Margery is not working on cases of elder abuse.
Which of the following pieces of evidence, if any, would make it *reasonably certain* that the conclusion drawn is true?

A. Elder abuse and recreational programs are unrelated fields
B. Nobody at the elder agency who works on cases of elder abuse works on recreation programs
C. Nobody at the elder agency who works on recreational programs works on cases of elder abuse
D. None of these

9. Summary of Evidence Collected to Date: 9.____
   I. St. Leo's Cathedral is not as tall as the FarCorp building.
   II. The FarCorp building and the Hyatt Uptown are the same height.
Prematurely Drawn Conclusion: The FarCorp building is not in Springfield.
Which of the following pieces of evidence, if any, would make it *reasonably certain* that the conclusion drawn is true?

A. No buildings in Springfield are as tall as the Hyatt Uptown
B. The Hyatt Uptown is not in Springfield
C. St. Leo's Cathedral is the oldest building in Springfield
D. None of these

Questions 10-14

Questions 10 through 14 refer to Map #1 and measure your ability to orient yourself within a given section of town, neighborhood or particular area. Each of the questions describes a starting point and a destination. Assume that you are driving a car in the area shown on the map accompanying the questions. Use the map as a basis for the shortest way to get from one point to another without breaking the law.

On the map, a street marked by arrows, or by arrows and the words "One Way," indicates one-way travel, and should be assumed to be one-way for the entire length, even when there are breaks or jogs in the street.

4 (#1)

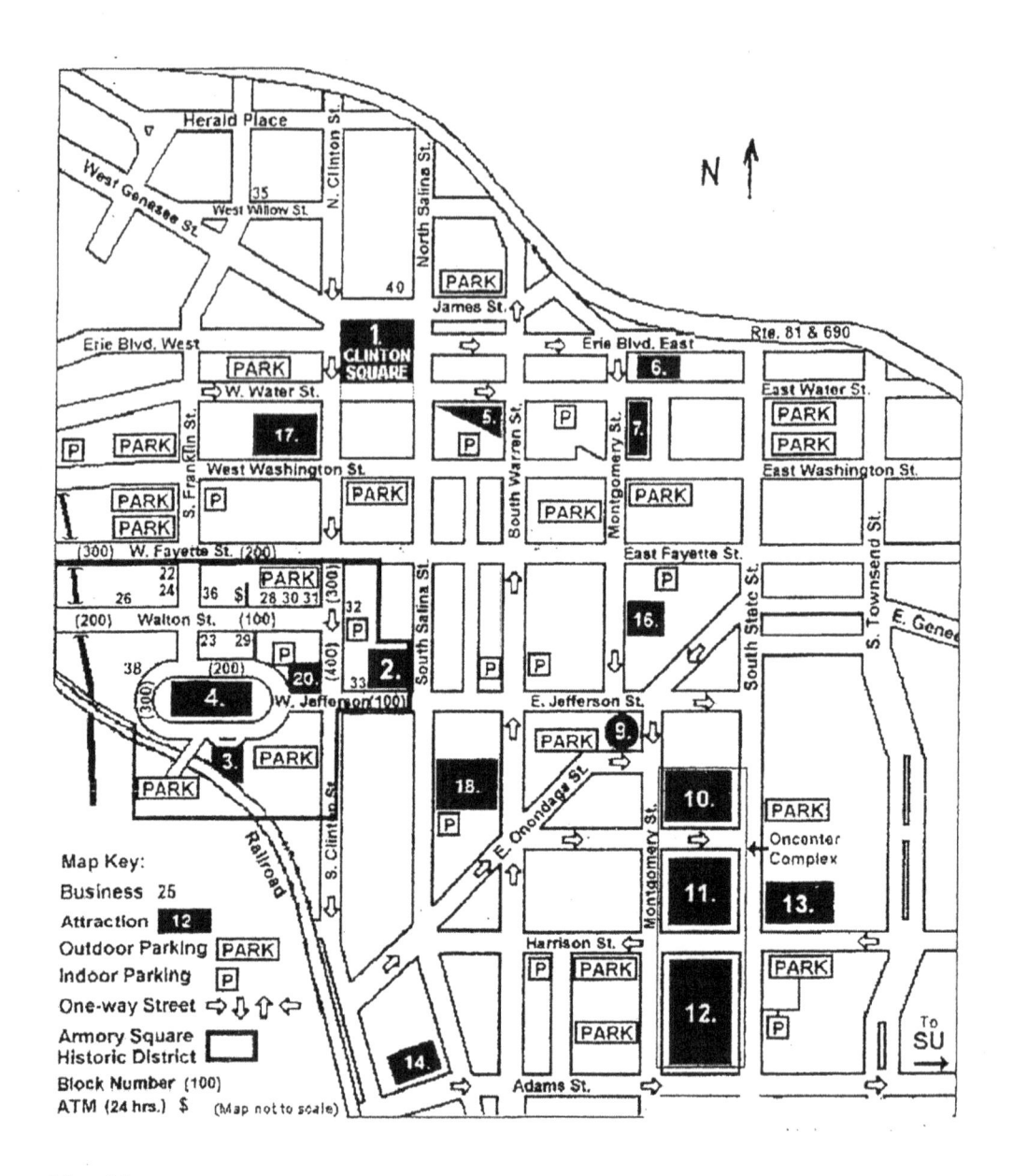

Map #1

1. Clinton Square
2. Landmark Theatre
3. OnTrack Commuter Rail Service
4. Museum of Science and Technology
5. Hanover Square
6. Erie Canal Museum
7. City Hall
9. Columbus Circle
10. Mulroy Civic Center Theaters
11. War Memorial
12. Convention Center
13. Everson Museum of Art
14. Convention and Visitors Bureau
16. Onondaga Historical Association
17. Federal Plaza
18. Galleries of Syracuse

5 (#1)

10. The shortest legal way from Columbus Circle to Federal Plaza is   10._____

    A. west on Jefferson St., north on Salina St., west on Water St.
    B. east on Jefferson St., north on State St., west on Washington St.
    C. north on Montgomery St., west on Washington St.
    D. south on Montgomery St., west on Harrison St., north on Salina St., west on Washington St.

11. The shortest legal way from Clinton Square to the Museum of Science and Technology is   11._____

    A. south on Clinton St., west on Fayette St., south on Franklin St.
    B. west on Erie Blvd., south on Franklin St.
    C. south on Clinton St., west on Water St., south on Franklin St.
    D. south on Clinton St., west on Jefferson St.

12. The shortest legal way from Hanover Square to Landmark Theatre is   12._____

    A. west on Water St., south on Salina St.
    B. east on Water St., south on Montgomery St., west on Fayette St., south on Salina St.
    C. east on Water St., south on Montgomery St., west on Fayette St., south on Clinton St., east on Jefferson St.
    D. south on Warren St., west on Jefferson St.

13. The shortest legal way from the Convention Center to the Erie Canal Museum is   13._____

    A. north on State St., west on Washington St., north on Montgomery St.
    B. north on Montgomery St., jog west on Jefferson St., north on Montgomery St.
    C. north on State St., west on Fayette St., north on Warren St., east on Water St.
    D. north on State St., west on Water St.

14. The shortest legal way from City Hall to Clinton Square is   14._____

    A. west on Washington St., north on Salina St.
    B. south on Montgomery St., west on Fayette St., north on Salina St.
    C. north on Montgomery St., west on Erie Blvd.
    D. west on Water St.

6 (#1)

Questions 15-19

Questions 15 through 19 refer to Figure #1, on the following page, and measure your ability to understand written descriptions of events. Each question presents a description of an accident or event and asks you which of the five drawings in Figure #1 BEST represents it.

In the drawings, the following symbols are used:

Moving vehicle: ⌂   Non-moving vehicle: ⌂

Pedestrian or bicycle: ●

The path and direction of travel of a vehicle or pedestrian is indicated by a solid line.

The path and direction of travel of each vehicle or pedestrian directly involved in a collision from the point of impact is indicated by a dotted line.

In the space at the right, print the letter of the drawing that best fits the descriptions written below:

15. A driver heading north on Elm sideswipes a parked car, veers into the oncoming lane and travels through the intersection of Elm and Main. He then sideswipes an oncoming car, veers back into the northbound lane and flees. 15.____

16. A driver heading south on Elm sideswipes a car parked in the southbound lane, then loses control and veers through the intersection of Elm and Main. The driver then collides with the rear of another parked car, which is knocked forward after the impact. 16.____

17. A driver heading north on Elm strikes the rear of a parked car, which is knocked through the intersection of Elm and Main and strikes a parked car in the southbound lane head-on. 17.____

18. A driver heading north on Elm strikes the rear of a car that is stopped at a traffic light. The car at the light is knocked through the intersection of Elm and Main and strikes a parked car in the rear. 18.____

19. A driver heading south on Elm loses control and crosses into the other lane of traffic, where he sideswipes a car parked in the northbound lane, then veers back into the southbound lane, travels through the intersection of Elm and Main and collides with the rear end of a parked car. 19.____

FIGURE #1

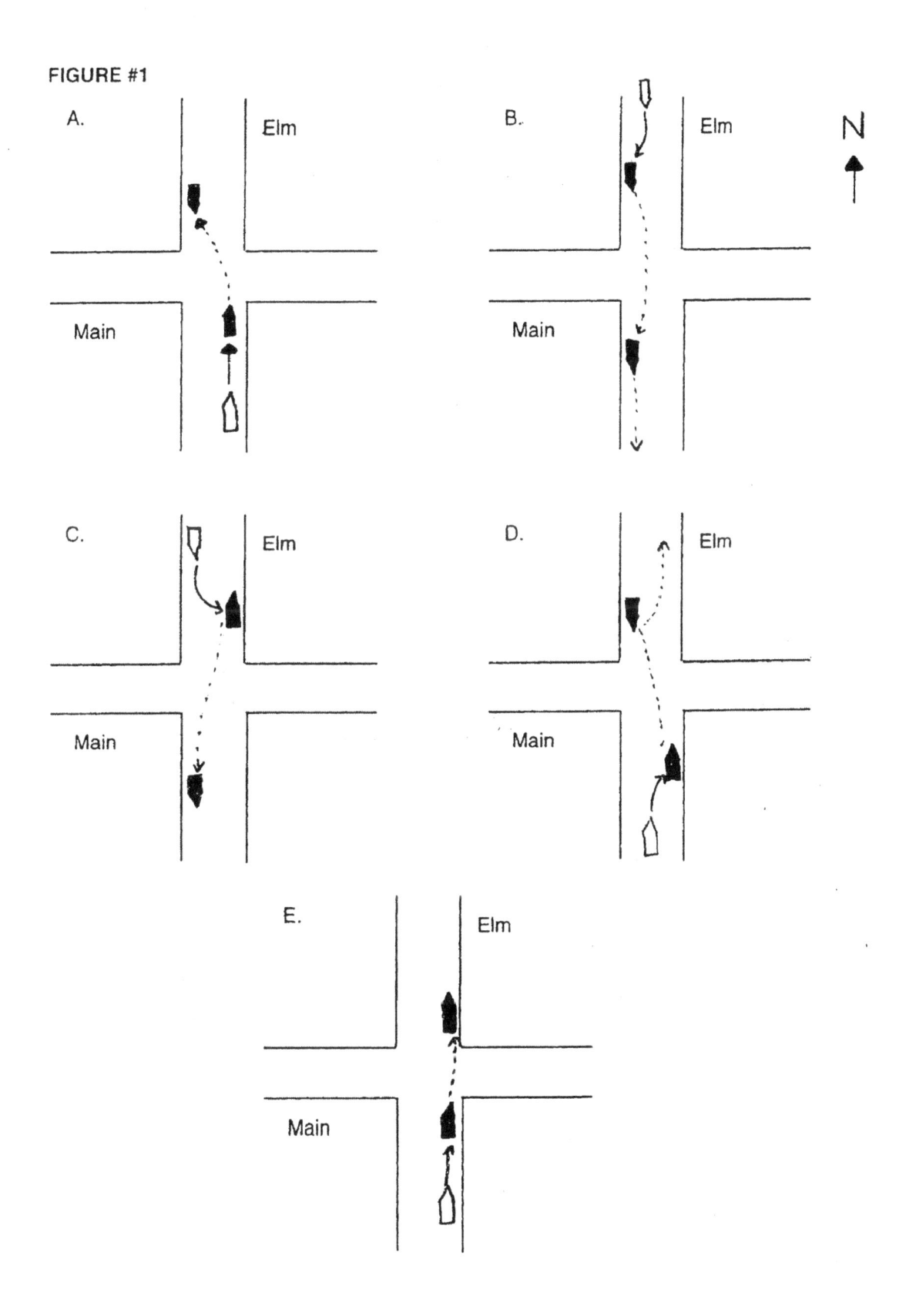

Questions 20-22

In questions 20 through 22, choose the word or phrase CLOSEST in meaning to the word or phrase printed in capital letters.

20. REDRESS

    A. suspend
    B. repeat
    C. compensate
    D. subdue

21. PRECEDENT

    A. cohort
    B. example
    C. obstruction
    D. elder

22. ADJUDICATION

    A. case
    B. judgment
    C. claim
    D. defendant

Questions 23-25

Questions 23 through 25 measure your ability to do fieldwork-related arithmetic. Each question presents a separate arithmetic problem for you to solve.

23. The Department of Sanitation purchased seven vehicles in the last year. Four of the vehicles were street sweepers that cost $95,000 each. Three were garbage compactors that cost $160,000 each. The average price of a vehicle purchased by the Department in the last year was about

    A. $98,000
    B. $108,000
    C. $122,000
    D. $145,000

24. Agent Frederick, whose car gets about 24 miles to the gallon, drives to Buffalo, 260 miles away. The average price of gasoline is $2.30 a gallon. How much did Agent Frederick spend on gas for the trip to Buffalo?

    A. $11   B. $25   C. $55   D. $113

25. Over the last four days, Precinct 11 has had 20 misdemeanor arrests each day. If the precinct records 15 misdemeanor arrests on the fifth day, what will its average daily number of misdemeanor arrests be?

    A. 16   B. 17   C. 18   D. 19

KEY (CORRECT ANSWERS)

1.	D		11.	A
2.	C		12.	B
3.	A		13.	C
4.	A		14.	A
5.	B		15.	D
6.	A		16.	B
7.	A		17.	A
8.	C		18.	E
9.	A		19.	C
10.	B		20.	C

21. B
22. B
23. C
24. B
25. D

TEST 2

DIRECTIONS: Each question or incomplete statement is followed by several suggested answers or completions. Select the one that BEST answers the question or completes the statement. *PRINT THE LETTER OF THE CORRECT ANSWER IN THE SPACE AT THE RIGHT.*

Questions 1-9

Questions 1 through 9 measure your ability to (1) determine whether statements from witnesses say essentially the same thing and (2) determine the evidence needed to make it reasonably certain that a particular conclusion is true.
To do well on this part of the test, you do NOT have to have a working knowledge of police procedures and techniques. Nor do you have to have any more familiarity with criminals and criminal behavior than that acquired from reading newspapers, listening to radio or watching TV. To do well in this part, you must read and reason carefully.

1. Which of the following pairs of statements say essentially the same thing in two different ways?

    I. All of the teachers at the school are wise, but some have proven to be bad-tempered.
    Teachers at the school are either wise or bad-tempered.
    II. If John can both type and do long division, he is qualified for this job.
    If John applies for this job, he can both type and do long division.

    A. I only
    B. I and II
    C. II only
    D. Neither I nor II

2. Which of the following pairs of statements say essentially the same thing in two different ways?

    I. If Carl rides the A train, the C train is down.
    Carl doesn't ride the A train unless the C train is down.
    II. If the three sides of a triangle are equal, the triangle is equilateral.
    A triangle is equilateral if the three sides are equal.

    A. I only
    B. I and II
    C. II only
    D. Neither I nor II

3. Which of the following pairs of statements say essentially the same thing in two different ways?

    I. If this dog has a red collar, it must be Slim.
    If this dog does not have a red collar, it can't be Slim.
    II. Dr. Slouka is not in his office during lunchtime.
    If it's not lunchtime, Dr. Slouka is in his office.

    A. I only
    B. I and II
    C. II only
    D. Neither I nor II

4. Which of the following pairs of statements say essentially the same thing in two different ways?

   I. At least one caseworker at Social Services has a degree in psychology.
      Not all the caseworkers at Social Services have a degree in psychology.
   II. If an officer doesn't pass the physical fitness test, he cannot be promoted.
      If an officer is not promoted, he hasn't passed the physical fitness test.

   A. I only
   B. I and II
   C. II only
   D. Neither I nor II

5. Summary of Evidence Collected to Date:
   I. All the Class II inspectors use multiplication when they inspect escalators.
   II. On some days, Fred, a Class II inspector, doesn't use multiplication at all.
   III. Fred's friend, Garth, uses multiplication every day.

   Prematurely Drawn Conclusion: Garth inspects escalators every day.
   Which of the following pieces of evidence, if any, would make it *reasonably certain* that the conclusion drawn is true?

   A. Garth is a Class II inspector
   B. Fred never inspects escalators
   C. Fred usually doesn't inspect escalators
   D. None of these

6. Summary of Evidence Collected to Date:
   I. Every one of the shelter's male pit bulls has been neutered.
   II. Some male pit bulls have also been muzzled.

   Prematurely Drawn Conclusion: Rex has been neutered.
   Which of the following pieces of evidence, if any, would make it *reasonably certain* that the conclusion drawn is true?

   A. Rex, a pit bull at the shelter, has been muzzled
   B. All of the pit bulls at the shelter are males
   C. Rex is one of the shelter's male pit bulls
   D. None of these

7. Summary of Evidence Collected to Date:
   I. Some of the social workers at the clinic have been welfare recipients.
   II. Some of the social workers at the clinic are college graduates.

   Prematurely Drawn Conclusion: Some of the social workers at the clinic who are college graduates have never received welfare benefits.
   Which of the following pieces of evidence, if any, would make it *reasonably certain* that the conclusion drawn is true?

   A. There are more college graduates at the clinic than those who have received welfare benefits
   B. There is an odd number of social workers at the clinic
   C. The number of college graduates and former welfare recipients at the clinic is the same
   D. None of these

8. <u>Summary of Evidence Collected to Date:</u>
Everyone who works at the library has read *War and Peace*. Most people who have read *War and Peace* have also read *Anna Karenina*.
<u>Prematurely Drawn Conclusion:</u> Marco has read *War and Peace*.
Which of the following pieces of evidence, if any, would make it *reasonably certain* that the conclusion drawn is true?

   A. Marco works at the library
   B. Marco has probably read *Anna Karenina*
   C. Everyone who has read *Anna Karenina* has read *War and Peace*
   D. None of these

8.____

9. <u>Summary of Evidence Collected to Date:</u>
Officer Skiles is working on the Martin investigation.
<u>Prematurely Drawn Conclusion:</u> Skiles is also working on the Bartlett case.
Which of the following pieces of evidence, if any, would make it *reasonably certain* that the conclusion drawn is true?

   A. Everyone who is working on the Martin investigation is also working on the Bartlett investigation
   B. Everyone who is working on the Bartlett investigation is also working on the Martin investigation
   C. The Martin investigation and Bartlett investigation are being conducted at the same time
   D. None of these

9.____

Questions 10-14

Questions 10 through 14 refer to Map #2 and measure your ability to orient yourself within a given section of town, neighborhood or particular area. Each of the questions describes a starting point and a destination. Assume that you are driving a car in the area shown on the map accompanying the questions. Use the map as a basis for the shortest way to get from one point to another without breaking the law.

On the map, a street marked by arrows, or by arrows and the words "One Way," indicates one-way travel, and should be assumed to be one-way for the entire length, even when there are breaks or jogs in the street. EXCEPTION: A street that does not have the same name over the full length.

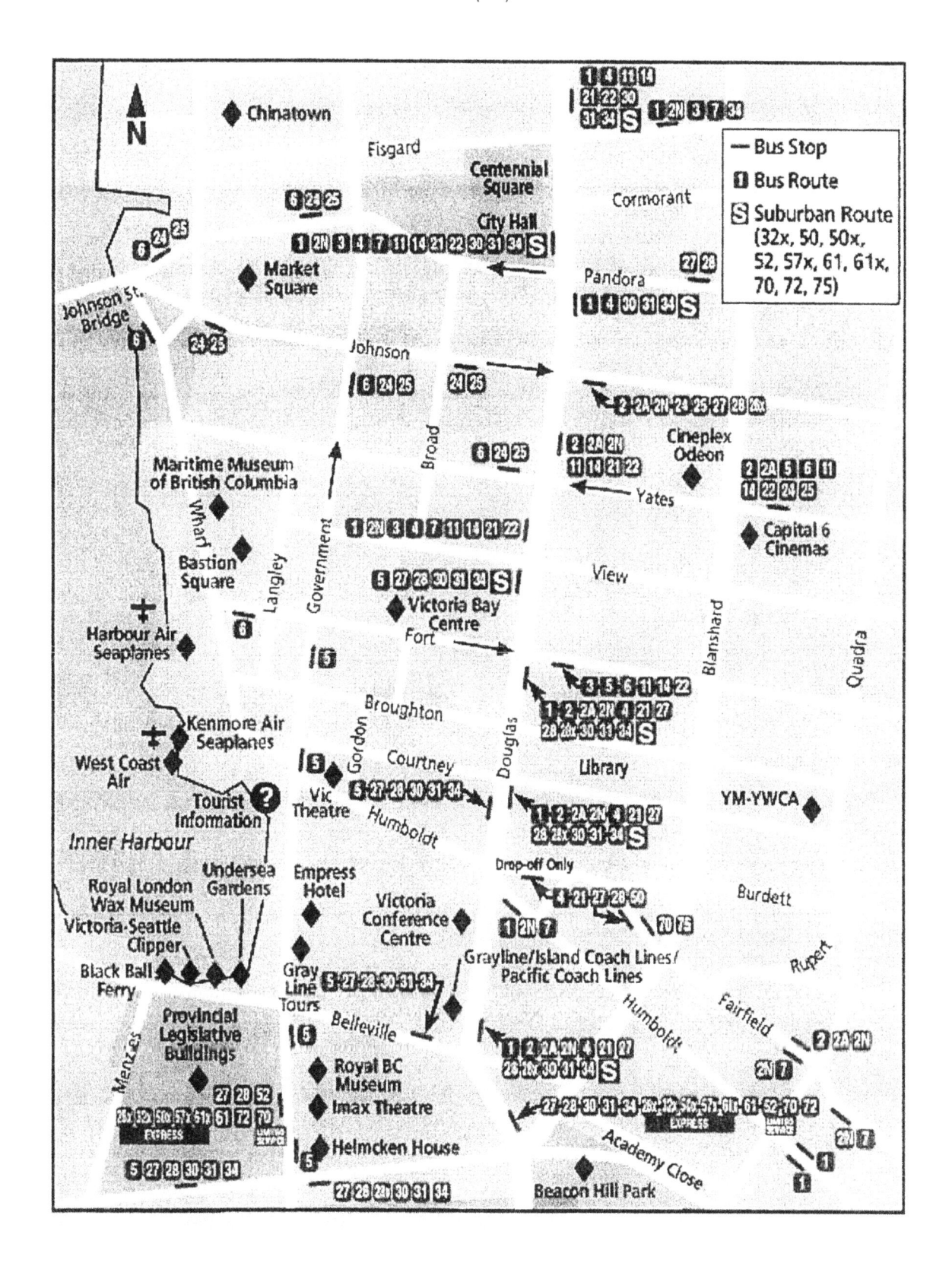

Map #2

5 (#2)

10. The shortest legal way from the Royal London Wax Museum to the Chinatown block is   10.____

    A. east on Belleville, north on Douglas, west on Broughton, north on Government
    B. east on Belleville, north on Government
    C. east on Belleville, north on Government, west on Yates, north on Wharf
    D. east on Belleville, north on Douglas, west on Fisgard

11. The shortest legal way from the Maritime Museum of British Columbia to the Victoria   11.____
    Conference Centre is

    A. north on Wharf, east on Yates, south on Douglas
    B. south and west on Wharf, north on Government, east on Broughton, south on Douglas
    C. south on Wharf, east on Fort, south on Douglas
    D. south and west on Wharf, south on Government, east on Belleville, north on Douglas

12. The shortest legal way from Market Square to City Hall is   12.____

    A. north on Government, east on Fisgard, south on Douglas
    B. east on Pandora, north on Douglas
    C. east on Johnson, north on Blanshard, west on Pandora, north on Douglas
    D. east on Johnson, north on Douglas

13. The shortest legal way from the Victoria Bay Centre to Bastion Square is   13.____

    A. east on Fort, south on Douglas, west on Broughton, north on Wharf
    B. west on Fort, north on Government, west on Yates, south on Wharf
    C. west on Fort, north on Wharf
    D. east on Fort, north on Douglas, west on Johnson, south on Wharf

14. The shortest legal way from The Empress Hotel to the YM-YWCA is   14.____

    A. north on Government, east on Broughton
    B. north on Government, east on Courtney
    C. north on Government, southeast on Humboldt, north on Quadra
    D. north on Government, west on Courtney

6 (#2)

Questions 15-19

Questions 15 through 19 refer to Figure #2, on the following page, and measure your ability to understand written descriptions of events. Each question presents a description of an accident or event and asks you which of the five drawings in Figure #2 BEST represents it.

In the drawings, the following symbols are used:

Moving vehicle: ◊   Non-moving vehicle: ◆

Pedestrian or bicycle: ●

The path and direction of travel of a vehicle or pedestrian is indicated by a solid line.

The path and direction of travel of each vehicle or pedestrian directly involved in a collision from the point of impact is indicated by a dotted line.

In the space at the right, print the letter of the drawing that best fits the descriptions written below:

15. A driver traveling north on Taylor strikes a parked car in the rear and knocks it forward, where it collides with a pedestrian in the crosswalk.   15.____

16. A driver headed south on Taylor strikes another car that is traveling east through the intersection of Taylor and Hayes. After the impact, the eastbound car veers to the right and strikes a pedestrian in the crosswalk on Jones.   16.____

17. A driver headed south on Taylor runs a red light and strikes another car that is headed east on Hayes. The eastbound car is knocked into a pedestrian that is using the crosswalk on Taylor   17.____

18. A driver traveling south on Taylor makes a sudden left turn onto Hayes. In the intersection, he strikes the front of an oncoming car and veers onto Hayes, where he strikes a pedestrian in the crosswalk.   18.____

19. A driver headed west on Hayes strikes a car that is traveling east through the intersection of Taylor and Hayes. After the impact, the eastbound car veers to the right and strikes a pedestrian in the crosswalk on Jones.   19.____

FIGURE #2

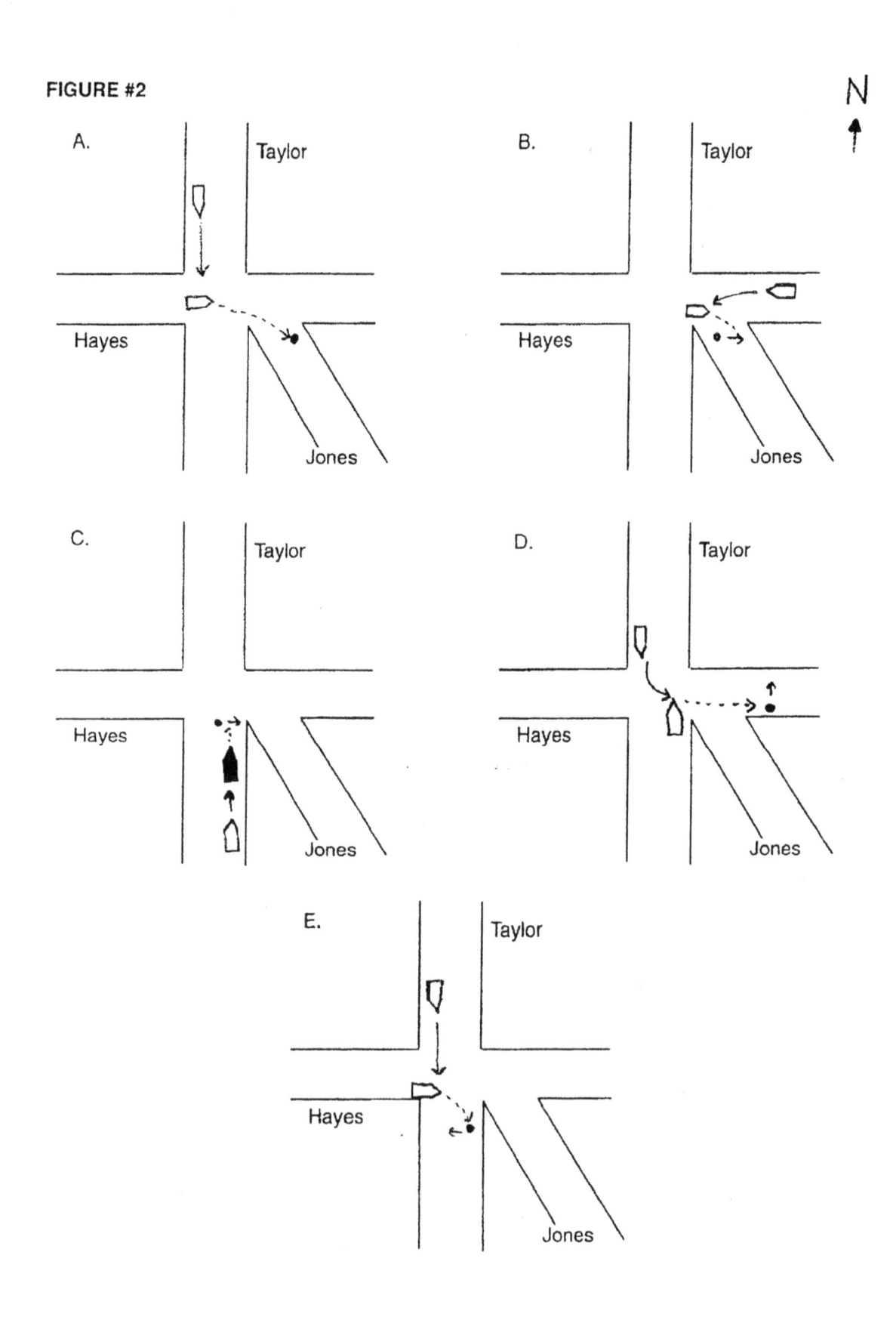

Questions 20-22

In questions 20 through 22, choose the word or phrase CLOSEST in meaning to the word or phrase printed in capital letters.

20. SEQUESTER

   A. follow
   B. separate
   C. endorse
   D. punish

21. EXECUTE

   A. carry out
   B. advance
   C. impede
   D. occur

22. SUPPRESS

   A. uphold
   B. convict
   C. forbid
   D. compensate

Questions 23-25

Questions 23 through 25 measure your ability to do fieldwork-related arithmetic. Each question presents a separate arithmetic problem for you to solve..

23. In the election for the presidency of Local Union 1134, Stan Fitz received 542 votes, Elizabeth Stuckey received 430 votes and Gene Sterner received 130 votes. Ninety percent of those eligible to vote did so. What was the number of eligible voters?

   A. 900
   B. 992
   C. 1102
   D. 1224

24. The Department of Records wants to sort its files alphabetically into boxes that hold an average of 50 files each. The Department has 1,110 records, an amount that is expected to double in the next ten years. To have enough boxes ten years from now, the Department should buy at least _____ boxes.

   A. 23   B. 38   C. 45   D. 47

25. The office's petty cash fund contains a total of $433 on Wednesday. At the beginning of the day, Arnold reimburses $270 that he had previously borrowed from the fund. Then Janet withdraws $158 for office supplies; Hank spends $87 on lunch for a committee meeting; and at the end of the day, Ernestine buys a new office calendar for $12. How much remains in the petty cash fund at the end of the day on Wednesday?

   A. $94   B. $257   C. $446   D. $527

KEY (CORRECT ANSWERS)

1.	D	11.	C
2.	B	12.	D
3.	A	13.	A
4.	D	14.	B
5.	A	15.	C
6.	C	16.	A
7.	D	17.	E
8.	A	18.	D
9.	A	19.	B
10.	B	20.	B

21. A
22. C
23. D
24. D
25. C

READING COMPREHENSION
UNDERSTANDING AND INTERPRETING WRITTEN MATERIAL
EXAMINATION SECTION
TEST 1

DIRECTIONS: Each question or incomplete statement is followed by several suggested answers or completions. Select the one that BEST answers the question or completes the statement. *PRINT THE LETTER OF THE CORRECT ANSWER IN THE SPACE AT THE RIGHT.*

Questions 1-4.

DIRECTIONS: Questions 1 through 4 are to be answered SOLELY on the basis of the information given in the paragraph below.

Abandoned cars—with tires gone, chrome stripped away, and windows smashed—have become a common sight on the city's streets. In 2000, more than 72,000 were deposited at curbs by owners who never came back, an increase of 15,000 from the year before and more than 30 times the number abandoned a decade ago. In January 2001, the city Environmental Protection Administrator asked the State Legislature to pass a law requiring a buyer of a new automobile to deposit $100 and an owner of an automobile at the time the law takes effect to deposit $50 with the State Department of Motor Vehicles. In return, they would be given a certificate of deposit which would be passed on to each succeeding owner. The final owner would get the deposit money back if he could present proof that he has disposed of his car *in an environmentally acceptable manner.* The Legislature has given no indication that it plans to rush ahead on the matter.

1. The number of cars abandoned in the city streets in 1990 was MOST NEARLY

    A. 2,500   B. 12,000   C. 27,500   D. 57,000

2. The proposed law would require a person who owned a car bought before the law was passed to deposit

    A. $100 with the State Department of Motor Vehicles
    B. $50 with the Environmental Protection Administration
    C. $100 with the State Legislature
    D. $50 with the State Department of Motor Vehicles

3. The proposed law would require the State to return the deposit money ONLY when the

    A. original owner of the car shows proof that he sold it
    B. last owner of the car shows proof that he got rid of the car in a satisfactory way
    C. owner of a car shows proof that he has transferred the certificate of deposit to the next owner
    D. last owner of a car returns the certificate of deposit

4. The MAIN idea or theme of the above article is that
   A. a proposed new law would make it necessary for car owners in the State to pay additional taxes
   B. the State Legislature is against a proposed law to require deposits from automobile owners to prevent them from abandoning their cars
   C. the city is trying to find a solution for the increasing number of cars abandoned on its streets
   D. to pay for the removal of abandoned cars the city's Environmental Protection Administrator has asked the State to fine automobile owners who abandon their vehicles

Questions 5-7.

DIRECTIONS: Questions 5 through 7 are to be answered SOLELY on the basis of the information given in the paragraph below.

The regulations applying to parking meters provide that the driver is required to deposit the appropriate coin immediately upon parking and it is illegal for him to return at a later period to extend the parking time. If there is unused time on a parking meter, another car may be parked for a period not to exceed the unused time without the deposit of a coin. Operators of commercial vehicles are not required to deposit coins while loading or unloading expeditiously. By definition, a vehicle is considered parked even though there is a driver at the wheel and the meter must be used by the driver of such car.

5. According to the above paragraph, the regulations applying to parking meters do NOT
   A. allow the driver of a parked vehicle to stay in his car
   B. consider any loading or unloading of a vehicle as parking
   C. make any distinction between an unoccupied car and one with the driver at the wheel
   D. permit a driver who has parked a car at a meter with unused parking time to put a coin in the meter

6. According to the above paragraph, it is a violation of the parking meter regulations to
   A. load and unload slowly
   B. park commercial vehicles except for loading and unloading
   C. put a second coin in the meter in order to park longer
   D. use a parking space at any time without depositing a coin

7. The above paragraph CLEARLY indicates
   A. the number of minutes a vehicle may be parked
   B. the value of the coin that is to be put in the meter
   C. what is meant by a commercial vehicle
   D. when a car may be parked free

Questions 8-13.

DIRECTIONS: Questions 8 through 13 are to be answered on the basis of the information given in the paragraph below.

There are many types of reports. One of these is the field report, which requests information specified and grouped under columns or headings. A detailed, printed form is often used in submitting field reports. However, these printed, standardized forms provide a limited amount of space. The field man is required to make the decision as to how much of the information he has should go directly into the report and how much should be left for clarification if and when he is called in to explain a reported finding. In many instances, the addition of a short explanation of the finding might relieve the reader of the report of the necessity to seek an explanation. Therefore, the basic factual information asked for by the printed report form should often be clarified by some simple explanatory statement. If this is done, the reported finding becomes meaningful to the reader of the report who is far from the scene of the subject matter dealt with in the report. The significance of that which is reported finds its expression in the adoption of certain policies, improvements, or additions essential to furthering the effectiveness of the program.

8. According to the above paragraph, the field report asks for

   A. a detailed statement of the facts
   B. field information which comes under the heading of technical data
   C. replies to well-planned questions
   D. specific information in different columns

9. According to the above paragraph, the usual printed field report form

   A. does not have much room for writing
   B. is carefully laid out
   C. is necessary for the collection of facts
   D. usually has from three to four columns

10. According to the above paragraph, the man in the field MUST decide if

    A. a report is needed at all
    B. he should be called in to explain a reported finding
    C. he should put all the information he has into the report
    D. the reader of the report is justified in seeking an explanation

11. According to the above paragraph, the man in the field may be required to

    A. be acquainted with the person or persons who will read his report
    B. explain the information he reports
    C. give advice on specific problems
    D. keep records of the amount of work he completes

12. According to the above paragraph, the value of an explanatory statement added to the factual information reported in the printed forms is that it

    A. allows the person making the report to express himself briefly
    B. forces the person making the report to think logically
    C. helps the report reader understand the facts reported
    D. makes it possible to turn in the report later

13. According to the above paragraph, the importance of the information given by the field man in his report is shown by the

   A. adoption of policies and improvements
   B. effectiveness of the field staff
   C. fact that such a report is required
   D. necessary cost studies to back up the facts

Questions 14-15.

DIRECTIONS: Questions 14 and 15 are to be answered on the basis of the information contained in the following paragraph.

The driver of the collection crew shall at all times remain in or on a department vehicle in which there is revenue. In the event such driver must leave the vehicle, he shall designate one of the other members of the crew to remain in or on the vehicle. The member of the crew so designated by the driver shall remain in or on the vehicle until relieved by the driver or another member of the crew. The vehicle may be left unattended only when there is no revenue contained therein provided, however, that in that event the vehicle shall be locked. The loss of any vehicle or any of its contents, including revenue, resulting from any deviation from this rule, shall be the responsibility of the member or members of crew who shall be guilty of such deviation.

14. The vehicle of a collection crew may be left with no one in it only if

   A. it is locked
   B. there is a crew member nearby
   C. there is no money in it
   D. there is only one member in the crew

15. If money is stolen from an unattended vehicle of a collection crew, the employee held responsible is the

   A. driver
   B. one who left the vehicle unattended
   C. one who left the vehicle unlocked
   D. one who relieved the driver

Questions 16-18.

DIRECTIONS: Questions 16 through 18 are to be answered SOLELY on the basis of the information given in the paragraph below.

Safety belts provide protection for the passengers of a vehicle by preventing them from crashing around inside if the vehicle is involved in a collision. They operate on the principle similar to that used in the packaging of fragile items. You become a part of the vehicle package, and you are kept from being tossed about inside if the vehicle is suddenly decelerated. Many injury-causing collisions at low speeds, for example at city intersections, could have been injury-free if the occupants had fastened their safety belts. There is a double advantage to the driver in that it not only protects him from harm, but prevents him from being yanked away from the wheel, thereby permitting him to maintain control of the car.

16. The principle on which seat belts work is that 16.____

   A. a car and its driver and passengers are fragile
   B. a person fastened to the car will not be thrown around when the car slows down suddenly
   C. the driver and passengers of a car that is suddenly decelerated will be thrown forward
   D. the driver and passengers of an automobile should be packaged the way fragile items are packaged

17. We can assume from the above passage that safety belts should be worn at all times because you can never tell when 17.____

   A. a car will be forced to turn off onto another road
   B. it will be necessary to shift into low gear to go up a hill
   C. you will have to speed up to pass another car
   D. a car may have to come to a sudden stop

18. Besides preventing injury, an ADDITIONAL benefit from the use of safety belts is that 18.____

   A. collisions are fewer
   B. damage to the car is kept down
   C. the car can be kept under control
   D. the number of accidents at city intersections is reduced

Questions 19-24.

DIRECTIONS: Questions 19 through 24 are to be answered on the basis of the following reading passage covering Procedures For Patrol.

PROCEDURES FOR PATROL

The primary function of all Parking Enforcement Agents assigned to patrol duty shall be to patrol assigned areas and issue summonses to violators of various sections of the City Traffic Regulations, which sections govern the parking or operation of vehicles. Parking Enforcement Agents occasionally may be called upon to distribute educational pamphlets and perform other work, at the discretion of the Bureau Chief.

Each Agent on patrol duty will be assigned a certain area (or areas) to be patrolled. These areas will be assigned during the daily roll call. Walking Cards will describe the street locations of the patrol and the manner in which the patrol is to be walked.

A Traffic Department vehicle will be provided for daily patrol assignments when necessary.

Each Agent shall accomplish an assigned field patrol in the following manner:

   a. Start each patrol at the location specified on the daily patrol sheet, and proceed as per walking instructions.
   b. Approach each metered space being utilized (each metered space in which a vehicle is parked). If the meter shows the expired flag, the member of the force shall prepare and affix a summons to the vehicle parked at meter.

c. Any vehicle in violation of any regulation governing the parking, standing, stopping, or movement of vehicles will be issued a summons.
d. No summons will be issued to a vehicle displaying an authorized vehicle identification plate of the Police Department unless the vehicle is parked in violation of the No Standing, No Stopping, Hydrant, Bus Stop, or Double Parking Regulations. Identification plates for Police Department automobiles are made of plastic and are of rectangular shape, 10 3/4" long, 3 3/4" high, black letters and numerals on a white background. The words *POLICE DEPT.* are printed on the face with the identification number. Identification plates for private automobiles are the same size and shape as those used on Police Department automobiles.

An Agent on patrol, when observing a person *feeding* a street meter (placing an additional coin in a meter so as to leave the vehicle parked for an additional period) shall prepare and affix a summons to the vehicle.

An Agent on patrol shall note on a computer card each missing or defective, out of order, or otherwise damaged meter.

19. Of the following, the work which the Parking Enforcement Agent performs MOST often is

    A. issuing summonses for parking violations
    B. distributing educational pamphlets
    C. assisting the Bureau Chief
    D. driving a city vehicle

20. The area to be covered by a Parking Enforcement Agent on patrol is

    A. determined by the Police Department
    B. regulated by the city Traffic Regulations
    C. marked off with red flags
    D. described on Walking Cards

21. A Parking Enforcement Agent reports a broken meter by

    A. issuing a summons
    B. making a mark on a computer card
    C. raising the flag on the broken meter
    D. attending a daily roll call

22. With respect to the use of an automobile for patrol duty,

    A. Parking Enforcement Agents must supply their own cars for patrol
    B. automobiles for patrol will be supplied by the Police Department
    C. Parking Enforcement Agents are permitted to park in a bus stop
    D. department vehicles will be provided when required for patrol

23. Parking Enforcement Agents sometimes issue summonses to drivers for *feeding* a street meter in violation of parking regulations.
    Which one of the following situations describes such a violation?
    A driver

    A. has moved from one metered space to another
    B. has parked next to a Police Department No Standing sign
    C. is parked by a meter which shows 30 minutes time still remaining
    D. has used a coin to reset the meter after his first time period expired

24. Vehicles displaying an authorized vehicle identification plate of the Police Department are allowed to park at expired meters.
Which one of the following statements describes the proper size of identification plates for private automobiles used for police work?
They

    A. are 10 3/4" long and 3 3/4" high
    B. have white letters and numerals on a black background
    C. are 3 3/4" long and 10 3/4" high
    D. have black letters and numerals on a white background

24.____

Questions 25-30.

DIRECTIONS: Questions 25 through 30 are to be answered on the basis of the following reading passage covering the Operation of Department Motor Vehicles.

OPERATION OF DEPARTMENT MOTOR VEHICLES

When operating a Traffic Department motor vehicle, a member of the force must show every courtesy to other drivers, obey all traffic signs and traffic regulations, obey all other lawful authority, and handle the vehicle in a manner which will foster safety practices in others and create a favorable impression of the Bureau, the Department, and the City. The operator and passengers MUST use the safety belts.

Driving Rules

    a. DO NOT operate a mechanically defective vehicle.
    DO NOT race engine on starting.
    DO NOT tamper with mechanical equipment.
    DO NOT run engine if there is an indication of low engine oil pressure, overheating, or no transmission oil.

    b. When parking on highway, all safety precautions must be observed.

    c. When parking in a garage or parking field, observe a maximum speed of 5 miles per hour. Place shift lever in park or neutral position, effectively apply hand brake, then shut off all ignition and light switches to prevent excess battery drain, and close all windows.

Reporting Defects

    a. Report all observed defects on Drivers' Vehicle Defect Card and on Monthly Vehicle Report Form 49 in sufficient detail so a mechanic can easily locate the source of trouble.
    b. Enter vehicle road service calls and actual time of occurrence on Monthly Vehicle Report.

Reporting Accidents

Promptly report all facts of each accident as follows: For serious accidents, including those involving personal injury, call your supervisor as soon as possible. Give all the appropriate information about the accident to your supervisor. Record vehicle registration information, including the name of the registered owner, the state, year, and serial number, and the classification marking on the license plates. Also record the operator's license number and other identifying information, and, if it applies, the injured person's age and sex. Give a full description of how the accident happened, and what happened following the accident, including the vehicles in collision, witnesses, police badge number, hospital, condition of road surface, time of day, weather conditions, location (near, far, center of intersection), and damage.

Repairs to Automobiles

When a Department motor vehicle requires repairs that cannot be made by the operator, or requires replacement of parts or accessories (including tires and tubes), or requires towing, the operator shall notify the District Commander.

When a Departmental motor vehicle is placed out of service for repairs, the Regional Commander shall assign another vehicle, if available.

Daily Operator's Report

The operator of a Department automobile shall keep a daily maintenance record of the vehicle, and note any unusual occurrences, on the Daily Operator's Report.

25. Parking Enforcement Agents who are assigned to operate Department motor vehicles on patrol are expected to

    A. disregard the posted speed limits to save time
    B. remove their seat belts on short trips
    C. show courtesy to other drivers on the road
    D. take the right of way at all intersections

26. The driver of a Department motor vehicle should

    A. leave the windows open when parking the vehicle in a garage
    B. drive the vehicle at approximately 10 miles per hour in a parking field
    C. be alert for indication of low engine oil pressure and overheated engine
    D. start a cold vehicle by racing the engine for 5 minutes

27. The reason that all defects on a Department vehicle that have been observed by its driver should be noted on a Monthly Vehicle Report Form 49 is:

    A. This action will foster better safety practices among other Agents
    B. The source of the defect may be located easily by a trained mechanic
    C. All the facts of an accident will be reported promptly
    D. The District Commander will not have to make road calls

28. If the driver of a Department vehicle is involved in an accident, an Accident Report should be made out. This Report should include a full description of how the accident happened.
Which of the following statements would PROPERLY belong in an Accident Report?

   A. The accident occurred at the intersection of Broadway and 42nd Street.
   B. The operator of the Department motor vehicle replaced the windshield wiper.
   C. The vehicle was checked for gas and water before the patrol began.
   D. A bus passed two parked vehicles.

29. When a Department vehicle is disabled, whom should the operator notify?
The

   A. Traffic Department garage
   B. Assistant Bureau Chief
   C. Police Department
   D. District Commander

30. The PROPER way for an operator of a Department vehicle to report unusual occurrences with respect to the operation of the vehicle is to

   A. follow the same procedures as for reporting a defect
   B. request the Regional Commander to assign another vehicle
   C. phone the Bureau Chief as soon as possible
   D. make a note of the circumstances on the Daily Operator's Report

---

KEY (CORRECT ANSWERS)

1.	A	16.	B
2.	D	17.	D
3.	B	18.	C
4.	C	19.	A
5.	C	20.	D
6.	C	21.	B
7.	D	22.	D
8.	D	23.	D
9.	A	24.	A
10.	C	25.	C
11.	B	26.	C
12.	C	27.	B
13.	A	28.	A
14.	C	29.	D
15.	B	30.	D

TEST 2

DIRECTIONS: Each question or incomplete statement is followed by several suggested answers or completions. Select the one that BEST answers the question or completes the statement. *PRINT THE LETTER OF THE CORRECT ANSWER IN THE SPACE AT THE RIGHT.*

Questions 1-4.

DIRECTIONS: Questions 1 through 4 are to be answered SOLELY on the basis of the information contained in the following passage.

Of those arrested in the city in 2003 for felonies or misdemeanors, only 32% were found guilty of any charge. Fifty-six percent of such arrestees were acquitted or had their cases dismissed. 11% failed to appear for trial, and 1% received other dispositions. Of those found guilty, only 7.4% received any sentences of over one year in jail. Only 50% of those found guilty were sentenced to any further time in jail. When considered with the low probability of arrests for most crimes, these figures make it clear that the crime control system in the city poses little threat to the average criminal. Delay compounds the problem. The average case took four appearances for disposition after arraignment. Twenty percent of all cases took eight or more appearances to reach a disposition. Forty-four percent of all cases took more than one year to disposition.

1. According to the above passage, crime statistics for 2003 indicate that

   A. there is a low probability of arrests for all crimes in the city
   B. the average criminal has much to fear from the law in the city
   C. over 10% of arrestees in the city charged with felonies or misdemeanors did not show up for trial
   D. criminals in the city are less likely to be caught than criminals in the rest of the country

2. The percentage of those arrested in 2003 who received sentences of over one year in jail amounted to MOST NEARLY

   A. .237 B. 2.4 C. 23.7 D. 24.0

3. According to the above passage, the percentage of arrestees in 2003 who were found guilty was

   A. 20% of those arrested for misdemeanors
   B. 11% of those arrested for felonies
   C. 50% of those sentenced to further time in jail
   D. 32% of those arrested for felonies or misdemeanors

4. According to the above paragraph, the number of appearances after arraignment and before disposition amounted to

   A. an average of four
   B. eight or more in 44% of the cases
   C. over four for cases which took more than a year
   D. between four and eight for most cases

Questions 5-6.

DIRECTIONS: Questions 5 and 6 are to be answered on the basis of the following paragraph.

A person who, with the intent to deprive or defraud another of the use and benefit of property or to appropriate the same to the use of the taker, or of any other person other than the true owner, wrongfully takes, obtains or withholds, by any means whatever, from the possession of the true owner or of any other person any money, personal property, thing in action, evidence of debt or contract, or article of value of any kind, steals such property and is guilty of larceny.

5. This definition from the Penal Law has NO application to the act of

   A. fraudulent conversion by a vendor of city sales tax money collected from purchasers
   B. refusing to give proper change after a purchaser has paid for an article in cash
   C. receiving property stolen from the rightful owner
   D. embezzling money from the rightful owner

6. According to the above paragraph, an auto mechanic who claimed to have a lien on an automobile for completed repairs and refused to surrender possession until the bill was paid

   A. *cannot* be charged with larceny because his repairs increased the value of the car
   B. *can* be charged with larceny because such actual possession can be construed to include intent to deprive the owner of use of the car
   C. *cannot* be charged with larceny because the withholding is temporary and such possession is not an evidence of debt
   D. *cannot* be charged with larceny because intent to defraud is lacking

Questions 7-12.

DIRECTIONS: Questions 7 through 12 are to be answered on the basis of the information given in the passage below. Assume that all questions refer to the same state described in the passage.

The courts and the police consider an *offense* as any conduct that is punishable by a fine or imprisonment. Such offenses include many kinds of acts—from behavior that is merely annoying, like throwing a noisy party that keeps everyone awake, all the way up to violent acts like murder. The law classifies offenses according to the penalties that are provided for them. In one state, minor offenses are called *violations*. A violation is punishable by a fine of not more than $250 or imprisonment of not more than 15 days, or both. The annoying behavior mentioned above is an example of a violation. More serious offenses are classified as *crimes*. Crimes are classified by the kind of penalty that is provided. A *misdemeanor* is a crime that is punishable by a fine of not more than $1,000 or by imprisonment of not more than 1 year, or both. Examples of misdemeanors include stealing something with a value of $100 or less, turning in a false alarm, or illegally possessing less than 1/8 of an ounce of a dangerous drug. A *felony* is a criminal offense punishable by imprisonment of more than 1 year. Murder is clearly a felony.

7. According to the above passage, any act that is punishable by imprisonment or by a fine is called a(n)   7._____

   A. offense   B. violation   C. crime   D. felony

8. According to the above passage, which of the following is classified as a crime?   8._____

   A. Offense punishable by 15 days imprisonment
   B. Minor offense
   C. Violation
   D. Misdemeanor

9. According to the above passage, if a person guilty of burglary can receive a prison sentence of 7 years or more, burglary would be classified as a   9._____

   A. violation   B. misdemeanor
   C. felony   D. violent act

10. According to the above passage, two offenses that would BOTH be classified as misdemeanors are   10._____

    A. making unreasonable noise, and stealing a $90 bicycle
    B. stealing a $75 radio, and possessing 1/16 of an ounce of heroin
    C. holding up a bank, and possessing 1/4 of a pound of marijuana
    D. falsely reporting a fire, and illegally double-parking

11. The above passage says that offenses are classified according to the penalties provided for them.   11._____
    On the basis of clues in the passage, who probably decides what the maximum penalties should be for the different kinds of offenses?

    A. The State lawmakers   B. The City police
    C. The Mayor   D. Officials in Washington, D.C.

12. Of the following, which BEST describes the subject matter of the passage?   12._____

    A. How society deals with criminals
    B. How offenses are classified
    C. Three types of criminal behavior
    D. The police approach to offenders

Questions 13-20.

DIRECTIONS: Questions 13 through 20 are to be answered SOLELY on the basis of the following passage.

Auto theft is prevalent and costly. In 2005, 486,000 autos valued at over $500 million were stolen. About 28 percent of the inhabitants of Federal prisons are there as a result of conviction of interstate auto theft under the Dyer Act. In California alone, auto thefts cost the criminal justice system approximately $60 million yearly.

The great majority of auto theft is for temporary use rather than resale, as evidenced by the fact that 88 percent of autos stolen in 2005 were recovered. In Los Angeles, 64 percent of stolen autos that were recovered were found within two days, and about 80 percent within a week. Chicago reports that 71 percent of the recovered autos were found within four miles of the point of theft. The FBI estimates that 8 percent of stolen cars are taken for the purpose of stripping them for parts, 12 percent for resale, and 5 percent for use in another crime. Auto thefts are primarily juvenile acts. Although only 21 percent of all arrests for nontraffic offenses in 2005 were of individuals under 18 years of age, 63 percent of auto theft arrests were of persons under 18. Auto theft represents the start of many criminal careers; in an FBI sample of juvenile auto theft offenders, 41 percent had no prior arrest record.

13. In the above passage, the discussion of the reasons for auto theft does NOT include the percent of

    A. autos stolen by prior offenders
    B. recovered stolen autos found close to the point of theft
    C. stolen autos recovered within a week
    D. stolen autos which were recovered

14. Assuming the figures in the above passage remain constant, you may logically estimate the cost of auto thefts to the California criminal justice system over a five-year period beginning in 2005 to have been about _____ million.

    A. $200   B. $300   C. $440   D. $500

15. According to the above passage, the percent of stolen autos in Los Angeles which were not recovered within a week was _____ percent.

    A. 12   B. 20   C. 29   D. 36

16. According to the above passage, MOST auto thefts are committed by

    A. former inmates of Federal prisons   B. juveniles
    C. persons with a prior arrest record   D. residents of large cities

17. According to the above passage, MOST autos are stolen for

    A. resale   B. stripping of parts
    C. temporary use   D. use in another crime

18. According to the above passage, the percent of persons arrested for auto theft who were under 18

    A. equals nearly the same percent of stolen autos which were recovered
    B. equals nearly two-thirds of the total number of persons arrested for nontraffic offenses
    C. is the same as the percent of persons arrested for nontraffic offenses who were under 18
    D. is three times the percent of persons arrested for nontraffic offenses who were under 18

19. An APPROPRIATE title for the above passage is

    A. HOW CRIMINAL CAREERS BEGIN
    B. RECOVERY OF STOLEN CARS
    C. SOME STATISTICS ON AUTO THEFT
    D. THE COSTS OF AUTO THEFT

20. Based on the above passage, the number of cars taken for use in another crime in 2005 was

    A. 24,300   B. 38,880   C. 48,600   D. 58,320

Questions 21-22.

DIRECTIONS: Questions 21 and 22 are to be answered SOLELY on the basis of the following paragraph.

If the second or third felony is such that, upon a first conviction, the offender would be punishable by imprisonment for any term less than his natural life, then such person must be sentenced to imprisonment for an indeterminate term, the minimum of which shall be not less than one-half of the longest term prescribed upon a first conviction, and the maximum of which shall be not longer than twice such longest term, provided, however, that the minimum sentence imposed hereunder upon such second or third felony offender shall in no case be less than five years; except that where the maximum punishment for a second or third felony offender hereunder is five years or less, the minimum sentence must be not less than two years.

21. According to the above paragraph, a person who has a second felony conviction shall receive as a sentence for that second felony an indeterminate term

    A. not less than twice the minimum term prescribed upon a first conviction as a maximum
    B. not less than one-half the maximum term of his first conviction as a minimum
    C. not more than twice the minimum term prescribed upon a first conviction as a minimum
    D. with a maximum of not more than twice the longest term prescribed for a first conviction for this crime

22. According to the above paragraph, if the term for this crime for a first offender is up to three years, the possible indeterminate term for this crime as a second or third felony shall have a _____ of not _____ than _____ years.

    A. minimum; less; five
    B. maximum; more; five
    C. minimum; less; one and one-half
    D. maximum; less; six

23. A statute states: *A person who steals an article worth $1,000 or less where no aggravating circumstances accompany the act is guilty of petit larceny. If the article is worth more than $1,000, it may be grand larceny.*
    If all you know is that Edward Smith stole an article worth $1,000, it may reasonably be said that

    A. Smith is guilty of petit larceny
    B. Smith is guilty of grand larceny
    C. Smith is guilty of neither petit larceny nor grand larceny
    D. precisely what charge will be placed against Smith is uncertain

Questions 24-25.

DIRECTIONS: Questions 24 and 25 are to be answered on the basis of the following section of a law.

A person who, after having been three times convicted within this state of felonies or attempts to commit felonies, or under the law of any other state, government, or country, of crimes which if committed within this state would be felonious, commits a felony, other than murder, first or second degree, or treason, within this state, shall be sentenced upon conviction of such fourth, or subsequent, offense to imprisonment in a state prison for an indeterminate term the minimum of which shall be not less than the maximum term provided for first offenders for the crime for which the individual has been convicted, but, in any event, the minimum term upon conviction for a felony as the fourth or subsequent, offense shall be not less than fifteen years, and the maximum thereof shall be his natural life.

24. Under the terms of the above law, a person must receive the increased punishment therein provided if

    A. he is convicted of a felony and has been three times previously convicted of felonies
    B. he has been three times previously convicted of felonies, regardless of the nature of his present conviction
    C. his fourth conviction is for murder, first or second degree, or treason
    D. he has previously been convicted three times of murder, first or second degree, or treason

25. Under the terms of the above law, a person convicted of a felony for which the penalty is imprisonment for a term not to exceed ten years, and who has been three times previously convicted of felonies in this state, shall be sentenced to a term, the MINIMUM of which shall be

    A. 10 years   B. 15 years
    C. indeterminate   D. his natural life

KEY (CORRECT ANSWERS)

1.	C		11.	A
2.	B		12.	B
3.	D		13.	A
4.	A		14.	B
5.	C		15.	B
6.	D		16.	B
7.	A		17.	C
8.	D		18.	D
9.	C		19.	C
10.	B		20.	A

21. D
22. C
23. D
24. A
25. B

READING COMPREHENSION
UNDERSTANDING AND INTERPRETING WRITTEN MATERIAL
EXAMINATION SECTION
TEST 1

DIRECTIONS: Each question or incomplete statement is followed by several suggested answers or completions. Select the one that BEST answers the question or completes the statement. *PRINT THE LETTER OF THE CORRECT ANSWER IN THE SPACE AT THE RIGHT.*

Questions 1-3.

DIRECTIONS: Questions 1 through 3 are to be answered SOLELY on the basis of the following passage.

Foot patrol has some advantages over all other methods of patrol. Maximum opportunity is provided for observation within range of the senses and for close contact with people and things that enable the patrolman to provide a maximum service as an information source and counselor to the public and as the eyes and ears of the police department. A foot patrolman loses no time in alighting from a vehicle, and the performance of police tasks is not hampered by responsibility for his vehicle while afoot. Foot patrol, however, does not have many of the advantages of a patrol car. Lack of both mobility and immediate communication with headquarters lessens the officer's value in an emergency. The area that he can cover effectively is limited and, therefore, this method of patrol is costly.

1. According to the above passage, the foot patrolman is the eyes and ears of the police department because he is
    A. in direct contact with the station house
    B. not responsible for a patrol vehicle
    C. able to observe closely conditions on his patrol post
    D. a readily available information source to the public

2. The MOST accurate of the following statements concerning the various methods of patrol, according to the above passage, is that
    A. foot patrol should sometimes be combined with a motor patrol
    B. foot patrol is better than motor patrol
    C. helicopter patrol has the same advantages as motor patrol
    D. motor patrol is more readily able to communicate with superior officers in an emergency

3. According to the above passage, it is CORRECT to state that foot patrol is
    A. economical since increased mobility makes more rapid action possible
    B. expensive since the area that can be patrolled is relatively small
    C. economical since vehicle costs need not be considered
    D. expensive since giving information to the public is time consuming

1.____

2.____

3.____

Questions 4-6.

DIRECTIONS: Questions 4 through 6 are to be answered SOLELY on the basis of the following passage.

All applicants for an original license to operate a catering establishment shall be fingerprinted. This shall include the officers, employees, and stockholders of the company and the members of a partnership. In case of a change, by addition or subtraction, occurring during the existence of a license, the person added or substituted shall be fingerprinted. However, in the case of a hotel containing more than 200 rooms, only the officer or manager filing the application is required to be fingerprinted. The police commissioner may also at his discretion exempt the employees and stockholders of any company. The fingerprints shall be taken on one copy of form C.E. 20 and on two copies of C.E. 21. One copy of form C.E. 21 shall accompany the application. Fingerprints are not required with a renewal application.

4. According to the above passage, an employee added to the payroll of a licensed catering establishment which is not in a hotel must
   A. always be fingerprinted
   B. be fingerprinted unless he has been previously fingerprinted for another license
   C. be fingerprinted unless exempted by the police commissioner
   D. be fingerprinted only if he is the manager or an officer of the company

4._____

5. According to the above passage, it would be MOST accurate to state that
   A. form C.E. 20 must accompany a renewal application
   B. form C.E. 21 must accompany all applications
   C. form C.E. 21 must accompany an original application
   D. both forms C.E. 20 and C.E. 21 must accompany all applications

5._____

6. A hotel of 270 rooms has applied for a license to operate a catering establishment on the premises.
   According to the instructions for fingerprinting given in the above passage, the _____ shall be fingerprinted.
   A. officers, employees, and stockholders
   B. officers and the manager
   C. employees
   D. officer filing the application

6._____

Questions 7-9.

DIRECTIONS: Questions 7 through 9 are to be answered SOLELY on the basis of the following passage.

It is difficult to instill in young people inner controls on aggressive behavior in a world marked by aggression. The slum child's environment, full of hostility, stimulates him to delinquency; he does that which he sees about him. The time to act against delinquency is before it is committed. It is clear that juvenile delinquency, especially when it is committed in groups or gangs, leads almost inevitably to an adult criminal life unless it is checked at once.

The first signs of vandalism and disregard for the comfort, health, and property of the community should be considered as storm warnings which cannot be ignored. The delinquent's first crime has the underlying element of testing the law and its ability to hit back.

7. A SUITABLE title for this entire paragraph based on the material it contains is
   A. The Need for Early Prevention of Juvenile Delinquency
   B. Juvenile Delinquency as a Cause of Slums
   C. How Aggressive Behavior Prevents Juvenile Delinquency
   D. The Role of Gangs in Crime

8. According to the above passage, an initial act of juvenile crime USUALLY involves a(n)
   A. group or gang activity
   B. theft of valuable property
   C. test of the strength of legal authority
   D. act of physical violence

9. According to the above passage, acts of juvenile delinquency are MOST likely to lead to a criminal career when they are
   A. acts of vandalism
   B. carried out by groups or gangs
   C. committed in a slum environment
   D. such as to impair the health of the neighborhood

Questions 10-12.

DIRECTIONS: Questions 10 through 12 are to be answered SOLELY on the basis of the following passage.

The police laboratory performs a valuable service in crime investigation by assisting in the reconstruction of criminal action and by aiding in the identification of persons and things. When studied by a technician, physical things found at crime scenes often reveal facts useful in identifying the criminal and in determining what has occurred. The nature of substances to be examined and the character of the examinations to be made vary so widely that the services of a large variety of skilled scientific persons are needed in crime investigations. To employ such a complete staff and to provide them with equipment and standards needed for all possible analyses and comparisons is beyond the means and the needs of any but the largest police departments. The search of crime scenes for physical evidence also calls for the services of specialists supplied with essential equipment and assigned to each tour of duty so as to provide service at any hour.

10. If a police department employs a large staff of technicians of various types in its laboratory, it will affect crime investigation to the extent that
    A. most crimes will be speedily solved
    B. identification of criminals will be aided
    C. search of crime scenes for physical evidence will become of less importance
    D. investigation by police officers will not usually be required

11. According to the above passage, the MOST complete study of objects found at the scenes of crimes is
    A. always done in all large police departments
    B. based on assigning one technician to each tour of duty
    C. probably done only in large police departments
    D. probably done in police departments of communities with low crime rates

12. According to the above passage, a large variety of skilled technicians is useful in criminal investigations because
    A. crimes cannot be solved without their assistance as a part of the police team
    B. large police departments need large staffs
    C. many different kinds of tests on various substances can be made
    D. the police cannot predict what methods may be tried by wily criminals

Questions 13-14.

DIRECTIONS: Questions 13 and 14 are to be answered SOLELY on the basis of the following passage.

The emotionally unstable person is always potentially a dangerous criminal, who causes untold misery to other persons and is a source of considerable trouble and annoyance to law enforcement officials. Like his fellow criminals, he will be a menace to society as long as he is permitted to be at large. Police activities against him serve to sharpen his wits and imprisonment gives him the opportunity to learn from others how to commit more serious crimes when he is released. This criminal's mental structure makes it impossible for him to profit by his experience with the police officials, by punishment of any kind or by sympathetic understanding and treatment by well-intentioned persons, professional and otherwise.

13. According to the above passage, the MOST accurate of the following statements concerning the relationship between emotional instability and crime is that
    A. emotional instability is proof of criminal activities
    B. the emotionally unstable person can become a criminal
    C. all dangerous criminals are emotionally unstable
    D. sympathetic understanding will prevent the emotionally unstable person from becoming a criminal

14. According to the above passage, the effect of police activities on the emotionally unstable criminal is that
    A. police activities aid this type of criminal to reform
    B. imprisonment tends to deter this type of criminal from committing future crimes
    C. contact with the police serves to assist sympathetic understanding and medical treatment
    D. police methods against this type of criminal develop him for further unlawful acts

Questions 15-17.

DIRECTIONS: Questions 14 through 17 are to be answered SOLELY on the basis of the following passage.

Proposals to license gambling operations are based on the belief that the human desire to gamble cannot be suppressed and, therefore, it should be licensed and legalized with the people sharing in the profits, instead of allowing the underworld to benefit. If these proposals are sincere, then it is clear that only one is worthwhile at all. Legalized gambling should be completely controlled and operated by the state with all the profits used for its citizens. A state agency should be set up to operate and control the gambling business. It should be as completely removed from politics as possible. In view of the inherent nature of the gambling business, with its close relationship to lawlessness and crime, only a man of the highest integrity should be eligible to become head of this agency. However, state gambling would encourage mass gambling with its attending social and economic evils in the same manner as other forms of legal gambling; but there is no justification whatever for the business of gambling to be legalized and then permitted to operate for private profit or for the benefit of any political organization.

15. The central thought of this passage may be CORRECTLY expressed as the   15.____
    A. need to legalize gambling in the state
    B. state operation of gambling for the benefit of the people
    C. need to license private gambling establishments
    D. evils of gambling

16. According to the above passage, a problem of legalized gambling which will   16.____
    still occur if the state operates the gambling business is
    A. the diversion of profits from gambling to private use
    B. that the amount of gambling will tend to diminish
    C. the evil effects of any form of mass gambling
    D. the use of gambling revenues for illegal purposes

17. According to the above passage, to legalize the business of gambling would be   17.____
    A. *justified*, because gambling would be operated only by a man of the highest integrity
    B. *justified*, because this would eliminate politics
    C. *unjustified* under any conditions because the human desire to gamble cannot be suppressed
    D. *unjustified* if operated for private or political profit

Questions 18-19.

DIRECTIONS: Questions 18 and 19 are to be answered SOLELY on the basis of the following passage.

For many years, slums had been recognized as breeding disease, juvenile delinquency, and crime which not only threatened the health and welfare of the people who lived there, but also weakened the structure of society as a whole. As far bac as 1834, a sanitary inspection report in New York City pointed out the connection between unsanitary, overcrowded housing and the spread of epidemics. Down through the years, evidence of slum-produced evils accumulated as the slums themselves continued to spread. This spread of slums was nationwide. Its symptoms and its ill effects were peculiar to no locality, but were characteristic of the country as a whole and imperiled the national welfare.

18. According to the above passage, people who live in slum dwellings 18.____
    A. cause slums to become worse
    B. are threatened by disease and crime
    C. create bad housing
    D. are the chief source of crime in the country

19. According to the above passage, the effects of juvenile delinquency and crime 19.____
    in slum areas were
    A. to destroy the structure of society
    B. noticeable in all parts of the country
    C. a chief cause of the spread of slums
    D. to spread unsanitary conditions in New York City

Questions 20-22.

DIRECTIONS: Questions 20 through 22 are to be answered SOLELY on the basis of the following passage.

Whenever, in the course of the performance of their duties in an emergency, members of the force operate the emergency power switch at any location on the transit system and thereby remove power from portions of the track, or they are on the scene where this has been done, they will bear in mind that, although power is removed, further dangers exist; namely, that a train may coast into the area even though the power is off, or that the rails may be energized by a train which may be in a position to transfer electricity from a live portion of the third rail through its shoe beams. Employees must look in each direction before stepping upon, crossing, or standing close to tracks, being particularly careful not to come into contact with the third rail.

20. According to the above passage, whenever an emergency occurs which has 20.____
    resulted in operating the emergency power switch, it is MOST accurate to state that
    A. power is shut off and employees may perform their duties in complete safety
    B. there may still be power in a portion of the third rail
    C. the switch will not operate if a portion of the track has been broken
    D. trains are not permitted to stop in the area of the emergency

21. An IMPORTANT precaution which this passage urges employees to follow after 21.____
    operating the emergency power switch is to
    A. look carefully in both directions before stepping near the rails
    B. inspect the nearest train which has stopped to see if the power is on
    C. examine the third rail to see if the power is on
    D. check the emergency power switch to make sure it has operated properly

22. A trackman reports to you, the patrolman, that a dead body is lying on the road bed. You operate the emergency power switch. A train which has been approaching comes to a stop near the scene.
In order to act in accordance with the instructions in the above passage, you should
   A. climb down to the road bed and remove the body
   B. direct the train motorman to back up to the point where his train will not be in position to transfer electricity through its shoe beams
   C. carefully cross over the road bed to the body, avoiding the third rail and watching for train movements
   D. have the train motorman check to see if power is on before crossing to the tracks

Questions 23-25.

DIRECTIONS: Questions 23 through 25 are to be answered SOLELY on the basis of the following passage.

Pickpockets operate most effectively when there are prospective victims in either heavily congested areas or in lonely places. In heavily populated areas, the large number of people about them covers the activities of these thieves. In lonely spots, they have the advantage of working unobserved. The main factor in the pickpocket's success is the selection of the *right* victim. A pickpocket's victim must, at the time of the crime, be inattentive, distracted, or unconscious. If any of these conditions exist, and if the pickpocket is skilled in his operations, the stage is set for a successful larceny. With the control of winter, the crowds move southward—and so do most of the pickpockets. However, some pickpockets will remain in certain areas all year around. They will concentrate on theater districts, bus and railroad terminals, hotels or large shopping centers. A complete knowledge of the methods of this type of criminal and the ability to recognize them come only from long years of experience in performing patient surveillance and trailing of them. This knowledge is essential for the effective control and apprehension of this type of thief.

23. According to the above passage, the pickpocket is LEAST likely to operate in a
   A. baseball park with a full capacity attendance
   B. subway station in an outlying area late at night
   C. moderately crowded dance hall
   D. overcrowded department store

24. According to the above passage, the one of the following factors which is NOT necessary for the successful operation of the pickpocket is that
   A. he be proficient in the operations required to pick pockets
   B. the *right* potential victims be those who have been the subject of such a theft previously
   C. his operations be hidden from the view of others
   D. the potential victim be unaware of the actions of the pickpocket

25. According to the above passage, it would be MOST correct to conclude that police officers who are successful in apprehending pickpockets
   A. are generally those who have had lengthy experience in recognizing all types of criminals
   B. must, by intuition, be able to recognize potential *right* victims
   C. must follow the pickpockets in their southward movement
   D. must have acquired specific knowledge and skills in this field

KEY (CORRECT ANSWERS)

1.	C		11.	C
2.	D		12.	C
3.	B		13.	B
4.	C		14.	D
5.	C		15.	B
6.	B		16.	C
7.	A		17.	D
8.	C		18.	D
9.	B		19.	B
10.	B		20.	B

21. A
22. C
23. C
24. B
25. D

TEST 2

DIRECTIONS: Each question or incomplete statement is followed by several suggested answers or completions. Select the one that BEST answers the question or completes the statement. *PRINT THE LETTER OF THE CORRECT ANSWER IN THE SPACE AT THE RIGHT.*

Questions 1-2.

DIRECTIONS: Questions 1 and 2 are to be answered SOLELY on the basis of the following passage.

The medical examiner may contribute valuable data to the investigator of fires which cause fatalities. By careful examination of the bodies of any victims, he not only establishes cause of death, but may also furnish, in many instances, answers to questions relating to the identity of the victim and the source and origin of the fire. The medical examiner is of greatest value to law enforcement agencies because he is able to determine the exact cause of death through an examination of tissue of apparent arson victims. Thorough study of a burned body or even of parts of a burned body will frequently yield information which illuminates the problems confronting the arson investigator and the police.

1. According to the above passage, the MOST important task of the medical examiner in the investigation of arson is to obtain information concerning the
   A. identity of arsonists
   B. cause of death
   C. identity of victims
   D. source and origin of fires

1.____

2. The central thought of the above passage is that the medical examiner aids in the solution of crimes of arson when
   A. a person is burnt to death
   B. identity of the arsonist is unknown
   C. the cause of the fire is known
   D. trained investigators are not available

2.____

Questions 3-6.

DIRECTIONS: Questions 3 through 6 are to be answered SOLELY on the basis of the following passage.

A foundling is an abandoned child whose identity is unknown. Desk officers shall direct the delivery, by a policewoman if available, of foundlings actually or apparently under two years of age to the American Foundling Hospital, or if actually or apparently two year of age or over to the Children's Center. In all other cases of dependent or neglected children, other than foundlings, requiring shelter, desk officers shall provide for obtaining such shelter as follows: between 9 A.M. and 5 P.M., Monday through Friday, by telephone direct to the Bureau of Child Welfare, in order to ascertain the shelter to which the child shall be sent; at all other time, direct the delivery of a child actually or apparently under two years of age to the American Foundling Hospital, or if the child is actually or apparently two years of age or over to the Children's Center.

3. According to the above passage, it would be MOST correct to state that
   A. a foundling as well as a neglected child may be delivered to the American Foundling Hospital
   B. a foundling but not a neglected child may be delivered to the Children's Center
   C. a neglected child requiring shelter, regardless of age, may be delivered to the Bureau of Child Welfare
   D. the Bureau of Child Welfare may determine the shelter to which a foundling may be delivered

4. According to the above passage, the desk officer shall provide for obtaining shelter for a neglected child apparently under two years of age by
   A. directing its delivery to Children's Center if occurrence is on a Monday between 9 A.M. and 5 P.M.
   B. telephoning the Bureau of Child Welfare if occurrence is on a Sunday
   C. directing its delivery to the American Foundling Hospital if occurrence is on a Wednesday at 4 P.M.
   D. telephoning the Bureau of Child Welfare if occurrence is at 10 A.M. on a Friday

5. According to the above passage, the desk officer should direct delivery to the American Foundling Hospital of any child who is
   A. actually under 2 years of age and requires shelter
   B. apparently under 2 years of age and is neglected or dependent
   C. actually 2 years of age and is a foundling
   D. apparently under 2 years of age and has been abandoned

6. A 12-year-old neglected child requiring shelter is brought to a police station on Thursday at 2 P.M.
   Such a child should be sent to
   A. a shelter selected by the Bureau of Child Welfare
   B. a shelter selected by the desk officer
   C. the Children's Center
   D. the American Foundling Hospital when a brother or sister under 2 years of age also requires shelter

Questions 7-10.

DIRECTIONS: Questions 7 through 10 are to be answered SOLELY on the basis of the following passage.

In addition to making the preliminary investigation of crimes, patrolmen should serve as eyes, ears, and legs for the detective division. The patrol division may be used for surveillance, to serve warrants and bring in suspects and witnesses, and to perform a number of routine tasks for the detectives which will increase the time available for tasks that require their special skills and facilities. It is to the advantage of individual detectives, as well as of the detective division, to have patrolmen working in this manner; more cases are cleared by arrest and a greater proportion of stolen property is recovered when, in addition to the detective regularly assigned, a number of patrolmen also work on the case. Detectives may stimulate the interest and participation of patrolmen by keeping them currently informed of the presence, identity or description, hangouts, associates, vehicles, and method of operation of each criminal known to be in the community.

7. According to the above passage, a patrolman should
    A. assist the detective in certain of his routine functions
    B. be considered for assignment as a detective on the basis of his patrol performance
    C. leave the scene once a detective arrives
    D. perform as much of the detective's duties as time permits

8. According to the above passage, patrolmen should aid detectives by   8.____
    A. accepting assignments from detectives which give promise of recovering stolen property
    B. making arrests of witnesses for the detective's interrogation
    C. performing all special investigative work for detectives
    D. producing for questioning individuals who may aid the detective in his investigation

9. According to the above passage, detectives can keep patrolmen interested by   9.____
    A. ascertaining that patrolmen are doing investigative work properly
    B. having patrolmen directly under his supervision during an investigation
    C. informing patrolmen of the value of their efforts in crime prevention
    D. supplying the patrolmen with information regarding known criminals in the community

10. Which of the following is NOT a result of cooperation between detectives and   10.____
patrolmen?
    A. A greater proportion of stolen property is recovered.
    B. Detectives have more time to make preliminary investigations.
    C. Detectives have more time to finish tasks requiring their special skills.
    D. Patrolmen may become more interested and participate more in solving the case.

Questions 11-12.

DIRECTIONS: Questions 11 and 12 are to be answered SOLELY on the basis of the following passage.

State motor vehicle registration departments should and do play a vital role in the prevention and detection of automobile thefts. The combatting of theft is, in fact, one of the primary purposes of the registration of motor vehicles. In 2020 there were approximately 61,309,000 motor vehicles registered in the United States. That same year some 200,000 of them were stolen. All but 6 percent have been or will be recovered. This is a very high recovery ratio compared to the percentage of recovery of other stolen personal property. The reason for this is that automobiles are carefully identified by the manufacturers and carefully registered by many of the states.

11. The central thought of this passage is that there is a close relationship between the
    A. number of automobiles registered in the United States and the number stolen
    B. prevention of automobile thefts and the effectiveness of police departments in the United States
    C. recovery of stolen automobiles and automobile registration
    D. recovery of stolen automobiles and of other stolen property

12. According to the above passage, the high recovery ratio for stolen automobiles is due to
    A. state registration and manufacturer identification of motor vehicles
    B. successful prevention of automobile thefts by state motor vehicle departments
    C. the fact that only 6% of stolen vehicles are not properly registered
    D. the high number of motor vehicles registered in the United States

Questions 13-16.

DIRECTIONS: Questions 13 through 16 are to be answered SOLELY on the basis of the following passage.

It is not always understood that the term *physical evidence* embraces any and all objects, living or inanimate. A knife, gun, signature, or burglar tool is immediately recognized as physical evidence. Less often is it considered that dust, microscopic fragments of all types, even an odor, may equally be physical evidence and often the most important of all. It is well established that the most useful types of physical evidence are generally microscopic in dimensions, that is, not noticeable by the eye and, therefore, most likely to be overlooked by the criminal and by the investigator. For this reason, microscopic evidence persists for months or years after all other evidence has been removed and found inconclusive. Naturally, there are limitations to the time of collecting microscopic evidence as it may be lost or decayed. The exercise of judgment as to the possibility or profit of delayed action in collecting the evidence is a field in which the expert investigator should judge.

13. The one of the following which the above passage does NOT consider to be physical evidence is a
    A. criminal thought   B. minute speck of dust
    C. raw onion smell   D. typewritten note

14. According to the above passage, the rechecking of the scene of a crime
    A. is useless when performed years after the occurrence of the crime
    B. is advisable chiefly in crimes involving physical evidence
    C. may turn up microscopic evidence of value
    D. should be delayed if the microscopic evidence is not subject to decay or loss

15. According to the above passage, the criminal investigator should
    A. give most of his attention to weapons used in the commission of the crime
    B. ignore microscopic evidence until a request is received from the laboratory
    C. immediately search for microscopic evidence and ignore the more visible objects
    D. realize that microscopic evidence can be easily overlooked

16. According to the above passage,
    A. a delay in collecting evidence must definitely diminish its value to the investigator
    B. microscopic evidence exists for longer periods of time than other physical evidence
    C. microscopic evidence is generally the most useful type of physical evidence
    D. physical evidence is likely to be overlooked by the criminal and by the investigator

Questions 17-20.

DIRECTIONS: Questions 17 through 20 are to be answered SOLELY on the basis of the following passage.

Sometimes, but not always, firing a gun leaves a residue of nitrate particles on the hands. This fact is utilized in the paraffin test which consists of applying melted paraffin and gauze to the fingers, hands, and wrists of a suspect until a cast of approximately 1/8 of an inch is built up. The heat of the paraffin causes the pores of the skin to open and release any particles embedded in them. The paraffin cast is then removed and tested chemically for nitrate particles. In addition to gunpowder, fertilizers, tobacco ashes, matches, and soot are also common sources of nitrates on the hands.

17. Assume that the paraffin test has been given to a person suspected of firing a gun and that nitrate particles have been found.
    It would be CORRECT to conclude that the suspect
    A. is guilty   B. is innocent
    C. may be guilty or innocent   D. is probably guilty

18. In testing for the presence of gunpowder particles on human hands, the characteristic of paraffin which makes it MOST serviceable is that it
    A. causes the nitrate residue left by a fired gun to adhere to the gauze
    B. is waterproof
    C. melts at a high temperature
    D. helps to distinguish between gunpowder nitrates and other types

19. According to the above passage, in the paraffin test the nitrate particles are removed from the pores because the paraffin
    A. enlarges the pores   B. contracts the pores
    C. reacts chemically with nitrates   D. dissolves the particles

20. The presence of a residue of nitrate particles on the hands is a COMMON result of 20._____
   A. the paraffin test
   B. handling fertilizer
   C. a bullet wound
   D. enlarged pores

KEY (CORRECT ANSWERS)

1.	B	11.	C
2.	A	12.	A
3.	A	13.	A
4.	D	14.	C
5.	D	15.	D
6.	A	16.	C
7.	A	17.	C
8.		18.	A
9.	D	19.	A
10.	B	20.	B

REPORT WRITING

EXAMINATION SECTION

TEST 1

DIRECTIONS: Each question or incomplete statement is followed by several suggested answers or completions. Select the one that BEST answers the question or completes the statement. *PRINT THE LETTER OF THE CORRECT ANSWER IN THE SPACE AT THE RIGHT.*

1. Following are six steps that should be taken in the course of report preparation:
   I. Outlining the material for presentation in the report
   II. Analyzing and interpreting the facts
   III. Analyzing the problem
   IV. Reaching conclusions
   V. Writing, revising, and rewriting the final copy
   VI. Collecting data

   According to the principles of good report writing, the CORRECT order in which these steps should be taken is:
   A. VI, III, II, I, IV, V
   B. III, VI, II, IV, I, V
   C. III, VI, II, I, IV, V
   D. VI, II, III, IV, I, V

   1.____

2. Following are three statements concerning written reports:
   I. Clarity is generally more essential in oral reports than in written reports.
   II. Short sentences composed of simple words are generally preferred to complex sentences and difficult words.
   III. Abbreviations may be used whenever they are customary and will not distract the attention of the reader.

   Which of the following choices correctly classifies the above statements in to those which are valid and those which are not valid?
   A. I and II are valid, but III is not valid
   B. I is valid, but II and III are not valid.
   C. II and III are valid, but I is not valid.
   D. III is valid, but I and II are not valid.

   2.____

3. In order to produce a report written in a style that is both understandable and effective, an investigator should apply the principles of unit, coherence, and emphasis.
   The one of the following which is the BEST example of the principle of coherence is
   A. interlinking sentences so that thoughts flow smoothly
   B. having each sentence express a single idea to facilitate comprehension
   C. arranging important points in prominent positions so they are not overlooked
   D. developing the main idea fully to insure complete consideration

   3.____

4. Assume that a supervisor is preparing a report recommending that a standard work procedure be changed.
Of the following, the MOST important information that he should include in this report is
   A. a complete description of the present procedure
   B. the details and advantages of the recommended procedure
   C. the type and amount of retraining needed
   D. the percentage of men who favor the change

5. When you include in your report on an inspection some information which you have obtained from other individuals, it is MOST important that
   A. this information have no bearing on the work these other people are performing
   B. you do not report as fact the opinions of other individuals
   C. you keep the source of the information confidential
   D. you do not tell the other individuals that their statements will be included in your report

6. Before turning in a report of an investigator of an accident, you discover some additional information you did not know about when you wrote the report.
Whether or not you re-write your report to include this additional information should depend MAINLY on the
   A. source of this additional information
   B. established policy covering the subject matter of the report
   C. length of the report and the time it would take you to re-write it
   D. bearing this additional information will have on the conclusions in the report

7. The MOST desirable *first* step in the planning of a written report is to
   A. ascertain what necessary information is readily available in the files
   B. outline the methods you will employ to get the necessary information
   C. determine the objectives and uses of the report
   D. estimate the time and cost required to complete the report

8. In writing a report, the practice of taking up the least important points and the most important points last is a
   A. *good* technique since the final points made in a report will make the greatest impression on the reader
   B. *good* technique since the material is presented in a more logical manner and will lead directly to the conclusions
   C. *poor* technique since the reader's time is wasted by having to review irrelevant information before finishing the report
   D. *poor* technique since it may cause the reader to lose interest in the report and arrive at incorrect conclusions about the report

3 (#1)

9. Which one of the following serves as the BEST guideline for you to follow for effective written reports?
Keep sentences
   A. short and limit sentences to one thought
   B. short and use as many thoughts as possible
   C. long and limit sentences to one thought
   D. long and use as many thoughts as possible

9.____

10. One method by which a supervisor might prepare written reports to management is to begin with the conclusions, results, or summary, and to follow this with the supporting data.
The BEST reason why management may *prefer* this form of report is that
   A. management lacks the specific training to understand the data
   B. the data completely supports the conclusions
   C. time is saved by getting to the conclusions of the report first
   D. the data contains all the information that is required for making the conclusions

10.____

11. When making written reports, it is MOST important that they be
   A. well-worded   B. accurate as to the facts
   C. brief   D. submitted immediately

11.____

12. Of the following, the MOST important reason for a supervisor to prepare good written reports is that
   A. a supervisor is rated on the quality of his reports
   B. decisions are often made on the basis of the reports
   C. such reports take less time for superiors to review
   D. such reports demonstrate efficiency of department operations

12.____

13. Of the following, the BEST test of a good report is whether it
   A. provides the information needed
   B. shows the good sense of the writer
   C. is prepared according to a proper format
   D. is grammatical and neat

13.____

14. When a supervisor writes a report, he can BEST show that he has a understanding of the subject of the report by
   A. including necessary facts and omitting nonessential details
   B. using statistical data
   C. giving his conclusions but not the data on which they are based
   D. using a technical vocabulary

14.____

15. Suppose you and another supervisor on the same level are assigned to work together on a report. You disagree strongly with one of the recommendations the other supervisor wants to include in the report but you cannot change his views.

15.____

167

Of the following, it would be BEST that
- A. you refuse to accept responsibility for the report
- B. you ask that someone else be assigned to this project to replace you
- C. each of you state his own ideas about this recommendation in the report
- D. you give in to the other supervisor's opinion for the sake of harmony

16. Standardized forms are often provided for submitting reports.
Of the following, the MOST important advantage of using standardized forms for reports is that
- A. they take less time to prepare than individually written reports
- B. the person making the report can omit information he considers unimportant
- C. the responsibility for preparing these reports can be turned over to subordinates
- D. necessary information is less likely to be omitted

16._____

17. A report which may BEST be classed as a *periodic* report is one which
- A. requires the same type of information at regular intervals
- B. contains detailed information which is to be retained in permanent records
- C. is prepared whenever a special situation occurs
- D. lists information in graphic form

17._____

18. In the writing of reports or letters, the ideas presented in a paragraph are usually of unequal importance and require varying degrees of emphasis.
All of the following are methods of placing extra stress on an idea EXCEPT
- A. repeating it in a number of forms
- B. placing it in the middle of the paragraph
- C. placing it either at the beginning or at the end of a paragraph
- D. underlining it

18._____

Questions 19-25.

DIRECTIONS: Questions 19 through 25 concern the subject of report writing and are based on the information and incidents described in the following paragraph. (In answering these questions, assume that the facts and incidents in the paragraph are true.)

On December 15, at 8 A.M., seven Laborers reported to Foreman Joseph Meehan in the Greenbranch Yard in Queens. Meehan instructed the men to load some 50-pound boxes of books on a truck for delivery to an agency building in Brooklyn. Meehan told the men that, because the boxes were rather heavy, two men should work together, helping each other lift and load each box. Since Michael Harper, one of the Laborers, was without a partner, Meehan helped him with the boxes for a while. When Meehan was called to the telephone in a nearby building, however, Harper decided to lift a box himself. He appeared able to lift the box, but, as he got the box halfway up, he cried out that he had a sharp pain in his back. Another Laborer, Jorge Ortiz, who was passing by, ran over to help Harper put the box down. Harper suddenly dropped the box, which fell on Ortiz' right foot. By this time, Meehan had come out of the building. He immediately helped get the box off Ortiz' foot and had both men lie down. Meehan covered the men with blankets and called an ambulance, which arrived a half hour later. At the hospital, the doctor said that the X-ray results showed that Ortiz' right foot was broken in three places.

19. What would be the BEST term to use in a report describing the injury of Jorge Ortiz?
    A. Strain　　B. Fracture　　C. Hernia　　D. Hemorrhage

    19._____

20. Which of the following would be the MOST accurate summary for the Foreman to put in his report of the incident?
    A. Ortiz attempted to help Harper carry a box which was too heavy for one person, but Harper dropped it before Ortiz got there.
    B. Ortiz tried to help Harper carry a box but Harper got a pain in his back and accidentally dropped the box on Ortiz' foot.
    C. Harper refused to follow Meehan's orders and lifted a box too heavy for him; he deliberately dropped it when Ortiz tried to help him carry it.
    D. Harper lifted a box and felt a pain in his back; Ortiz tried to help Harper put the box down but Harper accidentally dropped it on Ortiz' foot.

    20._____

21. One of the Laborers at the scene of the accident was asked his version of the incident.
    Which information obtained from this witness would be LEAST important for including in the accident report?
    A. His opinion as to the cause of the accident
    B. How much of the accident he saw
    C. His personal opinion of the victims
    D. His name and address

    21._____

22. What should be the MAIN objective of writing a report about the incident described in the above paragraph? To
    A. describe the important elements in the accident situation
    B. recommend that such Laborers as Ortiz be advised not to interfere in another's work unless given specific instructions
    C. analyze the problems occurring when there are not enough workers to perform a certain task
    D. illustrate the hazards involved in performing routine everyday tasks

    22._____

23. Which of the following is information *missing* from the above passage but which *should* be included in a report of the incident? The
    A. name of the Laborer's immediate supervisor
    B. contents of the boxes
    C. time at which the accident occurred
    D. object or action that caused the injury to Ortiz' foot

    23._____

24. According to the description of the incident, the accident occurred because
    A. Ortiz attempted to help Harper who resisted his help
    B. Harper failed to follow instructions given him by Meehan
    C. Meehan was not supervising his men as closely as he should have
    D. Harper was not strong enough to carry the box once he lifted it

    24._____

25. Which of the following is MOST important for a foreman to avoid when writing up an official accident report?
    A. Using technical language to describe equipment involved in the accident
    B. Putting in details which might later be judged unnecessary
    C. Giving an opinion as to conditions that contributed to the accident
    D. Recommending discipline for employees who, in his opinion, caused the accident

KEY (CORRECT ANSWERS)

1.	B		11.	B
2.	C		12.	B
3.	A		13.	A
4.	B		14.	A
5.	B		15.	C
6.	D		16.	D
7.	C		17.	A
8.	D		18.	B
9.	A		19.	B
10.	C		20.	D

21. C
22. A
23. C
24. B
25. D

TEST 2

DIRECTIONS: Each question or incomplete statement is followed by several suggested answers or completions. Select the one that BEST answers the question or completes the statement. *PRINT THE LETTER OF THE CORRECT ANSWER IN THE SPACE AT THE RIGHT.*

1. Lieutenant X is preparing a report to submit to his commanding officer in order to get approval of a plan of operation he has developed.
   The report starts off with the statement of the problem and continues with the details of the problem. It contains factual information gathered with the help of field and operational personnel. It contains a final conclusion and recommendation for action. The recommendation is supplemented by comments from other precinct staff members on how the recommendations will affect their areas of responsibility. The report also includes directives and general orders ready for the commanding officer's signature. In addition, it has two statements of objections presented by two precinct staff members.
   Which one of the following, if any, is either an item that Lieutenant X should have included in his report and which is not mentioned above, or is an item which Lieutenant X improperly did include in his report?
   A. Considerations of alternative courses of action and their consequences should have been covered in the report.
   B. The additions containing undocumented objections to the recommended course of action should not have been included as part of the report.
   C. A statement on the qualifications of Lieutenant X, which would support his expertness in the field under consideration, should have been included in the report.
   D. The directives and general orders should not have been prepared and included in the report until the commanding officer had approved the recommendations.
   E. None of the above, since Lieutenant X's report was both proper and complete.

2. During a visit to a section, the district supervisor criticizes the method being used by the assistant foreman to prepare a certain report and orders him to modify the method. This change ordered by the district supervisor is in direct conflict with the specific orders of the foreman.
   In this situation, it would be BEST for the assistant foreman to
   A. change the method and tell the foreman about the change at the first opportunity
   B. change the method and rely on the district supervisor to notify the foreman
   C. report the matter to the foreman and delay the preparation of the report
   D. ask the district supervisor to discuss the matter with the foreman but use the old method for the time being

3. A department officer should realize that the MOST usual reason for writing a report is to
   A. give orders and follow up their execution
   B. establish a permanent record
   C. raise questions
   D. supply information

3._____

4. A very important report which is being prepared by a department officer will soon be due on the desk of the district supervisor. No typing help is available at this time for the officer.
   For the officer to write out this report in longhand in such a situation would be
   A. *bad*; such a report would not make the impression a typed report would
   B. *good*; it is important to get the report in on time
   C. *bad*; the district supervisor should not be required to read longhand reports
   D. *good*; it would call attention to the difficult conditions under which this section must work

4._____

5. In a well-written report, the length of each paragraph in the report should be
   A. varied according to the content
   B. not over 300 words
   C. pretty nearly the same
   D. gradually longer as the report is developed and written

5._____

6. A clerk in the headquarters office complains to you about the way in which you are filing out a certain report.
   It would be BEST for you to
   A. tell the clerk that you are following official procedures in filling out the report
   B. ask to be referred to the clerk's superior
   C. ask the clerk exactly what is wrong with the way in which you are filling out the report
   D. tell the clerk that you are following the directions of the district supervisor

6._____

7. The use of an outline to help in writing a report is
   A. *desirable*, in order to insure good organization and coverage
   B. *necessary*, so it can be used as an introduction to the report itself
   C. *undesirable*, since it acts as a straightjacket and may result in an unbalanced report
   D. *desirable*, if you know your immediate supervisor reads reports with extreme care and attention

7._____

8. It is advisable that a department officer do his paper work and report writing as soon as he has completed an inspection MAINLY because
   A. there are usually deadlines to be met
   B. it insures a steady work-flow
   C. he may not have time for this later
   D. the facts are then freshest in his mind

8._____

9. Before you turn in a report you have written of an investigation that you have made, you discover some additional information you didn't know about before. Whether or not you re-write the report to include this additional information should depend MAINLY on the
    A. amount of time remaining before the report is due
    B. established policy of the department covering the subject matter of the report
    C. bearing this information will have on the conclusions of the report
    D. number of people who will eventually review the report

10. When a supervisory officer submits a periodic report to the district supervisor, he should realize that the CHIEF importance of such a report is that it
    A. is the principal method of checking on the efficiency of the supervisor and his subordinates
    B. is something to which frequent reference will be made
    C. eliminates the need for any personal follow-up or inspection by higher echelons
    D. permits the district supervisor to exercise his functions of direction, supervision, and control better

11. Conclusions and recommendations are usually placed at the end rather than at the beginning of a report because
    A. the person preparing the report may decide to change some of the conclusions and recommendations before he reaches the end of the report
    B. they are the most important part of the report
    C. they can be judged better by the person to whom the report is sent after he reads the facts and investigators which come earlier in the report
    D. they can be referred to quickly when needed without reading the rest of the report

12. The use of the same method of record-keeping and reporting by all agency sections is
    A. *desirable*, MAINLY because it saves time in section operations
    B. *undesirable*, MAINLY because it kills the initiative of the individual section foreman
    C. *desirable*, MAINLY because it will be easier for the administrator to evaluate and compare section operations
    D. *undesirable*, MAINLY because operations vary from section to section and uniform record-keeping and reporting is not appropriate

13. The GREATEST benefit the section officer will have from keeping complete and accurate records and reports of section operations is that
    A. he will find it easier to run his section efficiently
    B. he will need less equipment
    C. he will need less manpower
    D. the section will run smoothly when he is out

4 (#2)

14. You have prepared a report to your superior and are ready to send it forward. But on re-reading it, you think some parts are not clearly expressed and your superior ay have difficulty getting your point.
Of the following, it would be BEST for you to
    A. give the report to one of your men to read, and if he has no trouble understanding it send it through
    B. forward the report and call your superior the next day to ask whether it was all right
    C. forward the report as is; higher echelons should be able to understand any report prepared by a section officer
    D. do the report over, re-writing the sections you are in doubt about

14.____

15. The BEST of the following statements concerning reports is that
    A. a carelessly written report may give the reader an impression of inaccuracy
    B. correct grammar and English are unimportant if the main facts are given
    C. every man should be required to submit a daily work report
    D. the longer and more wordy a report is, the better it will read

15.____

16. In writing a report, the question of whether or not to include certain material could be determined BEST by considering the
    A. amount of space the material will occupy in the report
    B. amount of time to be spent in gathering the material
    C. date of the material
    D. value of the material to the superior who will read the report

16.____

17. Suppose you are submitting a fairly long report to your superior.
The one of the following sections that should come FIRST in this report is a
    A. description of how you gathered material
    B. discussion of possible objections to your recommendations
    C. plan of how your recommendations can be put into practice
    D. statement of the problem dealt with

17.____

Questions 18-20.

DIRECTIONS: A foreman is asked to write a report on the incident described in the following passage. Answer Questions 18 through 20 based on the following information.

On March 10, Henry Moore, a laborer, was in the process of transferring some equipment from the machine shop to the third floor. He was using a dolly to perform this task and, as he was wheeling the material through the machine shop, laborer Bob Greene called to him. As Henry turned to respond to Bob, he jammed the dolly into Larry Mantell's leg, knocking Larry down in the process and causing the heavy drill that Larry was holding to fall on Larry's foot. Larry started rubbing his foot and then, infuriated, jumped up and punched Henry in the jaw. The force of the blow drove Henry's head back against the wall. Henry did not fight back; he appeared to be dazed. An ambulance was called to take Henry to the hospital, and the ambulance attendant told the foreman that it appeared likely that Henry had suffered a concussion. Larry's injuries consisted of some bruises, but he refused medical attention.

18. An adequate report of the above incident should give as minimum information the names of the persons involved, the names of the witnesses, the date and the time that each event took place, and the   18._____
    A. names of the ambulance attendants
    B. names of all the employees working in the machine shop
    C. location where the accident occurred
    D. nature of the previous safety training each employee had been given

19. The only one of the following which is NOT a fact is   19._____
    A. Bob called to Henry
    B. Larry suffered a concussion
    C. Larry rubbed his foot
    D. the incident took place in the machine shop

20. Which of the following would be the MOST accurate summary of the incident for the foreman to put in his report of the accident?   20._____
    A. Larry Mantell punched Henry Moore because a drill fell on his foot and he was angry. Then Henry fell and suffered a concussion.
    B. Henry Moore accidentally jammed a dolly into Larry Mantell's foot, knocking Larry down. Larry punched Henry, pushing him into the wall and causing him to bang his head against the wall.
    C. Bob Greene called Henry Moore. A dolly than jammed into Larry Mantell and knocked him down. Larry punched Henry who tripped and suffered some bruises. An ambulance was called.
    D. A drill fell on Larry Mantell's foot. Larry jumped up suddenly and punched Henry Moore and pushed him into the wall. Henry may have suffered a concussion as a result of falling.

Questions 21-25.

DIRECTIONS: Questions 21 through 25 are to be answered ONLY on the basis of the information provided in the following passage.

A written report is a communication of information from one person to another. It is an account of some matter especially investigated, however routine that matter may be. The ultimate basis of any good written report is facts, which become known through observation and verification. Good written reports may seem to be no more than general ideas and opinions. However, in such cases, the facts leading to these opinions were gathered, verified, and reported earlier, and the opinions are dependent upon these facts. Good style, proper form, and emphasis cannot make a good written report out of unreliable information and bad judgment; but, on the other hand, solid investigation and brilliant thinking are not likely to become very useful until they are effectively communicated to others. If a person's work calls for written reports, then his work is often no better than his written reports.

21. Based on the information in the above passage, it can be concluded that opinions expressed in a report should be
    A. based on facts which are gathered and reported
    B. emphasized repeatedly when they result from a special investigation
    C. kept to a minimum
    D. separated from the body of the report

21.____

22. In the above passage, the one of the following which is mentioned as a way of establishing facts is
    A. authority
    B. communication
    C. reporting
    D. verification

22.____

23. According to the above passage, the characteristic shared by ALL written reports is that they are
    A. accounts of routine matters
    B. transmissions of information
    C. reliable and logical
    D. written in proper form

23.____

24. Which of the following conclusions can logically be drawn from the information given in the above passage?
    A. Brilliant thinking can make up for unreliable information in a report.
    B. One method of judging an individual's work is the quality of the written reports he is required to submit.
    C. Proper form and emphasis can make a good report out of unreliable information.
    D. Good written reports that seem to be no more than general ideas should be rewritten.

24.____

25. Which of the following suggested titles would be MOST appropriate for this passage?
    A. Gathering and Organizing Facts
    B. Techniques of Observation
    C. Nature and Purpose of Reports
    D. Reports and Opinions: Differences and Similarities

25.____

KEY (CORRECT ANSWERS)

1.	A		11.	C
2.	A		12.	C
3.	D		13.	A
4.	B		14.	D
5.	A		15.	A
6.	C		16.	D
7.	A		17.	D
8.	D		18.	C
9.	C		19.	B
10.	D		20.	B

21. A
22. D
23. B
24. B
25. C

TEST 3

DIRECTIONS: Each question or incomplete statement is followed by several suggested answers or completions. Select the one that BEST answers the question or completes the statement. *PRINT THE LETTER OF THE CORRECT ANSWER IN THE SPACE AT THE RIGHT.*

Questions 1-5.

DIRECTIONS: The following is an accident report similar to those used in departments for reporting accidents. Questions 1 through 5 are be answered using ONLY the information given in this report.

ACCIDENT REPORT

FROM: John Doe	DATE OF REPORT: June 23	
TITLE: Sanitation Worker		
DATE OF ACCIDENT: June 22 time 3 AM PM	CITY: Metropolitan	
PLACE: 1489 Third Avenue		
VEHICLE NO. 1	VEHICLE NO. 2	
OPERATOR: John Doe, Sanitation Worker Title	OPERATOR: Richard Roe	
VEHICLE CODE NO: 14-238	ADDRESS: 498 High Street	
LICENSE NO.: 0123456	OWNER: Henry Roe ADDRESS:786 E.83 St.	LIC. NO.: 5N1492
DESCRIPTION OF ACCIDENT: Light green Chevrolet sedan while trying to pass drove in to rear side of sanitation truck which had stopped to collect garbage. No one was injured but there was property damage.		
NATURE OF DAMAGE TO PRIVATE VEHICLE: Right front fender crushed, bumper bent		
DAMAGE TO CITY VEHICLE: Front of left rear fender pushed in. Paint scraped.		
NAME OF WITNESS: Frank Brown	ADDRESS: 48 Kingsway	
SIGNATURE OF PERSON MAKING THIS REPORT *John Doe*	BADGE NO.: 428	

1. Of the following, the one which has been omitted from this accident report is the   1.____
   A. location of the accident
   B. drivers of the vehicles involved
   C. traffic situation at the time of the accident
   D. owners of the vehicles involved

2. The address of the driver of Vehicle No. 1 is not required because he   2.____
   A. is employed by the department   B. is not the owner of the vehicle
   C. reported the accident   D. was injured in the accident

3. The report indicates that the driver of Vehicle No. 2 was PROBABLY   3.____
   A. passing on the wrong side of the truck
   B. not wearing his glasses
   C. not injured in the accident
   D driving while intoxicated

178

4. The number of people *specifically* referred to in this report is 4.____
   A. 3   B. 4   C. 5   D. 6

5. The license number of Vehicle No. 1 is 5.____
   A. 428   B. 5N1492   C. 14-238   D. 0123456

6. In a report of unlawful entry into department premises, it is LEAST important to include the 6.____
   A. estimated value of the property missing
   B. general description of the premises
   C. means used to get into the premises
   D. time and date of entry

7. In a report of an accident, it is LEAST important to include the 7.____
   A. name of the insurance company of the person injured in the accident
   B. probable cause of the accident
   C. time and place of the accident
   D. names and addresses of all witnesses of the accident

8. Of the following, the one which is NOT required in the preparation of a weekly functional expense report is the 8.____
   A. hourly distribution of the time by proper heading in accordance with the actual work performed
   B. signatures of officers not involved in the preparation of the report
   C. time records of the men who appear on the payroll of the respective locations
   D. time records of men working in other districts assigned to this location

KEY (CORRECT ANSWERS)

1. C   5. D
2. A   6. B
3. C   7. A
4. B   8. B

PREPARING WRITTEN MATERIAL

EXAMINATION SECTION

TEST 1

DIRECTIONS: Each question consists of a sentence which may or may not be an example of good English usage. Examine each sentence, considering grammar, punctuation, spelling, capitalization, and awkwardness. Then choose the correct statement about it from the four choices below it. If the English usage in the sentence given is better than any of the changes suggested in choices B, C, or D, pick choice A. (Do not pick a choice that will change the meaning of the sentence.) *PRINT THE LETTER OF THE CORRECT ANSWER IN THE SPACE AT THE RIGHT.*

1. We attended a staff conference on Wednesday the new safety and fire rules were discussed.
   A. This is an example of acceptable writing.
   B. The words "safety," "fire," and "rules" should begin with capital letters.
   C. There should be a comma after the word "Wednesday."
   D. There should be a period after the word "Wednesday" and the word "the" should begin with a capital letter.

2. Neither the dictionary or the telephone directory could be found in the office library.
   A. This is an example of acceptable writing.
   B. The word "or" should be changed to "nor."
   C. The word "library" should be spelled "libery."
   D. The word "neither" should be changed to "either."

3. The report would have been typed correctly if the typist could read the draft.
   A. This is an example of acceptable writing.
   B. The word "would" should be removed.
   C. The word "have" should be inserted after the word "could."
   D. The word "correctly" should be changed to "correct."

4. The supervisor brought the reports and forms to an employees desk.
   A. This is an example of acceptable writing.
   B. The word "brought" should be changed to "took."
   C. There should be a comma after the word "reports" and a comma after the word "forms."
   D. The word "employees" should be spelled "employee's."

5. It's important for all the office personnel to submit their vacation schedules on time.
   A. This is an example of acceptable writing.
   B. The word "It's" should be spelled "Its."
   C. The word "their" should be spelled "they're."
   D. The word "personnel" should be spelled "personal."

6. The report, along with the accompanying documents, were submitted for review.
   A. This is an example of acceptable writing.
   B. The words "were submitted" should be changed to "was submitted."
   C. The word "accompanying" should be spelled "accompaning."
   D. The comma after the word "report" should be taken out.

7. If others must use your files, be certain that they understand how the system works, but insist that you do all the filing and refiling.
   A. This is an example of acceptable writing.
   B. There should be a period after the word "works," and the word "but" should start a new sentence.
   C. The words "filing" and "refiling" should be spelled "fileing" and "refileing."
   D. There should be a comma after the word "but."

8. The appeal was not considered because of its late arrival.
   A. This is an example of acceptable writing.
   B. The word "its" should be changed to "it's."
   C. The word "its" should be changed to "the."
   D. The words "late arrival" should be changed to "arrival late."

9. The letter must be read carefuly to determine under which subject it should be filed.
   A. This is an example of acceptable writing.
   B. The word "under" should be changed to "at."
   C. The word "determine" should be spelled "determin."
   D. The word "carefuly" should be spelled "carefully."

10. He showed potential as an office manager, but he lacked skill in delegating work.
    A. This is an example of acceptable writing.
    B. The word "delegating" should be spelled "delagating."
    C. The word "potential" should be spelled "potencial."
    D. The words "he lacked" should be changed to "was lacking."

KEY (CORRECT ANSWERS)

1.	D	6.	B
2.	B	7.	A
3.	C	8.	A
4.	D	9.	D
5.	A	10.	A

TEST 2

DIRECTIONS: Each question consists of a sentence which may or may not be an example of good English usage. Examine each sentence, considering grammar, punctuation, spelling, capitalization, and awkwardness. Then choose the correct statement about it from the four choices below it. If the English usage in the sentence given is better than any of the changes suggested in choices B, C, or D, pick choice A. (Do not pick a choice that will change the meaning of the sentence.) *PRINT THE LETTER OF THE CORRECT ANSWER IN THE SPACE AT THE RIGHT.*

1. The supervisor wants that all staff members report to the office at 9:00 A.M. 1.____
    A. This is an example of acceptable writing.
    B. The word "that" should be removed and the word "to" should be inserted after the word "members."
    C. There should be a comma after the word "wants" and a comma after the word "office."
    D. The word "wants" should be changed to "want" and the word "shall" should be inserted after the word "members."

2. Every morning the clerk opens the office mail and distributes it. 2.____
    A. This is an example of acceptable writing.
    B. The word "opens" should be changed to "open."
    C. The word "mail" should be changed to "letters."
    D. The word "it" should be changed to "them."

3. The secretary typed more fast on a desktop computer than on a laptop computer. 3.____
    A. This is an example of acceptable writing.
    B. The words "more fast" should be changed to "faster."
    C. There should be a comma after the words "desktop computer."
    D. The word "than" should be changed to "then."

4. The new stenographer needed a desk a computer, a chair and a blotter. 4.____
    A. This is an example of acceptable writing.
    B. The word "blotter" should be spelled "blodder."
    C. The word "stenographer" should begin with a capital letter.
    D. There should be a comma after the word "desk."

5. The recruiting officer said, "There are many different goverment jobs available." 5.____
    A. This is an example of acceptable writing.
    B. The word "There" should not be capitalized.
    C. The word "government" should be spelled "government."
    D. The comma after the word "said" should be removed.

6. He can recommend a mechanic whose work is reliable. 6.____
    A. This is an example of acceptable writing.
    B. The word "reliable" should be spelled "relyable."
    C. The word "whose" should be spelled "who's."
    D. The word "mechanic should be spelled "mecanic."

183

7. She typed quickly; like someone who had not a moment to lose.   7._____
    A. This is an example of acceptable writing.
    B. The word "not" should be removed.
    C. The semicolon should be changed to a comma.
    D. The word "quickly" should be placed before instead of after the word "typed."

8. She insisted that she had to much work to do.   8._____
    A. This is an example of acceptable writing.
    B. The word "insisted" should be spelled "incisted."
    C. The word "to" used in front of "much" should be spelled "too."
    D. The word "do" should be changed to "be done."

9. He excepted praise from his supervisor for a job well done.   9._____
    A. This is an example of acceptable writing.
    B. The word "excepted" should be spelled "accepted."
    C. The order of the words "well done" should be changed to "done well."
    D. There should be a comma after the word "supervisor."

10. What appears to be intentional errors in grammar occur several times in the passage.   10._____
    A. This is an example of acceptable writing.
    B. The word "occur" should be spelled "occurr."
    C. The word "appears" should be changed to "appear."
    D. The phrase "several times" should be changed to "from time to time."

KEY (CORRECT ANSWERS)

1.	B	6.	A
2.	A	7.	C
3.	B	8.	C
4.	D	9.	B
5.	C	10.	C

TEST 3

DIRECTIONS: Each question consists of a sentence which may or may not be an example of good English usage. Examine each sentence, considering grammar, punctuation, spelling, capitalization, and awkwardness. Then choose the correct statement about it from the four choices below it. If the English usage in the sentence given is better than any of the changes suggested in choices B, C, or D, pick choice A. (Do not pick a choice that will change the meaning of the sentence.) *PRINT THE LETTER OF THE CORRECT ANSWER IN THE SPACE AT THE RIGHT.*

1. The clerk could have completed the assignment on time if he knows where these materials were located.
    A. This is an example of acceptable writing.
    B. The word "knows" should be replaced by "had known."
    C. The word "were" should be replaced by "had been."
    D. The words "where these materials were located" should be replaced by "the location of these materials."

1.____

2. All employees should be given safety training. Not just those who accidents.
    A. This is an example of acceptable writing.
    B. The period after the word "training" should be changed to a colon.
    C. The period after the word "training" should be changed to a semicolon, and the first letter of the word "Not" should be changed to a small "n."
    D. The period after the word "training" should be changed to a comma, and the first letter of the word "Not" should be changed to a small "n."

2.____

3. This proposal is designed to promote employee awareness of the suggestion program, to encourage employee participation in the program, and to increase the number of suggestions submitted.
    A. This is an example of acceptable writing.
    B. The word "proposal" should be spelled "proposal."
    C. The words "to increase the number of suggestions submitted" should be changed to "an increase in the number of suggestions is expected."
    D. The word "promote" should be changed to "enhance" and the word "increase" should be changed to "add to."

3.____

4. The introduction of inovative managerial techniques should be preceded by careful analysis of the specific circumstances and conditions in each department.
    A. This is an example of acceptable writing.
    B. The word "technique" should be spelled "techneques."
    C. The word "inovative" should be spelled "innovative."
    D. A comma should be placed after the word "circumstances" and after the word "conditions."

4.____

185

5. This occurrence indicates that such criticism embarrasses him. 5._____
    A. This is an example of acceptable writing.
    B. The word "occurrence" should be spelled "occurence."
    C. The word "criticism" should be spelled "critisism.
    D. The word "embarrasses" should be spelled "embarasses.

KEY (CORRECT ANSWERS)

1. B
2. D
3. A
4. C
5. A

PREPARING WRITTEN MATERIAL
EXAMINATION SECTION
TEST 1

DIRECTIONS: Each question or incomplete statement is followed by several suggested answers or completions. Select the one that BEST answers the question or completes the statement. *PRINT THE LETTER OF THE CORRECT ANSWER IN THE SPACE AT THE RIGHT.*

Questions 1-4.

DIRECTIONS: Questions 1 through 4 each consist of a sentence which may or may not be an example of good English. The underlined parts of each sentence may be correct or incorrect. Examine each sentence, considering grammar, punctuation, spelling, and capitalization. If the English usage in the underlined parts of the sentence given is better than any of the changes in the underlined words suggested in options B, C, or D, choose option A. If the changes in the underlined words suggested in options B, C, or D would make the sentence correct, choose the correct option. Do not choose an option that will change the meaning of the sentence.

1. This Fall, the office will be closed on Columbus Day, October 9th.   1._____
   A. Correct as is
   B. fall...Columbus Day; October
   C. Fall...columbus day, October
   D. fall...Columbus Day – October

2. There weren't no paper in the supply closet.   2._____
   A. Correct as is
   B. weren't any
   C. wasn't any
   D. wasn't no

3. The alphabet, or A to Z sequence are the basis of most filing systems.   3._____
   A. Correct as is
   B. alphabet, or A to Z sequence, is
   C. alphabet, or A to Z sequence, are
   D. alphabet, or A too Z sequence, is

4. The Office Aide checked the register and finding the date of the meeting.   4._____
   A. Correct as is
   B. regaster and finding
   C. register and found
   D. regaster and found

Questions 5-10.

DIRECTIONS: Questions 5 through 10 consist of sentences which contain examples of correct or incorrect English usage. Examine each sentence with reference to grammar, spelling, punctuation, and capitalization. Chooses one of the following options that would be BEST for correct English usage:

187

2 (#1)

   A. The sentence is correct
   B. There is one mistake
   C. There are two mistakes
   D. There are three mistakes

5. Mrs. Fitzgerald came to the 59th Precinct to retreive her property which were stolen earlier in the week.   5.____

6. The two officer's responded to the call, only to find that the perpatrator and the victim have left the scene.   6.____

7. Mr. Coleman called the 61st Precinct to report that, upon arriving at his store, he discovered that there was a large hole in the wall and that three boxes of radios were missing.   7.____

8. The Administrative Leiutenant of the 62nd Precinct held a meeting which was attended by all the civilians, assigned to the Precinct.   8.____

9. Three days after the robbery occurred the detective apprahended two suspects and recovered the stolen items.   9.____

10. The Community Affairs Officer of the 64th Precinct is the liaison between the Precinct and the community; he works closely with various community organizations, and elected officials,   10.____

Questions 11-18.

DIRECTIONS: Questions 11 through 18 are to be answered on the basis of the following paragraph, which contains some deliberate errors in spelling and/or grammar and/or punctuation. Each line of the paragraph is preceded by a number. There are 9 lines and 9 numbers.

Line No.	Paragraph Line
1	The protection of life and proporty are, one of
2	the oldest and most important functions of a city.
3	New York City has it's own full-time police Agency.
4	The police Department has the power an it shall
5	be there duty to preserve the Public piece,
6	prevent crime detect and arrest offenders, supress
7	riots, protect the rites of persons and property, etc.
8	The maintainance of sound relations with the community they
9	serve is an important function of law enforcement officers

11. How many errors are contained in line one?   11.____

12. How many errors are contained in line two?   12.____

13. How many errors are contained in line three?   13.____

14. How many errors are contained in line four? 14._____

15. How many errors are contained in line five? 15._____

16. How many errors are contained in line six? 16._____

17. How many errors are contained in line seven? 17._____

18. How many errors are contained in line eight? 18._____

19. In the sentence, *The candidate wants to file his application for preference before it is too late*, the word *before* is used as a(n) 19._____
    A. preposition   B. subordinating conjunction
    C. pronoun   D. adverb

20. The one of the following sentences which is grammatically PREFERABLE to the others is: 20._____
    A. Our engineers will go over your blueprints so that you may have no problems in construction.
    B. For a long time he had been arguing that we, not he, are to blame for the confusion.
    C. I worked on this automobile for two hours and still cannot find out what is wrong with it.
    D. Accustomed to all kinds of hardships, fatigue seldom bothers veteran policemen.

KEY (CORRECT ANSWERS)

1.	A	11.	C
2.	C	12.	D
3.	B	13.	C
4.	C	14.	B
5.	C	15.	C
6.	D	16.	B
7.	A	17.	A
8.	C	18.	A
9.	C	19.	B
10.	B	20.	A

TEST 2

DIRECTIONS: Each question or incomplete statement is followed by several suggested answers or completions. Select the one that BEST answers the question or completes the statement. *PRINT THE LETTER OF THE CORRECT ANSWER IN THE SPACE AT THE RIGHT.*

1. The plural of
    A. turkey is turkies
    B. cargo is cargoes
    C. bankruptcy is bankruptcys
    D. son-in-law is son-in-laws

    1.____

2. The abbreviation *viz.* means MOST NEARLY
    A. namely   B. for example   C. the following   D. see

    2.____

3. In the sentence, *A man in a light-grey suit waited thirty-five minutes in the ante-room for the all-important document,* the word IMPROPERLY hyphenated is
    A. light-grey   B. thirty-five   C. ante-room   D. all-important

    3.____

4. The MOST accurate of the following sentences is:
    A. The commissioner, as well as his deputy and various bureau heads, were present.
    B. A new organization of employers and employees have been formed.
    C. One or the other of these men have been selected.
    D. The number of pages in the book is enough to discourage a reader.

    4.____

5. The MOST accurate of the following sentences is:
    A. Between you and me, I think he is the better man.
    B. He was believed to be me.
    C. Is it us that you wish to see?
    D. The winners are him and her.

    5.____

Questions 6-13.

DIRECTIONS: The sentences numbered 6 through 13 deal with some phase of police activity. They may be classified most appropriately under one of the following four categories.

    A. Faulty because of incorrect grammar
    B. Faulty because of incorrect punctuation
    C. Faulty because of incorrect use of a word
    D. Correct

Examine each sentence carefully. Then, in the space at the right, print the capital letter preceding the option which is the BEST of the four suggested above. All incorrect sentences contain only one type of error. Consider a sentence correct if it contains none of the types of errors mentioned, even though there may be other correct ways of expressing the same thought.

2 (#2)

6. The Department Medal of Honor is awarded to a member of the Police Force who distinguishes himself inconspicuously in the line of police duty by the performance of an act of gallantry.

6._____

7. Members of the Detective Division are charged with the prevention of crime, the detection and arrest of criminals and the recovery of lost or stolen property,

7._____

8. Detectives are selected from the uniformed patrol forces after they have indicated by conduct, aptitude and performance that they are qualified for the more intricate duties of a detective.

8._____

9. The patrolman, pursuing his assailant, exchanged shots with the gunman and immortally wounded him as he fled into a nearby building.

9._____

10. The members of the Traffic Division has to enforce the Vehicle and Traffic Law, the Traffic Regulations and ordinances relating to vehicular and pedestrian traffic.

10._____

11. After firing a shot at the gunman, the crowd dispersed from the patrolman's line of fire.

11._____

12. The efficiency of the Missing Persons Bureau is maintained with a maximum of public personnel due to the specialized training given to its members.

12._____

13. Records of persons arrested for violations of Vehicle and Traffic Regulations are transmitted upon request to precincts, courts and other authorized agencies.

13._____

14. Following are two sentences which may or may not be written in correct English:
    I. Two clients assaulted the officer.
    II. The van is illegally parked.
    Which one of the following statements is CORRECT?
    A. Only Sentence I is written in correct English.
    B. Only Sentence II is written in correct English.
    C. Sentences I and II are both written in correct English.
    D. Neither Sentence I nor Sentence II is written in correct English.

14._____

15. Following are two sentences which may or may not be written in correct English:
    I. Security Officer Rollo escorted the visitor to the patrolroom.
    II. Two entry were made in the facility logbook.
    Which one of the following statements is CORRECT?
    A. Only Sentence I is written in correct English.
    B. Only Sentence II is written in correct English.
    C. Sentences I and II are both written in correct English.
    D. Neither Sentence I nor Sentence II is written in correct English.

15._____

16. Following are two sentences which may or may not be written in correct English:
    I. Officer McElroy putted out a small fire in the wastepaper basket.
    II. Special Officer Janssen told the visitor where he could obtained a pass.
    Which one of the following statements is CORRECT?
    A. Only Sentence I is written in correct English.
    B. Only Sentence II is written in correct English.
    C. Sentences I and II are both written in correct English.
    D. Neither Sentence I nor Sentence II is written in correct English.

16.____

17. Following are two sentences which may or may not be written in correct English:
    I. Security Officer Warren observed a broken window while he was on his post in Hallway C.
    II. The worker reported that two typewriters had been stolen from the office,
    Which one of the following statements is CORRECT?
    A. Only Sentence I is written in correct English.
    B. Only Sentence II is written in correct English.
    C. Sentences I and II are both written in correct English.
    D. Neither Sentence I nor Sentence II is written in correct English,

17.____

18. Following are two sentences which may or may not be written in correct English:
    I. Special Officer Cleveland was attempting to calm an emotionally disturbed visitor.
    II. The visitor did not stop crying and calling for his wife.
    Which one of the following statements is CORRECT?
    A. Only Sentence I is written in correct English.
    B. Only Sentence II is written in correct English.
    C. Sentences I and II are both written in correct English.
    D. Neither Sentence I nor Sentence II is written in correct English.

18.____

19. Following are two sentences that may or may not be written in correct English:
    I. While on patrol, I observes a vagrant loitering near the drug dispensary.
    II. I escorted the vagrant out of the building and off the premises.
    Which one of the following statements is CORRECT?
    A. Only Sentence I is written in correct English.
    B. Only Sentence II is written in correct English.
    C. Sentences I and II are both written in correct English.
    D. Neither Sentence I nor Sentence II is written in correct English.

19.____

20. Following are two sentences which may or may not be written in correct English:
    I. At 4:00 P.M., Sergeant Raymond told me to evacuate the waiting area immediately due to a bomb threat.
    II. Some of the clients did not want to leave the building.
    Which one of the following statements is CORRECT?
    A. Only Sentence I is written in correct English.
    B. Only Sentence II is written in correct English.
    C. Sentences I and II are both written in correct English.
    D. Neither Sentence I nor Sentence II is written in correct English.

20.____

KEY (CORRECT ANSWERS)

1.	B	11.	A
2.	A	12.	C
3.	C	13.	D
4.	D	14.	C
5.	A	15.	A
6.	C	16.	D
7.	B	17.	A
8.	D	18.	A
9.	C	19.	B
10.	A	20.	C

PREPARING WRITTEN MATERIALS
EXAMINATION SECTION
TEST 1

DIRECTIONS: Each question consists of a sentence which may be classified appropriately under one of the following four categories:
- A. Incorrect because of faulty grammar or sentence structure.
- B. Incorrect because of faulty punctuation.
- C. Incorrect because of faulty spelling or capitalization.
- D. Correct

Examine each sentence carefully. Then, in the space at the right, print the capital letter preceding the option which is the BEST of the four suggested above. All incorrect sentences contain only one type of error. Consider a sentence correct if it contains none of the types of errors mentioned, although there may be other correct ways of expressing the same thought.

1. The fire apparently started in the storeroom, which is usually locked.   1._____
2. On approaching the victim two bruises were noticed by this officer.   2._____
3. The officer, who was there examined the report with great care.   3._____
4. Each employee in the office had a separate desk.   4._____
5. The suggested procedure is similar to the one now in use.   5._____
6. No one was more pleased with the new procedure than the chauffeur.   6._____
7. He tried to pursuade her to change the procedure.   7._____
8. The total of the expenses charged to petty cash were high.   8._____
9. An understanding between him and I was finally reached.   9._____
10. It was at the supervisor's request that the clerk agreed to postpone his vacation.   10._____
11. We do not believe that it is necessary for both he and the clerk to attend the conference.   11._____
12. All employees, who display perseverance, will be given adequate recognition.   12._____
13. He regrets that some of us employees are dissatisfied with our new assignments.   13._____

195

2 (#1)

14. "Do you think that the raise was merited," asked the supervisor? 14.____

15. The new manual of procedure is a valuable supplament to our rules and regulation. 15.____

16. The typist admitted that she had attempted to pursuade the other employees to assist her in her work. 16.____

17. The supervisor asked that all amendments to the regulations be handled by you and I. 17.____

18. They told both he and I that the prisoner had escaped. 18.____

19. Any superior officer, who, disregards the just complaints of his subordinates, is remiss in the performance of his duty. 19.____

20. Only those members of the national organization who resided in the Middle west attended the conference in Chicago. 20.____

21. We told him to give the investigation assignment to whoever was available. 21.____

22. Please do not disappoint and embarass us by not appearing in court. 22.____

23. Despite the efforts of the Supervising mechanic, the elevator could not be started. 23.____

24. The U.S. Weather Bureau, weather record for the accident date was checked. 24.____

KEY (CORRECT ANSWERS)

1.	D	11.	A
2.	A	12.	B
3.	B	13.	D
4.	D	14.	B
5.	D	15.	C
6.	D	16.	C
7.	C	17.	A
8.	A	18.	A
9.	A	19.	B
10.	D	20.	C

21.	D
22.	C
23.	C
24.	B

TEST 2

DIRECTIONS: Each question consists of a sentence. Some of the sentences contain errors in English grammar or usage, punctuation, spelling, or capitalization. A sentence does not contain an error simply because it could be written in a different manner. Choose answer:
- A. If the sentence contains an error in English grammar or usage.
- B. if the sentence contains an error in punctuation.
- C. If the sentence contains an error in spelling or capitalization
- D. If the sentence does not contain any errors.

1. The severity of the sentence prescribed by contemporary statutes—including both the former and the revised New York Penal Laws—do not depend on what crime was intended by the offender.

2. It is generally recognized that two defects in the early law of attempt played a part in the birth of burglary: (1) immunity from prosecution for conduct short of the last act before completion of the crime, and (2) the relatively minor penalty imposed for an attempt (it being a common law misdemeanor) vis-à-vis the completed offense.

3. The first sentence of the statute is applicable to employees who enter their place of employment, invited guests, and all other persons who have an express or implied license or privilege to enter the premises.

4. Contemporary criminal codes in the United States generally divide burglary into various degrees, differentiating the categories according to place, time and other attendent circumstances.

5. The assignment was completed in record time but the payroll for it has not yet been prepaid.

6. The operator, on the other hand, is willing to learn me how to use the mimeograph.

7. She is the prettiest of the three sisters.

8. She doesn't know; if the mail has arrived.

9. The doorknob of the office door is broke.

10. Although the department's supply of scratch pads and stationery have diminished considerably, the allotment for our division has not been reduced.

11. You have not told us whom you wish to designate as your secretary.

12. Upon reading the minutes of the last meeting, the new proposal was taken up for consideration.

2 (#2)

13. Before beginning the discussion, we locked the door as a precautionery measure.   13.____

14. The supervisor remarked, "Only those clerks, who perform routine work, are permitted to take a rest period."   14.____

15. Not only will this duplicating machine make accurate copies, but it will also produce a quantity of work equal to fifteen transcribing typists.   15.____

16. "Mr. Jones," said the supervisor, "we regret our inability to grant you an extention of your leave of absence."   16.____

17. Although the employees find the work monotonous and fatigueing, they rarely complain.   17.____

18. We completed the tabulation of the receipts on time despite the fact that Miss Smith our fastest operator was absent for over a week.   18.____

19. The reaction of the employees who attended the meeting, as well as the reaction of those who did not attend, indicates clearly that the schedule is satisfactory to everyone concerned.   19.____

20. Of the two employees, the one in our office is the most efficient.   20.____

21. No one can apply or even understand, the new rules and regulations.   21.____

22. A large amount of supplies were stored in the empty office.   22.____

23. If an employee is occassionally asked to work overtime, he should do so willingly.   23.____

24. It is true that the new procedures are difficult to use but, we are certain that you will learn them quickly.   24.____

25. The office manager said that he did not know who would be given a large allotment under the new plan.   25.____

KEY (CORRECT ANSWERS)

1.	A		11.	D
2.	D		12.	A
3.	D		13.	C
4.	C		14.	B
5.	C		15.	A
6.	A		16.	C
7.	D		17.	C
8.	B		18.	B
9.	A		19.	D
10.	A		20.	A

21. B
22. A
23. C
24. B
25. D

TEST 3

DIRECTIONS: Each of the following sentences may be classified MOST appropriately under one of the following categories:
A. Faulty because of incorrect grammar
B. Faulty because of incorrect punctuation
C. Faulty because of incorrect capitalization
D. Correct

Examine each sentence carefully. Then, in the space at the right, print the capital letter preceding the option which is the BEST of the four suggested above. All incorrect sentence contain but one type of error. Consider a sentence correct if it contains none of the types of errors mentioned, even though there may be other correct ways of expressing the same thought.

1. The desk, as well as the chairs, were moved out of the office. 1.____

2. The clerk whose production was greatest for the month won a day's vacation as first prize. 2.____

3. Upon entering the room, the employees were found hard at work at their desks. 3.____

4. John Smith our new employee always arrives at work on time. 4.____

5. Punish whoever is guilty of stealing the money. 5.____

6. Intelligent and persistent effort lead to success no matter what the job may be. 6.____

7. The secretary asked, "can you call again at three o'clock?" 7.____

8. He told us, that if the report was not accepted at the next meeting, it would have to be rewritten. 8.____

9. He would not have sent the letter if he had known that it would cause so much excitement. 9.____

10. We all looked forward to him coming to visit us. 10.____

11. If you find that you are unable to complete the assignment please notify me as soon as possible. 11.____

12. Every girl in the office went home on time but me; there was still some work for me to finish. 12.____

13. He wanted to know who the letter was addressed to, Mr. Brown or Mr. Smith. 13.____

14. "Mr. Jones, he said, please answer this letter as soon as possible." 14.____

201

15. The new clerk had an unusual accent inasmuch as he was born and educated in the south.   15.____

16. Although he is younger than her, he earns a higher salary.   16.____

17. Neither of the two administrators are going to attend the conference being held in Washington, D.C.   17.____

18. Since Miss Smith and Miss Jones have more experience than us, they have been given more responsible duties.   18.____

19. Mr. Shaw the supervisor of the stock room maintains an inventory of stationery and office supplies.   19.____

20. Inasmuch as this matter affects both you and I, we should take joint action.   20.____

21. Who do you think will be able to perform this highly technical work?   21.____

22. Of the two employees, John is considered the most competent.   22.____

23. He is not coming home on tuesday; we expect him next week.   23.____

24. Stenographers, as well as typists must be able to type rapidly and accurately.   24.____

25. Having been placed in the safe we were sure that the money would not be stolen.   25.____

KEY (CORRECT ANSWERS)

1.	A		11.	B
2.	D		12.	D
3.	A		13.	A
4.	B		14.	B
5.	D		15.	C
6.	A		16.	A
7.	C		17.	A
8.	B		18.	A
9.	D		19.	B
10.	A		20.	A

21. D
22. A
23. C
24. B
25. A

TEST 4

DIRECTIONS: Each of the following sentences consist of four sentences lettered A, B, C, and D. One of the sentences in each group contains an error in grammar or punctuation. Indicate the INCORRECT sentence in each group. *PRINT THE LETTER OF THE CORRECT ANSWER IN THE SPACE AT THE RIGHT.*

1. A. Give the message to whoever is on duty.
   B. The teacher who's pupil won first prize presented the award.
   C. Between you and me, I don't expect the program to succeed.
   D. His running to catch the bus caused the accident.

   1.____

2. A. The process, which was patented only last year is already obsolete.
   B. His interest in science (which continues to the present) led him to convert his basement into a laboratory.
   C. He described the book as "verbose, repetitious, and bombastic".
   D. Our new director will need to possess three qualities: vision, patience, and fortitude.

   2.____

3. A. The length of ladder trucks varies considerably.
   B. The probationary fireman reported to the officer to who he was assigned.
   C. The lecturer emphasized the need for we firemen to be punctual.
   D. Neither the officers nor the members of the company knew about the new procedure.

   3.____

4. A. Ham and eggs is the specialty of the house.
   B. He is one of the students who are on probation.
   C. Do you think that either one of us have a chance to be nominated for president of the class?
   D. I assume that either he was to be in charge or you were.

   4.____

5. A. Its a long road that has no turn.
   B. To run is more tiring than to walk.
   C. We have been assigned three new reports: namely, the statistical summary, the narrative summary, and the budgetary summary.
   D. Had the first payment been made in January, the second would be due in April.

   5.____

6. A. Each employer has his own responsibilities.
   B. If a person speaks correctly, they make a good impression.
   C. Every one of the operators has had her vacation.
   D. Has anybody filed his report?

   6.____

7. A. The manager, with all his salesmen, was obliged to go.
   B. Who besides them is to sign the agreement?
   C. One report without the others is incomplete.
   D. Several clerks, as well as the proprietor, was injured.

   7.____

2 (#4)

8. A. A suspension of these activities is expected. 8._____
    B. The machine is economical because first cost and upkeep are low.
    C. A knowledge of stenography and filing are required for this position.
    D. The condition in which the goods were received shows that the packing was not done properly.

9. A. There seems to be a great many reasons for disagreement. 9._____
    B. It does not seem possible that they could have failed.
    C. Have there always been too few applicants for these positions?
    D. There is no excuse for these errors.

10. A. We shall be pleased to answer your question. 10._____
    B. Shall we plan the meeting for Saturday?
    C. I will call you promptly at seven.
    D. Can I borrow your book after you have read it?

11. A. You are as capable as I. 11._____
    B. Everyone is willing to sign but him and me.
    C. As for he and his assistant, I cannot praise them too highly.
    D. Between you and me, I think he will be dismissed.

12. A. Our competitors bid above us last week. 12._____
    B. The survey which was began last year has not yet been completed.
    C. The operators had shown that they understood their instructions.
    D. We have never ridden over worse roads.

13. A. Who did they say was responsible? 13._____
    B. Whom did you suspect?
    C. Who do you suppose it was?
    D. Whom do you mean?

14. A. Of the two propositions, this is the worse. 14._____
    B. Which report do you consider the best—the one in January or the one in July?
    C. I believe this is the most practicable of the many plans submitted.
    D. He is the youngest employee in the organization.

15. A. The firm had but three orders last week. 15._____
    B. That doesn't really seem possible.
    C. After twenty years scarcely none of the old business remains.
    D. Has he done nothing about it?

KEY (CORRECT ANSWERS)

1.	B	6.	B	11.	C
2.	A	7.	D	12.	B
3.	C	8.	C	13.	A
4.	C	9.	A	14.	B
5.	A	10.	D	15.	C

PREPARING WRITTEN MATERIAL

EXAMINATION SECTION

TEST 1

DIRECTIONS: Each question or incomplete statement is followed by several suggested answers or completions. Select the one that BEST answers the question or completes the statement. *PRINT THE LETTER OF THE CORRECT ANSWER IN THE SPACE AT THE RIGHT.*

1. The one of the following sentences which is LEAST acceptable from the viewpoint of correct usage is:
   A. The police thought the fugitive to be him.
   B. The criminals set a trap for whoever would fall into it.
   C. It is ten years ago since the fugitive fled from the city.
   D. The lecturer argued that criminals are usually cowards.
   E. The police removed four bucketfuls of earth from the scene of the crime.

1.____

2. The one of the following sentences which is LEAST acceptable from the viewpoint of correct usage is:
   A. The patrolman scrutinized the report with great care.
   B. Approaching the victim of the assault, two bruises were noticed by the patrolman.
   C. As soon as I had broken down the door, I stepped into the room.
   D. I observed the accused loitering near the building, which was closed at the time.
   E. The storekeeper complained that his neighbor was guilty of violating a local ordinance.

2.____

3. The one of the following sentences which is LEAST acceptable from the viewpoint of correct usage is:
   A. I realized immediately that he intended to assault the woman, so I disarmed him.
   B. It was apparent that Mr. Smith's explanation contained many inconsistencies.
   C. Despite the slippery condition of the street, he managed to stop the vehicle before injuring the child.
   D. Not a single one of them wish, despite the damage to property, to make a formal complaint.
   E. The body was found lying on the floor.

3.____

4. The one of the following sentences which contains NO error in usage is:
   A. After the robbers left, the proprietor stood tied in his chair for about two hours before help arrived.
   B. In the cellar I found the watchman's hat and coat.
   C. The persons living in adjacent apartments stated that they had heard no unusual noises.

4.____

D. Neither a knife or any firearms were found in the room.
E. Walking down the street, the shouting of the crowd indicated that something was wrong.

5. The one of the following sentences which contains NO error in usage is:
   A. The policeman lay a firm hand on the suspect's shoulder.
   B. It is true that neither strength nor agility are the most important requirement for a good patrolman.
   C. Good citizens constantly strive to do more than merely comply the restraints imposed by society.
   D. No decision was made as to whom the prize should be awarded.
   E. Twenty years is considered a severe sentence for a felony.

6. Which of the following sentences is NOT expressed in standard English usage?
   A. The victim reached a pay-phone booth and manages to call police headquarters.
   B. By the time the call was received, the assailant had left the scene.
   C. The victim has been a respected member of the community for the past eleven years.
   D. Although the lighting was bad and the shadows were deep, the storekeeper caught sight of the attacker.
   E. Additional street lights have since been installed, and the patrols have been strengthened.

7. Which of the following sentences is NOT expressed in standard English usage?
   A. The judge upheld the attorney's right to question the witness about the missing glove.
   B. To be absolutely fair to all parties is the jury's chief responsibility.
   C. Having finished the report, a loud noise in the next room startled the sergeant.
   D. The witness obviously enjoyed having played a part in the proceedings.
   E. The sergeant planned to assign the case to whoever arrived first.

8. In which of the following sentences is a word misused?
   A. As a matter of principle, the captain insisted that the suspect's partner be brought for questioning.
   B. The principle suspect had been detained at the station house for most of the day.
   C. The principal in the crime had no previous criminal record, but his closest associate had been convicted of felonies on two occasions.
   D. The interest payments had been made promptly, but the firm had been drawing upon the principal for these payments.
   E. The accused insisted that his high school principal would furnish him a character reference.

3 (#1)

9. Which of the following statements is ambiguous? 9.____
   A. Mr. Sullivan explained why Mr. Johnson had been dismissed from his job.
   B. The storekeeper told the patrolman he had made a mistake.
   C. After waiting three hours, the patients in the doctor's office were sent home.
   D. The janitor's duties were to maintain the building in good shape and to answer tenants' complaints.
   E. The speed limit should, in my opinion, be raised to sixty miles an hour on that stretch of road.

10. In which of the following is the punctuation or capitalization faulty? 10.____
    A. The accident occurred at an intersection in the Kew Gardens section of Queens, near the bus stop.
    B. The sedan, not the convertible, was struck in the side.
    C. Before any of the patrolmen had left the police car received an important message from headquarters.
    D. The dog that had been stolen was returned to his master, John Dempsey, who lived in East Village.
    E. The letter had been sent to 12 Hillside Terrace, Rutland, Vermont 05702.

Questions 11-25.

DIRECTIONS: Questions 11 through 25 are to be answered in accordance with correct English usage; that is, standard English rather than nonstandard or substandard. Nonstandard and substandard English includes words or expressions usually classified as slang, dialect, illiterate, etc., which are not generally accepted as correct in current written communication. Standard English also requires clarity, proper punctuation and capitalization and appropriate use of words. Write the letter of the sentence NOT expressed in standard English usage in the space at the right.

11. A. There were three witnesses to the accident. 11.____
    B. At least three witnesses were found to testify for the plaintiff.
    C. Three of the witnesses who took the stand was uncertain about the defendant's competence to drive.
    D. Only three witnesses came forward to testify for the plaintiff.
    E. The three witnesses to the accident were pedestrians.

12. A. The driver had obviously drunk too many martinis before leaving for home. 12.____
    B. The boy who drowned had swum in these same waters many times before.
    C. The petty thief had stolen a bicycle from a private driveway before he was apprehended.
    D. The detectives had brung in the heroin shipment they intercepted.
    E. The passengers had never ridden in a converted bus before.

13. A. Between you and me, the new platoon plan sounds like a good idea.
    B. Money from an aunt's estate was left to his wife and he.
    C. He and I were assigned to the same patrol for the first time in two months.
    D. Either you or he should check the front door of that store.
    E. The captain himself was not sure of the witness's reliability.

13.____

14. A. The alarm had scarcely begun to ring when the explosion occurred.
    B. Before the firemen arrived at the scene, the second story had been destroyed.
    C. Because of the dense smoke and heat, the firemen could hardly approach the now-blazing structure.
    D. According to the patrolman's report, there wasn't nobody in the store when the explosion occurred.
    E. The sergeant's suggestion was not at all unsound, but no one agreed with him.

14.____

15. A. The driver and the passenger they were both found to be intoxicated.
    B. The driver and the passenger talked slowly and not too clearly.
    C. Neither the driver nor his passengers were able to give a coherent account of the accident.
    D. In a corner of the room sat the passenger, quietly dozing.
    E. the driver finally told a strange and unbelievable story, which the passenger contradicted.

15.____

16. A. Under the circumstances I decided not to continue my examination of the premises.
    B. There are many difficulties now not comparable with those existing in 1960.
    C. Friends of the accused were heard to announce that the witness had better been away on the day of the trial.
    D. The two criminals escaped in the confusion that followed the explosion.
    E. The aged man was struck by the considerateness of the patrolman's offer.

16.____

17. A. An assemblage of miscellaneous weapons lay on the table.
    B. Ample opportunities were given to the defendant to obtain counsel.
    C. The speaker often alluded to his past experience with youthful offenders in the armed forces.
    D. The sudden appearance of the truck aroused my suspicions.
    E. Her studying had a good affect on her grades in high school.

17.____

18. A. He sat down in the theater and began to watch the movie.
    B. The girl had ridden horses since she was four years old.
    C. Application was made on behalf of the prosecutor to cite the witness for contempt.
    D. The bank robber, with his two accomplices, were caught in the act.
    E. His story is simply not credible.

18.____

5 (#1)

19. A. The angry boy said that he did not like those kind of friends.
    B. The merchant's financial condition was so precarious that he felt he must avail himself of any offer of assistance.
    C. He is apt to promise more than he can perform.
    D. Looking at the messy kitchen, the housewife felt like crying.
    E. A clerk was left in charge of the stolen property.

19.____

20. A. His wounds were aggravated by prolonged exposure to sub-freezing temperatures.
    B. The prosecutor remarked that the witness was not averse to changing his story each time he was interviewed.
    C. The crime pattern indicated that the burglars were adapt in the handling of explosives.
    D. His rigid adherence to a fixed plan brought him into renewed conflict with his subordinates.
    E. He had anticipated that the sentence would be delivered by noon.

20.____

21. A. The whole arraignment procedure is badly in need of revision.
    B. After his glasses were broken in the fight, he would of gone to the optometrist if he could.
    C. Neither Tom nor Jack brought his lunch to work.
    D. He stood aside until the quarrel was over.
    E. A statement in the psychiatrist's report disclosed that the probationer vowed to have his revenge.

21.____

22. A. His fiery and intemperate speech to the striking employees fatally affected any chance of a future reconciliation.
    B. The wording of the statute has been variously construed.
    C. The defendant's attorney, speaking in the courtroom, called the official a demagogue who contempuously disregarded the judge's orders.
    D. The baseball game is likely to be the most exciting one this year.
    E. The mother divided the cookies among her two children.

22.____

23. A. There was only a bed and a dresser in the dingy room.
    B. John was one of the few students that have protested the new rule.
    C. It cannot be argued that the child's testimony is negligible; it is, on the contrary, of the greatest importance.
    D. The basic criterion for clearance was so general that officials resolved any doubts in favor of dismissal.
    E. Having just returned from a long vacation, the officer found the city unbearably hot.

23.____

24. A. The librarian ought to give more help to small children.
    B. The small boy was criticized by the teacher because he often wrote careless.
    C. It was generally doubted whether the women would permit the use of her apartment for intelligence operations.
    D. The probationer acts differently every time the officer visits him.
    E. Each of the newly appointed officers has 12 years of service.

24.____

25. A. The North is the most industrialized region in the country.
    B. L. Patrick Gray 3d, the bureau's acting director, stated that, while "rehabilitation is fine" for some convicted criminals, "it is a useless gesture for those who resist every such effort."
    C. Careless driving, faulty mechanism, narrow or badly kept roads all play their part in causing accidents.
    D. The childrens' books were left in the bus.
    E. It was a matter of internal security; consequently, he felt no inclination to rescind his previous order.

25.____

KEY (CORRECT ANSWERS)

1.	C		11.	C
2.	B		12.	D
3.	D		13.	B
4.	C		14.	D
5.	E		15.	A
6.	A		16.	C
7.	C		17.	E
8.	B		18.	D
9.	B		19.	A
10.	C		20.	C

21. B
22. E
23. B
24. B
25. D

TEST 2

DIRECTIONS: Each question or incomplete statement is followed by several suggested answers or completions. Select the one that BEST answers the question or completes the statement. *PRINT THE LETTER OF THE CORRECT ANSWER IN THE SPACE AT THE RIGHT.*

Questions 1-6.

DIRECTIONS: Each of Questions 1 through 6 consists of a statement which contains a word (one of those underlined) that is either incorrectly used because it is not in keeping with the meaning the quotation is evidently intended to convey, or is misspelled. There is only one INCORRECT word in each quotation. Of the four underlined words, determine if the first one should be replaced by the word lettered A, the second replaced by the word lettered B, the third replaced by the word lettered C, or the fourth replaced by the word lettered D.

1. Whether one depends on fluorescent or artificial light or both, adequate standards should be maintained by means of systematic tests.
   A. natural B. safeguards C. established D. routine

2. A police officer has to be prepared to assume his knowledge as a social scientist in the community.
   A. forced B. role C. philosopher D. street

3. It is practically impossible to indicate whether a sentence is too long simply by measuring its length.
   A. almost B. tell C. very D. guessing

4. Strong leaders are required to organize a community for delinquency prevention and for dissemination of organized crime and drug addiction.
   A. tactics B. important C. control D. meetings

5. The demonstrators who were taken to the Criminal Courts building in Manhattan (because it was large enough to accommodate them), contended that the arrests were unwarranted.
   A. demonstraters
   B. Manhatten
   C. accomodate
   D. unwarranted

6. They were guaranteed a calm atmosphere, free from harassment, which would be conducive to quiet consideration of the indictments.
   A. guarenteed
   B. atmspher
   C. harassment
   D. inditements

Questions 7-11.

DIRECTIONS: Each of Questions 7 through 11 consists of a statement containing four words in capital letters. One of these words in capital letters is not in keeping with the meaning which the statement is evidently intended to carry. The four words in capital letters in each statement are reprinted after the statement. Print the capital letter preceding the one of the four words which does MOST to spoil the true meaning of the statement in the space at the right.

7. Retirement and pension systems are essential not only to provide employees with with a means of support in the future, but also to prevent longevity and CHARITABLE considerations from UPSETTING the PROMOTIONAL opportunities RETIRED members of the career service.
   A. charitable   B. upsetting   C. promotional   D. retired

7.____

8. Within each major DIVISION in a properly set up public or private organization, provision is made so that each NECESSARY activity is CARED for and lines of authority and responsibility are clear-cut and INFINITE.
   A. division   B. necessary   C. cared   D. infinite

8.____

9. In public service, the scale of salaries paid must be INCIDENTAL to the services rendered, with due CONSIDERATION for the attraction of the desired MANPOWER and for the maintenance of a standard of living COMMENSURATE with the work to be performed.
   A. incidental   B. consideration
   C. manpower   D. commensurate

9.____

10. An understanding of the AIMS of an organization by the staff will AID greatly in increasing the DEMAND of the correspondence work of the office, and will to a large extent DETERMINE the nature of the correspondence.
   A. aims   B. aid   C. demand   D. determine

10.____

11. BECAUSE the Civil Service Commission strongly feels that the MERIT system is a key factor in the MAINTENANCE of democratic government, it has adopted as one of its major DEFENSES the progressive democratization of its own procedures in dealing with candidates for positions in the public service.
   A. Because   B. merit   C. maintenance   D. defenses

11.____

Questions 12-14.

DIRECTIONS: Questions 12 through 14 consist of one sentence each. Each sentence contains an incorrectly used word. First, decide which is the incorrectly used word. Then, from among the options given, decide which word, when substituted for the incorrectly used word, makes the meaning of the sentence clear.
EXAMPLE:
The U.S. national income exhibits a pattern of long term deflection.
   A. reflection   B. subjection   C. rejoicing   D. growth

The word *deflection* in the sentence does not convey the meaning the sentence evidently intended to convey. The word *growth* (Answer D), when substituted for the word *deflection*, makes the meaning of the sentence clear. Accordingly, the answer to the question is D.

12. The study commissioned by the joint committee fell compassionately short of the mark and would have to be redone.
    A. successfully
    B. insignificantly
    C. experimentally
    D. woefully

12.____

13. He will not idly exploit any violation of the provisions of the order.
    A. tolerate   B. refuse   C. construe   D. guard

13.____

14. The defendant refused to be virile and bitterly protested service.
    A. irked   B. feasible   C. docile   D. credible

14.____

Questions 15-25.

DIRECTIONS: Questions 15 through 25 consist of short paragraphs. Each paragraph contains one word which is INCORRECTLY used because it is NOT in keeping with the meaning of the paragraph. Find the word in each paragraph which is INCORRECTLY used and then select as the answer the suggested word which should be substituted for the incorrectly used word.

SAMPLE QUESTION:
In determining who is to do the work in your unit, you will have to decide just who does what from day to day. One of your lowest responsibilities is to assign work so that everybody gets a fair share and that everyone can do his part well.
    A. new   B. old   C. important   D. performance

EXPLANATION:
The word which is NOT in keeping with the meaning of the paragraph is *lowest*. This is the INCORRECTLY used word. The suggested word *important* would be in keeping with the meaning of the paragraph and should be substituted for *lowest*. Therefore, the CORRECT answer is choice C.

15. If really good practice in the elimination of preventable injuries is to be achieved and held in any establishment, top management must refuse full and definite responsibility and must apply a good share of its attention to the task.
    A. accept   B. avoidable   C. duties   D. problem

15.____

16. Recording the human face for identification is by no means the only service performed by the camera in the field of investigation. When the trial of any issue takes place, a word picture is sought to be distorted to the court of incidents, occurrences, or events which are in dispute.
    A. appeals   B. description   C. portrayed   D. deranged

16.____

17. In the collection of physical evidence, it cannot be emphasized too strongly that a haphazard systematic search at the scene of the crime is vital. Nothing must be overlooked. Often the only leads in a case will come from the results of this search.
    A. important B. investigation C. proof D. thorough

18. If an investigator has reason to suspect that the witness is mentally stable, or a habitual drunkard, he should leave no stone unturned in his investigation to determine if the witness was under the influence of liquor or drugs, or was mentally unbalanced either at the time of the occurrence to which he testified or at the time of the trial.
    A. accused B. clue C. deranged D. question

19. The use of records is a valuable step in crime investigation and is the main reason every department should maintain accurate reports. Crimes are not committed through the use of departmental records alone but from the use of all records, of almost every type, wherever they may be found and whenever they give any incidental information regarding the criminal.
    A. accidental B. necessary C. reported D. solved

20. In the years since passage of the Harrison Narcotic Act of 1914, making the possession of opium amphetamines illegal in most circumstances, drug use has become a subject of considerable scientific interest and investigation. There is at present a voluminous literature on drug use of various kinds.
    A. ingestion B. derivatives C. addiction D. opiates

21. Of course, the fact that criminal laws are extremely patterned in definition does not mean that the majority of persons who violate them are dealt with as criminals. Quite the contrary, for a great many forbidden acts are voluntarily engaged in within situations of privacy and go unobserved and unreported.
    A. symbolic B. casual C. scientific D. broad-gauged

22. The most punitive way to study punishment is to focus attention on the pattern of punitive action: to study how a penalty is applied, too study what is done to or taken from an offender.
    A. characteristic B. degrading C. objective D. distinguished

23. The most common forms of punishment in times past have been death, physical torture, mutilation, branding, public humiliation, fines, forfeits of property, banishment, transportation, and imprisonment. Although this list is by no means differentiated, practically every form of punishment has had several variations and applications.
    A. specific B. simple C. exhaustive D. characteristic

5 (#2)

24. There is another important line of inference between ordinary and professional criminals, and that is the source from which they are recruited. The professional criminal seems to be drawn from legitimate employment and, in many instances, from parallel vocations or pursuits.
    A. demarcation   B. justification   C. superiority   D. reference

24.____

25. He took the position that the success of the program was insidious on getting additional revenue.
    A. reputed   B. contingent   C. failure   D. indeterminate

25.____

KEY (CORRECT ANSWERS)

1.	A		11.	D
2.	B		12.	D
3.	B		13.	A
4.	C		14.	C
5.	D		15.	A
6.	C		16.	C
7.	D		17.	D
8.	D		18.	C
9.	A		19.	D
10.	C		20.	B

21. D
22. C
23. C
24. A
25. B

TEST 3

DIRECTIONS: Each question or incomplete statement is followed by several suggested answers or completions. Select the one that BEST answers the question or completes the statement. *PRINT THE LETTER OF THE CORRECT ANSWER IN THE SPACE AT THE RIGHT.*

Questions 1-5.

DIRECTIONS: Questions 1 through 5 are to be answered on the basis of the following.

You are a supervising officer in an investigative unit. Earlier in the day, you directed Detectives Tom Dixon and Sal Mayo to investigate a reported assault and robbery in a liquor store within your area of jurisdiction.

Detective Dixon has submitted to you a preliminary investigative report containing the following information:

- At 1630 hours on 2/20, arrived at Joe's Liquor Store at 350 SW Avenue with Detective Mayo to investigate A & R.
- At store interviewed Rob Ladd, store manager, who stated that he and Joe Brown (store owner) had been stuck up about ten minutes prior to our arrival.
- Ladd described the robbers as male whites in their late teens or early twenties. Further stated that one of the robbers displayed what appeared to be an automatic pistol as he entered the store, and said, *Give us the money or we'll kill you*. Ladd stated that Brown then reached under the counter where he kept a loaded .38 caliber pistol. Several shots followed, and Ladd threw himself to the floor.
- The robbers fled, and Ladd didn't know if any money had been taken.
- At this point, Ladd realized that Brown was unconscious on the floor and bleeding from a head wound.
- Ambulance called by Ladd, and Brown was removed by same to General Hospital.
- Personally interviewed John White, 382 Dartmouth Place, who stated he was inside store at the time of occurrence. White states that he hid behind a wine display upon hearing someone say, *Give us the money*. He then heard shots and saw two young men run from the store to a yellow car parked at the curb. White was unable to further describe auto. States the taller of the two men drove the car away while the other sat on passenger side in front.
- Recovered three spent .38 caliber bullets from premises and delivered them to Crime Lab.
- To General Hospital at 1800 hours but unable to interview Brown, who was under sedation and suffering from shock and a laceration of the head.
- Alarm #12487 transmitted for car and occupants.
- Case Active.

Based solely on the contents of the preliminary investigation submitted by Detective Dixon, select one sentence from the following groups of sentences which is MOST accurate and is grammatically correct.

1. A. Both robbers were armed.
   B. Each of the robbers were described as a male white.
   C. Neither robber was armed.
   D. Mr. Ladd stated that one of the robbers was armed.

1._____

2. A. Mr. Brown fired three shots from his revolver.
   B. Mr. Brown was shot in the head by one of the robbers.
   C. Mr. Brown suffered a gunshot wound of the head during the course of the robbery.
   D. Mr. Brown was taken to General Hospital by ambulance.

2._____

3. A. Shots were fired after one of the robbers said, *Give us the money or we'll kill you.*
   B. After one of the robbers demanded the money from Mr. Brown, he fired a shot.
   C. The preliminary investigation indicated that although Mr. Brown did not have a license for the gun, he was justified in using deadly physical force.
   D. Mr. Brown was interviewed at General Hospital.

3._____

4. A. Each of the witnesses were customers in the store at the time of occurrence.
   B. Neither of the witnesses interviewed was the owner of the liquor store.
   C. Neither of the witnesses interviewed were the owner of the store.
   D. Neither of the witnesses was employed by Mr. Brown.

4._____

5. A. Mr. Brown arrived at General Hospital at about 5:00 P.M.
   B. Neither of the robbers was injured during the robbery.
   C. The robbery occurred at 3:30 P.M. on February 10.
   D. One of the witnesses called the ambulance.

5._____

Questions 6-10.

DIRECTIONS: Each of Questions 6 through 10 consists of information given in outline form and four sentences labeled A, B, C, and D. For each question, choose the one sentence which CORRECTLY expresses the information given in outline form and which also displays PROPER English usage.

6. Client's Name: Joanna Jones
   Number of Children: 3
   Client's Income: None
   Client's Marital Status: Single

6._____

   A. Joanna Jones is an unmarried client with three children who have no income.
   B. Joanna Jones, who is single and has no income, a client she has three children.
   C. Joanna Jones, whose three children are clients, is single and has no income.
   D. Joanna Jones, who has three children, is an unmarried client with no income.

3 (#3)

7. Client's Name: Bertha Smith
   Number of Children: 2
   Client's Rent: $1050 per month
   Number of Rooms: 4

   A. Bertha Smith, a client, pays $1050 per month for her four rooms with two children.
   B. Client Bertha Smith has two children and pays $1050 per month for four rooms.
   C. Client Bertha Smith is paying $1050 per month for two children with four rooms.
   D. For four rooms and two children client Bertha Smith pays $1050 per month.

7.____

8. Name of Employee: Cynthia Dawes
   Number of Cases Assigned: 9
   Date Cases were Assigned: 12/16
   Number of Assigned Cases Completed: 8

   A. On December 16, employee Cynthia Dawes was assigned nine cases; she has completed eight of these cases.
   B. Cynthia Dawes, employee on December 16, assigned nine cases, completed eight.
   C. Being employed on December 16, Cynthia Dawes completed eight of nine assigned cases.
   D. Employee Cynthia Dawes, she was assigned nine cases and completed eight, on December 16.

8.____

9. Place of Audit: Broadway Center
   Names of Auditors: Paul Cahn, Raymond Perez
   Date of Audit: 11/20
   Number of Cases Audited: 41

   A. On November 20, at the Broadway Center 41 cases was audited by auditors Paul Cahn and Raymond Perez.
   B. Auditors Raymond Perez and Paul Cahn has audited 41 cases at the Broadway Center on November 20.
   C. At the Broadway Center, on November 20, auditors Paul Cahn and Raymond Perez audited 41 cases.
   D. Auditors Paul Cahn and Raymond Perez at the Broadway Center, on November 20, is auditing 41 cases.

9.____

10. Name of Client: Barbra Levine
    Client's Monthly Income: $2100
    Client's Monthly Expenses: $4520

    A. Barbra Levine is a client, her monthly income is $2100 and her monthly expenses is $4520.
    B. Barbra Levine's monthly income is $2100 and she is a client, with whose monthly expenses are $4520.

10.____

C. Barbra Levine is a client whose monthly income is $2100 and whose monthly expenses are $4520.
D. Barbra Levine, a client, is with a monthly income which is $2100 and monthly expenses which are $4520.

Questions 11-13.

DIRECTIONS: Questions 11 through 13 involve several statements of fact presented in a very simple way. These statements of fact are followed by 4 choices which attempt to incorporate all of the facts into one logical statement which is properly constructed and grammatically correct.

11.
   I. Mr. Brown was sweeping the sidewalk in front of his house.
   II. He was sweeping it because it was dirty.
   III. He swept the refuse into the street.
   IV. Police Officer gave him a ticket.

   Which one of the following BEST presents the information given above?
   A. Because his sidewalk was dirty, Mr. Brown received a ticket from Officer Green when he swept the refuse into the street.
   B. Police Officer Green gave Mr. Brown a ticket because his sidewalk was dirty and he swept the refuse into the street.
   C. Police Officer Green gave Mr. Brown a ticket for sweeping refuse into the street because his sidewalk was dirty.
   D. Mr. Brown, who was sweeping refuse from his dirty sidewalk into the street, was given a ticket by Police Officer Green.

12.
   I. Sergeant Smith radioed for help.
   II. The sergeant did so because the crowd was getting larger.
   III. It was 10:00 A.M. when he made his call.
   IV. Sergeant Smith was not in uniform at the time of occurrence.

   Which one of the following BEST presents the information given above?
   A. Sergeant Smith, although not on duty at the time, radioed for help at 10 o'clock because the crowd was getting uglier.
   B. Although not in uniform, Sergeant Smith called for help at 10:00 A.M. because the crowd was getting uglier.
   C. Sergeant Smith radioed for help at 10:00 A.M. because the crowd was getting larger.
   D. Although he was not in uniform, Sergeant Smith radioed for help at 10:00 A.M. because the crowd was getting larger.

13.
   I. The payroll office is open on Fridays.
   II. Paychecks are distributed from 9:00 A.M. to 12 Noon.
   III. The office is open on Fridays because that's the only day the payroll staff is available.
   IV. It is open for the specified hours in order to permit employees to cash checks at the bank during lunch hour.

The choice below which MOST clearly and accurately presents the above idea is:
- A. Because the payroll office is open on Fridays from 9:00 A.M. to 12 Noon, employees can cash their checks when the payroll staff is available.
- B. Because the payroll staff is only available on Fridays until noon, employees can cash their checks during their lunch hour.
- C. Because the payroll staff is available only on Fridays, the office is open from 9:00 A.M. to 12 Noon to allow employees to cash their checks.
- D. Because of payroll staff availability, the payroll office is open on Fridays. It is open from 9:00 A.M. to 12 Noon so that distributed paychecks can be cashed at the bank while employees are on their lunch hour.

Questions 14-16.

DIRECTIONS: In each of Questions 14 through 6, the four sentences are from a paragraph in a report. They are not in the right order. Which of the following arrangements is the BEST one?

14.
   I. An executive may answer a letter by writing his reply on the face of the letter itself instead of having a return letter typed.
   II. This procedure is efficient because it saves the executive's time, the typist's time, and saves office file space.
   III. Copying machines are used in small offices as well as large offices to save time and money in making brief replies to business letters.
   IV. A copy is made on a copy machine to go into the company files, while the original is mailed back to the sender.

   The CORRECT answer is:
   A. I, II, IV, III   B. I, IV, II, III   C. III, I, IV, II   D. III, IV, II, I

14.____

15.
   I. Most organizations favor one of the types but always include the others to a lesser degree.
   II. However, we can detect a definite trend toward greater use of symbolic control.
   III. We suggest that our local police agencies are today primarily utilizing material control.
   IV. Control can be classified into three types: physical, material, and symbolic.

   The CORRECT answer is:
   A. IV, II, III, I   B. II, I, IV, III   C. III, IV, II, I   D. IV, I, III, II

15.____

16.
   I. They can and do take advantage of ancient political and geographical boundaries, which often give them sanctuary from effective policy activity.
   II. This country is essentially a country of small police forces, each operating independently within the limits of its jurisdiction.
   III. The boundaries that define and limit police operations do not hinder the movement of criminals, of course.
   IV. The machinery of law enforcement in America is fragmented, complicated, and frequently overlapping.

16.____

The CORRECT answer is:
A. III, I, IV   B. II, IV, I, III   C. IV, II, III, I   D. IV, III, II, I

17. Examine the following sentence, and then choose from below the words which should be inserted in the blank spaces to produce the best sentence.
The unit has exceeded _____ goals and the employees are satisfied with _____ accomplishments.
A. their, it's   B. it's; it's   C. its, there   D. its, their

18. Examine the following sentence, and then choose from below the words which should be inserted in the blank spaces to produce the best sentence.
Research indicates that employees who _____ no opportunity for close social relationships often find their work unsatisfying, and this _____ of satisfaction often reflects itself in low production.
A. have; lack   B. have; excess   C. has; lack   D. has; excess

19. Words in a sentence must be arranged properly to make sure that the intended meaning of the sentence is clear.
The sentence below that does NOT make sense because a clause has been separated from the word on which its meaning depends is:
A. To be a good writer, clarity is necessary.
B. To be a good writer, you must write clearly.
C. You must write clearly to be a good writer.
D. Clarity is necessary to good writing.

Questions 20-21.

DIRECTIONS: Each of Questions 20 and 21 consists of a statement which contains a word (one of those underlined) that is either incorrectly used because it is not in keeping with the meaning the quotation is evidently intended to convey, or is misspelled. There is only one INCORRECT word in each quotation. Of the four underlined words, determine if the first one should be replaced by the word lettered A, the second one replaced by the word lettered B, the third one replaced by the word lettered C, or the fourth one replaced by the word lettered D.

20. The alleged killer was occasionally permitted to exoercise in the corridor.
A. alledged   B. ocasionally   C. permited   D. exercise

21. Defense counsel stated, in affect, that their conduct was permissible under the First Amendment.
A. council   B. effect   C. there   D. permissable

Question 22.

DIRECTIONS: Question 22 consists of one sentence. This sentence contains an incorrectly used word. First, decide which is the incorrectly used word. Then, from among the options given, decide which word, when substituted for the incorrectly used word, makes the meaning of the sentence clear.

22. As today's violence has no single cause, so its causes have no single scheme. 22.____
    A. deference   B. cure   C. flaw   D. relevance

23. In the sentence, *A man in a light-grey suit waited thirty-five minutes in the ante-room for the all-important document*, the word IMPROPERLY hyphenated is 23.____
    A. light-grey
    B. thirty-five
    C. ante-room
    D. all-important

24. In the sentence, *The candidate wants to file his application for preference before it is too late*, the word *before* is used as a(n) 24.____
    A. preposition
    B. subordinating conjunction
    C. pronoun
    D. adverb

25. In the sentence, *The perpetrators ran from the scene*, the word *from* is a 25.____
    A. preposition   B. pronoun   C. verb   D. conjunction

KEY (CORRECT ANSWERS)

1.	D	11.	D
2.	D	12.	D
3.	A	13.	D
4.	B	14.	C
5.	D	15.	D
6.	D	16.	C
7.	B	17.	D
8.	A	18.	A
9.	C	19.	A
10.	C	20.	D

21. B
22. B
23. C
24. B
25. A

PREPARING WRITTEN MATERIAL

PARAGRAPH REARRANGEMENT
COMMENTARY

The sentences that follow are in scrambled order. You are to rearrange them in proper order and indicate the letter choice containing the correct answer at the space at the right.

Each group of sentences in this section is actually a paragraph presented in scrambled order. Each sentence in the group has a place in that paragraph; no sentence is to be left out. You are to read each group of sentences and decide upon the best order in which to put the sentences so as to form a well-organized paragraph.

The questions in this section measure the ability to solve a problem when all the facts relevant to its solution are not given.

More specifically, certain positions of responsibility and authority require the employee to discover connection between events sometimes, apparently, unrelated. In order to do this, the employee will find it necessary to correctly infer that unspecified events have probably occurred or are likely to occur. This ability becomes especially important when action must be taken on incomplete information.

Accordingly, these questions require competitors to choose among several suggested alternatives, each of which presents a different sequential arrangement of the events. Competitors must choose the MOST logical of the suggested sequences.

In order to do so, they may be required to draw on general knowledge to infer missing concepts or events that are essential to sequencing the given events. Competitors should be careful to infer only what is essential to the sequence. The plausibility of the wrong alternatives will always require the inclusion of unlikely events or of additional chains of events which are NOT essential to sequencing the given events.

It's very important to remember that you are looking for the best of the four possible choices, and that the best choice of all may not even be one of the answers you're given to choose from.

There is no one right way to solve these problems. Many people have found it helpful to first write out the order of the sentences, as they would have arranged them, on their scrap paper before looking at the possible answers. If their optimum answer is there, this can save them some time. If it isn't, this method can still give insight into solving the problem. Others find it most helpful to just go through each of the possible choices, contrasting each as they go along. You should use whatever method feels comfortable and works for you.

While most of these types of questions are not that difficult, we've added a higher percentage of the difficult type, just to give you more practice. Usually there are only one or two questions on this section that contain such subtle distinctions that you're unable to answer confidently. And you then may find yourself stuck deciding between two possible choices, neither of which you're sure about.

EXAMINATION SECTION
TEST 1

DIRECTIONS: The sentences that follow are in scrambled order. You are to rearrange them in proper order and indicate the letter choice containing the correct answer. *PRINT THE LETTER OF THE CORRECT ANSWER IN THE SPACE AT THE RIGHT.*

1. Below are four statements labeled W, X, Y and Z.
   W. He was a strict and fanatic drillmaster.
   X. The word is always used in a derogatory sense and generally shows resentment and anger on the part of the user.
   Y. It is from the name of this Frenchman that we derive our English word, martinet.
   Z. Jean Martinet was the Inspector-General of Infantry during the reign of King Louis XIV.
   The PROPER order in which these sentences should be placed in a paragraph is:
   A. X, Z, W, Y   B. X, Z, Y, W   C. Z, W, Y, X   D. Z, Y, W, X

   1._____

2. In the following paragraph, the sentences, which are numbered, have been jumbled.
   I. Since then it has undergone changes.
   II. It was incorporated in 1955 under the laws of the State of New York.
   III. Its primary purposes, a cleaner city, has, however, remained the same.
   IV. The Citizens Committee works in cooperation with the Mayor's Inter-departmental Committee for a Clean City.
   The order in which these sentences should be arranged to form a well-organized paragraph is:
   A. II, IV, I, III   B. III, IV, I, II   C. IV, II, I, III   D. IV, III, II, I

   2._____

   3._____

Questions 3-5.

DIRECTIONS: The sentences listed below are part of a meaningful paragraph but they are not given in their proper order. You are to decide what would be the BEST order in which to put the sentences so as to form a well-organized paragraph. Each sentence has a place in the paragraph; there are no extra sentences. You are then to answer Questions 3 through 5 inclusive on the basis of your rearrangements of these scrambled sentences into a properly organized paragraph.

In 1887 some insurance companies organized an Inspection Department to advise their clients on all phases of fire prevention and protection. Probably this has been due to the smaller annual fire losses in Great Britain than in the United States. It tests various fire prevention devices and appliances and determines manufacturing hazards and their safeguards. Fire research began earlier in the United States and is more advanced than in Great Britain. Later they established a laboratory specializing in electrical, mechanical, hydraulic, and chemical fields.

227

2 (#1)

3. When the five sentences are arranged in proper order, the paragraph starts with the sentence which begins
   A. "In 1887…" B. "Probably this…" C. "It tests…"
   D. "Fire research…" E. "Later they…"

3._____

4. In the last sentence listed above, "they" refers to
   A. the insurance companies
   B. the United States and Great Britain
   C. the Inspection Department
   D. clients
   E. technicians

4._____

5. When the above paragraph is properly arranged, it ends with the words
   A. "…and protection."
   B. "…the United States."
   C. "…their safeguards."
   D. "…in Great Britain."
   E. "…chemical fields."

5._____

KEY (CORRECT ANSWERS)

1. C
2. C
3. D
4. A
5. C

TEST 2

DIRECTIONS: In each of the questions numbered I through V, several sentences are given. For each question, choose as your answer the group of number that represents the MOST logical order of these sentences if they were arranged in paragraph form. *PRINT THE LETTER OF THE CORRECT ANSWER IN THE SPACE AT THE RIGHT.*

1. I. It is established when one shows that the landlord has prevented the tenant's enjoyment of his interest in the property leased.
    II. Constructive eviction is the result of a breach of the covenant of quiet enjoyment implied in all leases.
    III. In some parts of the United States, it is not complete until the tenant vacates within a reasonable time.
    IV. Generally, the acts must be of such serious and permanent character as to deny the tenant the enjoyment of his possessing rights.
    V. In this event, upon abandonment of the premises, the tenant's liability for that ceases.
    The CORRECT answer is:
    A. II, I, IV, III, V
    B. V, II, III, I, IV
    C. IV, III, I, II, V
    D. I, III, V, IV, II

    1.____

2. I. The powerlessness before private and public authorities that is the typical experience of the slum tenant is reminiscent of the situation of blue-collar workers all through the nineteenth century.
    II. Similarly, in recent years, this chapter of history has been reopened by anti-poverty groups which have attempted to organize slum tenants to enable them to bargain collectively with their landlords about the conditions of their tenancies.
    III. It is familiar history that many of the worker remedied their condition by joining together and presenting their demands collectively.
    IV. Like the workers, tenants are forced by the conditions of modern life into substantial dependence on these who possess great political aid and economic power.
    V. What's more, the very fact of dependence coupled with an absence of education and self-confidence makes them hesitant and unable to stand up for what they need from those in power.
    The CORRECT answer is:
    A. V, IV, I, II, III
    B. II, III, I, V, IV
    C. III, I, V, IV, II
    D. I, IV, V, III, II

    2.____

3. I. A railroad, for example, when not acting as a common carrier may contract away responsibility for its own negligence.
    II. As to a landlord, however, no decision has been found relating to the legal effect of a clause shifting the statutory duty of repair to the tenant.
    III. The courts have not passed on the validity of clauses relieving the landlord of this duty and liability.
    IV. They have, however, upheld the validity of exculpatory clauses in other types of contracts.

    3.____

229

V. Housing regulations impose a duty upon the landlord to maintain leased premises in safe condition.
VI. As another example, a bailee may limit his liability except for gross negligence, willful acts, or fraud.

The CORRECT answer is:
A. II, I, VI, IV, III, V
B. I, III, IV, V, VI, II
C. III, V, I, IV, II, VI
D. V, III, IV, I, VI, II

4.
I. Since there are only samples in the building, retail or consumer sales are generally eschewed by mart occupants, and in some instances, rigid controls are maintained to limit entrance to the mart only to those persons engaged in retailing.
II. Since World War I, in many larger cities, there has developed a new type of property, called the mart building.
III. It can, therefore, be used by wholesalers and jobbers for the display of sample merchandise.
IV. This type of building is most frequently a multi-storied, finished interior property which is a cross between a retail arcade and a loft building.
V. This limitation enables the mart occupants to ship the orders from another location after the retailer or dealer makes his selection from the samples.

The CORRECT answer is:
A. II, IV, III, I, V
B. IV, III, V, I, II
C. I, III, II, IV, V
D. I, IV, II, III, V

5.
I. In general, staff-line friction reduces the distinctive contribution of staff personnel.
II. The conflicts, however, introduce an uncontrolled element into the managerial system.
III. On the other hand, the natural resistance of the line to staff innovations probably usefully restrains over-eager efforts to apply untested procedures on a large scale.
IV. Under such conditions, it is difficult to know when valuable ideas are being sacrificed.
V. The relatively weak position of staff, requiring accommodation to the line, tends to restrict their ability to engage in free, experimental innovation.

The CORRECT answer is:
A. IV, II, III, I, V
B. I, V, III, II, IV
C. V, III, I, II, IV
D. II, I, IV, V, III

KEY (CORRECT ANSWERS)

1. A
2. D
3. D
4. A
5. B

TEST 3

DIRECTIONS: Questions 1 through 4 consist of six sentences which can be arranged in a logical sequence. For each question, select the choice which places the numbered sentences in the MOST logical sequent. *PRINT THE LETTER OF THE CORRECT ANSWER IN THE SPACE AT THE RIGHT.*

1. I. The burden of proof as to each issue is determined before trial and remains upon the same party throughout the trial.
    II. The jury is at liberty to believe one witness' testimony as against a number of contradictory witnesses.
    III. In a civil case, the party bearing the burden of proof is required to prove his contention by a fair preponderance of the evidence.
    IV. However, it must be noted that a fair preponderance of evidence does not necessarily mean a greater number of witnesses.
    V. The burden of proof is the burden which rests upon one of the parties to an action to persuade the trier of the facts, generally the jury, that a proposition he asserts is true.
    VI. If the evidence is equally balanced, or if it leaves the jury in such doubt as to be unable to decide the controversy either way, judgment must be given against the party upon whom the burden of proof rests.
    The CORRECT answer is:
    A. III, II, V, IV, I, VI   B. I, II, VI, V, III, IV
    C. III, IV, V, I, II, VI   D. V, I, III, VI, IV, II

    1.____

2. I. If a parent is without assets and is unemployed, he cannot be convicted of the crime of non-support of a child.
    II. The term "sufficient ability" has been held to mean sufficient financial ability.
    III. It does not matter if his unemployment is by choice or unavoidable circumstances.
    IV. If he fails to take any steps at all, he may be liable to prosecution for endangering the welfare of a child.
    V. Under the penal law, a parent is responsible for the support of his minor child only if the parent is "of sufficient ability."
    VI. An indigent parent may meet his obligation by borrowing money or by seeking aid under the provisions of the Social Welfare Law.
    The CORRECT answer is:
    A. VI, I, V, III, II, IV   B. I, III, V, II, IV, VI
    C. V, II, I, III, VI, IV   D. I, VI, IV, V, II, III

    2.____

3. I. Consider, for example, the case of a rabble rouser who urges a group of twenty people to go out and break the windows of a nearby factory.
    II. Therefore, the law fills the indicated gap with the crime of inciting to riot.
    III. A person is considered guilty of inciting to riot when he urges ten or more persons to engage in tumultuous and violent conduct of a kind likely to create public alarm.
    IV. However, if he has not obtained the cooperation of at least four people, he cannot be charged with unlawful assembly.

    3.____

231

2 (#3)

V. The charge of inciting to riot was added to the law to cover types of conduct which cannot be classified as either the crime of "riot" or the crime of "unlawful assembly."
VI. If he acquires the acquiescence of at least four of them, he is guilty of unlawful assembly even if the project does not materialize.
The CORRECT answer is:
 A. III, V, I, VI, IV, II   B. V, I, IV, VI, II, III
 C. III, IV, I, V, II, VI   D. V, I, IV, VI, III, II

4. I. If, however, the rebuttal evidence presents an issue of credibility, it is for the jury to determine whether the presumption has, in fact, been destroyed.
II. Once sufficient evidence to the contrary is introduced, the presumption disappears from the trial.
III. The effect of a presumption is to place the burden upon the adversary to come forward with evidence to rebut the presumption.
IV. When a presumption is overcome and ceases to exist in the case, the fact or facts which gave rise to the presumption still remain.
V. Whether a presumption has been overcome is ordinarily a question for the court.
VI. Such information may furnish a basis for a logical inference.
The CORRECT answer is:
 A. IV, VI, II, V, I, III   B. III, II, V, I, IV, VI
 C. V, III, VI, IV, II, I   D. V, IV, I, II, VI, III

KEY (CORRECT ANSWERS)

1. D
2. C
3. A
4. B

EXAMINATION SECTION

TEST 1

DIRECTIONS: Each question consists of several sentences which can be arranged in a logical sequence. For each question, select the choice which places the numbered sentences in the MOST logical sequence. *PRINT THE LETTER OF THE CORRECT ANSWER IN THE SPACE AT THE RIGHT.*

1.
   I. A body was found in the woods.
   II. A man proclaimed innocence.
   III. The owner of a gun was located.
   IV. A gun was traced.
   V. The owner of a gun was questioned.
   The CORRECT answer is:
   A. IV, III, V, II, I   B. II, I, IV, III, V   C. I, IV, III, V, II
   D. I, III, V, II, IV   E. I, II, IV, III, V

   1.____

2.
   I. A man is in a hunting accident.
   II. A man fell down a flight of steps.
   III. A man lost his vision in one eye.
   IV. A man broke his leg.
   V. A man had to walk with a cane.
   The CORRECT answer is:
   A. II, IV, V, I, III   B. IV, V, I, III, II   C. III, I, IV, V, II
   D. I, III, V, II, IV   E. I, III, II, IV, V

   2.____

3.
   I. A man is offered a new job.
   II. A woman is offered a new job.
   III. A man works as a waiter.
   IV. A woman works as a waitress.
   V. A woman gives notice.
   The CORRECT answer is:
   A. IV, II, V, III, I   B. IV, II, V, I, III   C. II, IV, V, III, I
   D. III, I, IV, II, V   E. IV, III, II, V, I

   3.____

4.
   I. A train let the station late.
   II. A man was late for work.
   III. A man lost his job.
   IV. Many people complained because the train was late.
   V. There was a traffic jam.
   The CORRECT answer is:
   A. V, II, I, IV, III   B. V, I, IV, II, III   C. V, I, II, IV, III
   D. I, V, IV, II, III   E. II, I, IV, V, III

   4.____

233

2 (#1)

5. I. The burden of proof as to each issue is determined before trial and remains upon the same party throughout the trial.
    II. The jury is at liberty to believe one witness' testimony as against a number of contradictory witnesses.
    III. In a civil case, the party bearing the burden of proof is required to prove his contention by a fair preponderance of the evidence.
    IV. However, it must be noted that a fair preponderance of evidence does not necessarily mean a greater number of witnesses.
    V. The burden of proof is the burden which rests upon one of the parties to an action to persuade the trier of the facts, generally the jury, that a proposition he asserts is true.
    VI. If the evidence is equally balanced, or if it leaves the jury in such doubt as to be unable to decide the controversy either way, judgment must be given against the party upon whom the burden of proof rests.
    The CORRECT answer is:
    A. III, II, V, IV, I, VI   B. I, II, VI, V, III, IV   C. III, IV, V, I, II, VI
    D. V, I, III, VI, IV, II   E. I, V, III, VI, IV, II

    5.____

6. I. If a parent is without assets and is unemployed, he cannot be convicted of the crime of non-support of a child.
    II. The term *sufficient ability* has been held to mean sufficient financial ability.
    III. It does not matter if his unemployment is by choice or unavoidable circumstances.
    IV. If he fails to take any steps at all, he may be liable to prosecution for endangering the welfare of a child.
    V. Under the penal law, a parent is responsible for the support of his minor child only if the parent is of *sufficient ability*.
    VI. An indigent parent may meet his obligation by borrowing money or by seeking aid under the provisions of the Social Welfare Law.
    The CORRECT answer is:
    A. VI, I, V, III, II, IV   B. I, III, V, II, IV, VI   C. V, II, I, III, VI, IV
    D. I, VI, IV, V, II, III   E. II, V, I, III, VI, IV

    6.____

7. I. Consider, for example, the case of a rabble rouser who urges a group of twenty people to go out and break the windows of a nearby factory.
    II. Therefore, the law fills the indicated gap with the crime of *inciting to riot*.
    III. A person is considered guilty of inciting to riot when he urges ten or more persons to engage in tumultuous and violent conduct of a kind likely to create public alarm.
    IV. However, if he has not obtained the cooperation of at least four people, he cannot be charged with unlawful assembly.
    V. The charge of inciting to riot was added to the law to cover types of conduct which cannot be classified as either the crime of *riot* or the crime of *unlawful assembly*.
    VI. If he acquires the acquiescence of at least four of them, he is guilty of unlawful assembly even if the project does not materialize.
    The CORRECT answer is:
    A. III, V, I, VI, IV, II   B. V, I, IV, VI, II, III   C. III, IV, I, V, II, VI
    D. V, I, IV, VI, III, II   E. V, III, I, VI, IV, II

    7.____

8. I. If, however, the rebuttal evidence presents an issue of credibility, it is for the jury to determine whether the presumption has, in fact, been destroyed.
    II. Once sufficient evidence to the contrary is introduced, the presumption disappears from the trial.
    III. The effect of a presumption is to place the burden upon the adversary to come forward with evidence to rebut the presumption.
    IV. When a presumption is overcome and ceases to exist in the case, the fact or facts which gave rise to the presumption still remain.
    V. Whether a presumption has been overcome is ordinarily a question for the court.
    VI. Such information may furnish a basis for a logical inference.
    The CORRECT answer is:
    A. IV, VI, II, V, I, III   B. III, II, V, I, IV, VI   C. V, III, VI, IV, II, I
    D. V, IV, I, II, VI, III   E. II, III, V, I, IV, VI

8.____

9. I. An executive may answer a letter by writing his reply on the face of the letter itself instead of having a return letter typed.
    II. This procedure is efficient because it saves the executive's time, the typist's time, and saves office file space.
    III. Copying machines are used in small offices as well as large offices to save time and money in making brief replies to business letters.
    IV. A copy is made on a copying machine to go into the company files, while the original is mailed back to the sender.
    The CORRECT answer is:
    A. I, II, IV, III   B. I, IV, II, III   C. III, I, IV, II   D. III, IV, II, I

9.____

10. I. Most organizations favor one of the types but always include the others to a lesser degree.
    II. However, we can detect a definite trend toward greater use of symbolic control.
    III. We suggest that our local police agencies are today primarily utilizing material control.
    IV. Control can be classified into three types: physical, material, and symbolic.
    The CORRECT answer is:
    A. IV, II, III, I   B. II, I, IV, III   C. III, IV, II, I   D. IV, I, III, II

10.____

11. I. Project residents had first claim to this use, followed by surrounding neighborhood children.
    II. By contrast, recreation space within the project's interior was found to be used more often by both groups.
    III. Studies of the use of project grounds in many cities showed grounds left open for public use were neglected and unused, both by residents and by members of the surrounding community.
    IV. Project residents had clearly laid claim to the play spaces, setting up and enforcing unwritten rules for use.
    V. Each group, by experience, found their activities easily disrupted by other groups, and their claim to the use of space for recreation difficult to enforce.

11.____

4 (#1)

The CORRECT answer is:
A. IV, V, I, II, III
B. V, II, IV, III, I
C. I, IV, III, II, V
D. III, V, II, IV, I

12. I. They do not consider the problems correctable within the existing subsidy formula and social policy of accepting all eligible applicants regardless of social behavior.
    II. A recent survey, however, indicated that tenants believe these problems correctable by local housing authorities and management within the existing financial formula.
    III. Many of the problems and complaints concerning public housing management and design have created resentment between the tenant and the landlord.
    IV. This same survey indicated that administrators and managers do not agree with the tenants.
    The CORRECT answer is:
    A. II, I, III, IV
    B. I, III, IV, II
    C. III, II, IV, I
    D. IV, II, I, III

12._____

13. I. In single-family residences, there is usually enough distance between tenants to prevent occupants from annoying one another.
    II. For example, a certain small percentage of tenant families has one or more members addicted to alcohol.
    III. While managers believe in the right of individuals to live as they choose, the manager becomes concerned when the pattern of living jeopardizes others' rights.
    IV. Still others turn night into day, staging lusty entertainments which carry on into the hours when most tenants are trying to sleep.
    V. In apartment buildings, however, tenants live so closely together that any misbehavior can result in unpleasant living conditions.
    VI. Other families engage in violent argument.
    The CORRECT answer is:
    A. III, II, V, IV, VI, I
    B. I, V, II, VI, IV, III
    C. II, V, IV, I, III, VI
    D. IV, II, V, VI, III, I

13._____

14. I. Congress made the commitment explicit in the Housing Act of 194, establishing as a national goal the realization of a *decent home and suitable environment for every American family*.
    II. The result has been that the goal of decent home and suitable environment is still as far distant as ever for the disadvantaged urban family.
    III. In spite of this action by Congress, federal housing programs have continued to be fragmented and grossly underfunded.
    IV. The passage of the National Housing Act signaled a few federal commitment to provide housing for the nation's citizens.
    The CORRECT answer is:
    A. I, IV, III, II
    B. IV, I, III, II
    C. IV, I, II, III
    D. II, IV, I, III

14._____

15. I. The greater expense does not necessarily involve *exploitation*, but it is often perceived as exploitative and unfair by those who are aware of the price differences involved, but unaware of operating costs.
II. Ghetto residents believe they are *exploited* by local merchants, and evidence substantiates some of these beliefs.
III. However, stores in low-income areas were more likely to be small independents, which could not achieve the economies available to supermarket chains and were, therefore, more likely to charge higher prices, and the customers were more likely to buy smaller-sized packages which are more expensive per unit of measure.
IV. A study conducted in one city showed that distinctly higher prices were charged for goods sold in ghetto stores in other areas.
The CORRECT answer is:
   A. IV, II, I, III   B. IV, I, III, II   C. II, IV, III, I   D. II, III, IV, I

15.____

KEY (CORRECT ANSWERS)

1.	C	6.	C	11.	D
2.	E	7.	A	12.	C
3.	B	8.	B	13.	B
4.	B	9.	C	14.	B
5.	D	10.	D	15.	C

ARITHMETICAL REASONING

EXAMINATION SECTION

TEST 1

DIRECTIONS: Each question or incomplete statement is followed by several suggested answers or completions. Select the one that BEST answers the question or completes the statement. *PRINT THE LETTER OF THE CORRECT ANSWER IN THE SPACE AT THE RIGHT.*

1. Traffic Enforcement Agents begin their daily patrol by taking at least 75 new blank summonses out into the field with them. However, agents may issue more or less than 75 summonses per day. Below is a list of the number of summonses Agent Wilson took out into the field with him at the start of his patrol and the number of summonses he had issued by the end of his patrol.

Day	Blank Summonses At Start of Patrol	Summonses Issued By the End of Patrol
Monday	75	65
Tuesday	75	70
Wednesday	100	90

   Agent Wilson needs to know the total number of summonses he has left, that is, the total number of summonses he has not issued, following his Monday-Wednesday patrol.
   Which one of the following formulas should he use?
   A. (65+70+90) – (75+75+100)
   B. (75+65) – (75+70) – (100+90)
   C. (75+75+100) – (65+70+90)
   D. (76-65) + (75-70) + (100+90)

   1.____

2. Traffic Enforcement Agent Jackson begins his patrol with 3 packages of summonses. Each package contains 25 summonses. At the end of the work day, Agent Jackson returns with 1 package of summonses.
   How many summonses did he issue?
   A. 25   B. 35   C. 50   D. 75

   2.____

3. Traffic Enforcement Agent Phillips began his day with 5 packages of unused summonses. Each package contains 25 summonses. At the end of the day, Agent Phillips has 9 unused summonses. Agent Phillips has to tell his supervisor how many summonses he used that day.
   Which one of the following formulas should Agent Phillips use to calculate how many summonses he issued?
   A. (25-9) × 5   B. (5×25) – 9   C. (25-9)/5   D. (5×25) + 9

   3.____

239

4. Six employees drive six passenger cars with Transit Authority decals into the Jamaica Yard parking lot after displaying their passes to the Agent. An hour later, two of those employees drive two of the cars out of the lot. Ten minutes later, two of those employees leave in one of the cars. A half hour after that, the other two employees leave in one of the cars with three other employees seated in the back.
How many of the six cars that entered together remain in the lot?
A. 1   B. 2   C. 3   D. 4

Questions 5-9.

DIRECTIONS: Questions 5 through 9 are to be answered on the basis of the following information.

The Classon City Bridge and Tunnel Authority requires that all officers collect tolls when on duty. Toll collection is an important part of the job, and all transactions should be accurate.

5. A car with a trailer attached to it arrives at the toll booth of Officer Anderson. Officer Anderson tells the driver that the toll for this vehicle and trailer is $1.40. The driver hands Officer Anderson a $5.00 bill.
How much change should Officer Anderson return to the driver?
A. $3.40   B. $3.50   C. $3.60   D. $3.70

6. Mr. Eric Knoll arrives at the toll booth of Officer Piton. The correct toll for his vehicle is $3.85. Knoll mistakenly gives Officer Piton $2.55.
Officer Piton should collect an additional
A. $1.15   B. $1.30   C. $1.35   D. $1.65

7. A truck driver comes into the lane of Officer Enid. The toll for his vehicle is $2.85. He informs Officer Enid that he also wants to pay for the truck immediately behind his. The toll for the second truck is also $2.85.
If the truck driver paid for both vehicles, the CORRECT change from $20 bill would be
A. $14.30   B. $14.45   C. $14.60   D. $15.30

8. A funeral procession of 8 cars approaches Officer Bragg's lane. The driver of the lead car asks Officer Bragg to charge him for all 8 cars. The toll for each individual car is $.75.
How much change should Officer Bragg return after receiving a $10.00 bill?
A. $2.00   B. $3.80   C. $4.00   D. $4.50

9. A truck driver approaches Officer Kendall's lane. The toll for the truck is $7.20. After the driver hands Officer Kendall a $10.00 bill, he drives away, forgetting his change.
How much change should the driver have received?
A. $1.80   B. $2.20   C. $2.60   D. $2.80

3 (#1)

10. How much change should a motorist receive from a $20.00 bill if his toll for using a tunnel is $2.65? 10._____
    A. $16.35 B. $16.65 C. $17.25 D. $17.35

11. On certain days, there are motorists who fail to pay the appropriate toll. On one day, this occurred four times. The unpaid tolls consisted of one for $2.15, two for $3.70 each, and another for $4.10. 11._____
    The TOTAL amount of tolls not paid was
    A. $9.95 B. $13.15 C. $13.65 D. $13.85

12. While assigned to Toll Lane 3, Bridge and Tunnel Officer Johnson sees a convoy of military vehicles approaching the toll plaza. Capt. Hernandez, the driver of the first vehicle, tells Officer Johnson that he will pay for all of the vehicles in the convoy. Capt. Hernandez gives Officer Johnson the following for payment of the toll: 12._____
    2 prepaid tickets at $2.00 each
    3 prepaid tickets at $3.75 each
    1 $50 bill
    Which one of the following methods should Officer Johnson use to determine how much payment he was given?
    A. Multiply the two tickets by $2.00, then multiply the three tickets by $3.75, then add those amounts to $50.00
    B. Add the number of tickets and bills, then add the two ticket amounts, then multiply the two amounts, then add $50.00
    C. Multiply one by $2.00, then multiply two by $3.75, then multiply three by $50.00, then add the three amounts
    D. Multiply the two tickets by $2.00, then multiply the three tickets by $3.75, then add the sums

13. Bridge and Tunnel Officer Storm is collecting tolls in Lane 7 of the Miller Bridge. A group of vehicles arrive in his lane in a single line. The driver of the first vehicle hands the following list to Officer Storm: 2 cars – Class 1; 3 vans – Class 2; 1 truck – Class 4; 2 cars with trailers – Class 5. 13._____

Vehicle Class	Toll Amount
1	$1.00
2	$1.50
3	$2.25
4	$3.00

    In order for Officer Storm to determine the CORRECT toll amount to collect from the driver, he should
    A. add the number of vehicles in each class to the toll amount for the class, then add the four amounts together
    B. add the number of vehicles, then add the amounts of toll per class, then multiply the two amounts together

C. multiply one × $1.00, then multiply two × $1.50, then multiply four × $2.25, then multiply five × $3.00, then add the four amounts together
D. multiply two × $1.00, then multiply three × $1.50, then multiply one × $2.25, then multiply two × $3.00, then add those amounts

Questions 14-18.

DIRECTIONS: Questions 14 through 18 are to be answered on the basis of the following information.

Bridge and Tunnel Officers must calculate the correct change to return to a motorist. Assume that the toll for each vehicle is $1.75. Determine the correct amount of change that should be returned to the driver for the following transactions.

14. A $20.00 bill is given to pay the toll for one vehicle. 14.____
    The change returned should be
    A. $18.25   B. $18.75   C. $19.25   D. $19.75

15. A $20 bill is given to pay the toll for three vehicles. 15.____
    The change returned should be
    A. $14.75   B. $15.25   C. $15.75   D. $18.25

16. A $5.00 bill is given to pay the toll for one vehicle. 16.____
    The change returned should be
    A. $2.50   B. $2.75   C. $3.00   D. $3.25

17. A $50.00 bill is given to pay the toll for ten vehicles. 17.____
    The change returned should be
    A. $25.00   B. $30.50   C. $32.50   D. $42.50

18. A $10.00 bill is given for payment of toll for six vehicles. 18.____
    The Bridge and Tunnel Officer should NEXT
    A. return $6.50 to the driver
    B. return $1.75 to the driver
    C. ask the driver for an additional fifty cents
    D. allow the vehicles to go through since the toll is paid in full

Questions 19-20.

DIRECTIONS: Questions 19 and 20 are to be answered SOLELY on the basis of the following information.

Bridge and Tunnel Officers are required to sell rolls of tokens.

5 (#1)

19. Bridge and Tunnel Officer Victor began collecting tolls at 7:00 A.M. with 50 fares. During his tour, Officer Victor was issued 25 additional fares three times. When Officer Victor completed his toll collecting assignment, he returned 13 fares.
How many fares did Officer Victor sell?
   A. 62   B. 112   C. 137   D. 138

19._____

20. Bridge and Tunnel Officer Smith was issued 100 fares at the start of her toll collecting assignment. During her tour, she was given an additional 30 fares. Officer Smith sold a total of 93 fares.
How many fares did Officer Smith have at the end of her tour?
   A. 7   B. 34   C. 37   D. 39

20._____

KEY (CORRECT ANSWERS)

1. CORRECT ANSWER: C
   Number of summonses left = (75+75+100) – (65+70+90), which is 25.

2. CORRECT ANSWER: C
   (3-1)(25) = 50 summonses

3. CORRECT ANSWER: B
   (5×25) – 9 = 116 summonses were issued.

4. CORRECT ANSWER: B
   6 – 2 – 1 – 1 = 2 cars remain in the lot.

5. CORRECT ANSWER: C
   $5.00 - $1.40 = $3.60 change

6. CORRECT ANSWER: B
   $3.05 - $2.55 = $1.30 owed.

7. CORRECT ANSWER: A
   $20.00 – (2)($2.85) = $14.30 change

8. CORRECT ANSWER: C
   $10.00 – (8)(.75) = $4.00 change

9. CORRECT ANSWER: D
   $10.00 - $7.20 = $2.80 change

10. CORRECT ANSWER: D
    $20.00 - $2.65 = $17.35 change

11. CORRECT ANSWER: C
    Unpaid amount = $2.15 + (2)($3.70) + $4.10 = $13.65

12. CORRECT ANSWER: A
    Payment = (2)($2.00) + (3)($3.75) + $50.00, which is $65.25

13. CORRECT ANSWER: D
    Toll amount = (2)($1.00) + (3)($1.50) + (1)($2.25) + (2)($3.00), which is $14.75

14. CORRECT ANSWER: A
    $20.00 - $1.75 = $18.25 change

15. CORRECT ANSWER: A
    $20.00 – (3)($1.75) = $14.75

7 (#1)

16. CORRECT ANSWER: D
    $5.00 - $1.75 = $3.25 change

17. CORRECT ANSWER: C
    $50.00 – (10)($1.75) = $32.50 change

18. CORRECT ANSWER: C
    Since (6)($1.75) = $10.50, the driver needs to pay an additional fifty cents

19. CORRECT ANSWER: B
    50 + (3)(25) – 13 = 112 fares sold

20. CORRECT ANSWER: C
    100 + 30 – 93 = 37 fares left

TEST 2

DIRECTIONS: Each question or incomplete statement is followed by several suggested answers or completions. Select the one that BEST answers the question or completes the statement. *PRINT THE LETTER OF THE CORRECT ANSWER IN THE SPACE AT THE RIGHT.*

1. The operator of a Transit Authority van hands Protection Agent Johnson a Material Pass listing the following: 31 boxes of No. 10 letter envelopes, 11 boxes – each containing 24 bottles of correction fluid, 18 packages of 14-inch photocopy paper, 12 packages of 11-inch photocopy paper, and 10 packages of paper towels. Agent Johnson counts the boxes and packages and finds a total of 79.
How many boxes or packages are missing?
   A. 2   B. 3   C. 4   D. 5

2. If a turnstile counter shows 28,841 at 10:00 P.M. and 1,348 passengers passed through that turnstile between 4:00 P.M. and 10:00 P.M., what was the reading at 4:00 P.M.?
   A. 27,303   B. 27,393   C. 17,403   D. 27,493

3. If a turnstile counter shows 49,739 at 11:00 A.M. and 2,157 passengers pass through that turnstile during the next three hours, what will be the reading at 2:00 P.M.?
   A. 41,896   B. 51,887   C. 51,896   D. 51,897

4. A squad of patrolmen assigned to enforce a new parking regulation in a particular area issued tag summonses on a particular day as follows: four patrolmen issued 16 summonses each; three issued 19 each; one issued 22; seven issued 25 each; eleven issued 28 each; ten issued 30 each; two issued 36 each; one issued 41; and three issued 45 each.
The average number of summonses issued by a member of this squad was MOST NEARLY
   A. 6.2   B. 17.2   C. 21.0   D. 27.9

5. A water storage tank is 75 feet long and 30 feet wide and has a depth of 6½ feet. Each cubic foot of the tank holds 9½ gallons.
The TOTAL capacity of the tank is _____ gallons.
   A. 73,125½   B. 131,625   C. 138,937½   D. 146,250

6. The price of admission to a PAL entertainment was $.25 each for adults and $.10 for chidren; the turnstile at the entrance showed that 358 persons entered and the gate receipts were $62.65.
The number of children who attended was
   A. 170   B. 175   C. 179   D. 183

7. A patrol car travels six times as fast as a bicycle.
If the patrol car goes 168 miles sin two hours less time than the bicycle requires to go 42 miles, their respective rates of speed are _____ miles per hour.
   A. 36 and 6   B. 42 and 7   C. 63 and 104   D. 126 and 21

8. The radiator of an automobile already contains six quarts of a 10% solution of alcohol. In order to make a mixture of 20% alcohol, it will be necessary to add _____ quarts of alcohol.
   A. ¾   B. 1¾   C. 2½   D. 3

9. A man received an inheritance of $80,000 and wanted to invest it so that it would produce an annual income sufficient to pay his rent of $400 a month. In order to do this, he will have to receive interest or dividends at the rate of
   A. 3%   B. 4%   C. 5¾%   D. 6%

10. If the price of a bus ticket varies directly as the mileage involved, and a ticket to travel 135 miles costs $29.70, a ticket for a 30 mile trip will cost
    A. $15.20   B. $13.40   C. $6.60   D. $2.20

11. A man owed a debt of $5,800. After a first payment of $100, he agreed to pay the balance by monthly payments in which each payment after this first would be $20 more than that of the preceding month.
If no interest charge is made, he will have to make, including the first payment, a total of _____ monthly payments.
    A. 16   B. 20   C. 24   D. 28

12. The written test of a civil service examination has a weight of 30, the oral test a weight of 20, experience a weight of 20, and the physical test a weight of 30. A candidate received ratings of 76 on the written test, 84 on the oral, and 80 for experience.
In order to attain an average of 85 on the examination, his rating on the physical test must be
    A. 86   B. 90   C. 94   D. 98

13. A family has an income of $3,200 per month. It spends 22% of this amount for rent, 36% for food, 16% for clothing, and 12% for additional household expenses. After meeting these expenses, 50% of the balance is deposited in the bank.
The amount deposited MONTHLY is
    A. $224.00   B. $366.00   C. $448.00   D. $520.00

14. Upon retirement last July, a patrolman bought a farm of 64 acres for $1,800 per acre. He made a down payment of $61,200 and agreed to pay the balance in installments of $750 a month commencing on August 1, 2008.
Disregarding interest, he will make his LAST payment on
    A. July 2014   B. August 2016
    C. January 2018   D. April 2021

15. 40% of those who commit a particular crime are subsequently arrested and convicted. 75% of those convicted receive sentences of 10 years or more. Assuming that those arrested for the first time serve less than 10 years, the percentage of those committing this crime who receive sentences of ten years or more is MOST NEARLY
A. 20%   B. 30%   C. 40%   D. 50%

15.____

16. Assume that in 2008 there were 21,580 vehicular highway accidents resulting in 713 deaths. This represents a 17% decrease over the year 2001.
If the year 2009 indicates a 6.5% decrease over 2001, the number of highway accidents taking place in 2009 is MOST NEARLY
A. 23,846   B. 24,817   C. 24,310   D. 22,983

16.____

17. Of 35 patrolmen assigned to Precinct P,
   5 have 2 years of service,
   5 have 4 years of service,
   9 have 6 years of service
   4 have 8 years of service
   7 have 12 years of service, and
   5 have 16 years of service.
The average number of years of service in the Police Department for the 35 patrolmen is MOST NEARLY
A. 6   B. 8   C. 7   D. 9

17.____

18. A patrolman purchases a two-family house for $318,000 and immediately rents one apartment to a tenant for $1,500 a month. At the end of two years, he sells the house for $352,000. Taxes, repairs, insurance, interest, and other expenses cost him $31,840. His total gain from renting and selling, based on his original investment, is MOST NEARLY
A. 6%   B. 8%   C. 10%   D. 12%

18.____

19. Precincts S, T, W, and Y are located in the county. The total number of patrolmen assigned to these precincts is 430. Precinct S has 7 patrolmen more than Precinct Y; Precinct T has 7 patrolmen less than Precinct Y; Precinct W has twice as many patrolmen as Precinct Y.
The number of patrolmen assigned to Precinct Y is MOST NEARLY
A. 82   B. 86   C. 92   D. 96

19.____

20. Two radio patrol cars, coming from different directions, are rushing to the scene of a crime. The first car proceeds at the rate of 45 miles an hour and arrives there in 4 minutes. Although the second car travels a route which is longer by ¾ of a mile, it arrives only ½ minute later.
The speed of the second patrol car, expressed in miles per hour, is MOST NEARLY
A. 50   B. 55   C. 60   D. 65

20.____

4 (#2)

KEY (CORRECT ANSWERS)

1. CORRECT ANSWER: B
   31 + 11 + 18 + 12 + 10 – 79 = 3 missing

2. CORRECT ANSWER: D
   28,841 – 1348 = 27,493 at 4:00 P.M.

3. CORRECT ANSWER: C
   49,739 + 2,157 = 51,896 at 2:00 P.M.

4. CORRECT ANSWER: D
   Average number of summonses = [(4)(16) + (3)(19) + (1)(22) + (7)(25) + (11)(28) + (10)(30) + (2)(36) + (1)(41) + (3)(45)] ÷ 42 ≈ 2795, closest to 27.9.

5. CORRECT ANSWER: C
   Total capacity = (75)(30)(6½)(9½) = 138,937½ gallons

6. CORRECT ANSWER: C
   Let x = number of children, 358-x = number of adults
   Then, .10x + (.25)(358-x) = $62.65.
   Solving, x = 179
   (Note: There were also 179 adults.)

7. CORRECT ANSWER: B
   Let x = rate of patrol car, 1/6x = rate of bike. Then, 168/x + 2 = 42/ 1/6x. Solving for x and 1/6x, we get 42 and 7.

8. CORRECT ANSWER: A
   Originally, there are (.10)(6) = .6 qts. of alcohol and 5.4 qts. of water. Let x = added qts. of alcohol. Then, (.6+x)/(6+x) = .20. Simplifying, .6 + x = 1.2 + .2x. Solving, x = ¾.

9. CORRECT ANSWER: D
   ($400)(12) = $4,800. Then, $4,800/$80,000 = 6%

10. CORRECT ANSWER: C
    Cost = ($29.80)(30/135) = .00

11. CORRECT ANSWER: B
    $100 + $120 + $140 + ... = $5,800. The formula for an arithmetic series is
    S = n/2[2a+(n-1)d], where n = number of terms, a = 1st term, d = difference, S = sum. So,
    $5,800 = n/2[(2)($100) + (n-1)($20)]. Simplifying, $n^2 + 9n – 5800 = 0$. Solving, n = 200

12. CORRECT ANSWER: D
    Let x = score on the physical test. Then, (76)(.30) + (84)(.20) + (80)(.20) + (x)(.30) = 85.
    Solving, x = 98.

5 (#2)

13. CORRECT ANSWER: A
    1 - .22 - .36 - .16 - .12 = .14. Then, (1/2)(.14)($3,200) = $224.00 is deposited monthly.

14. CORRECT ANSWER: A
    (64)($1800) = $115,200. Then, $115,200 - $61,200 = $54,000 to be paid in $750 monthly amounts. This would require $54,000/$750 = 72 monthly payments. Since his first payment is August 1, 2008, his last one is July 2014.

15. CORRECT ANSWER: B
    (.40)(.75) = 30%

16. CORRECT ANSWER: C
    Number of accidents in 2001 = 21,580 ÷ 83 = 26,000. Then, number of accidents in 2009 = (26,000)(.935) = 24,410.

17. CORRECT ANSWER: B
    Average = [(5)(2)+(5)(4)+(9)(6)+(4)(8)+(7)(12)+(5)(16)] ÷ 35 = 8 years

18. CORRECT ANSWER: D
    ($1,500)(I12)(2) + $352,000 - $318,000 - $31,840 = $38,160 gain. This represents $38,160/$318,000 = 12%.

19. CORRECT ANSWER: B
    Let x = number in Precinct Y, x+7 = number in Precinct S, x-7 = number in Precinct T, 2x = number in Precinct W. Then, 2x + x + x+ 7 + x + 7 = 430. Solving, x = 86.

20. CORRECT ANSWER: A
    The distance traveled by 1st patrol car = (45)(4/60) = 3 miles. The 2nd patrol car travels 3¾ miles in 4½ minutes. The speed of the 2nd car, in mph, is (3¾)(60/4½) = 50.

TEST 3

DIRECTIONS: Each question or incomplete statement is followed by several suggested answers or completions. Select the one that BEST answers the question or completes the statement. *PRINT THE LETTER OF THE CORRECT ANSWER IN THE SPACE AT THE RIGHT.*

1. A radio motor patrol car has to travel a distance of 15 miles in an emergency. If it does the first two-thirds of the distance at 40 m.p.h. and the last third at 60 m.p.h., the total number of minutes required for the entire run is MOST NEARLY
   A. 15   B. 20   C. 22½   D. 25

2. A patrol car had 11½ gallons of gasoline at the beginning of a trip of 196 miles and 5½ gallons at the end of the trip. During the trip, gasoline was bought for $21.70 at a cost of $3.10 per gallon.
   The average number of miles driven per gallon of gasoline was MOST NEARLY
   A. 14   B. 14.5   C. 15   D. 15.5

3. There are 15 patrolmen assigned to a certain operation. One-third earn $42,000 per year, three earn $44,100 per year, one earns $49,350 per year, and the rest earn $55,810 per year.
   The average annual salary of these patrolmen is MOST NEARLY
   A. $47,500   B. $48,000   C. $48,500   D. $49,000

4. In 2006, the cost of patrol car maintenance and repair was $5,000 more than in 2005, representing an increase of 10%.
   The cost of patrol car maintenance and repair in 2006 was MOST NEARLY
   A. $5,500   B. $45,000   C. $50,000   D. $55,000

5. A police precinct has an assigned strength of 180 men. Of this number, 25% are not available for duty due to illness, vacations, and other reasons. Of those who are available for duty, 1/3 are assigned outside of the precinct for special emergency duty.
   The ACTUAL available strength of the precinct in terms of men immediately available for precinct duty is
   A. 45   B. 60   C. 90   D. 135

6. Five police officers are taking target practice. The number of rounds fired by each and the percentage of perfect shots is as follows:

Officer	Rounds Fired	Perfect Shots
R	80	30%
S	70	40%
T	75	60%
U	92	25%
V	96	66⅔%

   The average number of perfect shots fired by them is MOST NEARLY
   A. 30   B. 36   C. 42   D. 80

2 (#3)

7. A dozen 5-gallon cans of paint weigh 494 pounds. Each can, when empty, weighs 3 pounds.
The weight of one gallon of paint is MOST NEARLY _____ lbs.
A. 5   B. 6 ½   C. 7½   D. 8

7._____

8. A radio motor patrol car finds it necessary to travel at 90 miles per hour for a period of 1 minute and 40 seconds.
The number of miles which the car travels during this period is
A. 1⁵⁄₆   B. 2   C. 24   D. 3¾

8._____

9. A parade is marching up an avenue for 60 city blocks. A sample count of the number of people watching the parade on one side of the street in the block is taken, first in a block near the end of the parade and then in a block at the middle; the former count is 4,000; the latter is 6,000.
If the average for the entire parade is assumed to be the average of the two samples, then the estimated number of persons watching the entire parade is MOST NEARLY
A. 240,000   B. 300,000   C. 480,000   D. 600,000

9._____

10. Suppose that the revenue from parking meters in a city was 5% greater in 2002 than in 2001 and 2% less in 2003 than in 2002.
If the revenue in 2001 was $1,500,000, then the revenue in 2003 was
A. $1,541,500   B. $1,542,000   C. $1,542,500   D. $1,543,500

10._____

11. A radio motor patrol car completes a ten mile trip in twenty minutes.
If it does one-half the distance at a speed of twenty miles an hour, its speed, in miles per hour, for the remainder of the distance must be
A. 30   B. 40   C. 50   D. 60

11._____

12. A public beach has two parking areas. Their capacities are in the ratio of two to one, and on a certain day are filled to 60% and 40% of capacity, respectively.
The entire parking facilities of the beach on that day are MOST NEARLY _____ filled.
A. 38%   B. 43%   C. 48%   D. 53%

12._____

13. While on foot patrol, a patrolman walks north for eleven blocks, turns around and walks south for six blocks, turns around and walks north for two blocks, then makes a right turn and walks one block.
In relation to his starting point, he is now _____ blocks away and facing _____.
A. twenty; east   B. seven; east   C. seven; west   D. nine; north

13._____

14. A block has metered parking for 19 cars from 7 A.M. to 9 P.M. at a charge of $1.00 per hour.
Assuming that each car that is parked remains for a full hour and that on an average, for each hour of parking, there is a vacancy of five minutes for each meter, the amount of revenue from the meters for a day will be MOST NEARLY
A. $100   B. $150   C. $200   d. $250

14._____

15. The standard formula for the stopping distance of a car with all four wheels locked is:

$$S = \frac{V \text{ times } V}{30W}$$

where S is the stopping distance in feet, V the speed of the car in miles per hour at the moment the brakes are applied, and W is a number which depends on the friction between the tires and the road.
If the speed of a car is 50 miles per hour and W is equal to 5/3, the stopping distance will be MOST NEARLY _____ feet.
   A. 30   B. 40   C. 50   D. 60

16. The radiator of a police car contains 20 quarts of a mixture consisting of 80% water and 20% antifreeze compound. Assume that you have been ordered to draw off some of the mixture and add pure antifreeze compound until the mixture is 75% water and 25% antifreeze compound.
The number of quarts of the mixture which should be removed is MOST NEARLY
   A. 1   B. 3   C. 4   D. 5

17. Assume that a parking space for six cars is to be outlined with white paint. The total area to be outlined is 24 feet by 40 feet, and the space for each car, also marked off by white lines, is to be 8 feet by 20 feet.
The total length of white lines to be painted is MOST NEARLY
   A. 128   B. 156   C. 184   D. 232

18. A police car is ordered to report to the scene of a crime 5 miles away.
If the car travels at an average rate of 40 miles per hour, the length of time it will take to reach its destination is MOST NEARLY _____ minutes.
   A. 3   B. 7   C. 10   D. 13

19. During the first nine months of the year, an officer spent an average of $270 a month. In October and November, he spent an average of $315 a month. In December, he spent $385.
His average monthly spending during the year was MOST NEARLY
   A. $254   B. $287   C. $323   D. $3,000

20. In 2005, there were 8,270 arrests in a certain city. The number of arrests increased by 12½% in 2006. In 2007, the number of arrests decreased 5% from the 2006 figures.
The number of arrests in 2007 was MOST NEARLY
   A. 8,840   B. 9,770   C. 6,870   D. 7,600

21. Assume that parking space is to be provided for 25% of the tenants in a new housing development. The project will have five 6-story buildings, having seven tenants on each floor, and eight 11-story buildings, having eight tenants on each floor.
The number of parking spaces needed is MOST NEARLY
   A. 215   B. 230   C. 700   D. 895

22. A stolen vehicle traveling at 60 miles per hour passes by a police car, which is standing still with the engine running. The police car immediately starts out in pursuit, and one minute later, having covered a distance of half a mile, it reaches a speed of 90 miles per hour and continues at this speed.
In how many minutes after the stolen vehicle passes the police car will the police car overtake it?
   A. 1 B. 1½ C. 2 D. 3

23. A police officer found his 42-hour work week was divided as follows: 1/6 of his time in investigating incidents on his patrol post, ½ of his time patrolling his post, and 1/8 of his time in special traffic duty. The rest of his time was devoted to assignments at precinct headquarters.
The percentage of his work week which was spent at precinct headquarters is MOST NEARLY
   A. 10% B. 15% C. 20% D. 25%

24. Last year, the Department of Sanitation towed away 8,430 cars which were abandoned or illegally parked on city streets.
If the value of the abandoned cars was $1,038,200 and that of the illegally parked cars was $6,234,800, then the average value of one of the towed-away cars was MOST NEARLY
   A. $400 B. $720 C. $860 D. 1,100

25. Two percent of all school children are problem children. Some 80% of these problem children become delinquents, and about 80% of the delinquent children become criminals.
If the school population is 1,000,000 children, the number of this group who will eventually become criminals, according to this analysis, is
   A. 12,800 B. 1,280 C. 640 D. 128

5 (#3)

KEY (CORRECT ANSWERS)

1. CORRECT ANSWER: B
   10/40 + 5/60 = 1/3 hr. = 20 min.

2. CORRECT ANSWER: C
   Number of gallons used = 11½ - 5½ + $21.70/$3.10 = 13
   Average miles per gallon = 196 ÷ 13 ≈ 15

3. CORRECT ANSWER: C
   Average annual salary = [(5)($42,000)+(3)($44,100)+(1)($49,350)+(6)($55,810) ÷ 15 = $48,434, closest to $48,500.

4. CORRECT ANSWER: D
   Cost in 2005 = $5,000 ÷ .10 = $50,000.
   Thus, the cost in 2006 = $50,000 + $5,000 = $55,000

5. CORRECT ANSWER: C
   180 – (.25)(180) = 135. Then, (135)(2/3) = 90 immediately available

6. CORRECT ANSWER: B
   [(80)(.30)+(70)(.40)+(75)(.60)+(92)(.25)+(96)(2/3)] ÷ 5 = 184 ÷ 5 = 36.8 ≈ 37

7. CORRECT ANSWER: C
   Each full can weighs 494 ÷ 12 = 41$^{1}/_{6}$ lbs. Since an empty can weighs 3 lbs., 5 gallons of paint weighs 38$^{1}/_{6}$ lbs. Thus, 1 gallon weighs 38$^{1}/_{6}$ ÷ 5 ≈ 7½ lbs.

8. CORRECT ANSWER: C
   (90)(1 2/3/60) = 2½ miles

9. CORRECT ANSWER: D
   Total estimate = (2)(5000)(60) = 600,000

10. CORRECT ANSWER: D
    Revenue in 2002 = ($1,500,000)(1.05) = $1,575,000
    Revenue in 2003 = ($1,575,000)(.98) = $1,543,500

11. CORRECT ANSWER: D
    20 mi/hr means 5/20 = ¼ hr. = 15 min. to go 5 miles. Then, the car must go 5 miles i 20 – 15 = 5 min. This means 6 mph.

12. CORRECT ANSWER: D
    Let 2x = capacity of larger parking area, x = capacity of smaller area.
    Then, [(.60)(2x)+(.40)(x)] ÷ 1.6/3 ≈ 53%

13. CORRECT ANSWER: B
    He has walked 11 – 6 + 2 = 7 blocks north and is facing east.

6 (#3)

14. CORRECT ANSWER: D
There will be 13 hours of parking time at each meter, due to the 5 min. vacancy for each of the 14 hrs. of operation. Then, $(13)(1.00)(19) = \$247 \approx \$250$

15. CORRECT ANSWER: C
$S = (50)(50)/(30)(5/3) = 50$ ft.

16. CORRECT ANSWER: A
The original mixture has 16 qts. water and 4 qts. antifreeze. Drawing out x qts. means that the 20-x qts. mixture will contain 16-.8x qts. of wter and 4-.2x qts. of antifreeze. Now add x qts. of pure antifreeze, so that now we have 4-.2x+x = 4+.8x qts. of antifreeze and 20-x+x = 20 qts. of the mixture. Finally, (4+8x)/20 = .25. Solving, x = 1.25

17. CORRECT ANSWER: D
Total length of white lines = (24')(3)+(40')(4) = 232 ft.

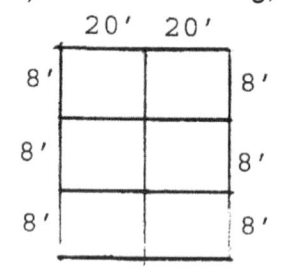

18. CORRECT ANSWER: B
Time = (5)(60/40) = 7½ min., closest to 7

19. CORRECT ANSWER: B
Average = [($270)(9)+($315)(2)+(1)($385)] ÷ 12 ≈ $287

20. CORRECT ANSWER: A
Number of arrests in 2007 = (8,270)(1.125)(.95) ≈ 8,840

21. CORRECT ANSWER: B
Number of parking spaces = (.25)[(5)(6)(7)+(8)(11)(8)] ≈ 230

22. CORRECT ANSWER: C
After 1 minute, the stolen car has traveled 1 mile, while the police car has traveled ½ mile. Let x = additional minutes required. Since the police car will travel ½ extra mile from the point at which it reaches 90 mph, (1 mi./min.)(x) = (1½ mi./min.)(x) − ½. Solving, x = 1. Total time = 2 min.

23. CORRECT ANSWER: C
1 − ⅙ − ½ - ⅛ = ⁵⁄₂₅ 20%

24. CORRECT ANSWER: C
Average value = ($6,234,800+$1,038,200) ÷ 8,430 ≈ $860

25. CORRECT ANSWER: A
(1,000,000)(.02)(.80)(.80) = 12,800 projected to be criminals.

EXAMINATION SECTION
TEST 1

DIRECTIONS: Questions 1 through 5 are to be answered on the basis of the information, instructions, and sample question given below. Each question contains a GENERAL RULE, EXCEPTIONS, a PROBLEM, and the ACTION actually taken.

The GENERAL RULE explains what the special officer (security officer) should or should not do.

The EXCEPTIONS describe circumstances under which a special officer (security officer) should take action contrary to the GENERAL RULE.

However, an unusual emergency may justify taking an action that is not covered either by the GENERAL RULE or by the stated EXCEPTIONS.

The PROBLEM describes a situation requiring some action by the special officer (security officer).

ACTION describes what a special officer (security officer) actually did in that particular case.

Read carefully the GENERAL RULE and EXCEPTIONS, the PROBLEM, and the ACTION, and the mark A, B, C, or D in the space at the right in accordance with the following instructions:

I. If an action is clearly justified under the general rule, mark your answer A.
II. If an action is not justified under the general rule, but is justified under a stated exception, mark your answer B.
III. If an action is not justified either by the general rule or by a stated exception, but does seem strongly justified by an unusual emergency situation, mark your answer C.
IV. If an action does not seem justified for any of these reasons, mark your answer D.

SAMPLE QUESTION:

GENERAL RULE: A special officer (security officer) is not empowered to stop a person and search him for hidden weapons.
EXCEPTION: He may stop a person and search him if he has good reason to believe that he may be carrying a hidden weapon. Good reasons to believe he may be carrying a hidden weapon include (a) notification through official channels that a person may be armed, (b) a statement directly to the special officer (security officer) by the person himself that he is armed, and (c) the special officer's (security officer's) own direct observation.

PROBLEM: A special officer (security officer) on duty at a hospital clinic is notified by a woman patient at the clinic that a man sitting near her is making muttered threats that he has a gun and is going to shoot his doctor if the doctor gives him any trouble. Although the woman is upset, she seems to be telling the truth, and two other waiting patients con-

firm this. However, the special officer (security officer) approaches the man and sees no sign of a hidden weapon. The man tells the officer that he has no weapon.
ACTION: The special officer (security officer) takes the man aside into an empty office and proceeds to frisk him for a concealed weapon.

ANSWER: The answer cannot be A, because the general rule is that a special officer (security officer) is not empowered to search a person for hidden weapons. The answer cannot be B, because the notification did not come through official channels, the man did not tell the special officer (security officer) that he had a weapon, and the special officer (security officer) did not observe any weapon. However, since three people have confirmed that the man has said he has a weapon and is threatening to use it, this is pretty clearly an emergency situation that calls for action. Therefore, the answer is C.

1. GENERAL RULE: A special officer (security officer) on duty at a certain entrance is not to leave his post unguarded at any time.
EXCEPTION: He may leave the post for a brief period if he first summons a replacement. He may also leave if it is necessary for him to take prompt emergency action to prevent injury to persons or property.
PROBLEM: The special officer (security officer) sees a man running down a hall with a piece of iron pipe in his hand, chasing another man who is shouting for help. By going in immediate pursuit, there is a good chance that the special officer (security officer) can stop the man with the pipe.
ACTION: The special officer (security officer) leaves his post unguarded and pursues the man.

The CORRECT answer is:

A. I B. II C. III D. IV

2. GENERAL RULE: Special officers (security officers) assigned to a college campus are instructed not to arrest students for minor violations such as disorderly conduct; instead, the violation should be stopped and the incident should be reported to the college authorities, who will take disciplinary action.
EXCEPTION: A special officer (security officer) may arrest a student or take other appropriate action if failure to do so is likely to result in personal injury or property damage, or disruption of school activities, or if the incident involves serious criminal behavior.
PROBLEM: A special officer (security officer) is on duty in a college building where evening classes are being held. He is told that two students are causing a disturbance in a classroom. He arrives and finds that a fist fight is in progress and the classroom is in an uproar. The special officer (security officer) separates the two students who are fighting and takes them out of the room. Both of them seem to be intoxicated. They both have valid student ID cards.
ACTION: The special officer (security officer) takes down their names and addresses for his report, then tells them to leave the building with a warning not to return this evening.

The CORRECT answer is:

A. I B. II C. III D. IV

3. GENERAL RULE: A special officer (security officer) is not permitted to carry a gun while on duty.
   EXCEPTION: A special officer (security officer) who disarms a person must keep the weapon in his possession for the brief period before he can turn it over to the proper authorities. A special officer (security officer) who is NOT on duty may, like any other citizen, own and carry a gun if he has a proper permit from the Police Department.
   PROBLEM: A special officer (security officer) is assigned to a post where there have been a series of violent incidents in the past few days. He feels that these incidents could have been controlled much more easily if the people involved had seen that the special officer (security officer) had a gun. He has a gun at home, for which he has a valid permit.
   ACTION: The special officer (security officer) brings his gun when he goes on duty. He does not plan to use it, but just show people that he has it so that they will not start any trouble.

   The CORRECT answer is:

   A. I   B. II   C. III   D. IV

4. GENERAL RULE: No one except a licensed physician or someone acting directly under a physician's orders may legally administer medicine to another person.
   EXCEPTION: In a first aid situation, the special officer (security officer) is allowed to help a person suffering from a heart condition or other disease to take medicine which the person has in his possession, provided that the person is conscious and requests this assistance.
   PROBLEM: A special officer (security officer) on duty at a public building is told that a man has collapsed in the elevator. When the special officer (security officer) arrives at the scene, the man is barely conscious. He cannot speak, but he points to his pocket. The special officer (security officer) finds a pill bottle that says *one capsule in ease of need*. The man nods.
   ACTION: The special officer (security officer) puts one capsule in the man's hand and guides the man's hand to his mouth.

   The CORRECT answer is:

   A. I   B. II   C. III   D. IV

5. GENERAL RULE: In case of a fire drill or fire alarm, special officers (security officers) on patrol in a building are to remain in their assigned areas to assist in the evacuation of persons from the building and to make sure that no one takes advantage of the situation by stealing property that is left unguarded.
   EXCEPTION: Should there be an actual fire, special officers (security officers) will follow whatever instructions are given by the firefighters or police officers who arrive on the scene to take charge.
   PROBLEM: A special officer (security officer) is on duty patroling the fifth floor of a building when a fire alarm sounds. The fire is in a supply closet at one end of the fifth floor. All personnel have been evacuated from the floor. Neither police nor firemen have yet shown up.
   ACTION: The special officer (security officer) stays on the fifth floor at a safe distance from the supply closet.

   The CORRECT answer is:

   A. I   B. II   C. III   D. IV

KEY (CORRECT ANSWERS)

1. B
2. A
3. D
4. B
5. A

EXAMINATION SECTION
TEST 1

DIRECTIONS: Each question or incomplete statement is followed by several suggested answers or completions. Select the one that BEST answers the question or completes the statement. *PRINT THE LETTER OF THE CORRECT ANSWER IN THE SPACE AT THE RIGHT.*

1. The officer who investigates accidents is always required to make a complete and accurate report.
   Of the following, the BEST reason for this procedure is to

   A. protect the operating agency against possible false claims
   B. provide a file of incidents which can be used as basic material for an accident prevention campaign
   C. provide the management with concrete evidence of violations of the rules by employees
   D. indicate what repairs need to be made

   1.____

2. It is suggested that an officer keep all persons away from the area of an accident until an investigation has been completed.
   This suggested procedure is

   A. *good;* witnesses will be more likely to agree on a single story
   B. *bad;* such action blocks traffic flow and causes congestion
   C. *good;* objects of possible use as evidence will be protected from damage or loss
   D. *bad;* the flow of normal pedestrian traffic provides an opportunity for an investigator to determine the cause of the accident

   2.____

3. A man having business with your agency is arguing with you and accuses you of being prejudiced against him. Although you explain to him that this is not so, he demands to see your supervisor.
   Of the following, the BEST course of action for you to take is to

   A. continue arguing with him until you have worn him out or convinced him
   B. take him to your supervisor
   C. ignore him and walk away from him to another part of the office
   D. escort him out of the office

   3.____

4. An officer receives instructions from his supervisor which he does not fully understand.
   For the officer to ask for a further explanation would be

   A. *good;* chiefly because his supervisor will be impressed with his interest in his work
   B. *poor;* chiefly because the time of the supervisor will be needlessly wasted
   C. *good;* chiefly because proper performance depends on full understanding of the work to be done
   D. *poor;* chiefly because officers should be able to think for themselves

   4.____

5. A person is making a complaint to an officer which seems unreasonable and of little importance.
   Of the following, the BEST action for the officer to take is to

   5.____

A. criticize the person making the complaint for taking up his valuable time
B. laugh over the matter to show that the complaint is minor and silly
C. tell the person that anyone responsible for his grievance will be prosecuted
D. listen to the person making the complaint and tell him that the matter will be investigated

6. A member of the department shall not indulge in intoxicating liquor while in uniform. A member of the department is not required to wear a uniform, and a uniformed member while out of uniform shall not indulge in intoxicants to an extent unfitting him for duty.
Of the following, the MOST correct interpretation of this rule is that a

   A. member, off duty, not in uniform, may drink intoxicating liquor
   B. member, not on duty, but in uniform, may drink intoxicating liquor
   C. member, on duty, in uniform, may drink intoxicants
   D. uniformed member, in civilian clothes, may not drink intoxicants

7. You have a suggestion for an important change which you believe will improve a certain procedure in your agency. Of the following, the next course of action for you to take is to

   A. try it out yourself
   B. submit the suggestion to your immediate supervisor
   C. write a letter to the head of your agency asking for his approval
   D. wait until you are asked for suggestions before submitting this one

8. An officer shall study maps and literature concerning his assigned area and the streets and points of interest nearby.
Of the following, the BEST reason for this rule is that

   A. the officer will be better able to give correct information to persons desiring it
   B. the officer will be better able to drive a vehicle in the area
   C. the officer will not lose interest in his work
   D. supervisors will not need to train the officers in this subject

9. In asking a witness to a crime to identify a suspect, it is a common practice to place the suspect with a group of persons and ask the witness to pick out the person in question.
Of the following, the BEST reason for this practice is that it will

   A. make the identification more reliable than if the witness were shown the suspect alone
   B. protect the witness against reprisals
   C. make sure that the witness is telling the truth
   D. help select other participants in the crime at the same time

10. It is most important for all officers to obey the "Rules and Regulations" of their agency.
Of the following, the BEST reason for this statement is that

    A. supervisors will not need to train their new officers
    B. officers will never have to use their own judgment
    C. uniform procedures will be followed
    D. officers will not need to ask their supervisors for assistance

Questions 11-13.

DIRECTIONS: Answer questions 11 to 13 SOLELY on the basis of the following paragraph.

All members of the police force must recognize that the people, through their representatives, hire and pay the police and that, as in any other employment, there must exist a proper employer-employee relationship. The police officer must understand that the essence of a correct police attitude is a willingness to serve, but at the same time, he should distinguish between service and servility, and between courtesy and softness. He must be firm but also courteous, avoiding even an appearance of rudeness. He should develop a position that is friendly and unbiased, pleasant and sympathetic, in his relations with the general public, but firm and impersonal on occasions calling for regulation and control. A police officer should understand that his primary purpose is to prevent violations, not to arrest people. He should recognize the line of demarcation between a police function and passing judgment which is a court function. On the other side, a public that cooperates with the police, that supports them in their efforts and that observes laws and regulations, may be said to have a desirable attitude.

11. In accordance with this paragraph, the PROPER attitude for a police officer to take is to   11.____

    A. be pleasant and sympathetic at all times
    B. be friendly, firm, and impartial
    C. be stern and severe in meting out justice to all
    D. avoid being rude, except in those cases where the public is uncooperative

12. Assume that an officer is assigned by his superior officer to a busy traffic intersection and is warned to be on the lookout for motorists who skip the light or who are speeding. According to this paragraph, it would be proper for the officer in this assignment to   12.____

    A. give a summons to every motorist whose ear was crossing when the light changed
    B. hide behind a truck and wait for drivers who violate traffic laws
    C. select at random motorists who seem to be impatient and lecture them sternly on traffic safety
    D. stand on post in order to deter violations and give offenders a summons or a warning as required

13. According to this paragraph, a police officer must realize that the primary purpose of police work is to   13.____

    A. provide proper police service in a courteous manner
    B. decide whether those who violate the law should be punished
    C. arrest those who violate laws
    D. establish a proper employer-employee relationship

Questions 14-15.

DIRECTIONS: Answer questions 14 and 15 SOLELY on the basis of the following paragraph.

If a motor vehicle fails to pass inspection, the owner will be given a rejection notice by the inspection station. Repairs must be made within ten days after this notice is issued. It is not necessary to have the required adjustment or repairs made at the station where the inspection occurred. The vehicle may be taken to any other garage. Re-inspection after repairs may be made at any official inspection station, not necessarily the same station which made the initial inspection. The registration of any motor vehicle for which an inspection sticker has not been obtained as required, or which is not repaired and inspected within ten days after inspection indicates defects, is subject to suspension. A vehicle cannot be used on public highways while its registration is under suspension.

14. According to the above paragraph, the owner of a car which does NOT pass inspection must   14.____

    A. have repairs made at the same station which rejected his car
    B. take the car to another station and have it re-inspected
    C. have repairs made anywhere and then have the car re-inspected
    D. not use the car on a public highway until the necessary repairs have been made

15. According to the above paragraph, the one of the following which may be cause for suspension of the registration of a vehicle is that   15.____

    A. an inspection sticker was issued before the rejection notice had been in force for ten days
    B. it was not re-inspected by the station that rejected it originally
    C. it was not re-inspected either by the station that rejected it originally or by the garage which made the repairs
    D. it has not had defective parts repaired within ten days after inspection

Questions 16-20.

DIRECTIONS: Answer questions 16 to 20 SOLELY on the basis of the following paragraph.

If we are to study crime in its widest social setting, we will find a variety of conduct which, although criminal in the legal sense, is not offensive to the moral conscience of a considerable number of persons. Traffic violations, for example, do not brand the offender as guilty of moral offense. In fact, the recipient of a traffic ticket is usually simply the subject of some good-natured joking by his friends. Although there may be indignation among certain groups of citizens against gambling and liquor law violations, these activities are often tolerated, if not openly supported, by the more numerous residents of the community. Indeed, certain social and service clubs regularly conduct gambling games and lotteries for the purpose of raising funds. Some communities regard violations involving the sale of liquor with little concern in order to profit from increased license fees and taxes paid by dealers. The thousand and one forms of political graft and corruption which infest our urban centers only occasionally arouse public condemnation and official action.

16. According to the paragraph, all types of illegal conduct are   16.____

    A. condemned by all elements of the community
    B. considered a moral offense, although some are tolerated by a few citizens
    C. violations of the law, but some are acceptable to certain elements of the community
    D. found in a social setting which is not punishable by law

17. According to the paragraph, traffic violations are generally considered by society as   17.____

    A. crimes requiring the maximum penalty set by the law
    B. more serious than violations of the liquor laws

C. offenses against the morals of the community
D. relatively minor offenses requiring minimum punishment

18. According to the paragraph, a lottery conducted for the purpose of raising funds for a church

    A. is considered a serious violation of law
    B. may be tolerated by a community which has laws against gambling
    C. may be conducted under special laws demanded by the more numerous residents of a community
    D. arouses indignation in most communities

19. On the basis of the paragraph, the MOST likely reaction in the community to a police raid on a gambling casino would be

    A. more an attitude of indifference than interest in the raid
    B. general approval of the raid
    C. condemnation of the raid by most people
    D. demand for further action since this raid is not sufficient to end gambling activities

20. The one of the following which BEST describes the central thought of this paragraph and would be MOST suitable as a title for it is

    A. CRIME AND THE POLICE
    B. PUBLIC CONDEMNATION OF GRAFT AND CORRUPTION
    C. GAMBLING IS NOT ALWAYS A VICIOUS BUSINESS
    D. PUBLIC ATTITUDE TOWARD LAW VIOLATIONS

Questions 21-23.

DIRECTIONS: Answer questions 21 to 23 SOLELY on the basis of the following paragraph.

The law enforcement agency is one of the most important agencies in the field of juvenile delinquency prevention. This is so not because of the social work connected with this problem, however, for this is not a police matter, but because the officers are usually the first to come in contact with the delinquent. The manner of arrest and detention makes a deep impression upon him and affects his life-long attitude toward society and the law. The juvenile court is perhaps the most important agency in this work. Contrary to the general opinion, however, it is not primarily concerned with putting children into correctional schools. The main purpose of the juvenile court is to save the child and to develop his emotional make-up in order that he can grow up to be a decent and well-balanced citizen. The system of probation is the means whereby the court seeks to accomplish these goals.

21. According to this paragraph, police work is an important part of a program to prevent juvenile delinquency because

    A. social work is no longer considered important in juvenile delinquency prevention
    B. police officers are the first to have contact with the delinquent
    C. police officers jail the offender in order to be able to change his attitude toward society and the law
    D. it is the first step in placing the delinquent in jail

22. According to this paragraph, the CHIEF purpose of the juvenile court is to   22.____

    A. punish the child for his offense
    B. select a suitable correctional school for the delinquent
    C. use available means to help the delinquent become a better person
    D. provide psychiatric care for the delinquent

23. According to this paragraph, the juvenile court directs the development of delinquents   23.____
    under its care CHIEFLY by

    A. placing the child under probation
    B. sending the child to a correctional school
    C. keeping the delinquent in prison
    D. returning the child to his home

Questions 24-27.

DIRECTIONS: Answer questions 24 to 27 SOLELY on the basis of the following paragraph.

When a vehicle has been disabled in the tunnel, the officer on patrol in this zone shall press the EMERGENCY TRUCK light button. In the fast lane, red lights will go on throughout the tunnel; in the slow lane, amber lights will go on throughout the tunnel. The yellow zone light will go on at each signal control station throughout the tunnel and will flash the number of the zone in which the stoppage has occurred. A red flashing pilot light will appear only at the signal control station at which the EMERGENCY TRUCK button was pressed. The emergency garage will receive an audible and visual signal indicating the signal control station at which the EMERGENCY TRUCK button was pressed. The garage officer shall acknowledge receipt of the signal by pressing the acknowledgment button. This will cause the pilot light at the operated signal control station in the tunnel to cease flashing and to remain steady. It is an answer to the officer at the operated signal control station that the emergency truck is responding to the call.

24. According to this paragraph, when the EMERGENCY TRUCK light button is pressed,   24.____

    A. amber lights will go on in every lane throughout the tunnel
    B. emergency signal lights will go on only in the lane in which the disabled vehicle happens to be
    C. red lights will go on in the fast lane throughout the tunnel
    D. pilot lights at all signal control stations will turn amber

25. According to this paragraph, the number of the zone in which the stoppage has occurred   25.____
    is flashed

    A. immediately after all the lights in the tunnel turn red
    B. by the yellow zone light at each signal control station
    C. by the emergency truck at the point of stoppage
    D. by the emergency garage

26. According to this paragraph, an officer near the disabled vehicle will know that the emer-   26.____
    gency tow truck is coming when

    A. the pilot light at the operated signal control station appears and flashes red
    B. an audible signal is heard in the tunnel

C. the zone light at the operated signal control station turns red
D. the pilot light at the operated signal control station becomes steady

27. Under the system described in the paragraph, it would be CORRECT to come to the conclusion that

   A. officers at all signal control stations are expected to acknowledge that they have received the stoppage signal
   B. officers at all signal control stations will know where the stoppage has occurred
   C. all traffic in both lanes of that side of the tunnel in which the stoppage has occurred must stop until the emergency truck has arrived
   D. there are two emergency garages, each able to respond to stoppages in traffic going in one particular direction

Questions 28-30.

DIRECTIONS: Answer questions 28 to 30 SOLELY on the basis of the following paragraphs.

In cases of accident, it is most important for an officer to obtain the name, age, residence, occupation, and a full description of the person injured, names and addresses of witnesses. He shall also obtain a statement of the attendant circumstances. He shall carefully note contributory conditions, if any, such as broken pavement, excavation, tights not burning, snow and ice on the roadway, etc. He shall enter all facts in his memorandum book and on Form 17 or Form 18 and promptly transmit the original of the form to his superior officer and the duplicate to headquarters.

An officer shall render reasonable assistance to sick or injured persons. If the circumstances appear to require the services of a physician, he shall summon a physician by telephoning the superior officer on duty and notifying him of the apparent nature of the illness or accident and the location where the physician will be required. He may summon other officers to assist if circumstances warrant.

In case of an accident or where a person is sick on city property, an officer shall obtain the information necessary to fill out card Form 18 and record this in his memorandum book and promptly telephone the facts to his superior officer. He shall deliver the original card at the expiration of his tour to his superior officer and transmit the duplicate to headquarters.

28. According to this quotation, the MOST important consideration in any report on a case of accident or injury is to

   A. obtain all the facts
   B. telephone his superior officer at once
   C. obtain a statement of the attendant circumstances
   D. determine ownership of the property on which the accident occurred

29. According to this quotation, in the case of an accident on city property, the officer should always

   A. summon a physician before filling out any forms or making any entries in his memorandum book
   B. give his superior officer on duty a prompt report by telephone

C. immediately bring the original of Form 18 to his superior officer on duty
D. call at least one other officer to the scene to witness conditions

30. If the procedures stated in this quotation were followed for all accidents in the city, an impartial survey of accidents occurring during any period of time in this city may be MOST easily made by

   A. asking a typical officer to show you his memorandum book
   B. having a superior officer investigate whether contributory conditions mentioned by witnesses actually exist
   C. checking all the records of all superior officers
   D. checking the duplicate card files at headquarters

Questions 31-55.

DIRECTIONS: In each of questions 31 to 55, select the lettered word or phrase which means MOST NEARLY the same as the first word in the row.

31. RENDEZVOUS

   A. parade   B. neighborhood
   C. meeting place   D. wander about

32. EMINENT

   A. noted   B. rich   C. rounded   D. nearby

33. CAUSTIC

   A. cheap   B. sweet   C. evil   D. sharp

34. BARTER

   A. annoy   B. trade   C. argue   D. cheat

35. APTITUDE

   A. friendliness   B. talent
   C. conceit   D. generosity

36. PROTRUDE

   A. project   B. defend   C. choke   D. boast

37. FORTITUDE

   A. disposition   B. restlessness
   C. courage   D. poverty

38. PRELUDE

   A. introduction   B. meaning
   C. prayer   D. secret

39. SECLUSION

   A. primitive   B. influence
   C. imagination   D. privacy

40. RECTIFY
    A. correct   B. construct   C. divide   D. scold

41. TRAVERSE
    A. rotate   B. compose   C. train   D. cross

42. ALLEGE
    A. raise   B. convict   C. declare   D. chase

43. MENIAL
    A. pleasant   B. unselfish
    C. humble   D. stupid

44. DEPLETE
    A. exhaust   B. gather   C. repay   D. close

45. ERADICATE
    A. construct   B. advise   C. destroy   D. exclaim

46. CAPITULATE
    A. cover   B. surrender   C. receive   D. execute

47. RESTRAIN
    A. restore   B. drive   C. review   D. limit

48. AMALGAMATE
    A. join   B. force   C. correct   D. clash

49. DEJECTED
    A. beaten   B. speechless
    C. weak   D. low-spirited

50. DETAIN
    A. hide   B. accuse   C. hold   D. mislead

KEY (CORRECT ANSWERS)

1.	A	11.	B	21.	B	31.	C	41.	D
2.	C	12.	D	22.	C	32.	A	42.	C
3.	B	13.	A	23.	A	33.	D	43.	C
4.	C	14.	C	24.	C	34.	B	44.	A
5.	D	15.	D	25.	B	35.	B	45.	C
6.	A	16.	C	26.	D	36.	A	46.	B
7.	B	17.	D	27.	B	37.	C	47.	D
8.	A	18.	B	28.	A	38.	A	48.	A
9.	A	19.	A	29.	B	39.	D	49.	D
10.	C	20.	D	30.	D	40.	A	50.	C

TEST 2

DIRECTIONS: Each question or incomplete statement is followed by several suggested answers or completions. Select the one that BEST answers the question or completes the statement. *PRINT THE LETTER OF THE CORRECT ANSWER IN THE SPACE AT THE RIGHT.*

1. AMPLE 1.____
   A. necessary   B. plentiful   C. protected   D. tasty

2. EXPEDITE 2.____
   A. sue   B. omit   C. hasten   D. verify

3. FRAGMENT 3.____
   A. simple tool   B. broken part
   C. basic outline   D. weakness

4. ADVERSARY 4.____
   A. thief   B. partner   C. loser   D. foe

5. ACHIEVE 5.____
   A. accomplish   B. begin   C. develop   D. urge

Questions 6-10.

DIRECTIONS: Answer Questions 6 to 10 on the basis of the information given in the table on the following page. The numbers which have been omitted from the table can be calculated from the other numbers which are given.

NUMBER OF DWELLING UNITS CONSTRUCTED

Year	Private one-family houses	In private apt. houses	In public housing	Total dwelling units
1996	4,500	500	600	5,600
1997	9,200	5,300	2,800	17,300
1998	8,900	12,800	6,800	28,500
1999	12,100	15,500	7,100	34,700
2000	?	12,200	14,100	39,200
2001	10,200	26,000	8,600	44,800
2002	10,300	17,900	7,400	35,600
2003	11,800	18,900	7,700	38,400
2004	12,700	22,100	8,400	43,200
2005	13,300	24,300	8,100	45,700
TOTALS	105,900	?	?	?

6. According to this table, the average number of public housing units constructed yearly during the period 1996 through 2005 was 6.____

   A. 7,160   B. 6,180   C. 7,610   D. 6,810

271

7. Of the following, the two years in which the number of private one-family homes constructed was GREATEST for the two years together is

   A. 1998 and 1999
   B. 1997 and 2003
   C. 1998 and 2004
   D. 2001 and 2002

8. For the entire period of 1996 through 2005, the total of all private one-family houses constructed exceeded the total of all public housing units constructed by

   A. 34,300   B. 45,700   C. 50,000   D. 83,900

9. Of the total number of private apartment house dwelling units constructed in the ten years given in the table, the percentage which was constructed in 2002 was MOST NEARLY

   A. 5%   B. 11%   C. 16%   D. 21%

10. Considering dwelling units of all types, the average number constructed annually in the period from 2001 through 2005 was GREATER than the average number constructed annually in the period from 1996 through 2000 by

    A. 16,480   B. 33,320   C. 79,300   D. 82,400

11. A car speeds through the toll entrance of a 2 1/4 mile long bridge without paying the toll and reaches the other end of the bridge 1 minute and 30 seconds later. The car was traveling MOST NEARLY at a rate of _____ miles per hour.

    A. 60   B. 70   C. 80   D. 90

12. During one week, 21,500 vehicles passed through the toll booths of a certain bridge. Of these, 550 were buses, 2,230 were trucks, and the rest were passenger cars. The toll charges were $3.50 for a passenger car, $7 for a truck and $14 for a bus. The total income for the week was

    A. $80,850   B. $88,830   C. $102,550   D. $109,550

13. A bullet fired from a revolver travels 100 feet the first second, and each succeeding second it travels a distance 10% less than during the immediately preceding second. The number of feet the bullet will have traveled at the end of the fourth second is MOST NEARLY

    A. 272   B. 320   C. 344   D. 360

14. An officer receives a uniform allowance of $500 a year in a lump sum. Of this amount, he spends $180 for a winter jacket and 40% of the remainder for two pairs of trousers. The officer now wishes to buy a winter overcoat which costs $240.
    The percentage of the purchase price of the overcoat by which he will be short is

    A. 20%   B. 25%   C. 48%   D. 60%

15. It has been suggested that small light cars can be used for certain kinds of police work. These light vehicles can run 30 miles per gallon of gasoline as contrasted with standard cars which run only 15 miles per gallon. Assume gasoline costs the city $3.75 per gallon. During 9,000 miles of travel, use of the small light car in preference to the standard car would result in a saving in gasoline costs of MOST NEARLY

    A. $1,125   B. $1,500   C. $1,875   D. $2,250

16. Out of a total of 34,750 felony complaints in 2006, 14,200 involved burglary. In 2005, there was a total of 32,300 felony complaints of which 12,800 were burglary.
Of the increase in felonies from 2005 to 2006, the increase in burglaries comprised APPROXIMATELY

    A. 27%   B. 37%   C. 47%   D. 57%

16.____

17. A certain city department has two offices which issue permits, one office handling twice as many applicants as the other. The smaller office grants permits to 40% of its applicants. The larger office handling twice as many applicants grants permits to 60% of its applicants.
If there were 900 applicants at both offices together on a given day, the total number of permits granted by both offices would be MOST NEARLY

    A. 420   B. 450   C. 480   D. 510

17.____

18. If a co-worker is not breathing after receiving an electric shock but is no longer in contact with the electricity, it is MOST important for you to

    A. avoid moving him
    B. wrap the victim in a blanket
    C. start artificial respiration promptly
    D. force him to take hot liquids

18.____

19. Employees using supplies from one of the first-aid kits available throughout the building are required to submit an immediate report of the occurrence.
Logical reasoning shows that the MOST important reason for this report is so that the

    A. supplies used will be sure to be replaced
    B. first-aid kit can be properly sealed again
    C. employee will be credited for his action
    D. record of first-aid supplies will be up-to-date

19.____

20. The BEST IMMEDIATE first-aid treatment for a scraped knee is to

    A. apply plain vaseline   B. wash it with soap and water
    C. apply heat   D. use a knee splint

20.____

21. Artificial respiration after a severe electrical shock is ALWAYS necessary when the shock results in

    A. unconsciousness   B. stoppage of breathing
    C. bleeding   D. a burn

21.____

22. The authority gives some of its maintenance employees instruction in first aid.
The MOST likely reason for doing this is to

    A. eliminate the need for calling a doctor in case of accident
    B. provide temporary emergency treatment in case of accident
    C. lower the cost of accidents to the authority
    D. reduce the number of accidents

22.____

23. The BEST IMMEDIATE first aid if a chemical solution splashes into the eyes is to

    A. protect the eyes from the light by bandaging
    B. rub the eyes dry with a towel

23.____

C. cause tears to flow by staring at a bright light
D. flush the eyes with large quantities of clean water

24. If you had to telephone for an ambulance because of an accident, the MOST important information for you to give the person who answered the telephone would be the

A. exact time of the accident
B. cause of the accident
C. place where the ambulance is needed
D. names and addresses of those injured

25. If a person has a deep puncture wound in his finger caused by a sharp nail, the BEST IMMEDIATE first aid procedure would be to

A. encourage bleeding by exerting pressure around the injured area
B. stop all bleeding
C. prevent air from reaching the wound
D. probe the wound for steel particles

26. In addition to cases of submersion, artificial respiration is a recommended first aid procedure for

A. sunstroke   B. electrical shock   C. chemical poisoning   D. apoplexy

27. Assume that you are called on to render first aid to a man injured in an accident. You find he is bleeding profusely, is unconscious, and has a broken arm. There is a strong odor of alcohol about him.
The FIRST thing for which you should treat him is the

A. bleeding   B. unconsciousness   C. broken arm   D. alcoholism

28. In applying first aid for removal of a foreign body in the eye, an important precaution to be observed is NOT to

A. attempt to wash out the foreign body
B. bring the upper eyelid down over the lower
C. rub the eye
D. touch or attempt to remove a speck on the lower lid

29. The one of the following symptoms which is LEAST likely to indicate that a person involved in an accident requires first aid for shock is that

A. he has fainted twice
B. his face is red and flushed
C. his skin is wet with sweat
D. his pulse is rapid

30. When giving first aid to a person suffering from shock as a result of an auto accident, it is MOST important to

A. massage him in order to aid blood circulation
B. have him sip whiskey
C. prop him up in a sitting position
D. cover the person and keep him warm

Questions 31-34.

DIRECTIONS: Answer questions 31 to 34 SOLELY on the basis of the following paragraph.

Assume that you are an officer assigned to one large office which issues and receives applications for various permits and licenses. The office consists of one section where the necessary forms are issued; another section where fees are paid to a cashier; and desks where applicants are interviewed and their forms reviewed and completed. There is also a section containing tables and chairs where persons may sit and fill out their applications before being interviewed or paying the fees. your duties consist of answering simple questions, directing the public to the correct section of the office, and maintaining order.

31. A man who speaks English poorly asks you for assistance in obtaining and filling out an application for a permit. You should

    A. send him to an interviewer who can assist him
    B. try to determine what permit he wants and fill out the form for him
    C. refer the man to the office supervisor
    D. ask another applicant to help this person

31._____

32. The office becomes noisy and crowded, with people milling around waiting for service at the various sections.
Of the following, the BEST action for you to take is to

    A. stand in a prominent place and in a loud voice request the people to be quiet
    B. direct all the people not being served to wait at the unoccupied tables until you call them
    C. line up the people in front of each section and keep the lines in good order
    D. tell the people to form a single line outside the office and let in a few at a time

32._____

33. A man who has just been denied a permit becomes angry and shouts that if he "knew the right people" he too could get a permit. His behavior is disturbing the office.
Of the following, the BEST action for you to take is to

    A. order the man to leave at once since his business is done
    B. tell the man to be quiet and file another application
    C. suggest to the supervisor that a pamphlet be prepared explaining the requirements for permits in simple language
    D. ask an interviewer to explain the requirements for his permit to the person and his right of appeal

33._____

34. Just before the close of business, a man rushes in and insists on being interviewed for a permit because his present one expires that night.
Of the following, the BEST action for you to take is to

    A. tell the man that the office is closed
    B. tell the man that there will be no penalty if he returns early the next morning
    C. inquire if an interviewer is still available to take care of him and send him to that desk
    D. tell the cashier to collect the fee and tell the man to return the next morning for an interview

34._____

35. Fingerprints are often taken of applicants for licenses. Of the following, the MOST valid reason for this procedure is that

    A. the license of someone who commits a crime can be more readily revoked
    B. applicants can be checked for possible criminal records
    C. it helps to make sure that the proper license fee is paid
    D. a complete employment record of the applicant is obtained

36. Assume that an officer is on patrol at 2 A.M. He notices that the night light inside one of the stores in a public building is out. The store is locked.
    Of the following, the FIRST action for him to take at this time is to

    A. continue on his patrol since the light probably burned out
    B. enter the store by any means possible so he can check it
    C. report the matter to his superior
    D. shine his flashlight through the window to look for anything unusual

37. In questioning a man suspected of having committed a theft, the BEST procedure for an officer to follow is to

    A. induce the man to express his feelings about the police, the courts, and his home environment
    B. threaten him with beatings when he refuses to answer your questions
    C. make any promises necessary to get him to confess
    D. remain calm and objective

38. As an officer, you are on duty in one of the offices of a large public building. A woman who has just finished her business with this office comes to you and reports that her son who was with her is missing.
    The one of the following which is the BEST action for you to take FIRST is to

    A. tell the mother that the child is probably all right and ask her to go to the local police station for help in finding the boy
    B. suggest that the mother wait in the office until the child turns up
    C. check nearby offices in an attempt to locate the child
    D. telephone the local police station and ask if any reports fitting the description of the child have been received

39. An officer assigned to patrol inside a public building at night has observed two men standing outside the doorway. Of the following, the MOST appropriate action for the officer to take FIRST is to

    A. approach the two men and ask them why they are standing there
    B. hide and wait for the two men to take some action
    C. phone the local police station and ask for help since these men may be planning criminal action
    D. check all the entrance doors of the building to make sure that they are locked

40. It is standard practice for special officers to inspect the restrooms in public buildings. This is done at regular intervals while on patrol.
    Of the following, the BEST reason for this practice is to

    A. inspect sanitary conditions
    B. discourage loiterers and potential criminals

C. check the ventilation
D. determine if all the equipment and plumbing is working properly

41. While on duty in the evening as an officer assigned to a public building, you receive a report that a card game is going on in one of the offices. Gambling is forbidden on government property.
Of the following, the BEST course of action for you to take is to

    A. go to the office and order the card players to leave
    B. ignore the complaint since this is probably just harmless social card playing
    C. report the matter to the building manager the next day
    D. go to the office and, if warranted, issue an appropriate warning

42. It has been suggested that special officers establish good working relationships with the local police officers of the police department on duty in the neighborhood.
Of the following, the MOST valid reason for this practice is that

    A. a spirit of good feeling and high morale will be created among members of the police department
    B. local police officers will probably cooperate more readily with the special officer
    C. local police officers can take over the building patrol duties of the special officer in case he is absent
    D. special officers have an even stronger obligation than ordinary citizens to cooperate with the police

43. It has been proposed that an officer assigned to a public building at night remain at one location in the building, instead of walking on patrol through the building.
This proposal is

    A. *bad;* chiefly because the officer would probably sit instead of stand at the proper location
    B. *good;* chiefly because the officer could do a better job of watching the entire building from one point
    C. *bad;* chiefly because anyone seeking to enter the building for illegal purposes might be able to do so at a point other than where the special officer is on duty
    D. *good;* chiefly because his supervisors would know exactly where to find him

44. In a busy office, an officer has been assigned the duty of making sure that the public is served in the order of their arrival at the office and that some employee is always taking care of a person desiring help.
Of the following, the BEST method for the officer to follow is to

    A. line up the persons in the waiting room
    B. give a numbered ticket to each person waiting and call out the numbers, in order, when an employee becomes available
    C. loudly announce "next" when an employee is available to serve someone
    D. seat one person next to each employee's desk and let the others wait for the first vacant seat

45. Two men have broken into and entered a building at night. The officer on duty at this building sees them, chases them out, and then observes them in the adjoining building. Of the following, the BEST course of action for the officer to take is to

   A. notify the local police station and be ready to aid the police
   B. enter the adjoining building to find the men
   C. notify the manager of his own building
   D. continue on duty since these men have left the building for which he is responsible

45.____

46. While an officer is on duty in a crowded waiting room, he finds a woman's purse on the floor.
Of the following, the FIRST course of action for him to take is to

   A. hold it up in the air, ask who owns it, and give it to whoever claims it
   B. keep the purse until someone claims it
   C. immediately deliver the purse to the "lost and found" desk
   D. ask the lady who is nearest to him if she lost a purse

46.____

47. Special officers often have the power of arrest.
Of the following, the BEST reason for this practice is to

   A. have the officer always arrest any person who refuses to obey his orders
   B. aid in maintaining order in places where he is assigned
   C. promote good public relations
   D. aid in preventing illegal use of public buildings by tenants or employees

47.____

48. An officer has told a mother that he found her son writing on the walls of the building with chalk. The mother tells the officer that he should be more concerned with "crooks" than with children's minor pranks.
Of the following, the BEST answer for the officer to make to this woman is that

   A. children should be taught good conduct by their parents
   B. damage to public property means higher taxes
   C. serious criminals often begin their careers with minor violations
   D. it is his duty to enforce all rules and regulations

48.____

49. A man asks you, a special officer, where to get a certain kind of license not issued in your office. You don't know where such licenses are issued.
Of the following, the BEST procedure for you to follow is to

   A. refer him to the manager of the office
   B. get the information if you can and give it to the man
   C. tell the man to inquire at any police station house
   D. tell the man that you just do not know

49.____

50. Special officers are not permitted to ask private citizens to buy tickets for dances or other such social functions, not even when such functions are operated by charitable organizations. Of the following, the BEST reason for this rule is that

   A. private citizens are under no obligation to buy any such tickets
   B. not all groups are allowed equal opportunity in the sale of their tickets
   C. private citizens might complain to officials
   D. private citizens might feel they would not get proper service unless they bought such tickets

50.____

KEY (CORRECT ANSWERS)

1.	B	11.	D	21.	B	31.	A	41.	D
2.	C	12.	B	22.	B	32.	C	42.	B
3.	B	13.	C	23.	D	33.	D	43.	C
4.	D	14.	A	24.	C	34.	C	44.	B
5.	A	15.	A	25.	A	35.	B	45.	A
6.	A	16.	D	26.	B	36.	D	46.	C
7.	C	17.	C	27.	A	37.	D	47.	B
8.	A	18.	C	28.	C	38.	C	48.	D
9.	B	19.	A	29.	B	39.	D	49.	B
10.	A	20.	B	30.	D	40.	B	50.	D

SOLUTIONS TO ARITHMETIC PROBLEMS

11. $2\frac{1}{4}$ miles are completed in 1 1/2 minutes (1 minute and 30 seconds)

    $\therefore 2\frac{1}{4} \div 1\frac{1}{2}$ = rate per minute

    $= \frac{9}{4} \div 1\frac{1}{2}$

    $= \frac{9}{4} \div \frac{3}{2}$

    $= \frac{9}{4} \times \frac{2}{3}$

    $= \frac{3}{2}$ miles per minute

    $\therefore \frac{3}{2} \times 60$ (minutes in an hour) = rate per hour = 90 miles per hour

    (Ans. D)

12. 550 + 2230 = 2780; 21,500 - 2780 = 18,720 passengers

550 buses at $14.00	=	$ 7,700
2230 trucks at $7.00	=	15,610
18720 passengers at $3.50	=	65,520
		$88,830

    (Ans. B)

13. Given: speed = 100 feet the first second

100 - 10 (10% of 100)	=	90 feet - the second second
90 - 9 (10% of 90)	=	81 feet - the third second
81 - 8.1 (10% of 81)	=	72.9 feet - the fourth second
		343.9 (total at end of the fourth second)

    (Ans. C)

14. Given: 500 = uniform allowance

    $500 - 180 = $320   (amount left after buying winter jacket)
    $320 × 40% = $128   (amount spent for two pairs of trousers)
    $320 - 128 = $192   (amount now left)

    Since the winter overcoat costs $240, he is now short $48 ($240 - 192) or 20% of the purchase price of the overcoat. (48/240 = $\frac{1}{5}$ = 20%)

(Ans. A)

15. Light care: 9000(miles)÷30(miles per gallon)×3.75(per gallon)

$$= \frac{9000}{30} \times 3.75$$
$$= 300 \times 3.75$$
$$= \$1,125 \text{ (total gasoline cost)}$$

Standard cars: 9000 (miles) ÷ 15 (miles per gallon) x 3.75

$$= \frac{9000}{15} \times 3.75$$
$$= 600 \times 3.75$$
$$= \$2,250 \text{ (total gasoline cost)}$$

∴ use of light car would result in a saving in gasoline costs of $1,125 ($2,250 - $1,125).

(Ans. A)

16. 2006: 14,200   (burglary)
    2005: 12,800   (burglary)
           1,400   (increase in burglaries)

    2006: 34,750   (felony)
    2005: 32,300   (felony)
           2,450   (increase in felonies

$$\therefore 1400 \div 2450 = \frac{1400}{2450} = .57$$

WORK

```
         .57
2450 ) 1400.0
       1225.0
        175.00
        171.50
```

(Ans. D)

17. Given: smaller office: grants permits to 40% of 1/3 of the total number of applicants (900)

    larger office: grants permits to 60% of 2/3 of the total number of applicants (900)

    Solving: smaller office: $.40 \times \frac{1}{3} \times 900 = 120$ permits

    larger office: $.60 \times \frac{2}{3} \times 900 = \underline{360}$ permits
    $\phantom{larger office: .60 \times \frac{2}{3} \times 900 =}$ 480 permits (total)

(Ans. C)

EXAMINATION SECTION
TEST 1

DIRECTIONS: Each question or incomplete statement is followed by several suggested answers or completions. Select the one that BEST answers the question or completes the statement. *PRINT THE LETTER OF THE CORRECT ANSWER IN THE SPACE AT THE RIGHT.*

Questions 1-4.

DIRECTIONS: Questions 1 through 4 are based on the picture entitled *Contents of a Woman's Handbag.* Assume that all of the contents are shown in the picture.

CONTENTS OF A WOMAN'S HANDBAG

283

1. Where does Gladys Constantine live?

    A. Chalmers Street in Manhattan
    B. Summer Street in Manhattan
    C. Summer Street in Brooklyn
    D. Chalmers Street in Brooklyn

2. How many keys were in the handbag?

    A. 2   B. 3   C. 4   D. 5

3. How much money was in the handbag? _____ dollar(s).

    A. Exactly five   B. More than five
    C. Exactly ten   D. Less than one

4. The sales slip found in the handbag shows the purchase of which of the following?

    A. The handbag   B. Lipstick
    C. Tissues   D. Prescription medicine

Questions 5-8.

DIRECTIONS: Questions 5 through 8 are based on the floor plan below.

FLOOR PLAN

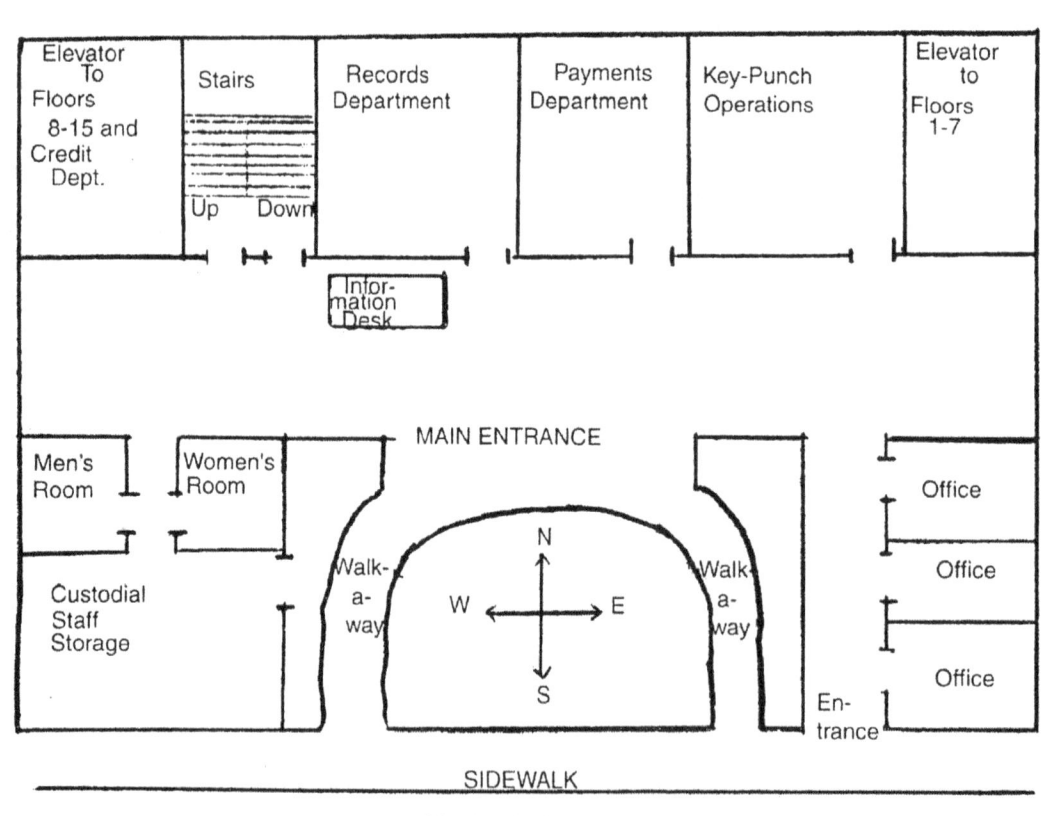

5. A special officer (security officer) on duty at the main entrance must be aware of other outside entrances to his area of the building. These unguarded entrances are usually kept locked, but they are important in case of fire or other emergency.
    Besides the main entrance, how many OTHER entrances shown on the floor plan directly face Forty-ninth Street?
    _____ other entrances.

    A. No B. One C. Two D. Three

6. A person who arrives at the main entrance and asks to be directed to the Credit Department SHOULD be told to

    A. take the elevator on the left
    B. take the elevator on the right
    C. go to a different entrance
    D. go up the stairs on the left

7. On the east side of the entrance can be found

    A. a storage room   B. offices
    C. toilets   D. stairs

8. The space DIRECTLY BEHIND the Information Desk in the floor plan is occupied by

    A. up and down stairs   B. key punch operations
    C. toilets   D. the records department

Questions 9-12.

DIRECTIONS: Answer Questions 9 to 12 on the basis of the information given in the passage below.

The public often believes that the main job of a uniformed officer is to enforce laws by simply arresting people. In reality, however, many of the situations that an officer deals with do not call for the use of his arrest power. In the first place, an officer spends much of his time preventing crimes from happening, by spotting potential violations or suspicious behavior and taking action to prevent illegal acts. In the second place, many of the situations in which officers are called on for assistance involve elements like personal arguments, husband-wife quarrels, noisy juveniles, or mentally disturbed persons. The majority of these problems do not result in arrests and convictions, and often they do not even involve illegal behavior. In the third place, even in situations where there seems to be good reason to make an arrest, an officer may have to exercise very good judgment. There are times when making an arrest too soon could touch off a riot, or could result in the detention of a minor offender while major offenders escaped, or could cut short the gathering of necessary on-the-scene evidence.

9. The above passage IMPLIES that most citizens

    A. will start to riot if they see an arrest being made
    B. appreciate the work that law enforcement officers do
    C. do not realize that making arrests is only a small part of law enforcement
    D. never call for assistance unless they are involved in a personal argument or a husband-wife quarrel

10. According to the passage, one way in which law enforcement officers can prevent crimes from happening is by

   A. arresting suspicious characters
   B. letting minor offenders go free
   C. taking action on potential violations
   D. refusing to get involved in husband-wife fights

11. According to the passage, which of the following statements is NOT true of situations involving mentally disturbed persons?

   A. It is a waste of time to call on law enforcement officers for assistance in such situations.
   B. Such situations may not involve illegal behavior
   C. Such situations often do not result in arrests.
   D. Citizens often turn to law enforcement officers for help in such situations.

12. The last sentence in the passage mentions *detention of minor offenders.*
    Of the following, which BEST explains the meaning of the word *detention* as used here?

   A. Sentencing someone
   B. Indicting someone
   C. Calling someone before a grand jury
   D. Arresting someone

Questions 13-28.

DIRECTIONS: In answering Questions 13 through 28, assume that *you* means a special officer (security officer) on duty. Your basic responsibilities are safeguarding people and property and maintaining order in the area to which you are assigned. You are in uniform, and you are not armed. You keep in touch with your supervisory station either by telephone or by a two-way radio (walkie-talkie).

13. It is a general rule that if the security alarm goes off showing that someone has made an unlawful entrance into a building, no officer responsible for security shall proceed to investigate alone. Each officer must be accompanied by at least one other officer.
    Of the following, which is the MOST probable reason for this rule?

   A. It is dangerous for an officer to investigate such a situation alone.
   B. The intruder might try to bribe an officer to let him go.
   C. One officer may be inexperienced and needs an experienced partner.
   D. Two officers are better than one officer in writing a report of the investigation.

14. You are on weekend duty on the main floor of a public building. The building is closed to the public on weekends, but some employees are sometimes asked to work weekends. You have been instructed to use cautious good judgment in opening the door for such persons.
    Of the following, which one MOST clearly shows the poorest judgment?

A. Admitting an employee who is personally known to you without asking to see any identification except the permit slip signed by the employee's supervisor
B. Refusing to admit someone whom you do not recognize but who claims left his identification at home
C. Admitting to the building only those who can give a detailed description of their weekend work duties
D. Leaving the entrance door locked for a while to make regulation security checks of other areas in the building with the result that no one can either enter or leave during these periods

15. You are on duty at a public building. An office employee tells you that she left her purse in her desk when she went out to lunch, and she has just discovered that it is gone. She has been back from lunch for half an hour and has not left her desk during this period. What should you do FIRST?

    A. Warn all security personnel to stop any suspicious-looking person who is seen with a purse
    B. Ask for a description of the purse
    C. Call the Lost and Found and ask if a purse has been turned in
    D. Obtain statements from any employees who were in the office during the lunch hour

16. You are patrolling your assigned area in a public building. You hear a sudden crash and the sound of running footsteps. You investigate and find that someone has forced open a locked entrance to the building. What is the FIRST thing you should do?

    A. Close the door and try to fix the lock so that no one else can get in
    B. Use your two-way radio to report the emergency and summon help
    C. Chase after the person whose running footsteps you heard
    D. Go immediately to your base office and make out a brief written report

17. You and another special officer (security officer) are on duty in the main waiting area at a welfare center. A caseworker calls both of you over and whispers that one of the clients, Richard Roe, may be carrying a gun. Of the following, what is the BEST action for both of you to take?

    A. You should approach the man, one on each side, and one of you should say loudly and clearly, "Richard Roe, you are under arrest."
    B. Both of you should ask the man to go with you to a private room, and then find out if he is carrying a gun
    C. Both of you should grab him, handcuff him, and take him to the nearest precinct station house
    D. Both of you should watch him carefully but not do anything unless he actually pulls a gun

18. You are on duty at a welfare center. You are told that a caseworker is being threatened by a man with a knife. You go immediately to the scene, and you find the caseworker lying on the floor with blood spurting from a wound in his arm. You do not know who the attacker is. What should you do FIRST?

    A. Ask the caseworker for a description of the attacker so that you can set out in pursuit and try to catch him
    B. Take down the names and addresses of any witnesses to the incident

C. Give first aid to the caseworker, if you can, and immediately call for an ambulance
D. Search the people standing around in the room for the knife

19. As a special officer (security officer), you have been patrolling a special section of a hospital building for a week. Smoking is not allowed in this section because the oxygen tanks in use here could easily explode. However, you have observed that some employees sneak into the linen-supply room in this section in order to smoke without anybody seeing them.
Of the following, which is the BEST way for you to deal with this situation?

    A. Whenever you catch anyone smoking, call his supervisor immediately
    B. Request the Building Superintendent to put a padlock on the door of the linen-supply room
    C. Ignore the smoking because you do not want to get a reputation for interfering in the private affairs of other employees
    D. Report the situation to your supervisor and follow his instructions

19.____

20. You are on duty at a hospital. You have been assigned to guard the main door, and you are responsible for remaining at your post until relieved. On one of the wards for which you are not responsible, there is a patient who was wounded in a street fight. This patient is under arrest for killing another man in this fight, and he is supposed to be under round-the-clock police guard. A nurse tells you that one of the police officers assigned to guard the patient has suddenly taken ill and has to periodically leave his post to go to the washroom. The nurse is worried because she thinks the patient might try to escape.
Of the following, which is the BEST action for you to take?

    A. Tell the nurse to call you whenever the police officer leaves his post so that you can keep an eye on the patient while the officer is gone
    B. Assume that the police officer probably knows his job, and that there is no reason for you to worry
    C. Alert your supervisor to the nurse's report
    D. Warn the police officer that the nurse has been talking about him

20.____

21. You are on night duty at a hospital where you are responsible for patrolling a large section of the main building. Your supervisor tells you that there have been several nighttime thefts from a supply room in your section and asks you to be especially alert for suspicious activity near this supply room.
Of the following, which is the MOST reasonable way to carry out your supervisor's direction?

    A. Check the supply room regularly at half-hour intervals
    B. Make frequent checks of the supply room at irregular intervals
    C. Station yourself by the door of the supply room and stay at this post all night
    D. Find a hidden spot from which you can watch the supply room and stay there all night

21.____

22. You are on duty at a vehicle entrance to a hospital. Parking space on the hospital grounds is strictly limited, and no one is ever allowed to park there unless they have an official parking permit. You have just stopped a driver who does not have a parking permit, but he explains that
he is a doctor and he has a patient in the hospital. What should you do?

22.____

A. Let him park since he has explained that he is a doctor
B. Ask in a friendly way, *"Can I check your identification?"*
C. Call the Information Desk to make sure there is such a patient in the hospital
D. Tell the driver politely but firmly that he will have to park somewhere else

23. You are on duty at a public building. A man was just mugged on a stairway. The mugger took the man's wallet and started to run down the stairs but tripped and fell. Now the mugger is lying unconscious at the bottom of the stairs and bleeding from the mouth.
The FIRST thing you should do is to

A. search him to see if he is carrying any other stolen property
B. pick him up and carry him away from the stairs
C. try and revive him for questioning
D. put in a call for an ambulance and police assistance

24. After someone breaks into an employee's locker at a public building, you interview the employee to determine what is missing from the locker. The employee becomes hysterical and asks why you are *wasting time with all these questions* instead of going after the thief.
The MOST reasonable thing for you to do is

A. tell the employee that it is very important to have an accurate description of the missing articles
B. quietly tell the employee to calm down and stop interfering with your work
C. explain to the employee that you are only doing what you were told to do and that you don't make the rules
D. assure the employee that there are a lot of people working on the case and that someone else is probably arresting the thief right now

25. You are on duty at a public building. An employee reports that a man has just held her up and taken her money. The employee says that the man was about 25 years old, with short blond hair and a pale complexion and was wearing blue jeans.
Of the following additional facts, which one would probably be MOST valuable to officers searching the building for the suspect?

A. The man was wearing dark glasses.
B. He had on a green jacket.
C. He was about 5 feet 8 inches tall.
D. His hands and fingernails were very dirty.

26. When the fire alarm goes off, it is your job as a special officer (security officer) to see that all employees leave the building quickly by the correct exits. A fire alarm has just sounded, and you are checking the offices on one of the floors. A supervisor in one office tells you, *"This is probably just another fire drill. I've sent my office staff out, but I don't want to stop my own work."*
What should you do?

A. Insist politely but firmly that the supervisor must obey the fire rules.
B. Tell the supervisor that it is all right this time but that the rules must be followed in the future.
C. Tell the supervisor that he is under arrest.
D. Allow the supervisor to do as he sees fit since he is in charge of his own office.

27. You are on duty on the main floor of a public building. You have been informed that a briefcase has just been stolen from an office on the tenth floor. You see a man getting off the elevator with a briefcase that matches the description of the one that was stolen.
What is the FIRST action you should take?

    A. Arrest the man and take him to the nearest public station
    B. Stop the man and say politely that you want to take a look at the briefcase
    C. Take the briefcase from the man and tell him that he cannot have it back unless he can prove that it is his
    D. Do not stop the man but note down his description and the exact time he got off the elevator

27._____

28. You are on duty at a welfare center. You have been told that two clients are arguing with a caseworker and making loud threats. You go to the scene, but the caseworker tells you that everything is now under control. The two clients, who are both mean-looking characters, are still there but seem to be acting normally.
What SHOULD you do?

    A. Apologize for having made a mistake and go away.
    B. Arrest the two men for having caused a disturbance.
    C. Insist on standing by until the interview is over, then escort the two men from the building.
    D. Leave the immediate scene but watch for any further developments.

28._____

29. You are on duty at a welfare center. A client comes up to you and says that two men just threatened him with a knife and made him give them his money. The client has alcohol on his breath and he is shabbily dressed. He points out the two men he says took the money.
Of the following, which is the BEST action to take?

    A. Arrest the two men on the client's complaint.
    B. Ignore the client's complaint since he doesn't look as if he could have had any money.
    C. Suggest to the client that he may be imagining things.
    D. Investigate and find out what happened.

29._____

Questions 30-35.

DIRECTIONS: Answer Questions 30 through 35 on the basis of the information given in the passage below. Assume that all questions refer to the same state described in the passage.

The courts and the police consider an "offense" as any conduct that is punishable by a fine or imprisonment. Such offenses include many kinds of acts - from behavior that is merely annoying, like throwing a noisy party that keeps everyone awake, all the way up to violent acts like murder. The law classifies offenses according to the penalties that are provided for them. In one state, minor offenses are called "violations." A violation is punishable by a fine of not more than $250 or imprisonment of not more than. 15 days, or both. The annoying behavior mentioned above is an example of a violation. More serious offenses are classified as "crimes." Crimes are classified by the kind of penalty that is provided. A "misdemeanor" is a crime that is punishable by a fine of not more than $1,000 or by imprisonment of not more than one year, or both. Examples of misdemeanors include stealing something with a value of $100 or less, turning in a false alarm, or illegally possessing less than 1/8 of an ounce of a dangerous drug. A "felony" is a criminal offense punishable by imprisonment of more than one year. Murder is clearly a felony.

30. According to the above passage, any act that is punishable by imprisonment or by a fine is called a(n)

   A. offense   B. violation   C. crime   D. felony

31. According to the above passage, which of the following is classified as a crime?

   A. Offense punishable by 15 days imprisonment
   B. Minor offense
   C. Violation
   D. Misdemeanor

32. According to the above passage, if a person guilty of burglary can receive a prison sentence of 7 years or more, burglary would be classified as a

   A. violation   B. misdemeanor
   C. felony   D. violent act

33. According to the above passage, two offenses that would BOTH be classified as misdemeanors are

   A. making unreasonable noise and stealing a $90 bicycle
   B. stealing a $75 radio and possessing 1/16 of an ounce of heroin
   C. holding up a bank and possessing 1/4 of a pound of marijuana
   D. falsely reporting a fire and illegally double-parking

34. The above passage says that offenses are classified according to the penalties provided for them.
   On the basis of clues in the passage, who probably decides what the maximum penalties should be for the different kinds of offenses?

   A. The State lawmakers   B. The City police
   C. The Mayor   D. Officials in Washington, B.C.

35. Of the following, which BEST describes the subject matter of the passage?

   A. How society deals with criminals
   B. How offenses are classified
   C. Three types of criminal behavior
   D. The police approach to offenders

KEY (CORRECT ANSWERS)

1.	C	16.	B
2.	C	17.	B
3.	B	18.	C
4.	D	19.	D
5.	B	20.	C
6.	A	21.	B
7.	B	22.	D
8.	D	23.	D
9.	C	24.	A
10.	C	25.	C
11.	A	26.	A
12.	D	27.	B
13.	A	28.	D
14.	C	29.	D
15.	B	30.	A

31.	D
32.	C
33.	B
34.	A
35.	B

TEST 2

DIRECTIONS: Each question or incomplete statement is followed by several suggested answers or completions. Select the one that BEST answers the question or completes the statement. *PRINT THE LETTER OF THE CORRECT ANSWER IN THE SPACE AT THE RIGHT.*

Questions 1-5.

DIRECTIONS: Questions 1 through 5 are based on the drawing below showing a view of a waiting area in a public building.

1. A desk is shown in the drawing. Which of the following is on the desk? A(n)   1.____

    A. plant
    B. telephone
    C. In-Out file
    D. *Information* sign

2. On which floor is the waiting area?

   A. Basement
   B. Main floor
   C. Second floor
   D. Third floor

3. The door IMMEDIATELY TO THE RIGHT of the desk is a(n)

   A. door to the Personnel Office
   B. elevator door
   C. door to another corridor
   D. door to the stairs

4. Among the magazines on the tables in the waiting area are

   A. TIME and NEWSWEEK
   B. READER'S DIGEST and T.V. GUIDE
   C. NEW YORK and READER'S DIGEST
   D. TIME and T.V. GUIDE

5. One door is partly open. This is the door to

   A. the Director's office
   B. the Personnel Manager's office
   C. the stairs
   D. an unmarked office

Questions 6-9.

DIRECTIONS: Questions 6 through 9 are based on the drawing below showing the contents of a male suspect's pockets.

CONTENTS OF A MALE SUSPECT'S POCKETS

3 (#2)

6. The suspect had a slip in his pockets showing an appointment at an out-patient clinic on   6._____

   A. February 9, 2013   B. September 2, 2013
   C. February 19, 2013   D. September 12, 2013

7. The MP3 player that was found on the suspect was made by   7._____

   A. RCA   B. GE   C. Sony   D. Zenith

8. The coins found in the suspect's pockets have a TOTAL value of   8._____

   A. 56¢   B. 77¢   C. $1.05   D. $1.26

9. All except one of the following were found in the suspect's pockets.   9._____
   Which was NOT found? A

   A. ticket stub   B. comb
   C. subway fare   D. pen

Questions 10-18

DIRECTIONS: In answering Questions 10 through 18, assume that *you* means a special officer (security officer) on duty. Your basic responsibilities are safeguarding people and property and maintaining order in the area to which you are assigned. You are in uniform, and you are not armed. You keep in touch with your supervisory station either by telephone or by a two-way radio (a walkie-talkie).

10. You are on duty at a center run by the Department of Social Services. Two teenaged   10._____
    boys are on their way out of the center. As they go past you, they look at you and laugh, and one makes a remark to you in Spanish. You do not understand Spanish, but you suspect it was a nasty remark.
    What SHOULD you do?

    A. Give the boys a lecture about showing respect for a uniform.
    B. Tell the boys that they had better stay away from the center from now on.
    C. Call for an interpreter and insist that the boy repeat the remark to the interpreter.
    D. Let the boys go on their way since they have done nothing requiring your intervention.

11. You are on duty at a shelter run by the Department of Social Services. You know that   11._____
    many of the shelter clients have drinking problems, drug problems, or mental health problems. You get a call for assistance from a caseworker who says a fight has broken out. When you arrive on the scene, you see that about a dozen clients are engaged in a free-for-all and that two or three of them have pulled knives.
    The BEST course of action is to

    A. call for additional assistance and order all bystanders away from the area
    B. jump into the center of the fighting group and try to separate the fighters
    C. pick up a heavy object and start swinging at anybody who has a knife
    D. try to find out what clients started the fight and place them under arrest

12. You have been assigned to duty at a children's shelter run by the Department of Social Services. The children range in age from 6 to 15, and many of them are at the shelter because they have no homes to go to.
   Of the following, which is the BEST attitude for you to take in dealing with these youngsters?

   A. Assume that they admire and respect anyone in uniform and that they will not usually give you much trouble
   B. Assume that they fear and distrust anyone in uniform and that they are going to give you a hard time unless you act tough
   C. Expect that many of them are going to become juvenile delinquents because of their bad backgrounds and that you should be suspicious of everything they do
   D. Expect that many of them may be emotionally upset and that you should be alert for unusual behavior

13. You are on duty outside the emergency room of a hospital. You notice that an old man has been sitting on a bench outside the room for a long time. He arrived alone, and he has not spoken to anyone at all.
   What SHOULD you do?

   A. Pay no attention to him since he is not bothering anyone.
   B. Tell him to leave since he does not seem to have any business there.
   C. Ask him if you can help him in any way.
   D. Do not speak to him, but keep an eye on him.

14. You are patrolling a section of a public building. An elderly woman carrying a heavy shopping bag asks you if you would watch the shopping bag for her while she keeps an appointment in the building.
   What SHOULD you do?

   A. Watch the shopping bag for her since her appointment probably will not take long.
   B. Refuse her request, explaining that your duties keep you on the move.
   C. Agree to her request just to be polite, but then continue your patrol after the woman is out of sight.
   D. Find a bystander who will agree to watch the shopping bag for her.

15. You are on duty at a public building. It is nearly 6:00 P.M., and most employees have left for the day.
   You see two well-dressed men carrying an office calculating machine out of the building. You SHOULD

   A. stop them and ask for an explanation
   B. follow them to see where they are going
   C. order them to put down the machine and leave the building immediately
   D. take no action since they do not look like burglars

16. You are on duty patrolling a public building. You have just tripped on the stairs and turned your ankle. The ankle hurts and is starting to swell.
   What is the BEST thing to do?

A. Take a taxi to a hospital emergency room, and from there have a hospital employee call your supervisor to explain the situation.
B. First try soaking your foot in cold water for half an hour, then go off duty if you really cannot walk at all.
C. Report the situation to your supervisor, explaining that you need prompt medical attention for your ankle.
D. Find a place where you can sit until you are due to go off duty, then have a doctor look at your ankle.

17. One of your duties as a special officer (security officer) on night patrol in a public building is to check the washrooms to see that the taps are turned off and that there are no plumbing leaks.
Of the following possible reasons for this inspection, which is probably the MOST important reason?

   A. If the floor gets wet, someone might slip and fall the next morning.
   B. A running water tap might be a sign that there is an intruder in the building.
   C. A washroom flood could leak through the ceilings and walls below and cause a lot of damage.
   D. Leaks must be reported quickly so that repairs can be scheduled as soon as possible.

17._____

18. You are on duty at a public building. A department supervisor tells you that someone has left a suspicious-looking package in the hallway on his floor. You investigate, and you hear ticking in the parcel. You think it could be a bomb.
The FIRST thing you should do is to

   A. rapidly question employees on this floor to get a description of the person who left the package
   B. write down the description of the package and the name of the department supervisor
   C. notify your security headquarters that there may be a bomb in the building and that all personnel should be evacuated
   D. pick up the package carefully and remove it from the building as quickly as you can

18._____

Questions 19-22.

DIRECTIONS: Answer Questions 19 through 22 on the basis of the Fact Situation and the Report of Arrest form below. Questions 19 through 22 ask how the report form should be filled in based on the information given in the Fact Situation.

FACT SITUATION

Jesse Stein is a special officer (security officer) who is assigned to a welfare center at 435 East Smythe Street, Brooklyn. He was on duty there Thursday morning, February 1. At 10:30 A.M., a client named Jo Ann Jones, 40 years old, arrived with her ten-year-old son, Peter. Another client, Mary Alice Wiell, 45 years old, immediately began to insult Mrs. Jones. When Mrs. Jones told her to "go away," Mrs. Wiell pulled out a long knife. The special officer (security officer) intervened and requested Mrs. Wiell to drop the knife. She would not, and he had to use necessary force to disarm her. He arrested her on charges of disorderly conduct, harassment, and possession of a dangerous weapon. Mrs. Wiell lives at 118 Heally Street,

Brooklyn, Apartment 4F, and she is unemployed. The reason for her aggressive behavior is not known.

REPORT OF ARREST	
01) _____ (Prisoner's surname) (first) (initial)	(08) _____ (Precinct)
(02) _____ (Address)	(09) _____ (Date of arrest) (Month, Day)
(03) _____ (04) _____ (05) _____ (Date of birth) (Age) (Sex)	(10) _____ (Time of arrest)
(06) _____ (07) _____ (Occupation) (Where employed)	(11) _____ (Place of arrest)
(12) _____ (Specific offenses)	
(13) _____ (Arresting Officer)	(14) _____ (Officer's No.)

19. What entry should be made in Blank 01?

    A. Jo Ann Jones B. Jones, Jo Ann
    C. Mary Wiell   D. Wiell, Mary A.

20. Which of the following should be entered in Blank 04?

    A. 40   B. 40's   C. 45   D. Middle-aged

21. Which of the following should be entered in Blank 09?

    A. Wednesday, February 1, 10:30 A.M.
    B. February 1
    C. Thursday morning, February 2
    D. Morning, February 4

22. Of the following, which would be the BEST entry to make in Blank 11?

    A. Really Street Welfare Center
    B. Brooklyn
    C. 435 E. Smythe St., Brooklyn
    D. 118 Heally St., Apt. 4F

Questions 23-27.

DIRECTIONS: Answer Questions 23 through 27 on the basis of the information given in the Report of Loss or Theft that appears below.

```
| REPORT OF LOSS OR THEFT          Date: 12/4      Time: 9:15 a.m. |
| Complaint made by: Richard Aldridge        [ ] Owner             |
|                    306 S. Walter St.       [x] Other - explain:  |
|                                            Head of Accty. Dept.  |
```

Type of property: _Computer_   Value: _$550.00_

Description: _Dell_

Location: _768 N Margin Ave., Accounting Dept., 3rd Floor_

Time: _Overnight 12/3 - 12/4_

Circumstances: _Mr. Aldridge reports he arrived at work 8:45 A.M., found office door open and machine missing. Nothing else reported missing. I investigated and found signs of forced entry: door lock was broken._   Signature of Reporting Officer: _B.L. Ramirez_

Notify:
 [ ] Building & Grounds Office, 768 N. Margin Ave.
 [ ] Lost Property Office, 110 Brand Ave.
 [x] Security Office, 703 N. Wide Street

23. The person who made this complaint is

    A. a secretary   B. a security officer
    C. Richard Aldridge   D. B.L. Ramirez

24. The report concerns a computer that has been

    A. lost   B. damaged   C. stolen   D. sold

25. The person who took the computer probably entered the office through

    A. a door   B. a window   C. the roof   D. the basement

26. When did the head of the Accounting Department first notice that the computer was missing?

    A. December 4 at 9:15 A.M.   B. December 4 at 8:45 A.M.
    C. The night of December 3   D. The night of December 4

27. The event described in the report took place at

    A. 306 South Walter Street   B. 768 North Margin Avenue
    C. 110 Brand Avenue   D. 703 North Wide Street

Questions 28-33.

DIRECTIONS: Answer Questions 28 through 33 on the basis of the instructions, the code, and the sample question given below.

Assume that a special officer (security officer) at a certain location is equipped with a two-way radio to keep him in constant touch with his security headquarters. Radio messages and replies are given in code form, as follows:

Radio Code for Situation	J	P	M	F	B
Radio Code for Action to be Taken	o	r	a	z	q
Radio Response for Action Being Taken	1	2	3	4	5

Assume that each of the above capital letters is the radio code for a particular type of situation, that the small letter below each capital letter is the radio code for the action a special officer (security officer) is directed to take, and that the number directly below each small letter is the radio response a special officer (security officer) should make to indicate what action was actually taken.

In each of the following Questions 28 through 33, the code letter for the action directed (Column 2) and the code number for the action taken (Column 3) should correspond to the capital letters in Column 1.

If only Column 2 is different from Column 1, mark your answer A.

If only Column 3 is different from Column 1, mark your answer B.

If both Column 2 and Column 3 are different from Column 1, mark your answer C.

If both Columns 2 and 3 are the same as Column 1, mark your answer D.

SAMPLE QUESTION

Column 1	Column 2	Column 3
JPFMB	orzaq	12453

The code letters in Column 2 are correct, but the numbers 53 in Column 3 should be 35. Therefore, the answer is B.

	Column 1	Column 2	Column 3	
28.	PBFJM	rqzoa	25413	28.____
29.	MPFBJ	zrqao	32541	29.____
30.	JBFPM	oqzra	15432	30.____
31.	BJPMF	qaroz	51234	31.____
32.	PJFMB	rozaq	21435	32.____
33.	FJBMP	zoqra	41532	33.____

Questions 34-40.

DIRECTIONS: Questions 34 through 40 are based on the instructions given below. Study the instructions and the sample question; then answer Questions 34 through 40 on the basis of this information

INSTRUCTIONS:

In each of the following Questions 34 through 40, the 3-line name and address in Column 1 is the master-list entry, and the 3-line entry in Column 2 is the information to be checked against the master list.

If there is one line that does not match, mark your answer A.

If there are two lines that do not match, mark your answer B.

If all three lines do not match, mark your answer C.

If the lines all match exactly, mark your answer D.

SAMPLE QUESTION:

Column 1	Column 2
Mark L. Field	Mark L. Field
11-09 Prince Park Blvd.	11-99 Prince Park
Bronx, N.Y. 11402	Bronx, N.Y. 11401

The first lines in each column match exactly. The second lines do not match, since 11-09 does not match 11-99 and Blvd. does not match Way. The third lines do not match either, since 11402 does not match 11401. Therefore, there are two lines that do not match and the correct answer is B.

	Column 1	Column 2	
34.	Jerome A. Jackson 1243 14th Avenue New York, N.Y. 10023	Jerome A. Johnson 1234 14th Avenue New York, N.Y. 10023	34.____
35.	Sophie Strachtheim 33-28 Connecticut Ave. Far Rockaway, N.Y. 11697	Sophie Strachtheim 33-28 Connecticut Ave. Far Rockaway, N.Y. 11697	35.____
36.	Elisabeth N.T. Gorrell 256 Exchange St. New York, N.Y. 10013	Elizabeth N.T. Gorrell 256 Exchange St. New York, N.Y. 10013	36.____
37.	Maria J. Gonzalez 7516 E. Sheepshead Rd. Brooklyn, N.Y. 11240	Maria J. Gonzalez 7516 N. Shepshead Rd. Brooklyn, N.Y. 11240	37.____
38.	Leslie B. Brautenweiler 21 57A Seller Terr. Flushing, N.Y. 11367	Leslie B. Brautenwieler 21-75A Seiler Terr. Flushing, N.J. 11367	38.____

39. Rigoberto J. Peredes   Rigoberto J. Peredes   39.___
    157 Twin Towers, #18F   157 Twin Towers, #18F
    Tottenville, S.I., N.Y.   Tottenville, S.I., N.Y.

40. Pietro F. Albino   Pietro F. Albina   40.___
    P.O. Box 7548   P.O. Box 7458
    Floral Park, N.Y. 11005   Floral Park, N.Y. 11005

KEY (CORRECT ANSWERS)

1.	D	11.	A	21.	B	31.	A
2.	C	12.	D	22.	C	32.	D
3.	B	13.	C	23.	C	33.	A
4.	D	14.	B	24.	C	34.	B
5.	B	15.	A	25.	A	35.	D
6.	A	16.	C	26.	B	36.	A
7.	C	17.	C	27.	B	37.	A
8.	D	18.	C	28.	D	38.	C
9.	D	19.	D	29.	C	39.	D
10.	D	20.	C	30.	B	40.	B

EXAMINATION SECTION
TEST 1

DIRECTIONS: Each question or incomplete statement is followed by several suggested answers or completions. Select the one that BEST answers the question or completes the statement. *PRINT THE LETTER OF THE CORRECT ANSWER IN THE SPACE AT THE RIGHT.*

1. Of the following, the MOST important single factor in any building security program is 1.____

    A. a fool-proof employee identification system
    B. an effective control of entrances and exits
    C. bright illumination of all outside areas
    D. clearly marking public and non-public areas

2. There is general agreement that the BEST criterion of what is a good physical security system in a large public building is 2.____

    A. the number of uniformed officers needed to patrol sensitive areas
    B. how successfully the system prevents rather than detects violations
    C. the number of persons caught in the act of committing criminal offenses
    D. how successfully the system succeeds in maintaining good public relations

3. Which one of the following statements most correctly expresses the CHIEF reason why women were originally made eligible for appointment to the position of officer? 3.____

    A. Certain tasks in security protection can be performed best by assigning women.
    B. More women than men are available to fill many vacancies in this position.
    C. The government wants more women in law enforcement because of their better attendance records.
    D. Women can no longer be barred from any government jobs because of sex.

4. The MOST BASIC purpose of patrol by officers is to 4.____

    A. eliminate as much as possible the opportunity for successful misconduct
    B. investigate criminal complaints and accident cases
    C. give prompt assistance to employees and citizens in distress or requesting their help
    D. take persons into custody who commit criminal offenses against persons and property

5. The highest quality of patrol service is MOST generally obtained by 5.____

    A. frequently changing the post assignments of each officer
    B. assigning officers to posts of equal size
    C. assigning problem officers to the least desirable posts
    D. assigning the same officers to the same posts

6. The one of the following requirements which is MOST essential to the successful performance of patrol duty by individual officers is their 6.____

    A. ability to communicate effectively with higher-level officers
    B. prompt signalling according to a prescribed schedule to insure post coverages at all times

C. knowledge of post conditions and post hazards
D. willingness to cover large areas during periods of critical manpower shortages

7. Officers on patrol are constantly warned to be on the alert for suspicious persons, actions, and circumstances.
   With this in mind, a senior officer should emphasize the need for them to

   A. be cautious and suspicious when dealing officially with any civilian regardless of the latter's overt actions or the circumstances surrounding his dealings with the police
   B. keep looking for the unusual persons, actions, and circumstances on their posts and pay less attention to the usual
   C. take aggressive police action immediately against any unusual person or condition detected on their posts, regardless of any other circumstances
   D. become thoroughly familiar with the usual on their posts so as to be better able to detect the unusual

8. Of primary importance in the safeguarding of property from theft is a good central lock and key issuance and control system.
   Which one of the following recommendations about maintaining such a control system would be LEAST acceptable?

   A. In selecting locks to be used for the various gates, building, and storage areas, consideration should be given to the amount of security desired.
   B. Master keys should have no markings that will identify them as such and the list of holders of these keys should be frequently reviewed to determine the continuing necessity for the individuals having them.
   C. Whenever keys for outside doors or gates or for other doors which permit access to important buildings and areas are misplaced, the locks should be immediately changed or replaced pending an investigation.
   D. Whenever an employee fails to return a borrowed key at the time specified, a prompt investigation should be made by the security force.

9. In a crowded building, a fire develops in the basement, and smoke enters the crowded rooms on the first floor. Of the following, the BEST action for an officer to take after an alarm is turned in is to

   A. call out a warning that the building is on fire and that everyone should evacuate because of the immediate danger
   B. call all of the officers together for an emergency meeting and discuss a plan of action
   C. immediately call for assistance from the local police station to help in evacuating the crowd
   D. tell everyone that there is a fire in the building next door and that they should move out onto the streets through available exits

10. Which of the following is in a key position to carry out successfully a safety program of an agency? The

    A. building engineer
    B. bureau chiefs
    C. immediate supervisors
    D. public relations director

11. It is GENERALLY considered that a daily roll call inspection, which checks to see that the officers and their equipment are in good order, is

    A. *desirable,* chiefly because it informs the superior officer what men will have to purchase new uniforms within a month
    B. *desirable,* chiefly because the public forms their impressions of the organization from the appearance of the officers
    C. *undesirable,* chiefly because this kind of daily inspection unnecessarily delays officers in getting to their assigned patrol posts
    D. *undesirable,* chiefly because roll call inspection usually misses individuals reporting to work late

12. A supervising officer in giving instructions to a group of officers on the principles of accident investigation remarked, "A conclusion that appears reasonable will often be changed by exploring a factor of apparently little importance".
    Which one of the following precautions does this statement emphasize as MOST important in any accident investigation?

    A. Every accident clue should be fully investigated.
    B. Accidents should not be too promptly investigated.
    C. Only specially trained officers should investigate accidents.
    D. Conclusions about accident causes are highly unreliable.

13. On a rainy day, a senior officer found that 9 of his 50 officers reported to work. What percentage of his officers was ABSENT?

    A. 18%   B. 80%   C. 82%   D. 90%

14. Officer A and Officer B work at the same post on the same days, but their hours are different. Officer A comes to work at 9:00 A.M. and leaves at 5:00 P.M., with a lunch period between 12:15 P.M. and 1:15 P.M. Officer B comes to work at 10:50 A.M. and works until 6:50 P.M., and he takes an hour for lunch between 3:00 P.M. and 4:00 P.M. What is the total amount of time between 9:00 A.M. and 6:50 P.M. that only ONE officer will be on duty?

    A. 4 hours
    B. 4 hours and 40 minutes
    C. 5 hours
    D. 5 hours and 40 minutes

15. An officer's log recorded the following attendance of 30 officers:

    | Monday | 20 | present; | 10 | absent |
    | Tuesday | 28 | present; | 2 | absent |
    | Wednesday | 30 | present; | 0 | absent |
    | Thursday | 21 | present; | 9 | absent |
    | Friday | 16 | present; | 14 | absent |
    | Saturday | 11 | present; | 19 | absent |
    | Sunday | 14 | present; | 16 | absent |

    On the average, how many men were present on the weekdays (Monday - Friday)?

    A. 21   B. 23   C. 25   D. 27

16. An angry woman is being questioned by an officer when she begins shouting abuses at him.
The BEST of the following procedures for the officer to follow is to

    A. leave the room until she has cooled off
    B. politely ignore anything she says
    C. place her under arrest by handcuffing her to a fixed object
    D. warn her that he will have to use force to restrain her making remarks

17. Of the following, which is NOT a recommended practice for an officer placing a woman offender under arrest?

    A. Assume that the offender is an innocent and virtuous person and treat her accordingly.
    B. Protect himself from attack by the woman.
    C. Refrain from using excessive physical force on the offender.
    D. Make the public aware that he is not abusing the woman.

Questions 18-21.

DIRECTIONS: Questions 18 through 21 are to be answered SOLELY on the basis of the following passage.

Specific measures for prevention of pilferage will be based on careful analysis of the conditions at each agency. The most practical and effective method to control casual pilferage is the establishment of psychological deterrents.

One of the most common means of discouraging casual pilferage is to search individuals leaving the agency at unannounced times and places. These spot searches may occasionally detect attempts at theft but greater value is realized by bringing to the attention of individuals the fact that they may be apprehended if they do attempt the illegal removal of property.

An aggressive security education program is an effective means of convincing employees that they have much more to lose than they do to gain by engaging in acts of theft. It is important for all employees to realize that pilferage is morally wrong no matter how insignificant the value of the item which is taken. In establishing any deterrent to casual pilferage, security officers must not lose sight of the fact that most employees are honest and disapprove of thievery. Mutual respect between security personnel and other employees of the agency must be maintained if the facility is to be protected from other more dangerous forms of human hazards. Any security measure which infringes on the human rights or dignity of others will jeopardize, rather than enhance, the overall protection of the agency.

18. The $100,000 yearly inventory of an agency revealed that $50 worth of goods had been stolen; the only individuals with access to the stolen materials were the employees. Of the following measures, which would the author of the preceding paragraph MOST likely recommend to a security officer?

    A. Conduct an intensive investigation of all employees to find the culprit.
    B. Make a record of the theft, but take no investigative or disciplinary action against any employee.
    C. Place a tight security check on all future movements of personnel.
    D. Remove the remainder of the material to an area with much greater security.

19. What does the passage imply is the percentage of employees whom a security officer should expect to be honest?

    A. No employee can be expected to be honest all of the time
    B. Just 50%
    C. Less than 50%
    D. More than 50%

20. According to the passage, the security officer would use which of the following methods to minimize theft in buildings with many exits when his staff is very small?

    A. Conduct an inventory of all material and place a guard near that which is most likely to be pilfered.
    B. Inform employees of the consequences of legal prosecution for pilfering.
    C. Close off the unimportant exits and have all his men concentrate on a few exits.
    D. Place a guard at each exit and conduct a casual search of individuals leaving the premises.

21. Of the following, the title BEST suited for this passage is:

    A. Control Measures for Casual Pilfering
    B. Detecting the Potential Pilferer
    C. Financial losses Resulting from Pilfering
    D. The Use of Moral Persuasion in Physical Security

22. Of the following first aid procedures, which will cause the GREATEST harm in treating a fracture?

    A. Control hemorrhages by applying direct pressure
    B. Keep the broken portion from moving about
    C. Reset a protruding bone by pressing it back into place
    D. Treat the suffering person for shock

23. During a snowstorm, a man comes to you complaining of frostbitten hands. PROPER first aid treatment in this case is to

    A. place the hands under hot running water
    B. place the hands in lukewarm water
    C. call a hospital and wait for medical aid
    D. rub the hands in melting snow

24. While on duty, an officer sees a woman apparently in a state of shock. Of the following, which one is NOT a symptom of shock?

    A. Eyes lacking luster
    B. A cold, moist forehead
    C. A shallow, irregular breathing
    D. A strong, throbbing pulse

25. You notice a man entering your building who begins coughing violently, has shortness of breath, and complains of severe chest pains.
    These symptoms are GENERALLY indicative of

    A. a heart attack   B. a stroke
    C. internal bleeding   D. an epileptic seizure

26. When an officer is required to record the rolled fingerprint impressions of a prisoner on the standard fingerprint form, the technique recommended by the F.B.I, as MOST likely to result in obtaining clear impressions is to roll

    A. all fingers away from the center of the prisoner's body
    B. all fingers toward the center of the prisoner's body
    C. the thumbs away from and the other fingers toward the center of the prisoner's body
    D. the thumbs toward and the other fingers away from the center of the prisoner's body

27. The principle which underlies the operation and use of a lie detector machine is that

    A. a person who is not telling the truth will be able to give a consistent story
    B. a guilty mind will unconsciously associate ideas in a very indicative manner
    C. the presence of emotional stress in a person will result in certain abnormal physical reactions
    D. many individuals are not afraid to lie

Questions 28-32.

DIRECTIONS: Questions 28 through 32 are based SOLELY on the following diagram and the paragraph preceding this group of questions. The paragraph will be divided into two statements. Statement one (1) consists of information given to the senior officer by an agency director; *this information will detail the specific security objectives the senior officer has to meet.* Statement two (2) gives the resources available to the senior officer.

NOTE: The questions are correctly answered only when all of the agency's objectives have been met and when the officer has used all his resources efficiently (i.e., to their maximum effectiveness) in meeting these objectives. All X's in the diagram indicate possible locations of officers' posts. Each X has a corresponding number which is to be used when referring to that location.

7 (#1)

DIAGRAM

Main entrance

⟶ Door
x .... Post Location

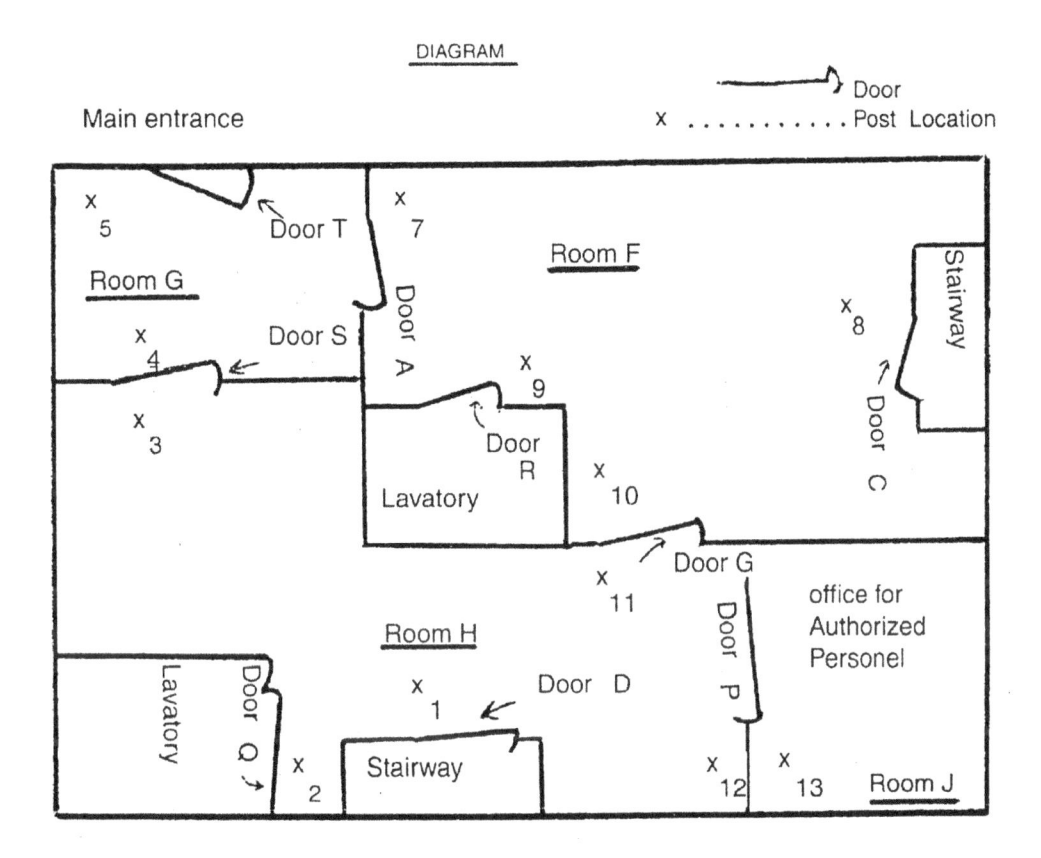

PARAGRAPH

PARAGRAPH

STATEMENT 1: Room G will be the public intake room from which persons will be directed to Room F or Room H; under no circumstances are they to enter the wrong room, and they are not to move from Room F to Room H or vice-versa. A minimum of two officers must be in each room frequented by the public at all times, and they are to keep unauthorized individuals from going to the second floor or into restricted areas. All usable entrances or exits must be covered.

STATEMENT 2: The senior officer can lock any door except the main entrance and stairway doors. He has a staff of five officers to carry out these operations.

NOTE: The senior officer is available for guard duty. Room J is an active office.

28. According to the instructions, how many officers should be assigned inside the office for authorized personnel (Room J)?   28.____

    A. 0   B. 1   C. 2   D. 3

29. In order to keep the public from moving between Room F and Room H, which door(s) can be locked without interfering with normal office operations? Door   29.____

    A. G   B. P   C. R and Q   D. S

309

30. When placing officers in Room H, the only way the senior officer can satisfy the agency's objectives and his manpower limitations is by placing men at locations

    A. 1 and 3   B. 1 and 12   C. 3 and 11   D. 11 and 12

31. In accordance with the instructions, the LEAST effective locations to place officers in Room F are locations

    A. 7 and 9   B. 7 and 10   C. 8 and 9   D. 9 and 10

32. In which room is it MOST difficult for each of the officers to see all the movements of the public? Room

    A. G   B. F   C. H   D. J

33. According to its own provisions, the Penal Law of the State has a number of general purposes.
    It would be LEAST accurate to state that one of these general purposes is to

    A. give fair warning of the nature of the conduct forbidden and the penalties authorized upon conviction
    B. define the act or omission and accompanying mental state which constitute each offense
    C. regulate the procedure which governs the arrest, trial and punishment of convicted offenders
    D. insure the public safety by preventing the commission of offenses through the deterrent influence of the sentences authorized upon conviction

34. Officers must be well-informed about the meaning of certain terms in connection with their enforcement duties. Which one of the following statements about such terms would be MOST accurate according to the Penal Law of the State? A(n)

    A. offense is always a crime
    B. offense is always a violation
    C. violation is never a crime
    D. felony is never an offense

35. According to the Penal Law of the State, the one of the following elements which must ALWAYS be present in order to justify the arrest of a person for criminal assault is

    A. the infliction of an actual physical injury
    B. an intent to cause an injury
    C. a threat to inflict a physical injury
    D. the use of some kind of weapon

36. A recent law of the State defines who are police officers and who are peace officers. The official title of this law is: The

    A. Criminal Code of Procedure
    B. Law of Criminal Procedure
    C. Criminal Procedure Law
    D. Code of Criminal Procedure

37. If you are required to appear in court to testify as the complainant in a criminal action, it would be MOST important for you to

   A. confine your answers to the questions asked when you are testifying
   B. help the prosecutor even if some exaggeration in your testimony may be necessary
   C. be as fair as possible to the defendant even if some details have to be omitted from your testimony
   D. avoid contradicting other witnesses testifying against the defendant

38. A senior officer is asked by the television news media to explain to the public what happened on his post during an important incident.
   When speaking with departmental permission in front of the tape recorders and cameras, the senior officer can give the MOST favorable impression of himself and his department by

   A. refusing to answer any questions but remaining calm in front of the cameras
   B. giving a detailed report of the wrong decisions made by his agency for handling the particular incident
   C. presenting the appropriate factual information in a competent way
   D. telling what should have been done during the incident and how such incidents will be handled in the future

39. Of the following suggested guidelines for officers, the one which is LEAST likely to be effective in promoting good manners and courtesy in their daily contacts with the public is:

   A. Treat inquiries by telephone in the same manner as those made in person
   B. Never look into the face of the person to whom you are speaking
   C. Never give misinformation in answer to any inquiry on a matter on which you are uncertain of the facts
   D. Show respect and consideration in both trivial and important contacts with the public

40. Assume you are an officer who has had a record of submitting late weekly reports and that you are given an order by your supervisor which is addressed to all line officers. The order states that weekly reports will be replaced by twice-weekly reports.
   The MOST logical conclusion for you to make, of the following, is:

   A. Fully detailed information was missing from your past reports
   B. Most officers have submitted late reports
   C. The supervisor needs more timely information
   D. The supervisor is attempting to punish you for your past late reports

41. A young man with long hair and "mod" clothing makes a complaint to an officer about the rudeness of another officer.
   If the senior officer is not on the premises, the officer receiving the complaint should

   A. consult with the officer who is being accused to see if the youth's story is true
   B. refer the young man to central headquarters
   C. record the complaint made against his fellow officer and ask the youth to wait until he can locate the senior officer
   D. search for the senior officer and bring him back to the site of the complainant

42. During a demonstration, which area should ALWAYS be kept clear of demonstrators? 42.___

    A. Water fountains
    B. Seating areas
    C. Doorways
    D. Restrooms

43. During demonstrations, an officer's MOST important duty is to 43.___

    A. aid the agency's employees to perform their duties
    B. promptly arrest those who might cause incidents
    C. promptly disperse the crowds of demonstrators
    D. keep the demonstrators from disrupting order

44. Of the following, what is the FIRST action a senior officer should take if a demonstration develops in his area without advance warning? 44.___

    A. Call for additional assistance from the police department
    B. Find the leaders of the demonstrators and discuss their demands
    C. See if the demonstrators intend to break the law
    D. Inform his superiors of the event taking place

45. If a senior officer is informed in the morning that a demonstration will take place during the afternoon at his assigned location, he should assemble his officers to discuss the nature and aspects of this demonstration. Of the following, the subject which it is LEAST important to discuss during this meeting is 45.___

    A. making a good impression if an officer is called before the television cameras for a personal interview
    B. the known facts and causes of the demonstration
    C. the attitude and expected behavior of the demonstrators
    D. the individual responsibilities of the officers during the demonstration

46. A male officer has probable reason to believe that a group of women occupying the ladies' toilet are using illicit drugs. 46.___
    The BEST action, of the following, for the officer to take is to

    A. call for assistance and, with the aid of such assistance, enter the toilet and escort the occupants outside
    B. ignore the situation but recommend that the ladies' toilet be closed temporarily
    C. immediately rush into the ladies' toilet and search the occupants therein
    D. knock on the door of the ladies' toilet and ask their permission to enter so that he will not be accused of trying to molest them

47. Assume that you know that a group of demonstrators will not cooperate with your request to throw handbills in a waste basket instead of on the sidewalk. You ask one of the leaders of the group, who agrees with you, to speak to the demonstrators and ask for their cooperation in this matter. 47.___
    Your request of the group leader is

    A. *desirable,* chiefly because an officer needs civilians to control the public since the officer is usually unfriendly to the views of public groups
    B. *undesirable,* chiefly because an officer should never request a civilian to perform his duties
    C. *desirable,* chiefly because the appeal of an acknowledged leader helps in gaining group cooperation

D. *undesirable,* chiefly because an institutional leader is motivated to maneuver a situation to gain his own personal advantage

48. A vague letter received from a female employee in the agency accuses an officer of improper conduct.
The initial investigative interview by the senior officer assigned to check the accusation should GENERALLY be with the

   A. accused officer
   B. female employee
   C. highest superior about disciplinary action against the officer
   D. immediate supervisor of the female employee

Questions 49-50.

DIRECTIONS: Questions 49 and 50 are to be answered SOLELY on the basis of the information in the following paragraph.

The personal conduct of each member of the Department is the primary factor in promoting desirable police-community relations. Tact, patience, and courtesy shall be strictly observed under all circumstances. A favorable public attitude toward the police must be earned; it is influenced by the personal conduct and attitude of each member of the force, by his personal integrity and courteous manner, by his respect for due process of law, by his devotion to the principles of justice, fairness, and impartiality.

49. According to the preceding paragraph, what is the BEST action an officer can take in dealing with people in a neighborhood?

   A. Assist neighborhood residents by doing favors for them.
   B. Give special attention to the community leaders in order to be able to control them effectively.
   C. Behave in an appropriate manner and give all community members the same just treatment.
   D. Prepare a plan detailing what he, the officer, wants to do for the community and submit it for approval.

50. As used in the paragraph, the word *impartiality* means *most nearly*

   A. observant　　　　　　　　　　B. unbiased
   C. righteousness　　　　　　　　D. honesty

KEY (CORRECT ANSWERS)

1. B	11. B	21. A	31. D	41. C
2. B	12. A	22. C	32. C	42. C
3. A	13. C	23. B	33. C	43. D
4. A	14. D	24. D	34. C	44. D
5. D	15. B	25. A	35. A	45. A
6. C	16. B	26. D	36. C	46. A
7. D	17. A	27. C	37. A	47. C
8. C	18. B	28. A	38. C	48. B
9. D	19. D	29. A	39. B	49. C
10. C	20. B	30. B	40. C	50. B

TEST 2

DIRECTIONS: Each question or incomplete statement is followed by several suggested answers or completions. Select the one that BEST answers the question or completes the statement. *PRINT THE LETTER OF THE CORRECT ANSWER IN THE SPACE AT THE RIGHT.*

Questions 1-5.

DIRECTIONS: Questions 1 through 5 consist of short paragraphs. Each paragraph contains one word which is INCORRECTLY used because it is NOT in keeping with the meaning of the paragraph. Find the word in each paragraph which is INCORRECTLY used, and then select as the answer the suggested word which should be substituted for the incorrectly used word.

SAMPLE QUESTION

In determining who is to do the work in your unit, you will have to decide just who does what from day to day. One of your lowest responsibilities is to assign work so that everybody gets a fair share and that everyone can do his part well.
   A. new   B. old   C. important   D. performance

EXPLANATION

The word which is NOT in keeping with the meaning of the paragraph is "lowest". This is the INCORRECTLY used word. The suggested word "important" would be in keeping with the meaning of the paragraph and should be substituted for "lowest". Therefore, the CORRECT answer is Choice C.

1. If really good practice in the elimination of preventable injuries is to be achieved and held in any establishment, top management must refuse full and definite responsibility and must apply a good share of its attention to the task.

   A. accept   B. avoidable   C. duties   D. problem

2. Recording the human face for identification is by no means the only service performed by the camera in the field of investigation. When the trial of any issue takes place, a word picture is sought to be distorted to the court of incidents, occurrences, or events which are in dispute.

   A. appeals   B. description
   C. portrayed   D. derangod

3. In the collection of physical evidence, it cannot be emphasized too strongly that a haphazard systematic search at the scene of the crime is vital. Nothing must be overlooked. Often the only leads in a case will come from the results of this search.

   A. important   B. investigation
   C. proof   D. thorough

4. If an investigator has reason to suspect that the witness is mentally stable or a habitual drunkard, he should leave no stone unturned in his investigation to determine if the witness was under the influence of liquor or drugs, or was mentally unbalanced either at the time of the occurrence to which he testified or at the time of the trial.

   A. accused   B. clue   C. deranged   D. question

5. The use of records is a valuable step in crime investigation and is the main reason every department should maintain accurate reports. Crimes are not committed through the use of departmental records alone but from the use of all records, of almost every type, wherever they may be found and whenever they give any incidental information regarding the criminal.

    A. accidental   B. necessary   C. reported   D. solved

Questions 6-8.

DIRECTIONS: Questions 6 through 8 are to be answered SOLELY on the basis of the following passage.

The mass media are an integral part of the daily life of virtually every American. Among these media, the youngest, television, is the most persuasive. Ninety-five percent of American homes have at least one television set, and on the average that set is in use for about 40 hours each week. The central place of television in American life makes this medium the focal point of a growing national concern over the effects of media portrayals of violence on the values, attitudes, and behavior of an ever increasing audience.

In our concern about violence and its causes, it is easy to make television a scapegoat. But we emphasise the fact that there is no simple answer to the problem of violence -- no single explanation of its causes, and no single prescription for its control. It should be remembered that America also experienced high levels of crime and violence in periods before the advent of television.

The problem of balance, taste, and artistic merit in entertaining programs on television are complex. We cannot countenance government censorship of television. Nor would we seek to impose arbitrary limitations on programming which might jeopardize television's ability to deal in dramatic presentations with controversial social issues. Nonetheless, we are deeply troubled by television's constant portrayal of violence, not in any genuine attempt to focus artistic expression on the human condition, but rather in pandering to a public preoccupation with violence that television itself has helped to generate.

6. According to the passage, television uses violence MAINLY

    A. to highlight the reality of everyday existence
    B. to satisfy the audience's hunger for destructive action
    C. to shape the values and attitudes of the public
    D. when it films documentaries concerning human conflict

7. Which one of the following statements is BEST supported by this passage?

    A. Early American history reveals a crime pattern which is not related to television.
    B. Programs should give presentations of social issues and never portray violent acts.
    C. Television has proven that entertainment programs can easily make the balance between taste and artistic merit a simple matter.
    D. Values and behavior should be regulated by governmental censorship.

8. Of the following, which word has the same meaning as countenance as it is used in the above passage?

    A. approve   B. exhibit   C. oppose   D. reject

Questions 9-12.

DIRECTIONS: Questions 9 through 12 are to be answered SOLELY on the basis of the following graph relating to the burglary rate in the city, 2003 to 2008, inclusive.

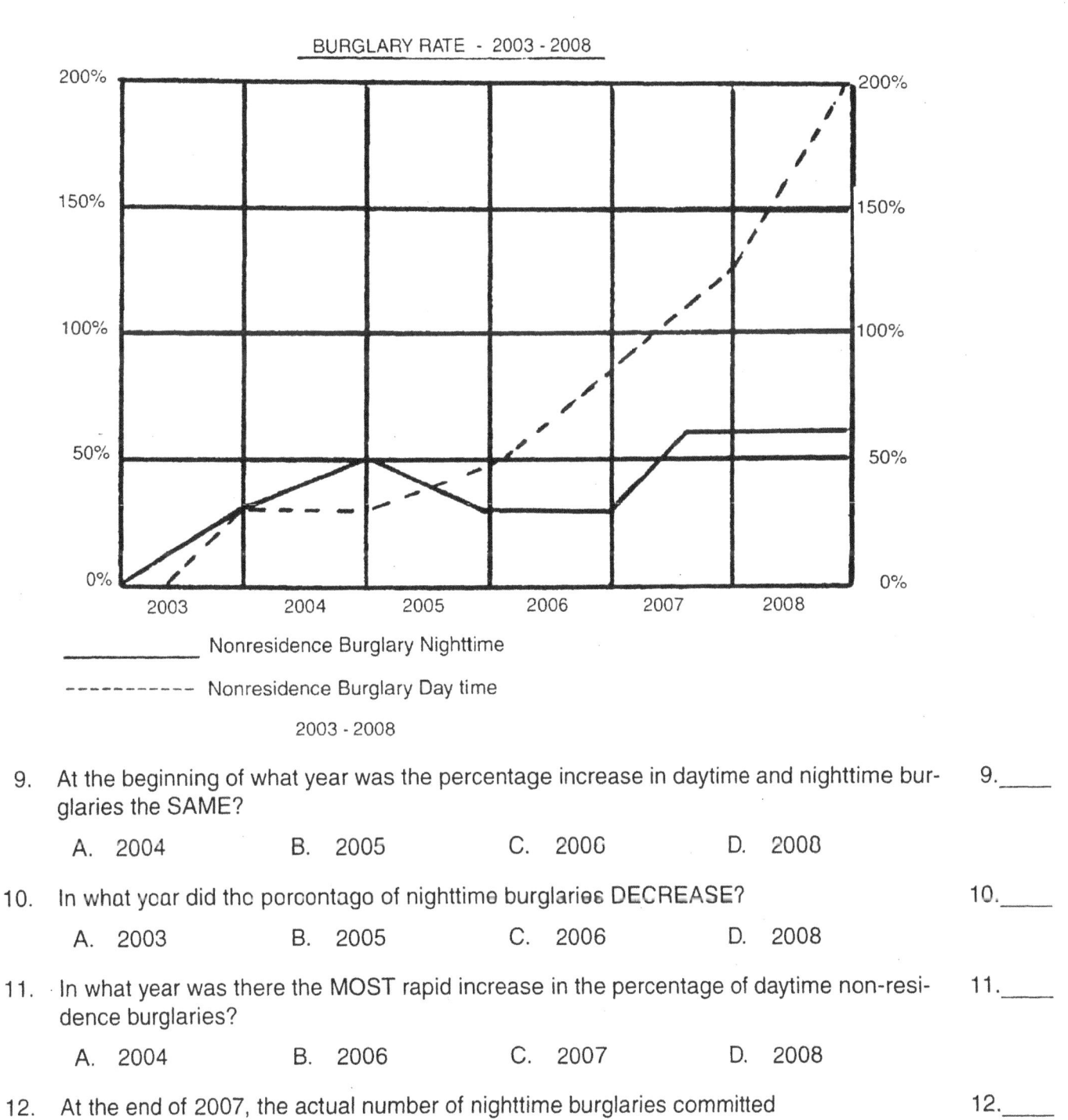

BURGLARY RATE - 2003 - 2008

———— Nonresidence Burglary Nighttime

- - - - - - - Nonresidence Burglary Day time

2003 - 2008

9. At the beginning of what year was the percentage increase in daytime and nighttime burglaries the SAME?

   A. 2004   B. 2005   C. 2006   D. 2008

10. In what year did the percentage of nighttime burglaries DECREASE?

    A. 2003   B. 2005   C. 2006   D. 2008

11. In what year was there the MOST rapid increase in the percentage of daytime non-residence burglaries?

    A. 2004   B. 2006   C. 2007   D. 2008

12. At the end of 2007, the actual number of nighttime burglaries committed

    A. was about 20%
    B. was 40%
    C. was 400
    D. cannot be determined from the information given

Questions 13-17.

DIRECTIONS: Questions 13 through 17 consist of two sentences numbered 1 and 2 taken from police officers' reports. Some of these sentences are correct according to ordinary formal English usage. Other sentences are incorrect because they contain errors in English usage or punctuation. Consider a sentence correct if it contains no errors in English usage or punctuation even if there may be other ways of writing the sentence correctly. Mark your answer to each question in the space at the right as follows:
  A. If only sentence 1 is correct, but not sentence 2
  B. If only sentence 2 is correct, but not sentence 1
  C. If sentences 1 and 2 are both correct
  D. If sentences 1 and 2 are both incorrect

SAMPLE QUESTION
  1. The woman claimed that the purse was her's.
  2. Everyone of the new officers was assigned to a patrol post.

EXPLANATION

Sentence 1 is INCORRECT because of an error in punctuation. The possessive words, "ours, yours, hers, theirs," do not have the apostrophe (').

Sentence 2 is CORRECT because the subject of the sentence is "Everyone" which is singular and requires the singular verb "was assigned".

Since only sentence 2 is correct, but not sentence 1, the CORRECT answer is B.

13. 1. Either the patrolman or his sergeant are always ready to help the public.   13.___
    2. The sergeant asked the patrolman when he would finish the report.

14. 1. The injured man could not hardly talk.   14.___
    2. Every officer had ought to hand in their reports on time.

15. 1. Approaching the victim of the assault, two large bruises were noticed by me.   15.___
    2. The prisoner was arrested for assault, resisting arrest, and use of a deadly weapon.

16. 1. A copy of the orders, which had been prepared by the captain, was given to each patrolman. 16.___
    2. It's always necessary to inform an arrested person of his constitutional rights before asking him any questions.

17. 1. To prevent further bleeding, I applied a tourniquet tothe wound.   17.___
    2. John Rano a senior officer was on duty at the time of the accident.

Questions 18-25.

DIRECTIONS: Answer each of Questions 18 through 25 SOLELY on the basis of the statement preceding the questions.

18. The criminal is one whose habits have been erroneously developed or, we should say,   18.___
    developed in anti-social patterns, and therefore the task of dealing with him is not one of punishment, but of treatment.
    The basic principle expressed in this statement is BEST illustrated by the

    A. emphasis upon rehabilitation in penal institutions
    B. prevalence of capital punishment for murder
    C. practice of imposing heavy fines for minor violations
    D. legal provision for trial by jury in criminal cases

19. The writ of habeas corpus is one of the great guarantees of personal liberty. Of the following, the BEST justification for this statement is that the writ of habeas corpus is frequently used to

    A. compel the appearance in court of witnesses who are outside the state
    B. obtain the production of books and records at a criminal trial
    C. secure the release of a person improperly held in custody
    D. prevent the use of deception in obtaining testimony of reluctant witnesses

20. Fifteen persons suffered effects of carbon dioxide asphyxiation shortly before noon recently in a seventh-floor pressing shop. The accident occurred in a closed room where six steam presses were in operation. Four men and one woman were overcome.
    Of the following, the MOST probable reason for the fact that so many people were affected simultaneously is that

    A. women evidently show more resistance to the effects of carbon dioxide than men
    B. carbon dioxide is an odorless and colorless gas
    C. carbon dioxide is lighter than air
    D. carbon dioxide works more quickly at higher altitudes

21. Lay the patient on his stomach, one arm extended directly overhead, the other arm bent at the elbow, and with the face turned outward and resting on hand or forearm.
    To the officer who is skilled at administering first aid, these instructions should IMMEDIATELY suggest

    A. application of artificial respiration
    B. treatment for third degree burns of the arm
    C. setting a dislocated shoulder
    D. control of capillary bleeding in the stomach

22. The soda and acid fire extinguisher is the hand extinguisher most commonly used by officers. The main body of the cylinder is filled with a mixture of water and bicarbonate of soda. In a separate interior compartment, at the top, is a small bottle of sulphuric acid. When the extinguisher is inverted, the acid spills into the solution below and starts a chemical reaction. The carbon dioxide thereby generated forces the solution from the extinguisher.
    The officer who understands the operation of this fire extinguisher should know that it is LEAST likely to operate properly

    A. in basements or cellars
    B. in extremely cold weather
    C. when the reaction is of a chemical nature
    D. when the bicarbonate of soda is in solution

23. Suppose that, at a training lecture, you are told that many of the men in our penal institutions today are second and third offenders.
    Of the following, the MOST valid inference you can make SOLELY on the basis of this statement is that

    A. second offenders are not easily apprehended
    B. patterns of human behavior are not easily changed
    C. modern laws are not sufficiently flexible
    D. laws do not breed crimes

24. In all societies of our level of culture, acts are committed which arouse censure severe enough to take the form of punishment by the government. Such acts are crimes, not because of their inherent nature, but because of their ability to arouse resentment and to stimulate repressive measures.
Of the following, the MOST valid inference which can be drawn from this statement is that

   A. society unjustly punishes acts which are inherently criminal
   B. many acts are not crimes but are punished by society because such acts threaten the lives of innocent people
   C. only modern society has a level of culture
   D. societies sometimes disagree as to what acts are crimes

25. Crime cannot be measured directly. Its amount must be inferred from the frequency of some occurrence connected with it; for example, crimes brought to the attention of the police, persons arrested, prosecutions, convictions, and other dispositions, such as probation or commitment. Each of these may be used as an index of the amount of crime.
SOLELY on the basis of the foregoing statement, it is MOST correct to state that

   A. the incidence of crime cannot be estimated with any accuracy
   B. the number of commitments is usually greater than the number of probationary sentences
   C. the amount of crime is ordinarily directly correlated with the number of persons arrested
   D. a joint consideration of crimes brought to the attention of the police and the number of prosecutions undertaken gives little indication of the amount of crime in a locality

KEY (CORRECT ANSWERS)

1. B
2. A
3. D
4. C
5. D

6. B
7. A
8. A
9. A
10. B

11. D
12. D
13. D
14. D
15. B

16. C
17. A
18. A
19. C
20. B

21. A
22. B
23. B
24. D
25. C

EXAMINATION SECTION
TEST 1

DIRECTIONS: Each question or incomplete statement is followed by several suggested answers or completions. Select the one that BEST answers the question or completes the statement. *PRINT THE LETTER OF THE CORRECT ANSWER IN THE SPACE AT THE RIGHT.*

NOTE: The title of Agent refers to Sanitation Enforcement Agent, the office title of Sergeant refers to Level I of Associate Sanitation Enforcement Agent, and the office title of Lieutenant refers to Level II of Associate Sanitation Enforcement Agent.

The terms *N.O.V.* and *summons* are used interchangeably to refer to a Notice of Violation; *B.C.C.* refers to the Bureau of Cleaning and Collection; *see* refers to an in-field meeting between a Sanitation Enforcement Agent and a supervisor; and *R.T.* refers to the Assault Response Team.

Questions 1-2.

DIRECTIONS: Questions 1 and 2 are to be answered on the basis of the following fact pattern.

While Agent Wells was issuing an N.O.V. in front of a store at 110 Washington Boulevard, a man ran by, grabbed the Agent's uniform hat, and ran around the corner into an apartment building at 159 Jefferson Street. Agent Wells then contacts Sergeant Murray, who reports to the location to investigate. Later that day, in the zone office, Sergeant Murray is filling out a Report of Lost and Stolen Equipment form.

1. What should Sergeant Murray enter on the Report of Lost and Stolen Equipment form to identify the location where the uniform hat was lost or stolen?

   A. 159 Washington Boulevard
   B. 159 Jefferson Street
   C. 110 Washington Boulevard
   D. 110 Jefferson Street

2. What should Sergeant Murray enter on the Report of Lost and Stolen Equipment form to describe how the uniform hat was lost or stolen?

   A. Hat lost in store.
   B. Hat grabbed off head.
   C. Hat blown away by wind.
   D. Hat stolen out of car.

Questions 3-5.

DIRECTIONS: Questions 3 through 5 are to be answered on the basis of Command Order No. 86-57AE (Enforcement Procedures -Local Law 30 regarding posting) and the fact pattern below.

While on routine patrol, Sergeant Simpson observes three men outside an unoccupied private construction site that is surrounded by a plywood fence. Two of the men are hanging posters advertising a Two Brothers concert that is being arranged by King of Music Promotions, Inc. One of these men is pasting the posters onto the fence, while the other is affixing posters to lampposts in front of the construction site. The third man is ripping down old posters from the fence and throwing them on the sidewalk. When Sergeant Simpson questions

2 (#1)

the three men, he is told that nobody from King of Music Promotions, Inc. has contacted the City Council, Board of Estimate, Bureau of Franchises, or any other city agent about the posters.

3. Which of the following actions should Sergeant Simpson take regarding the man ripping down the old posters?

   A. Personally serve the man ripping down the posters with a summons for littering.
   B. Serve the construction site with a summons for Dirty Sidewalk using alternative service.
   C. Personally serve the man ripping down the posters with a summons for Unlawful Removal of posters.
   D. Allow the man to proceed since there is no violation.

4. Which of the following actions should Sergeant Simpson take regarding the man affixing the posters to the lampposts?

   A. Personally serve the man affixing posters to the lampposts with a summons for illegal posting.
   B. Serve the President of King of Music Promotions, Inc. with a summons for illegal posting using alternative service.
   C. Refer the violation to the Enforcement Division Posting Unit.
   D. Allow the man to proceed since there is no violation.

5. Which of the following actions should Sergeant Simpson take regarding the man pasting posters onto the plywood fence?

   A. Personally serve the man pasting the posters on the fence with a summons for illegal posting.
   B. Serve the President of King of Music Promotions, Inc. with a summons for illegal posting using alternative service.
   C. Refer the violation to the Enforcement Division Posting Unit.
   D. Allow the man to proceed since there is no violation.

6. While Sergeant Saunders is investigating a complaint against Ward TV and Appliances, the manager attempts to hand a folded twenty dollar bill to Sergeant Saunders and asks him if this will take care of the problem.
   In accordance with Mayor's Executive Order 16, Sergeant Saunders should

   A. report the incident directly and without undue delay to the Commissioner or an Inspector General
   B. tell the store manager that he will receive a summons for attempted bribery the next time he offers money
   C. take the money to headquarters, submit it as evidence of the incident, and document his actions on his Daily Activity Report
   D. call the Zone Lieutenant to notify him of the incident

3 (#1)

7. There are many violations in a large public housing project located in one of Sergeant Washington's districts. Therefore, in accordance with Command Order 87-30E (regarding issuance to publicly owned property), Sergeant Washington should direct the assigned Agent to issue one summons

   A. each day until the violations are corrected
   B. each thirty-day period starting from the date of last issuance until the violations are corrected
   C. each fifteen-day period starting from the date of last issuance until the violations are corrected
   D. for each violation observed each day until the violations are corrected

7._____

Questions 8-11.

DIRECTIONS: Questions 8 through 11 are to be answered on the basis of the fact pattern below and the Worker's Compensation Board Form shown on the following page.

On July 6, 2006, Sergeant Parker is transporting Agent Donald Smith to Central County Hospital after an incident of assault against the Agent. The hospital is located at 1864 Shore Parkway, Bronx, N.Y. 10464. At the hospital, the attending physician, Dr. Larry Major, advises Agent Smith to remain overnight for observation. Agent Smith consents. Sergeant Parker then contacts headquarters to notify Agent Smith's nearest relative, Lillian Smith of 298 New Jersey Ave., Bronx, N.Y. 10450.

Later that day, Sergeant Parker is filling out a Worker's Compensation form for Agent Smith.

4 (#1)

WORKERS' COMPENSATION BOARD

			DATE OF ACCIDENT
Employer	THE CITY OF NEW YORK	Department Address	
Self Insured	THE CITY OF NEW YORK	LAW DEPARTMENT	
INJURED PERSON	(First) (Middle) (Last Name)	(Home Address)	

Civil Service Title of Injured Person

REMARKS: _____

Is injured still under care of a physician? _____ If so, give name of physician: _____
Has injured died? _____ If so, state date of death: _____
NAME and ADDRESS of nearest relative known: _____

DATE of this REPORT _____   THE CITY OF NEW YORK

Employee's S.S. No. _____   Signature _____
Official Title _____

8. Which one of the following should Sergeant Parker enter in the box headed *Civil Service Title of Injured Person*?

    A. Associate Sanitation Enforcement Agent
    B. Sanitation Enforcement Officer
    C. Sanitation Enforcement Agent
    D. Issuing Officer

9. Which one of the following should Sergeant Parker enter in the space *Name and Address of Nearest Relative Known*?

    A. Lillian Smith, 298 New Jersey Ave., Bronx, NY 10450
    B. Lillian Smith, 1864 Shore Parkway, Bronx, NY 10464
    C. Donald Smith, 298 New Jersey Ave., Bronx, NY 10450
    D. Donald Smith, 1864 Shore Parkway, Bronx, NY 10464

10. Which one of the following should be entered in the space *If so, give name of physician*?

    A. Dr. Garry Major   B. Dr. Larry Major
    C. Dr. Garry Mason   D. Dr. Larry Mason

11. Which one of the following should Sergeant Parker enter in the box headed *Date of Accident*?   11._____

    A. June 6, 2006
    B. June 7, 2006
    C. July 6, 2006
    D. July 7, 2006

12. Sergeant Bill Bradford is checking Agent Cynthia Taylor's summons book at an announced *see* location. He observes that Agent Taylor has issued two summonses for K09 violations that she observed while on her way to her assigned district.
    Sergeant Bradford should   12._____

    A. sign Agent Taylor's Daily Summons Summary Report since the summonses were issued appropriately
    B. issue an Official Letter of Warning to Agent Taylor for issuing summonses out of district
    C. void the summonses since they were issued by an Agent who was out of her assigned district
    D. order an Agent who is assigned to the district in which the violations occurred to reissue the summonses

13. At 11:45 A.M., Sergeant Paula Adams radios to Agent John McCoy to schedule a *see* at 1:30 P.M. At 1:25 P.M., Sergeant Adams arrives at the location of the scheduled *see* at Wood Street in Section 21. Sergeant Adams cannot located Agent McCoy anywhere in the immediate area. Sgt. Adams should   13._____

    A. start searching Section 21 for Agent McCoy
    B. call headquarters for further instructions
    C. call Agent McCoy on the radio to ask for his estimated time of arrival
    D. wait five minutes and, if Agent McCoy does not appear, resume patrol and question him later concerning his whereabouts

14. While on the way to a scheduled *see* location, Sergeant Clark observes a citizen who fails to remove his dog's waste from the sidewalk.
    Sergeant Clark should   14._____

    A. obtain identification from the citizen and issue an N.O.V., then continue to the *see* location
    B. radio the Agent assigned to that section to come to the location to issue an N.O.V., then detain the citizen until the Agent arrives
    C. obtain identification from the citizen and issue an N.O.V., then stake-out the area for additional canine violations
    D. radio the Agent assigned to that section to come to the location immediately to issue an N.O.V. before the citizen leaves the area, then continue to the *see* location

6 (#1)

Question 15.

DIRECTIONS: Question 15 is to be answered on the basis of the Notice of Violation and the Request to Void Summons Form and the fact pattern shown below and on the following page.

Agent Brown observes a Dirty Sidewalk violation at 1394 Gotham Boulevard, Long Island Railroad property. His attempts to locate a responsible party are to no avail. As Agent Brown is alternatively serving the summons at the location, Sergeant Harwood arrives for a *see*. Sergeant Harwood looks at the summons and tells Agent Brown that it must be voided. Sergeant Harwood directs Agent Brown to fill in the top part of a Request to Void Summons Form.

REQUEST TO VOID SUMMONS FORM
CITY OF NEW YORK DEPARTMENT OF SANITATION

TO: (ADJUDICATING AGENCY - ECB - PVB)
FROM: SUMMONS CONTROL UNIT
SUBJECT: REQUEST TO VOID SUMMONS

DATE 7/18/06

SUMMONS # E051245691

ISSUING OFFICER/AGENT
(print name) Jack Brown

VIOLATION 506

REGISTRY # 408813

ISSUING DATE 7/18/06

COMMAND Brooklyn West 12

TIME SERVED 1:30 p.m.

BOROUGH Brooklyn

PLACE OF OCCURRENCE 1394 Gotham Boulevard

REMARKS _____

ISSUING OFFICER/AGENT SIGNATURE _____

APPROVED BY _____
(Supv. Signature)

SUPV. TITLE _____

7 (#1)

No. E05 1 245 691 ENVIRONMENTAL CONTROL BOARD
NOTICE OF VIOLATION AND HEARING
FOR CIVIL PENALTIES ONLY

City of New York, Petitioner vs Respondent:

LAST NAME (Print)	FIRST NAME	INITIAL	Sex
Long Island Railroad			

STREET ADDRESS: 1394 Gotham Blvd.
Respondent is: 1 ☐ Owner or 2 ☐ Operator of Vehicle
CITY: Brooklyn STATE: NY ZIP: 11121

TYPE OF LICENSE / PERMIT OR IDENTIFICATION NUMBER

Date of Offense: 7/18/06 Time: 1:30 PM County: BX B.O. NO.: 12 Violation Code: S1016

SECTION: 16-118(2)

At Front of ☒ Place of Occurrence: 1394 Gotham Blvd.

DETAILS OF VIOLATION: Dirty sidewalk - I did observe pieces of glass, paper, cans, banana peels scattered on sidewalk.

☒ ALTERNATIVE SERVICE

Maximum Penalty For Violation: $250.00

Date of Appearance: 10th Day of Aug 2006 1 ☒ 2 3 4

RANK (TITLE) SIGNATURE OF COMPLAINANT: SEA Jack Brown
REPORT LEVEL: E K 1 2
COMPLAINANT'S NAME (Printed): Jack Brown
TAX REGISTRY NUMBER: 4018813
AGENCY: 827

IS AFFIDAVIT OF SERVICE ON REVERSE SIDE SIGNED? ☒ YES ☐ NO Date: 7/18/06   ECB

15. In order to complete the Request to Void Summons Form (DS 154), Sergeant Harwood must make an entry in the *Remarks* section and sign the form.
Which of the following should Sergeant Harwood enter in the *Remarks* section? No reissue -

    A. the Department only issues to Long Island Railroad property once every thirty days
    B. the Department only issues to Long Island Railroad property once every sixty days

15.____

C. only B.C.C. Supervisors are authorized to issue N.O.V.'s to Long Island Railroad property
D. Long Island Railroad is exempt from Sanitation Enforcement action

16. While Sergeant Lake is at the scene of an accident involving an injury to an Agent, he receives a radio transmission from Agent Marilyn Grant. Agent Grant informs him that she is attempting to issue a summons to a grocery store, but the owner refuses to give proper I.D. Agent Grant requests assistance.
Sergeant Lake informs the Agent that he is unable to assist her and should direct Agent Grant to

   A. resume patrol
   B. issue a nail-and-mail N.O.V.
   C. request assistance from another Agent
   D. radio headquarters to request assistance from a police sector car

17. During his 2:30 P.M. *see* with trainee Agent Grace Chan, Sergeant George Barry finds out that earlier in the afternoon she had written a nail-and-mail summons for three uncovered receptacles to a single-family dwelling.
In accordance with Department Violation Issuance Policies, Sergeant Barry should

   A. direct Agent Chan to issue summonses to other residences on the street
   B. advise Agent Chan that in this situation she can issue nail-and-mail summonses only if directed to do so by a District Superintendent or Enforcement Superior
   C. suggest that Agent Chan return to the street where the summons was issued and issue warning notices to the other residents on the street
   D. tell Agent Chan that she should have notified the District Superintendent or an Enforcement Supervisor directly after issuing the summons

18. Sergeant Glass is reviewing a summons that Agent Scott has just written to Teddy's Book Store for an *A* frame violation. Agent Scott explains that the summons was written in response to a letter of complaint from the Community Board, which states *check location for A frame and take corrective action*. Sergeant Glass then observes that the *A* frame is placed on a twelve foot wide sidewalk at the curb.
Sergeant Glass should inform Agent Scott that his action in writing the summons is

   A. *incorrect;* chiefly because the *A* frame was not a food-related *A* frame
   B. *correct;* chiefly because the community board asked the Department to take corrective action
   C. *incorrect;* chiefly because a warning should have been issued first
   D. *correct;* chiefly because the *A* frame should have been placed next to the building

19. When issuing personal service summonses, which of the following is ACCEPTABLE as primary proper identification?

   A. Social Security Card
   B. Voter Registration Card
   C. Current Motor Vehicle Registration
   D. Current New York City Pistol Permit

20. When issuing personal service summonses, which of the following is ACCEPTABLE as secondary proper identification? 20._____

    A. Utility bill
    B. Foreign passport
    C. New York State Notary Public Identification Card
    D. Business card with name, address, and telephone number

KEY (CORRECT ANSWERS)

1.	C	11.	C
2.	B	12.	A
3.	A	13.	C
4.	A	14.	A
5.	D	15.	D
6.	A	16.	B
7.	B	17.	B
8.	C	18.	C
9.	A	19.	D
10.	B	20.	C

EXAMINATION SECTION
TEST 1

DIRECTIONS: Each question or incomplete statement is followed by several suggested answers or completions. Select the one that BEST answers the question or completes the statement. *PRINT THE LETTER OF THE CORRECT ANSWER IN THE SPACE AT THE RIGHT.*

Questions 1-5.

DIRECTIONS: Questions 1 through 5 are to be answered SOLELY on the basis of the Memory Scene I on the next page. Study this scene for 5 minutes; then answer Questions 1 through 5.

MEMORY SCENE 1

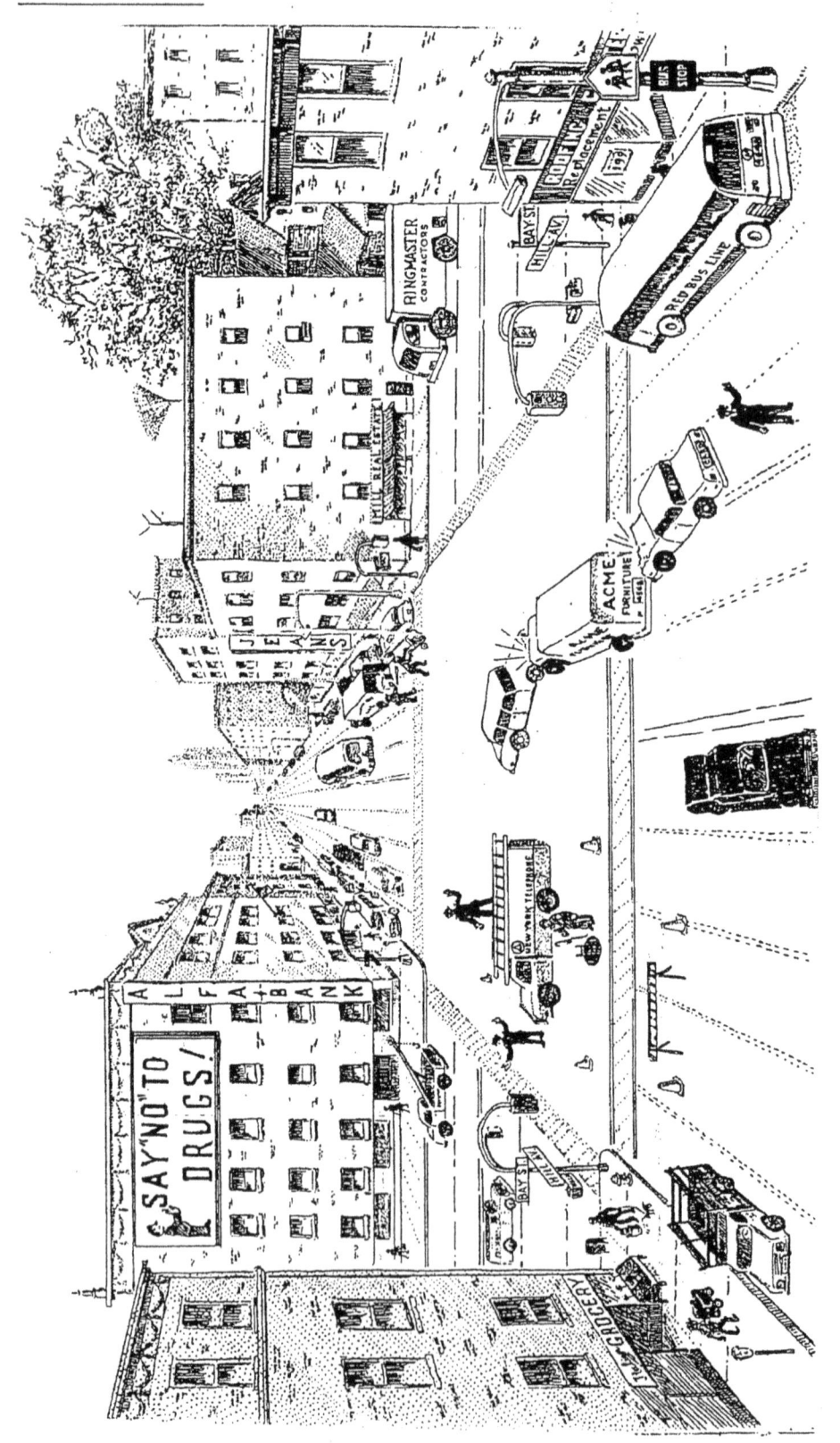

1. The utility truck in the intersection is

   A. Con Ed
   B. N.Y.C. Department of Water
   C. N.Y. Telephone
   D. N.Y.C. Department of Highways

2. The number of Traffic Enforcement Agents directing traffic is

   A. 2   B. 3   C. 4   D. 5

3. At which intersection did an accident take place?

   A. Bay Avenue and Hill Street
   B. Mill Street and Bay Avenue
   C. Hill Avenue and Bay Street
   D. Bay Street and Mill Avenue

4. How many vehicles were involved in the accident?

   A. 2   B. 3   C. 4   D. 5

5. Which one of the following is printed on the truck involved in the accident?

   A. ACME Furniture   B. Red Bus Line
   C. Ring Master   D. Bay Avenue Jeans

Questions 6-9.

DIRECTIONS: Questions 6 through 9 are to be answered SOLELY on the basis of the information in the Memory Narrative below. Study this paragraph for 2 minutes; then answer Questions 6 through 9.

MEMORY NARRATIVE

Traffic Enforcement Agent Hanks is assigned to Motorized Summons Patrol in Area 10, which covers 110th St. to 125th St. from Broadway to Amsterdam Avenue. At Roll Call, Lt. Wilson informs Agent Hanks that the agent should pay particular attention to double parkers in the Business District. The Business District in Area 10 runs on Broadway from 110th Street to 115th Street. Lt. Wilson also informs. Agent Hanks that there will be a funeral at St. Lukes Cathedral today from 10:00 A.M. to 11:30 A.M. Although the Cathedral has *No Standing Anytime* signs posted around it, the Lt. tells Agent Hanks not to enforce this restriction during the time that the funeral is in progress.

6. The Business District in Area 10 runs from

   A. 105th St. to 110th St. on Amsterdam Avenue
   B. 110th St. to 115th St. on Broadway
   C. 115th St. to 120th St. on Amsterdam Avenue
   D. 112th St. to 116th St. on Broadway

7. The funeral is scheduled to begin at _____ A.M.

   A. 9:00   B. 9:30   C. 10:00   D. 10:30

8. Which parking violations should Agent Hanks pay particular attention to? 8.____
   _____ violations.

   A. Fire hydrant   B. Double parking
   C. Meter   D. Drive-way

9. The funeral is being held at 9.____

   A. St. Luke's Cathedral   B. The Broadway Cathedral
   C. St. Mary's Cathedral   D. Our Lady of Mercy

10. While on patrol, Traffic Enforcement Agent Scott witnessed an incident. He recorded the 10.____
    following information:
    Place of Incident: Grand Central Parkway
    Time of Incident: 4:50 A.M.
    Cause of Incident: Falling debris struck a vehicle
    Vehicle Type: Buick
    License Plate Number: 403-QRM
    Agent Scott is about to radio Traffic Control regarding this incident.
    Which one of the following expresses the above information MOST clearly and accurately?

    A. A Buick, license plate number 403-QRM, was struck by falling debris on the Grand Central Parkway at 4:50 A.M.
    B. License plate number 403-QRM is a Buick. Falling debris struck the Grand Central Parkway at 4:50 A.M.
    C. On the Grand Central Parkway, falling debris struck license plate number 403-QRM at 4:50 A.M. The car was a Buick.
    D. Debris was falling at 4:50 A.M. A Buick, license plate number 403-QRM was on the Grand Central Parkway.

Questions 11-13.

DIRECTIONS: Questions 11 through 13 are to be answered SOLELY on the basis of the following passage.

Traffic Enforcement Agent Lewis, while on patrol, received a radio call from Lieutenant Oliva instructing him to proceed to 34th Street, between Madison and Park Avenues, in order to report on the traffic condition in that area.

When Agent Lewis arrived at the assigned location, he discovered approximately 100 demonstrators on the sidewalk in front of the Bamlian Mission to the United Nations located at 135 E. 34th Street. Agent Lewis radioed Lt. Oliva and informed him that traffic was moving very slowly because the demonstration had spilled out onto the street. Lt. Oliva responded that he understood the situation and would contact the Police Department, as well as send an additional agent to the scene.

Police Sergeant Rodriguez arrived at the Bamlian Mission along with several police officers and informed Agent Lewis that he was going to seal off the street between Madison and Park Avenues to contain the demonstration and prevent any demonstrators from being injured.

Agent McMillian arrived at the scene shortly after the police. He and Agent Lewis decided that to divert traffic from 34th Street, which has east and westbound traffic, Agent McMillian would go to the intersection of 34th Street and Madison Avenue and direct eastbound traffic north on to Madison Avenue. Meanwhile, Agent Lewis would position himself at the intersection of 34th Street and Park Avenue and direct westbound traffic south on to Park Avenue.

11. Agent Lewis was sent to 34th Street to

    A. direct traffic at the Bamlian Mission
    B. keep demonstrators out of the street
    C. report on the traffic condition
    D. assist the police

12. Police Sergeant Rodriguez closed 34th Street because he wanted to

    A. prevent injuries and wait for additional police officers
    B. contain the demonstration and wait for instructions from Lt. Oliva
    C. divert traffic and wait for additional police officers
    D. prevent injuries and contain the demonstration

13. Agent McMillian directed

    A. eastbound traffic north on to Madison Avenue
    B. westbound traffic south on to Park Avenue
    C. eastbound traffic south on to Madison Avenue
    D. westbound traffic north on to Park Avenue

Question 14.

DIRECTIONS: Question 14 is to be answered SOLELY on the basis of the following information.

A Traffic Enforcement Agent must obey the following rules when issuing a summons:

1. A summons must be issued once an agent starts writing out a summons for an observed violation.
2. An agent cannot cross out, erase, or change any part of a summons.
3. If an error is made when preparing a summons, the agent must immediately stop writing that summons.
4. The agent must enter the correct information on the next summons in the summons book and then must issue that summons to the violator.

14. Traffic Enforcement Agent Jones was on patrol in the downtown business district when he observed a double-parked vehicle. While writing a summons for this violation, Agent Jones realized he had made an error when he copied the license plate number. He was preparing a new summons when the motorist appeared. The motorist stated he would move his vehicle and insisted that he should not receive a summons because the summons was not yet completed. Agent Jones completed and issued the summons.
In this situation, the actions taken by the agent were

A. *proper,* primarily because the violation occurred in the downtown business district
B. *improper,* primarily because the agent made a mistake on the first summons
C. *proper,* primarily because a summons was in the process of being written
D. *improper,* primarily because the motorist appeared before the summons was completed

Questions 15-16.

DIRECTIONS: Questions 15 and 16 are to be answered SOLELY on the basis of the following passage.

Traffic Enforcement Agents who drive patrol cars are required to perform vehicle maintenance inspections twice a week. Maintenance inspections are conducted on Wednesdays and Saturdays under the direct supervision of a Traffic Enforcement Lieutenant. The main purpose of this program is to make sure that the vehicle fleet is working properly. The responsibility for vehicle maintenance lies first with the driver and then up through the supervisory chain within each command.

15. The MAIN purpose of the Vehicle Maintenance Inspections Program is to 15._____

   A. ensure that the vehicles operate properly
   B. assign responsibility for the operation of the vehicles
   C. reduce the amount of time between the initial reporting of defects and repairs
   D. set up a cost reduction policy whereby minor repairs are conducted at the command level

16. Who supervises maintenance inspections? 16._____
    A Traffic Enforcement

   A. Lieutenant   B. Agent
   C. Maintenance Specialist D. Captain

17. Before beginning her patrol, Traffic Enforcement Agent 17._____
    Flores inspects her patrol vehicle. She obtains the following information:
        Vehicle Number: 147
        Exterior Condition: Poor
                               (A) Dent in right front door
                               (B) Left front tire flat
        Interior Condition: Poor
                               (A) Seatbelts broken
                               (B) Rear Seat ripped
    Agent Flores is completing a report on her vehicle inspection. Which one of the following expresses the above information MOST CLEARLY and ACCURATELY?

   A. The rear seat is ripped and the exterior is in poor condition of vehicle 147. The seatbelts are broken. The interior is also in poor condition. The front tire on the left side is flat and the right front door is dented.
   B. The exterior shows a dented right front door and ripped rear seat. Vehicle 147 has a flat left front tire and broken seatbelts. The vehicles interior and exterior are both in poor condtion.

C. Vehicle 147 has a flat left front tire. The interior and exterior are in poor condition. Inside, the vehicle has a ripped rear seat and its seatbelts are broken. There is also a dent on the right front door.
D. Vehicle 147 is in poor condition. The exterior of the vehicle has a dent in the fight front door and a flat left front tire. The interior of the vehicle shows that the rear seat is ripped and the seatbelts are broken.

18. While on patrol, Traffic Enforcement Agent Gates observes the following: 18.____
    Violation: Parked in a *No Standing 7:00 A.M. to 7:00 P.M.* zone
    Place of Occurrence: 29-29 Park Lane
    License Plate Number: XZC-410
    Vehicle Type: Blue Dodge
    Assistance Needed: Tow truck

    Agent Gates is about to radio Traffic Control with this information.
    Which one of the following expresses the above information MOST clearly and accurately?

    A. At 29-29 Park Lane, a tow truck is needed between 7:00 A.M. and 7:00 P.M. A blue Dodge, licence plate number XZC-410 is parked in a *No Standing* zone.
    B. A blue Dodge, license plate number XZC-410, is parked in a *No Standing 7:00A.M. to 7:00 P.M.* zone at 29-29 Park Lane. A tow truck is needed.
    C. License plate number XZC-410 is parked in a *No Standing 7:00 A.M. to 7:00 P.M.* zone. A tow truck is needed for a blue Dodge, at 29-29 Park Lane.
    D. A tow truck is needed in a *No Standing 7:00 A.M. to 7:00 P.M.* zone at 29-29 Park Lane. License plate number XZC-410 is parked. It's a blue Dodge.

Questions 19-20.

DIRECTIONS: Questions 19 and 20 are to be answered SOLELY on the basis of the following information.

On Monday, July 11, Traffic Enforcement Agent Blake reports for roll call and is assigned to patrol Areas 1 and 2. Before leaving for the field, Agent Blake signs out 3 packages of summonses. Each package contains 25 summonses. Agent Blake patrols Area 1 and issues the following summonses:

- 5 for Bus Stop Violations
- 7 for Double Parking
- 4 for Expired Time on Parking Meters
- 4 for Fire Hydrant Violations

After patrolling Area 1, Agent Blake patrols Area 2 and issues the following summonses:

- 8 for Expired Time on Parking Meters
- 4 for Bus Stop Violations
- 8 for Double Parking
- 2 for Fire Hydrant Violations

19. How many summonses did Agent Blake issue in Area 2? 19._____

    A. 21   B. 22   C. 23   D. 24

20. After issuing summonses in Areas 1 and 2, how many summonses did Agent Blake have left? 20._____

    A. 30   B. 31   C. 32   D. 33

KEY (CORRECT ANSWERS)

1.	C	11.	C
2.	B	12.	D
3.	C	13.	A
4.	B	14.	C
5.	A	15.	A
6.	B	16.	A
7.	C	17.	D
8.	B	18.	B
9.	A	19.	B
10.	A	20.	D

TEST 2

DIRECTIONS: Each question or incomplete statement is followed by several suggested answers or completions. Select the one that BEST answers the question or completes the statement. *PRINT THE LETTER OF THE CORRECT ANSWER IN THE SPACE AT THE RIGHT.*

1. The following information relates to an accident observed by Traffic Enforcement Agent Taylor:

Place of Accident:	625 Hollings Avenue
Time of Accident:	2:00 P.M.
Drivers Involved:	Mrs. Jean Rodgers and Mr. John Cruz
Violation:	Failure to Obey a Stop Sign
Action Taken:	Summons served to Mrs. Jean Rodgers

   Agent Taylor is informing his Lieutenant about the facts of the accident.
   Which one of the following expresses the above information MOST clearly and accurately?

   1.____

   A. A summons was issued to Mrs. Jean Rodgers for driving at 2:00 P.M. in front of 625 Hollings Avenue. Mrs. Rodgers and Mr. John Cruz were involved in an accident and failed to obey a stop sign.
   B. Mrs. Jean Rodgers was issued a summons at 2:00 P.M. For failure to obey a stop sign, Mrs. Rodgers and Mr. John Cruz were involved in an accident at 625 Hollings Avenue.
   C. Mrs. Jean Rodgers and Mr. John Cruz were involved in an accident at 2:00 P.M. in front of 625 Hollings Avenue, and Mrs. Rodgers was issued a summons for failure to obey a stop sign.
   D. It was 2:00 P.M. when a summons was issued to Mrs. Jean Rodgers. For failure to obey a stop sign, Mrs. Rodgers and Mr. Cruz were involved in an accident. It was at 625 Hollings Avenue.

2. While directing traffic, Traffic Enforcement Agent Ross observed an accident and recorded the following information at the scene:

Place of Accident:	Intersection of White Plains Road and Pelham Parkway
Time of Accident:	4:48 P.M.
Name of Injured:	Kim Johnson
Name of Driver:	Kim Johnson
Description of Accident:	Car slid on ice and crashed into an elevated train support beam
Action Taken:	Notified Traffic Control to request police and ambulance

   Agent Ross is informing his Lieutenant about the accident.
   Which one of the following expresses the above information MOST clearly and accurately?

   2.____

   A. At the intersection of White Plains Road and Pelham Parkway, Kim Johnson injured herself on an elevated train support beam. When Traffic Control was notified that at 4:48 P.M. her car slid on the ice, police and an ambulance were requested.
   B. Kim Johnson was injured at the intersection of White Plains Road and Pelham Parkway. She injured herself and notified Traffic Control that her car hit a support beam at 4:48 P.M. when she slid on the ice into the train. A request for police and an ambulance was made.

341

C. At the intersection of White Plains Road and Pelham Parkway, Kim Johnson injured herself and Traffic Control was notified. Her car hit a support beam at 4:48 P.M., and she slid on the ice into the train. Traffic Control requested the police and an ambulance.
D. At 4:48 P.M., Kim Johnson was injured at the intersection of White Plains Road and Pelham Parkway when her car slid on the ice and crashed into an elevated train support beam. Traffic Control was notified to request police and an ambulance.

Question 3.

DIRECTIONS: Question 3 is to be answered SOLELY on the basis of the following information.

The following is a list of some common parking violations and their fines:

Double Parking	Fine
Between 23rd and 96th Street - Manhattan	$40.00
Remainder of New York City	$35.00

No Parking	
Between 23rd and 96th Street - Manhattan	$35.00
Remainder of New York City	$20.00

No Standing	
Between 23rd and 96th Street - Manhattan	$40.00
Remainder of New York City	$35.00

3. Agent Payne is on patrol on 26th Street on Staten Island when he observes a vehicle parked on a street covered by a *No Parking Anytime* sign. What is the amount of the fine?

   A. $20.00   B. $25.00   C. $35.00   D. $40.00

Question 4.

DIRECTIONS: Question 4 is to be answered SOLELY on the basis of the following information.

Traffic Lieutenant Hobbs orders Traffic Enforcement Agent Battista to improve the traffic flow in his assigned area by issuing summonses to double parked vehicles on West 142nd Street, vehicles parked at expired meters on West 138th Street, and vehicles parked at fire hydrants on East 136th Street. Lt. Hobbs informs Agent Battista that most double parking violations occur from 1:00 P.M. to 2:30 P.M.; most expired meter violations occur from 3:00 P.M. to 4:00 P.M.; and most fire hydrant violations occur between 4:30 P.M. to 6:00 P.M.

4. Agent Battista would be MOST likely to observe vehicles parked in violation of expired meters on

   A. West 138th Street from 3:00 P.M. - 4:00 P.M.
   B. East 142nd Street from 3:00 P.M. - 4:00 P.M.

C. West 138th Street from 1:00 P.M. - 2:30 P.M.
D. East 136th Street from 4:30 P.M. - 6:00 P.M.

Question 5.

DIRECTIONS: Question 5 is to be answered SOLELY on the basis of the following information.

When preparing a summons, a Traffic Enforcement Agent should enter the following information on the summons in the order given:
1. Description of vehicle
2. Time and date of violation
3. Place of occurrence
4. Law/code violated
5. Any necessary facts
6. Amount of fine
7. Name of issuing agent

5. On March 1, 2009, Agent Cole was patrolling in front of 619 Burke Avenue at 3:00 P.M. He saw a green Honda Civic parked by a fire hydrant and began to prepare a summons. He entered the following information: green Honda Civic, 3:00 P.M., March 1, 2009. What information should Agent Cole enter NEXT?

A. The agent's name
B. The amount of the fine
C. The type of violation
D. Where the violation took place

6. Traffic Enforcement Agent Smith is required to testify in court regarding a violation. The following facts relate to that incident:

Violator:	Ann Jones
Violation:	Dangerous Lane Change
Place of Issuance:	1st Avenue and 48th Street
Time of Issuance:	4:45 A.M.
Date of Issuance:	November 22, 2009
Action Taken:	Summons issued

Agent Smith needs to be accurate and clear when testifying.
Which one of the following expresses the above information MOST clearly and accurately?

A. At 4:45 A.M., I issued Ann Jones a summons. On November 22, 2009, she was dangerously changing lanes. This occurred at 1st Avenue and 48th Street.
B. I issued Ann Jones a summons for a dangerous lane change on November 22, 2009 at 4:45 A.M. at 1st Avenue and 48th Street.
C. On November 22, 2009, Ann Jones drove while I issued her a summons at 4:45 M. We were at 1st Avenue and 48th Street where she made a dangerous lane change.
D. At 1st Avenue and 48th Street, motorist Ann Jones issued a summons at 4:45 M. She had been changing lanes dangerously on November 22, 2009.

7. Traffic Enforcement Agent White notices that within his assigned patrol area most double parking violations occur on Pine Street and most expired parking meter violations occur on Bellemy Street. Agent White also notices that most expired parking meter violations occur on Tuesdays and Thursdays, and most double parking violations occur on Wednesdays and Fridays. Most double parking violations occur between 9:00 A.M. and 11:00 A.M., and most expired parking meter violations occur between 1:00 P.M. and 3:00 P.M.
Agent White would MOST likely be able to issue the GREATEST number of double parking summonses if he patrolled

    A. Pine Street, Wednesdays and Fridays, 9:00 A.M. to 11:00 A.M.
    B. Bellemy Street, Tuesdays and Thursdays, 1:00 P.M. to 3:00 P.M.
    C. Pine Street, Wednesdays and Thursdays, 9:30 A.M. to 11:00 A.M.
    D. Bellemy Street, Tuesdays and Wednesdays, 1:00 P.M. to 3:00 P.M.

7.____

8. Vehicles with special license plates, stickers, or parking permits are allowed to park in restricted parking areas when appropriate.
To which one of the following vehicles would it be MOST appropriate for a Traffic Enforcement Agent to issue a summons for illegal parking?

    A. A motorcycle with a police permit parked in a *Reserved-Police Parking* zone
    B. A car with doctors license plates parked in an *Emergency Only* zone by a hospital
    C. A car with a Board of Education permit parked by a fire hydrant
    D. A van with handicap license plates parked in a space reserved for disabled drivers

8.____

Questions 9-12.

DIRECTIONS: Questions 9 through 12 are to be answered SOLELY on the basis of the following passage.

    Traffic Enforcement Agent Krieg is assigned to direct traffic at the intersection of Frame and Taylor Streets, which is the only way into or out of the Reese Tunnel in the Bronx. At 2:25 P.M., a motorist, driving a blue Cadillac, exits the tunnel and informs Agent Krieg that a U.P.S. truck is on fire in an eastbound lane of the tunnel. Agent Krieg notifies Traffic Control that he has received an unconfirmed report of a fire in the Reese Tunnel. Traffic Control replies that once they receive confirmation of the fire, they will notify the Fire Department and also the District Office so that they may send additional agents and a tow truck to the scene. At 2:30 P.M., a motorist in a gray Ford exits the tunnel and informs Agent Krieg that the tunnel is filled with smoke and that driving is dangerous. Agent Krieg again informs Traffic Control of the situation. Traffic Control informs Agent Krieg that they have received confirmation of the fire from the Port Authority Police and that the Fire Department is on their way, as well as six Traffic Enforcement Agents and a tow truck. When the additional agents arrive, they close the tunnel to traffic in both directions in order to clear a path for the Fire Department and other emergency vehicles. Agent Krieg notifies Traffic Control that the Fire Department arrived at 2:45 P.M. and that the tunnel is closed. At 3:15 P.M., Lt. Backman of the Fire Department informs Agent Krieg that the fire has been extinguished, but that there are three vehicles in the tunnel that have to be towed, as well as the U.P.S. truck. At 3:20 P.M., the Fire Department leaves the scene, and the westbound lane is re-opened. At 3:40 P.M., the last vehicle is towed from the tunnel, arid Agent Krieg notifies Traffic Control that all lanes in the tunnel are re-opened to traffic.

9. What vehicle was reported to be on fire?   9._____
   A

   A. blue Cadillac   B. U.P.S. truck
   C. gray Ford   D. tow truck

10. From whom did Traffic Control receive confirmation that there was a fire?   10._____

    A. Agent Krieg   B. A motorist
    C. Lt. Backman   D. Port Authority Police

11. At what time was Agent Krieg informed that the fire was extinguished?   11._____
    _____ P.M.

    A. 2:25   B. 2:30   C. 3:15   D. 3:20

12. How many vehicles had to be towed out of the tunnel?   12._____

    A. 1   B. 2   C. 3   D. 4

13. Traffic Enforcement Agent Murray begins his patrol with 3 packages of summonses.   13._____
    Each package contains 25 summonses. Agent Murray issues all the summonses in the
    first two packages and 12 summonses from the third package.
    Which one of the following is the TOTAL number of summonses he issued?

    A. 57   B. 62   C. 65   D. 70

14. Traffic Enforcement Agent Gilmore is required to testify in court regarding a moving viola-   14._____
    tion. The following facts were recorded at the scene of the incident:
    Date of Occurrence: May 26
    Place of Occurrence: Intersection of W. 125th Street and Broadway
    Operator of Vehicle: George Underwood
    Charge: Failure to stop for a red light
    Vehicle: A blue 2014 Chevrolet sedan
    Action Taken: Summons issued

    Agent Gilmore needs to be accurate and clear when testifying.
    Which one of the following expresses the above information MOST clearly and accu-
    rately?

    A. On May 26, I issued a summons to George Underwood while driving a 2014
       blue Chevrolet sedan. He received the summons for failure to stop for a red light.
       This happened at the intersection of W. 125th Street and Broadway.
    B. For failure to stop a blue 2014 Chevrolet sedan for a red light, I issued a summons.
       George Underwood was at the intersection of W. 125th Street and Broadway on
       May 26.
    C. A 2014 blue Chevrolet sedan was driven by George Underwood, and I issued him
       a summons on May 26. He was on W. 125th St. when he failed to stop for a
       red light at the intersection of Broadway.
    D. On May 26, I issued a summons to George Underwood, who was driving a
       2014 blue Chevrolet sedan, for failure to stop for a red light at the intersection of W.
       125th St. and Broadway.

15. Traffic Enforcement Agent Jenkins was assigned to work from 7:00 A.M. to 3:00 P.M. He recorded his activities for the day on his Daily Field Patrol Sheet as follows:
    7:00 A.M. - 10:30 A.M. - On duty at Main Street
    10:30 A.M. - 11:00 A.M. - Off duty - lunch
    11:00 A.M. - 1:00 P.M. - On duty - special assignment
    1:00 P.M. - 3:30 P.M. - On duty - earned 1/2 hour overtime
    At the end of the day, Lieutenant Quinn asks Agent Jenkins how many hours he worked, not including lunch and overtime.
    Which one of the following formulas should Agent Jenkins use?
    Add the hours between 7:00 A.M. and

    A. 3:30 P.M., then subtract one hour
    B. 11:00 A.M., then add to that total the hours between 11:00 A.M. and 3:30 P.M., and then subtract 30 minutes
    C. 3:30 P.M., then subtract 30 minutes
    D. 10:30 A.M., then to that total add the hours between 10:30 A.M. and 3:30 P.M., then add 30 minutes

16. A Traffic Enforcement Agent will issue a code *1050* (agent in need of assistance) over the radio to his supervisor only when the agent feels him/herself in danger.
    In which one of the following situations would radioing for supervisory assistance be MOST appropriate?

    A. Jim Byers punches Agent Rodriguez as the agent is about to issue him a summons.
    B. Mary Akers screams at Agent Reese as he is about to issue her a summons.
    C. Jerry Smith drives off as Agent Garcia is about to issue him a summons.
    D. Kevin Dole verbally threatens Agent Monaham as the agent is about to issue him a summons.

17. Traffic Enforcement Agent Cohen witnessed an accident.
    He recorded the following information:
    Accident: Hit and run of a pedestrian
    Vehicle Make and Model: Plymouth station wagon
    License Plate Number: IJD-689
    Description of Driver: Male, white, black hair
    Time of Occurrence: 3:15 P.M.
    Place of Occurrence: Intersection of McLean Avenue and W. 249th Street
    Agent Cohen is preparing a report on this incident.
    Which one of the following expresses the above information MOST clearly and accurately?

    A. At 3:15 P.M., a Plymouth station wagon, license plate number IJD-689, driven by a white male with black hair, struck a pedestrian at the intersection of McLean Avenue and W. 249th Street.
    B. A Plymouth station wagon, license plate number IJD-689, struck a pedestrian. A white male with black hair was at the intersection of McLean Avenue and W. 249th St. at 3:15 P.M.

7 (#2)

C. A pedestrian struck a Plymouth station wagon, license plate number IJD-689, at the intersection of McLean Avenue and W. 249th Street. The driver was a white male with black hair.
D. A white male with black hair struck a pedestrian. At 3:15 P.M., he was driving a Plymouth station wagon, license plate number IJD-689 at the intersection of McLean Avenue and W. 249th Street.

18. The following facts relate to a vehicular accident observed by Traffic Enforcement Agent Webb:

   Date of Accident: February 13
   Time of Accident: 11:55 A.M.
   Place of Accident: Corner of Haven and Ridge Streets
   Driver in Violation: Mrs. Levin
   Violation: Driving the wrong way on a one-way street
   Other Driver: Mrs. Chang

Agent Webb is preparing a report on the accident.
Which one of the following expresses the above information MOST clearly and accurately?

A. Driving the wrong way on a one-way street on February 13 was Mrs. Levin. At the corner of Haven and Ridge Streets the other driver, was Mrs. Chang, caused an accident at 11:55 A.M.
B. Mrs. Chang was at the corner of Haven and Ridge Streets. On February 13 at 11:55 A.M., Mrs. Levin drove the wrong way on a one-way street and caused an accident with another driver.
C. On February 13 at 11:55 A.M., Mrs. Levin drove the wrong way on a one-way street and caused an accident with another driver, Mrs. Chang, on the corner of Haven and Ridge Streets.
D. Mrs. Chang was the other driver in an accident. Mrs. Levin drove the wrong way on a one-way street on February 13 on the corner of Haven and Ridge Streets at 11:55 A.M.

Questions 19-20.

DIRECTIONS: Questions 19 and 20 are to be answered SOLELY on the basis of the following passage.

Traffic Enforcement Agents Benjamin and O'Brien are assigned to direct traffic at the entrance of the eastbound side of the Smithsonian Bridge. While the agents are directing traffic, Agent Benjamin notices that eastbound traffic going onto the bridge is at a standstill. While Agent O'Brien remains at the intersection to direct traffic, Agent Benjamin goes onto the eastbound side of the bridge's lower level and observes a tractor trailer stopped in a lane. When Agent Benjamin reaches the trailer, she observes that it exceeds the height limit for vehicles to safely use the bridge. Agent Benjamin radios Traffic Control about the situation, and Traffic Control replies that they will notify the Bureau of Bridges but that in the meantime Agents Benjamin and O'Brien should try to handle the situation themselves. Agent Benjamin radios Agent O'Brien and tells him to stop all eastbound traffic from coming onto the bridge. Once this is done, Agent Benjamin then stops all westbound traffic at the site of the trailer. He then directs the eastbound vehicles behind the trailer to go around the trailer by using the westbound lane. Once all the traffic behind the tractor trailer has passed, Agent Benjamin has the trailer back off the bridge.

19. The tractor trailer did not proceed across the bridge because it was 19.____

    A. too high   B. too heavy
    C. too wide   D. out of fuel

20. Agent O'Brien was told to stop traffic heading in which direction? 20.____

    A. Northbound   B. Southbound
    C. Eastbound   D. Westbound

KEY (CORRECT ANSWERS)

1.	C	11.	C
2.	D	12.	D
3.	A	13.	B
4.	A	14.	D
5.	D	15.	A
6.	B	16.	A
7.	A	17.	A
8.	C	18.	C
9.	B	19.	A
10.	D	20.	C

EXAMINATION SECTION
TEST 1

DIRECTIONS: Each question or incomplete statement is followed by several suggested answers or completions. Select the one that BEST answers the question or completes the statement. *PRINT THE LETTER OF THE CORRECT ANSWER IN THE SPACE AT THE RIGHT.*

Questions 1-3.

DIRECTIONS: Questions 1 through 3 are to be answered SOLELY on the basis of the following map and information.

The flow of traffic is indicated by the arrows. If there is only one arrow shown, then traffic flows only in the direction indicated by the arrow. If there are two arrows, then traffic flows in both directions. You must follow the flow of traffic.

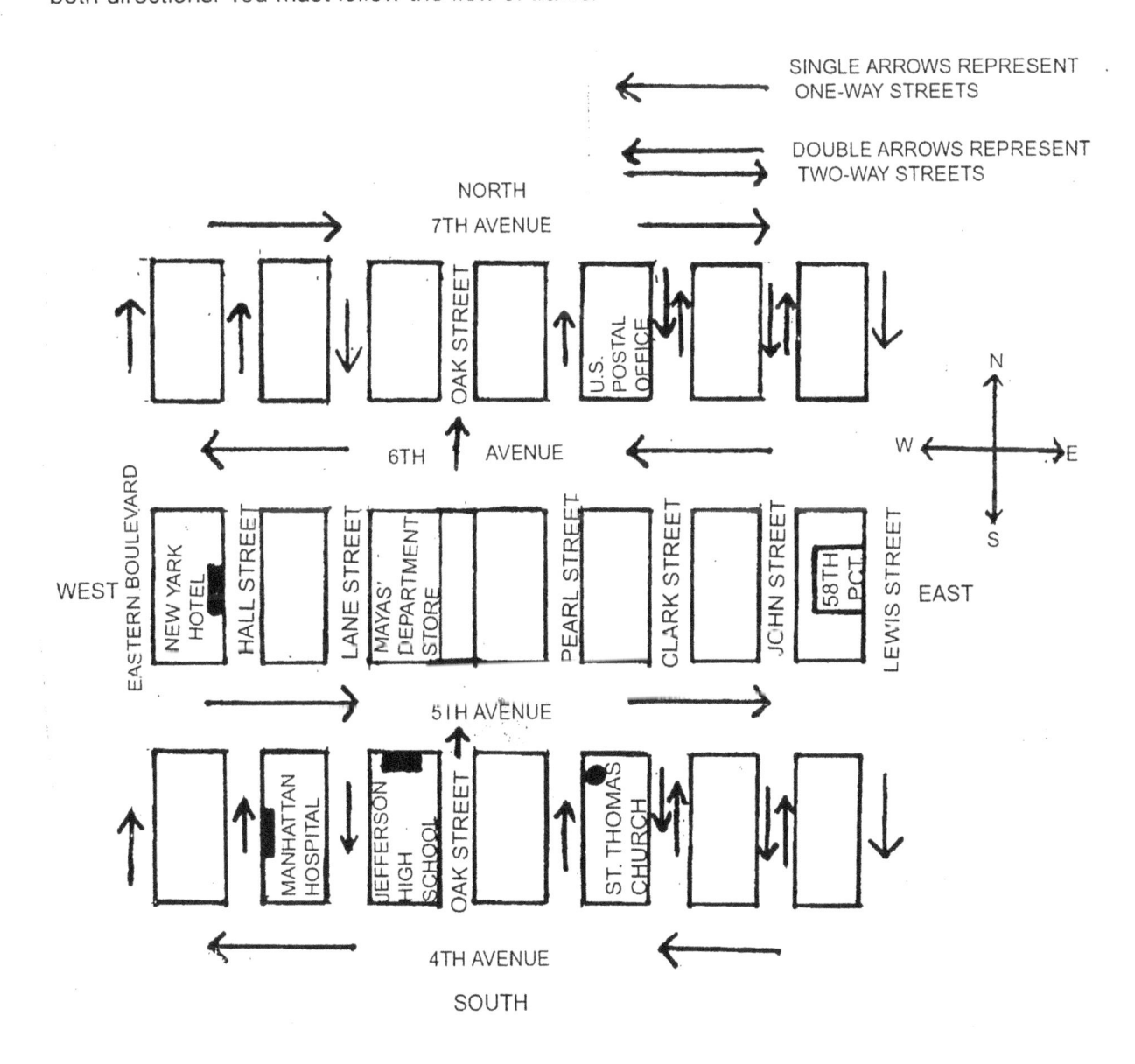

349

1. Traffic Enforcement Agent Fox was on foot patrol at John Street between 6th & 7th Avenues when a motorist driving southbound asked her for directions to the New York Hotel, which is located on Hall Street between 5th & 6th Avenues Which one of the following is the SHORTEST route for Agent Fox to direct the motorist to take, making sure to obey all traffic regulations?
   Travel _____ to the New York Hotel.

   A. north on John Street, then east on 7th Avenue, then north on Lewis Street, then west on 4th Avenue, then north on Eastern Boulevard, then east on 5th Avenue, then north on Hall Street
   B. south on John Street, then west on 6th Avenue, then south on Eastern Boulevard, then east on 5th Avenue, then north on Hall Street
   C. south on John Street, then west on 6th Avenue, then south on Clark Street, then east on 4th Avenue, then north on Eastern Boulevard, then east on 5th Avenue, then north on Hall Street
   D. south on John Street, then west on 4th Avenue, then north on Hall Street

2. Traffic Enforcement Agent Murphy is on motorized patrol on 7th Avenue between Oak Street and Pearl Street when Lt. Robertson radios him to go to Jefferson High School, located on 5th Avenue between Lane Street & Oak Street. Which one of the following is the SHORTEST route for Agent Murphy to take, making sure to obey all the traffic regulations?
   Travel east on 7th Avenue, then south on _____, then east on 5th Avenue to Jefferson High School.

   A. Clark Street, then west on 4th Avenue, then north on Hall Street
   B. Pearl Street, then west on 4th Avenue, then north on Lane Street
   C. Lewis Street, then west on 6th Avenue, then south on Hall Street
   D. Lewis Street, then west on 4th Avenue, then north on Oak Street

3. Traffic Enforcement Agent Vasquez was on 4th Avenue and Eastern Boulevard when a motorist asked him for directions to the 58th Police Precinct, which is located on Lewis Street between 5th & 6th Avenues.
   Which one of the following is the SHORTEST route for Agent Vasquez to direct the motorist to take, making sure to obey all traffic regulations?
   Travel north on Eastern Boulevard, then east on _____ on Lewis Street to the 58th Police Precinct.

   A. 5th Avenue, then north
   B. 7th Avenue, then south
   C. 6th Avenue, then north on Pearl Street, then east on 7th Avenue, then south
   D. 5th Avenue, then north on Clark Street, then east on 6th Avenue, then south

4. Traffic Enforcement Agent Mason was involved in a vehicular accident while on patrol. The following information relates to this accident:

Date of Accident:	March 3
Time of Accident:	3:45 P.M.
Damage to Traffic Vehicle #344:	Dented front fender
Driver of Other Vehicle:	Cindy Wasserman
Other Vehicle:	Gray Honda

   Agent Mason is preparing a report on the accident.
   Which one of the following expresses the above information MOST clearly and accurately?

A. At 3:45 P.M., a gray Honda and traffic car #344 collided causing dents on the front fender. Cindy Wasserman drove a car on March 3.
B. The other vehicle was a gray Honda and on March 3 at 3:45 P.M. dents on the front fender were caused by a collision between traffic car #344 and Cindy Wasserman.
C. There were dents on the front fender because on March 3 Cindy Wasserman drove a gray Honda at 3:45 P.M.
D. It was March 3 at 3:45 P.M. when a collision occurred between a gray Honda, driven by Cindy Wasserman, and traffic car #344. Car #344 suffered dents on the front fender.

5. Traffic Enforcement Agent Tonelli is working at an intersection when he observes the following:

    Condition: Disabled Vehicle
    Location: 41st Street exit of the Brooklyn-Queens Expressway
    Lane Affected: Southbound middle lane
    Type of Vehicle: Red Buick
    License Plate Number: 689-BCZ
    Assistance Needed: Tow truck

Agent Tonelli is about to radio Traffic Control with this information.
Which one of the following expresses the above information MOST clearly and accurately?

A. A tow truck, license plate number 689-BCZ, is needed in the southbound middle lane of the Brooklyn-Queens Expressway at the 41st Street exit. A red Buick is disabled.
B. At the 41st Street exit of the Brooklyn-Queens Expressway, a red Buick, license plate number 689-BCZ, is disabled in the southbound middle lane and a tow truck is needed.
C. A disabled vehicle requires a tow truck in the southbound middle lane. A red Buick, license plate number 689-BCZ, is at the 41st Street exit of the Brooklyn-Queens Expressway.
D. The 41st Street exit of the Brooklyn-Queens Expressway requires a tow truck. In the southbound middle lane there is a red Buick. The disabled vehicle's license plate number is 689-BCZ.

Question 6.

DIRECTIONS: Question 6 is to be answered SOLELY on the basis of the following information.

When dealing with vehicles with Board of Education parking permits, Traffic Enforcement Agents should:

1. Issue a summons to all vehicles parked in areas covered by a *No Parking 7:00 A.M. - 5:00 P.M. School Days* sign, even if they display a Board of Education parking permit.
2. Allow vehicles with Board of Education permits to park in areas covered by a *No Parking 7:00 A.M. - 5:00 P.M. Except Board of Education* sign.

6. On Wednesday, October 10 at 5:15 P.M., Traffic Enforcement Agent Smith is on patrol in front of Public School 24 where a car is parked in a *No Parking 7:00 A.M. -5:00 P.M. School Days* zone. The car has a Board of Education parking permit in the front windshield. Agent Smith sees the permit and proceeds to issue a summons.
In this situation, the action taken by Agent Smith was

   A. *proper*, primarily because the car was parked in front of the school on a school day
   B. *improper*, primarily because the car was legally parked
   C. *proper*, primarily because the car was parked illegally
   D. *improper*, primarily because there was a Board of Education permit displayed in the car window

7. Traffic Enforcement Agents begin their daily patrol by taking at least 75 new blank summonses out into the field with them. However, agents may issue more or less than 75 summonses per day. Below is a list of the number of summonses Agent Wilson took out into the field with him at the start of his patrol and the number of summonses he had issued by the end of his patrol.

Day	Blank Summonses At Start of Patrol	Summonses Issued by the end of Patrol
Monday	75	65
Tuesday	75	70
Wednesday	100	90

   Agent Wilson needs to know the total number of summonses he has left, that is, the total number of summonses he has not issued, following his Monday-Wednesday patrol.
   Which one of the following formulas should he use?
   A. (65+70+90) - (75+75+100)
   B. (75+65) - (75+70) - (100+90)
   C. (75+75+100) - (65+70+90)
   D. (75-65) + (75-70) + (100+90)

8. Traffic Enforcement Agent Dunn was on patrol when he observed the following:
   Violation: Parked by a fire hydrant
   Location: 263 E. 54th Street
   Vehicle Year and Model: 2008 Black Ford Taurus
   License Plate Number: YYJ-134
   Assistance Required: Tow truck

   Agent Dunn is about to radio this information to Traffic Control.
   Which one of the following expresses the above information MOST clearly and accurately?

   A. A tow truck is required by a fire hydrant at 263 E. 54th Street. A black Ford Taurus, license plate number YYJ-134 is parked.
   B. A tow truck, license plate number YYJ-134, is required at 263 E. 54th Street. A black Ford Taurus is parked by a fire hydrant.
   C. License plate number YYJ-134 is parked by a fire hydrant and a tow truck is required. A black Ford Taurus is at 263 E. 54th Street.
   D. A black Ford Taurus, license plate number YYJ-134, is parked by a fire hydrant at 263 E. 54th Street. A tow truck is required.

Question 9.

DIRECTIONS: Question 9 is to be answered SOLELY on the basis of the following information.

If anyone offers an agent money or anything else of value to not write a summons or perform the agent's duty, the agent should do the following in the order given:

1. Ask for the person's drivers license.
2. Check the vehicle registration.
3. Call a supervisor.
4. Request the Police and the Assault Investigation Squad to respond.

9. On February 17, Traffic Enforcement Agent Soto was on foot patrol when he observed a vehicle parked in a bus stop.
As Agent Soto started to prepare a summons for this violation, the operator of the vehicle appeared on the scene. The operator offered to give Agent Soto ten dollars if the agent did not issue him a summons for this violation. In this situation, Agent Soto should NEXT

A. call for a supervisor to respond to the scene
B. ask the operator of the vehicle for his drivers license
C. request the Police and the Assault Investigation Squad to respond to the scene
D. check the registration of the vehicle

Questions 10-12.

DIRECTIONS: Questions 10 through 12 are to be answered SOLELY on the basis of the following passage.

Traffic Enforcement Agents Miner and LaBatt are assigned to direct traffic at the intersection of 181st Street and Broadway. While directing traffic, Agent LaBatt is informed by a motorist that there is a brown Ford Escort partially blocking the 181st Street exit of the Cross Bronx Expressway. While Agent LaBatt proceeds to investigate this report, Agent Miner radios Traffic Control and informs Traffic Lieutenant Wesley that Agent LaBatt has left the intersection in order to investigate the motorist's report.

When Agent LaBatt arrives at the scene, he sees the reported vehicle partially blocking the 181st Street exit ramp. Agent LaBatt inspects the vehicle and discovers that the right front fender is missing and the left rear fender is dented. Upon further inspection, he finds that the license plates are missing, as well as the car's registration sticker. Agent LaBatt, believing that the car is abandoned, follows the procedures for an abandoned vehicle by writing his District Office number and the date and time on both rear fenders. Agent LaBatt also believes that the vehicle creates a hazard to safe traffic flow. He radios Traffic Control with this information and informs Lt. Wesley that a tow truck will be necessary. Lt. Wesley instructs Agent LaBatt to remain with the vehicle and direct exiting traffic off the expressway until the tow truck arrives.

10. The vehicle blocking the exit was missing its 10.___

   A. left rear fender, front license plate, and car registration sticker
   B. right rear fender, left rear fender, and license plates
   C. right front fender, license plates, and car registration sticker
   D. left front fender, rear license plate, and car registration sticker

11. Agent LaBatt was directed to remain with the vehicle 11.___

   A. to prevent the vehicle from being stripped
   B. so the tow truck driver would know where to go
   C. because traffic at 181st Street and Broadway was light
   D. to direct traffic off the expressway

12. What are the procedures to be followed regarding an abandoned vehicle? 12.___
    Write the date, time,

   A. and the District Office number on the left and right rear fenders
   B. District Office number and registration sticker number on both rear fenders
   C. and the District Office number on both front fenders
   D. the District Office number, and the license plate number on both front fenders

13. Traffic Enforcement Agent Jackson begins his patrol with 3 packages of summonses. 13.___
    Each package contains 25 summonses. At the end of the work day, Agent Jackson returns with 1 package of summonses.
    How many summonses did he issue?

   A. 25   B. 35   C. 50   D. 75

Question 14.

DIRECTIONS: Question 14 is to be answered SOLELY on the basis of the following information.

When driving a Department of Transportation vehicle, a Traffic Enforcement Agent is strictly prohibited from committing any of the following violations, regardless of the circumstances:

   1. Driving in the opposite direction of traffic
   2. Backing their vehicle into an intersection
   3. Passing through stop signs or signal lights
   4. Making illegal turns
   5. Speeding
   6. Making unsafe lane changes
   7. Entering the flow of traffic from the curb lane safely
   8. Interfering with traffic by driving slowly

14. Traffic Enforcement Agent Sloan has just reviewed the above regulations. Before going out on patrol, Agent Sloan is instructed by Lieutenant Smith to immediately issue a summons for any double parking violation he observes. While on patrol, Agent Sloan notices a double-parked car on a westbound one-way street. Agent Sloan decides to walk up the block to the car and issue a summons. However, before he reaches the car, he sees the driver enter the vehicle. Fearing that the motorist will leave the scene before a summons can be issued for the violation, Agent Sloan gets back in his car and drives eastbound on the street in order to block the vehicle's path.
In this situation, the actions taken by the agent were

   A. *proper,* primarily because Lt. Smith instructed the agent to issue summonses to double-parked vehicles
   B. *improper,* primarily because the motorist moved his vehicle before the agent began to prepare a summons
   C. *proper,* primarily because the double-parked vehicle was interfering with the flow of traffic
   D. *improper,* primarily because the agent committed a violation of a traffic regulation

15. Traffic Enforcement Agent Phillips began his day with 5 packages of unused summonses. Each package contains 25 summonses. At the end of the day, Agent Phillips has 9 unused summonses. Agent Phillips has to tell his supervisor how many summonses he used that day.
Which one of the following formulas should Agent Phillips use to calculate how many summonses he issued?

   A. (25-9) x 5   B. (5x25) - 9
   C. (25-9)/5   D. (5x25) + 9

16. Traffic Enforcement Agent Williams is about to testify in court. The following information was recorded:
   Date of Occurrence: January 18
   Time of Occurrence: 4:20 P.M.
   Place of Occurrence: Madison Avenue & 48th Street
   Motorist's Name: Joan Armstrong
   Vehicle: 2007 Chevrolet
   Violation: Driving in a bus lane
   Action Taken: Summons Issued

   Agent Williams needs to be clear and accurate when testifying.
   Which one of the following expresses the above information MOST clearly and accurately?

   A. On January 18, I issued a summons to Joan Armstrong for driving a 2007 Chevrolet in a bus lane on Madison Avenue and 48th Street at 4:20 P.M.
   B. On January 18, I issued Joan Armstrong a summons while driving in a bus lane on Madison Avenue and 48th Street, it was 4:20 P.M. and she was driving a 2007 Chevrolet.
   C. In a bus lane on Madison Avenue and 48th Street, I issued Joan Armstrong a summons for driving a 2007 Chevrolet on January 18 at 4:20 P.M.
   D. It was 4:20 P.M. when a 2007 Chevrolet drove in a bus lane on Madison Avenue and 48th Street. Joan Armstrong was issued a summons on January 18.

17. Traffic Enforcement Agents Cuff and O'Mara were directing traffic when Agent O'Mara was struck by a vehicle that then left the scene. The following information relates to this incident:

Incident:	Hit and run of Agent O'Mara
Place of Occurrence:	Intersection of Isham Street and Broadway
Time of Occurrence:	3:45 P.M.
Date of Occurrence:	July 9th
Description of Motorist:	Hispanic female; blonde hair
Description of Vehicle:	BMW sedan

Agent Cuff is testifying in Criminal Court about this incident.
Which one of the following expresses the above information MOST clearly and accurately?

A. On July 9th, Agent O'Mara was struck by an Hispanic female with blonde hair. She drove a BMW sedan at 3:45 P.M. at the intersection of Isham Street and Broadway.
B. On July 9th at 3:45 P.M., Agent O'Mara was struck by a BMW sedan at the intersection of Isham Street and Broadway. The driver of the vehicle was a Hispanic female with blonde hair.
C. At the intersection of Broadway and Isham Street, Agent O'Mara was struck at 3:45 P.M. A Hispanic female with blonde hair drove a BMW sedan on July 9th.
D. A BMW sedan was driven by a blonde haired Hispanic female at 3:45 P.M. On July 9th, Agent O'Mara was struck at the intersection of Isham Street and Broadway.

Questions 18-20.

DIRECTIONS: Questions 18 through 20 are to be answered SOLELY on the basis of the following passage.

Traffic Lieutenant Seaver informs Traffic Enforcement Agent Roberts that his assignment for the day is to direct traffic at the intersection of 72nd Street and Madison Avenue. At 11:30 A.M., Agent Roberts observes that the westbound lane at the corner of 120 E. 72nd Street is crumbling and water is pouring out of a huge crack in the street. Mrs. Perry, a resident at 140 E. 72nd Street is looking out her window at the time and immediately dials 911 to report the incident. Agent Roberts radios Traffic Control and informs them of the situation. He requests additional agents to respond to the scene. Traffic Control informs Agent Roberts that they will contact the appropriate utilities and city agencies. However, Agent Roberts is told that, until additional agents arrive, he should handle the situation. Fortunately for Agent Roberts, Mrs. Perry's call to 911 brought Police Officers Monroe and Lanier to the scene at 11:35 A.M. Since the crack is located in the westbound lane at 72nd Street and Madison Avenue, Police Officer Monroe proceeds to 72nd Street and 5th Avenue in order to divert westbound traffic before it reaches Madison Avenue. Police Officer Lanier proceeds to 71st Street and Madison Avenue to divert northbound traffic, while Agent Roberts diverts eastbound traffic at the 72nd Street and Madison Avenue intersection.

18. Police Officers Monroe and Lanier arrived at the scene at

   A. 11:00 P.M.   B. 11:15 A.M.
   C. 11:30 P.M.   D. 11:35 A.M.

9 (#1)

19. Who diverted traffic at 71st Street and Madison Avenue?   19.____

    A. Traffic Agent Roberts   B. Police Officer Lanier
    C. Lieutenant Seaver   D. Police Officer Monroe

20. The water is pouring out of the street at the corner of   20.____

    A. 120 W. 72nd   B. 140 E. 72nd
    C. 120 E. 72nd   D. 140 W. 72nd

KEY (CORRECT ANSWERS)

1. D	11. D
2. A	12. A
3. B	13. C
4. D	14. D
5. B	15. B
6. B	16. A
7. C	17. B
8. D	18. D
9. B	19. B
10. C	20. C

TEST 2

DIRECTIONS: Each question or incomplete statement is followed by several suggested answers or completions. Select the one that BEST answers the question or completes the statement. *PRINT THE LETTER OF THE CORRECT ANSWER IN THE SPACE AT THE RIGHT.*

Question 1.

DIRECTIONS: Question 1 is to be answered SOLELY on the basis of the following information.

According to the Department of Transportation's Rules and Regulations, a *sitter* is a motorist who parks a vehicle in violation of a parking regulation and then remains or has a passenger remain in the vehicle. A summons may be issued without warning for a parking violation even if someone is sitting in the vehicle at the time of the violation.

1. Traffic Enforcement Agent Overton is on patrol when he sees a double-parked car. Agent Overton approaches the car and informs Ms. Ruiz, the occupant, that she must move the car or he will have to issue a summons for the violation. Ms. Ruiz informs Agent Overton that she is not the driver of the car. However, she assures Agent Overton that the driver will be back shortly. Agent Overton proceeds to issue a summons. In this situation, the actions taken by the agent were

    A. *proper,* primarily because he warned Ms. Ruiz before issuing a summons
    B. *improper,* primarily because Ms. Ruiz informed the agent she was not the driver of the vehicle
    C. *proper,* primarily because the vehicle was parked illegally
    D. *improper,* primarily because the agent did not wait for the driver to return and move the car

1.____

Question 2.

DIRECTIONS: Question 2 is to be answered SOLELY on the basis of the following information.

When a Traffic Enforcement Agent issues a summons for a moving violation (which is an offense that occurs when the vehicle is in motion), the agent should do the following in the order given:

1. Request the motorist's license and registration.
2. Advise the motorist of the type of violation committed.
3. Issue the summons.
4. Return the license and registration to the motorist.
5. Inform the motorist of the court date.
6. Return to assigned post.

2. Traffic Enforcement Agent Butler is directing traffic at an intersection when Bill Lee drives through the intersection ignoring the agent's hand signal directing the motorist to stop. Agent Butler blows his whistle in order to get Mr. Lee's attention and directs him to pull his car over to the side of the street. Agent Butler asks Mr. Lee for his license and registration and then informs Mr. Lee that he committed a moving violation by continuing to drive past the agent after he signaled him to stop. Agent Butler then issues Mr. Lee a summons.
The NEXT step Agent Butler should take is to

   A. give back Mr. Lee's registration and license
   B. return to the intersection
   C. request Mr. Lee's license and registration
   D. inform Mr. Lee of when he is to appear in court

3. Traffic Enforcement Agents are often asked by members of the public to radio for the police. It is up to the agent to determine if a situation actually requires police assistance. In which one of the following situations would it be MOST appropriate for an agent to notify the police?

   A. Mr. Nicks tells Agent Jerrian he was just robbed.
   B. Ms. Clay tells Agent Zelig that she saw another Traffic Enforcement Agent leave a liquor store.
   C. Mr. Yee informs Agent Stewart that his car will not start.
   D. Agent Castellano sees a suspicious looking man walking out of a bank.

4. Traffic Enforcement Agent Michaels is assigned to an intersection where workmen are repairing the street. He obtains the following information:

Name of Utility:	Consolidated Union
Location:	Intersection of 207th Street and Miles Avenue
Lanes Closed by Utility:	Westbound lane of 207th Street
Traffic Condition:	Slow moving traffic
Permit Number:	P576201

   Agent Michaels is about to radio Traffic Control for a check of the permit number and to report the traffic condition.
   Which one of the following expresses the above information
   MOST clearly and accurately?

   A. Slow moving traffic has caused the closing of the westbound lane of 207th Street. Consolidated Union is working at the intersection of 207th Street and Miles Avenue. I request a check of permit number P576201.
   B. P576201 is the permit number I request to be checked. At the intersection of 207th Street and Miles Avenue, there is slow moving traffic in the closed westbound lane of 207th Street. Consolidated Union closed it down.
   C. Consolidated Union is working at the intersection of 207th Street and Miles Avenue. They have closed the westbound lane of 207th Street, and this has caused a slow moving traffic condition. I request that you check their permit number which is P576201.
   D. Consolidated Union's permit number is P576201. At the intersection of 207th Street and Miles Avenue, there is a slow moving traffic condition because the westbound lane of 207th Street is closed. I request you check their permit number.

5. Traffic Enforcement Agent James' patrol vehicle was damaged while he was on patrol in the vehicle. The following facts are related to this incident:

    Car Number: 829
    Damage: Broken rear axle
    Cause of Damage: Drove over a pothole
    Date of Occurrence: February 1
    Place of Occurrence: 49th Street and 11th Avenue
    Time of Occurrence: 4:20 P.M.

Agent James is preparing a report on the incident. Which one of the following expresses the above information MOST clearly and accurately?

    A. The car broke its rear axle on a pothole at 49th Street and 11th Avenue. I drove car 829 on February 1 at 4:20 P.M.
    B. It was 4:20 P.M. when on a pothole a broken rear axle occurred. On February 1 on 49th Street and 11th Avenue I drove car 829.
    C. On February 1, I drove car 829 over a pothole breaking the car's rear axle. This occurred on 49th Street and 11th Avenue.
    D. It was 4:20 P.M. when car 829 broke its rear axle. On 49th Street and 11th Avenue there was a pothole on February 1.

Question 6.

DIRECTIONS: Question 6 is to be answered SOLELY on the basis of the following information.

    Before issuing a summons for a double-parked vehicle, a Traffic Enforcement Agent should do the following in the order given:

    1. Check if a summons was already issued.
    2. Check the license plate number.
    3. Determine the vehicle type.
    4. Check for the time of offense.
    5. Determine the code number for the violation.

6. Agent Jefferson is on patrol when he notices a double-parked van in front of 14 E. 52nd Street. After observing that there were no summonses already issued to the vehicle, Agent Jefferson checks the license plate number.
The NEXT step Agent Jefferson should take is to

    A. check the dashboard for summonses
    B. determine the proper code number of the violation
    C. look at his watch for the time
    D. check what type of vehicle it is

7. Traffic Enforcement Agent Carter observes the following incident:

    Obstruction: Stalled bus
    Location: Intersection of Kent Avenue and 5th Street
    Traffic Condition: Slow moving traffic on 5th Street due to stalled bus
    Assistance Needed: Tow truck

Agent Carter is about to radio Traffic Control regarding this incident.
Which one of the following expresses the above information MOST clearly and accurately?

    A. There is slow moving traffic on 5th Street and at the intersection of Kent Avenue and 5th Street a stalled bus needs a tow truck.
    B. A tow truck is needed to remove slow moving traffic on 5th Street. There is a stalled bus at the intersection of Kent Avenue and 5th Street.
    C. At the intersection of Kent Avenue and 5th Street, a bus is stalled. A tow truck is needed because of slow moving traffic on 5th Street.
    D. A stalled bus at the intersection of Kent Avenue and 5th Street is causing slow moving traffic on 5th Street and a tow truck is needed.

Question 8.

DIRECTIONS: Question 8 is to be answered SOLELY on the basis of the following information.

When arriving at Traffic Court, a Traffic Enforcement Agent should do the following in the order given:

1. Sign his name in the log book.
2. Write the time he arrived in the log book.
3. Locate the court room where the hearing is to take place.
4. Notify the clerk in the court room that he is present.
5. Give testimony regarding the summons he issued.
6. Sign the log book stating what time he departed.

8. Agent Ginsberg arrives at Traffic Court to testify about a summons he wrote. After recording his name and the time of his arrival in the log book, Agent Ginsberg tries to find out what court room the hearing will be in. What should Agent Ginsberg do once he finds the court room?

    A. Testify as to why the summons was issued.
    B. Find the court clerk and inform him that he has arrived.
    C. Record the time he arrived.
    D. Sign out in the log book.

Questions 9-10.

DIRECTIONS: Questions 9 and 10 are to be answered SOLELY on the basis of the following passage.

5 (#2)

Traffic Enforcement Agent Murray was on patrol in his vehicle at the corner of Chambers and Church Streets when he noticed an accident between a white van and a green station wagon at the intersection of Church and Duane Streets. The two drivers were involved in a heated argument when Agent Murray approached them. He advised them to move their vehicles out of the intersection and over to the curb. Once at the curb, Ms. Ambrose, the driver of the station wagon, informed Agent Murray that the van had cut her off. The driver of the van, Mr. Hope, informed Agent Murray that he was simply trying to change lanes when the station wagon hit his van. Agent Murray asked both drivers for their drivers licenses and registrations. He informed them that since no one was injured and the damage to the vehicles was minor, they should have driven their cars from the intersection before arguing as to who was at fault. Since they failed to do so, he was going to issue both drivers a summons for obstructing traffic. At this point, Mr. Hope jumped into his van and raced up Reade Street. Agent Murray completed two summonses, one for Ms. Ambrose and the other for Mr. Hope. He issued Ms. Ambrose her summons and at the end of the day returned to his District Office and prepared a Summons Refusal Form. He then attached Mr. Hope's summons to the Summons Refusal Form so that the summons could be mailed to Mr. Hope.

9. At what intersection did the accident occur?

   A. Chambers Street and Church Street
   B. Church Street and Duane Street
   C. Chambers Street and Reade Street
   D. Reade Street and Duane Street

10. When Agent Murray arrived at the scene, the drivers involved in the accident were

    A. moving their vehicles to a side street
    B. exchanging insurance information
    C. involved in an argument
    D. waiting for an ambulance

11. Traffic Enforcement Agent Clark observes the following incident:
    Date of Occurrence: November 27
    Time of Occurrence: 5:00 P.M.
    Place of Occurrence: 38th Street and Madison Avenue
    Driver: Laura Benton
    Type of Vehicle: 2005 Mazda
    Violation: Illegal right turn
    Action Taken: Summons issued

    Agent Clark is required to testify in court about this incident.
    Which one of the following expresses the above information MOST clearly and accurately?

    A. Laura Benton made an illegal right turn at 38th Street and Madison Avenue. At 5:00 P.M. on November 22, she drove a 2005 Mazda and I issued her a summons.
    B. Making an illegal right turn, I issued Laura Benton a summons. A 2005 Mazda was on 38th Street and Madison Avenue on November 22.
    C. An illegal right turn was made on 38th Street and Madison Avenue and I issued a summons. On November 22 at 5:00 P.M. Laura Benton was driving a 2005 Mazda.

6 (#2)

D. On November 22 at 5:00 P.M., Laura Benton, while driving a 2005 Mazda, made an illegal right turn at the corner of Madison Avenue and 38th Street. I issued her a summons.

12. Traffic Enforcement Agent Rivera was offered $10.00 from a motorist if he did not issue a summons for a parking violation. The following facts relate to this incident:

Date of Incident:	December 12
Time of Incident:	2:35 P.M.
Location of Incident:	148 Sherman Avenue
Name of Motorist:	Arnold Pratt
Amount Offered to Not Issue Summons:	$10.00
Action Taken:	Notified Traffic Control

Agent Rivera is preparing a memo on this incident.
Which one of the following expresses the above information MOST clearly and accurately?

12.____

A. Arnold Pratt of 148 Sherman Avenue offered me $10.00 not to issue a summons. I notified Traffic Control on December 12 at 2:35 P.M.
B. Arnold Pratt notified Traffic Control that $10.00 was offered at 2:35 P.M. on December 12. It was at 148 Sherman Avenue.
C. On December 12 at 2:35 P.M., Arnold Pratt offered me $10.00 not to issue him a summons. This took place in front of 148 Sherman Avenue, and I notified Traffic Control.
D. At 148 Sherman Avenue, $10.00 was offered to not issue a summons on December 12 at 2:35 P.M. Traffic Control was notified that Arnold Pratt is the name of a motorist.

Question 13.

DIRECTIONS: Question 13 is to be answered SOLELY on the basis of the following information.

Before issuing a summons for a parking meter violation, a Traffic Enforcement Agent must do the following in the order given:

1. Read the traffic signs in the area.
2. Check to see if there is a special parking permit on the dashboard of the vehicle.
3. Check the meter to see if it is working properly.
4. Check for the number of the meter.
5. Check the time of day.
6. Check the violation code card to determine the code number for the violation.

13. Traffic Enforcement Agent Hernandez is on patrol when he notices a car parked at an expired meter. After checking the traffic signs, the agent looks at the dashboard for a parking permit and finds none. He then turns the meter knob to make sure it is working properly.
The NEXT step Agent Hernandez should take is to

13.____

A. look at his watch to see what time it is
B. check his code card for the violation number
C. check the meter for its number
D. read all the traffic signs

Question 14.

DIRECTIONS: Question 14 is to be answered SOLELY on the basis of the following information.

Code	Violation
70	Inspection Sticker Expired or Missing
71	Front or Back License Plate Missing
72	No Match between License Plate and
73	Registration Sticker

14. Traffic Enforcement Agent Pezzo has come across a parked vehicle with a flat right rear tire, an expired registration sticker, and an expired parking permit. In addition, the vehicle's license plate and inspection sticker do not match.
According to the information above, Agent Pezzo should issue a summons to the vehicle for a violation of code(s)

A. 70, but not 71, 72, or 73
B. 71 and 72, but not 70 or 73
C. 73, but not 70, 71, or 72
D. 70 and 73, but not 71 or 72

15. Traffic Enforcement Agent Barfield was directing traffic when he observed a robbery. The following facts relate to this incident:

Time of Robbery: 3:50 P.M.
Location of Robbery: Corner of Ludlow and Clasp Streets
Victim: Edna Walton
Suspect: Black male wearing a red sweatsuit
Action Taken: Requested Traffic Control to contact Police

Agent Barfield is writing a memo on the above incident. Which one of the following expresses the above information MOST clearly and accurately?

A. Edna Walton was the victim of a robbery at the corner of Ludlow and Clasp Streets. I requested that Traffic Control contact the police. At 3:50 P.M., a black male wore a red sweatsuit.
B. The corner of Ludlow and Clasp Streets was the location of a black male wearing a red sweatsuit and the robbery of Edna Walton at 3:50 P.M. I requested Traffic Control to contact the police.
C. I requested that Traffic Control contact the police at the corner of Ludlow and Clasp Streets. A black male wore a red sweatsuit while Edna Walton was robbed at 3:50 P.M.
D. At 3:50 P.M. on the corner of Ludlow and Clasp Streets, Edna Walton was robbed by a black male wearing a red sweatsuit. I requested Traffic Control to contact the police.

16. Traffic Enforcement Agent Burns witnessed an accident and recorded the following facts: 16._____
	Place of Accident: Intersection of 23rd Street and Park Avenue
	Time of Accident: 6:00 A.M.
	Drivers Involved: Curtis Aldan, Jack Forbes
	Violation: Speeding
	Action Taken: Summons issued to Curtis Aldan

   Agent Burns is informing his Lieutenant about the facts of the accident.
   Which one of the following expresses the above information MOST clearly and accurately?

   A. Curtis Aldan and Jack Forbes were involved in an accident at the intersection of 23rd Street and Park Avenue at 6:00 A.M. Mr. Aldan was issued a summons for speeding.
   B. It was 6:00 A.M. when a summons was issued to Curtis Aldan for speeding. At the intersection of 23rd Street and Park Avenue, Curtis Aldan and Jack Forbes were involved in an accident.
   C. Curtis Aldan and Jack Forbes were the drivers involved in an accident at 6:00 M. At the intersection of 23rd Street and Park Avenue, a summons was issued to Mr. Aldan for speeding.
   D. A summons was issued to Curtis Aldan while speeding. It was at the intersection of 23rd Street and Park Avenue at 6:00 A.M. that Mr. Aldan and Jack Forbes were involved in an accident.

Questions 17-18.

DIRECTIONS: Questions 17 and 18 are to be answered SOLELY on the basis of the following passage.

At 2:00 P.M., Traffic Enforcement Agent Black was on foot patrol on Hack Avenue when Mrs. Herbet approached him about a faulty parking meter. She complained that for the two quarters she deposited, she is supposed to get two hours of parking time and not just the forty minutes that the meter shows. Agent Black accompanied Mrs. Herbet to her car which was parked at 243 Chief Street. He tested the meter by turning the knob and found that the meter was broken because any amount of money deposited in the meter would register forty minutes of parking time. He searched for the serial number of the meter which was P26601 and recorded it along with the location of the meter on his Daily Field Patrol Sheet. Agent Black informed Mrs. Herbet that she would have two hours of parking time, the maximum amount of time she would have received if the meter were working properly. He also informed her that he was starting this two hour limit as of 2:05 P.M. and recorded this time and her license plate number (DRE-927) on his Daily Field Patrol Sheet. The agent told Mrs. Herbet that if her car was parked at the meter past the two hour limit, he would have to issue her a summons. Mrs. Herbet thanked the agent and said she would be gone long before the limit was up.

At 4:15 P.M., Agent Black was again on Chief Street when he saw that Mrs. Herbet's car was still parked at the meter. He issued her a summons for a meter violation and continued on his patrol.

9 (#2)

17. Which of the following is recorded on Agent Black's Daily Field Patrol Sheet? 17.____

    A. 243 Hack Avenue, P26611, 2:05 P.M., DRE-927
    B. 243 Chief Street, P26601, 2:05 P.M., DRE-927
    C. 243 Hack Street, P26661, 2:00 P.M., DRE-927
    D. 243 Chief Avenue, P26601, 2:05 P.M., DRF-927

18. Agent Black allowed Mrs. Herbet to park at the meter for two hours because 18.____

    A. it is the maximum amount of parking time allowed if the meter-were working properly
    B. he felt bad that she lost her money
    C. she was complaining to him
    D. she assured him she would be gone before the two hour limit was up

19. Traffic Enforcement Agent Edwards was directing traffic when he witnessed a vehicle accident. Agent Edwards recorded the following information: 19.____

    Accident: Hit and Run
    Vehicle Hit: Blue Saab
    Hit and Run Vehicle: Black Volvo
    Description of Hit and
      Run Driver: Male, White, blonde hair
    Time of Occurrence: 11:15 A.M.
    Place of Occurrence: 3rd Avenue and 33rd Street

    Agent Edwards is testifying in court regarding this incident.
    Which one of the following expresses the above information MOST clearly and accurately?

    A. At 11:15 A.M., a white male with blonde hair was driving a blue Saab on 3rd Avenue & 33rd Street. A black Volvo was hit.
    B. On 3rd Avenue and 33rd Street, a white male hit a blue Saab. He had blonde hair at 11:15 A.M. when he drove a black Volvo.
    C. At 11:15 A.M., a white male with blonde hair, driving a black Volvo, hit a blue Saab on 3rd Avenue and 33rd Street.
    D. It was a white male with blonde hair on 3rd Avenue and 33rd Street at 11:15 M. A blue Saab was struck by a black Volvo.

20. A Traffic Enforcement Agent is required to radio a supervisor if they become aware of a serious problem outside the agent's assigned patrol area. 20.____
    In which one of the following situations would it be MOST appropriate for an agent to radio a supervisor of a serious problem that occurs outside the agent's assigned area?

    A. A woman reports that her neighbors are constantly blocking her driveway with their car.
    B. A motorist reports that a school bus is on fire near Exit 5 of the expressway.
    C. A store owner reports that an abandoned vehicle has been parked in front of his store for 2 weeks.
    D. A woman reports that her car is stalled in the Grand Safe Shopping Center.

KEY (CORRECT ANSWERS)

1. C
2. A
3. A
4. C
5. C

6. D
7. D
8. B
9. B
10. C

11. D
12. C
13. C
14. A
15. D

16. A
17. B
18. A
19. C
20. B